JAPAN AND SINGAPORE IN THE WORLD ECONOMY

This pioneering work examines Japan's economic activities in Singapore from 1870 to 1965. Drawing upon a wide range of published and unpublished sources, the authors shed new light on issues such as:

- prostitution
- foreign trade by Kobe's overseas Chinese
- fishermen in the inter-war period
- Japanese economic activities during the Pacific War
- Japanese involvement in Singapore's post-war industrialisation plan
- the Lee Kuan Yew regime's policy towards Japan
- the 1960s Japanese investment boom

This important work challenges commonly held views on Japan's economic advance into Southeast Asia in general and Singapore in particular.

Shimizu Hiroshi is Professor of Asian Economic History at Aichi Shukutoku University, Japan. He has published widely on Japanese trade expansion.

Hirakawa Hitoshi is Professor of Asian Economics at Tokyo Keizai University, Japan. His research focus is Asian NIEs (newly industralising economies).

ROUTLEDGE STUDIES IN THE MODERN HISTORY OF ASIA

JAPAN AND SINGAPORE IN THE WORLD ECONOMY

Japan's Economic Advance into Singapore
1870–1965

Shimizu Hiroshi
and Hirakawa Hitoshi

London and New York

First published 1999
by Routledge
11 New Fetter Lane, London EC4P 4EE

Simultaneously published in the USA and Canada
by Routledge
29 West 35th Street, New York, NY 10001

Routledge is an imprint of the Taylor & Francis Group

© 1999 Shimizu Hiroshi and Hirakawa Hitoshi

© 1998 Shimizu Hiroshi and Hirakawa Hitoshi, *Karayuki-san to
Keizai Shinshutsu: Sekai Keizai no naka no Shingaporu Nihon Kankei-shi*
Published by Commons, Tokyo
Translated from the Japanese by Shimizu Hiroshi

Typeset in Garamond by
Exe Valley Dataset Ltd, Exeter
Printed and bound in Great Britain by
Biddles Ltd, Guildford and King's Lynn

British Library Cataloguing in Publication Data
A catalogue record for this book is available from the British Library

Library of Congress Cataloging in Publication Data
Shimizu, Hiroshi.
 [Karayukisan to keizai shinshutsu.   English]
 Japan and Singapore in the world economy: Japan's economic advance
into Singapore, 1870–1965 / Shimizu Hiroshi and
Hirakawa Hitoshi
   p.   cm.
 Includes bibliographical references and index.
 ISBN 0-415-19236-6 (hb)
   1. Japan—Foreign economic relations—Singapore. 2. Singapore—
Foreign economic relations—Japan. 3. Prostitution—Japan—History.
4. Prostitution—Singapore—History. 5. Japan—Economic conditions—
1868– 6. Singapore—Economic conditions. I. Hirakawa, Hitoshi,
1948– . II. Title. III. Title: Japan's economic advance into Singapore,
1870–1965.
HF1602.15.S55S5513   1999
337.5205957—dc21   98-48277
                                                            CIP

ISBN 0-415-19236-6

TO OUR WIVES, BÉATRIX AND MAYUMI

CONTENTS

CONTENTS

PLATES AND MAPS

FIGURES AND TABLES

ABBREVIATIONS

ACU	Asian Currency Unit
CDO	Contagious Disease Ordinance
CO	Colonial Office
COS	Colony of Singapore
DRO	Diplomatic Record Office
DSS	Department of Statistics Singapore
ECAFE	Economic Commission for Asia and the Far East
EDB	Economic Development Board
FO	Foreign Office
IBRD	International Bank for Reconstruction and Development
IHI	Ishikawajima-Harima Heavy Industries Ltd
NIDS	National Institute of Defence Studies
OCBC	Oversea-Chinese Banking Corporation Ltd
OHI	Oral History Interview
OUB	Overseas Union Bank Ltd
PAP	People's Action Party
PRO	Public Record Office
SCAP	Supreme Commander of the Allied Powers
SICC	Singapore International Chamber of Commerce
SLA	Singapore Legislative Assembly
SOS	State of Singapore
STB	Singapore Tourist Board
STPB	Singapore Tourist Promotion Board
UMNO	United Malays National Organisation

EXPLANATORY NOTES

1 As regards Chinese and Japanese names, the surname has been given before the personal name throughout.

2 The Japanese names of the three eras used are the Meiji era (1868–1912), the Taisho era (1912–26), and the Showa era (1926–89).

3 Macrons are omitted in romanised Japanese spellings.

4 Conventional or Wade-Giles spellings for the transliteration of Chinese names and place names have been used in this work.

5 The $ symbol denotes the Straits (Malayan) dollar, and one Straits (Malayan) dollar was equivalent in value to two shillings and four pence from 1906 to 1966. Other dollars are distinguished, for example, by US$ (American dollar) and HK$ (Hong Kong dollar).

6 One ton equals 2,240 lb (1016.1 kg), and one metric ton 1,000 kg. One *kati* is equal to $1\frac{1}{3}$ lb.

7 Figures in statistical tables have been rounded to the nearest whole number so that in some cases a total does not become 100 per cent.

8 For references, the Harvard reference system is used throughout the text. The author's surname, the year of publication, and the page reference are cited in this order in brackets. Where there are same surnames, personal names are added to make the references clear to the reader. For long names, shorter forms or abbreviations have been used – e.g. Maruzen Sekiyu Shashi Henshu Iinkai (The Editorial Committee of the Maruzen Oil Company History) is shortened as Maruzen Sekiyu, and the Singapore International Chamber of Commerce is abbreviated as SICC. As for unpublished materials and certain published works, special arrangements are made for the sake of clarity.

9 Southeast Asia was known in Japan as Nanyo (the South Seas) before World War II, and Nanpo (the Southern Regions) during the war.

10 Prior to World War II, the Straits Settlements comprised Singapore, Penang, Malacca, and (at various times) the small territories including Labuan and the Dindings.

11 Prior to World War II, the term British Malaya comprised the Straits Settlements and the Malay Peninsula (Federated Malay States and Unfederated Malay States). Malaya meant British Malaya except Singapore. It became the Malayan Union in 1946 and the Federation of Malaya from 1948 to 1963.

12 During the Japanese occupation period, Singapore was called Syonan (the Light of the South). Singapore became a crown colony in 1946, and gained self-government in 1959. From 1959 to 1963 it was the State of Singapore. In 1963 Singapore joined the Federation of Malaya to form Malaysia with North Borneo (Sabah) and Sarawak, but was separated from it in 1965 to become an independent state.

PREFACE AND
ACKNOWLEDGEMENTS

It has already been over half a century since the end of the Pacific War, but people's memories of the Japanese military rule over Singapore and other parts of Southeast Asia have recently been refreshed with the publication of large numbers of academic and non-academic works especially on the political, military and cultural aspects of the Japanese occupation. Indeed, in the history of Japan–Southeast Asia relations, the occupation period undoubtedly stands out. However, obviously this does not mean that other periods are insignificant. In the pre-war period, large numbers of Japanese were engaged in a wide variety of economic activities in the Southeast Asian region, while in the post-war period many Japanese firms have made direct investment there. Naturally, these periods, together with the occupation period, need to be studied critically and systematically in order to get a whole picture of Japan's economic relations with Southeast Asian countries over a long period. Unfortunately, as far as we are aware, there exists, at present, no major work on this theme, and we propose to fill part of the gap.

In 1819 Singapore was acquired by Britain, and in the next 150 years or so it went through a number of changes in its political status until 1965 when it finally became an independent state. Over the same period, Japan transformed herself from a feudal state with an agriculture-based economy to one of the major industrial powers in the world. Japan's economic advance into the British colony began in the last quarter of the nineteenth century but the composition of Japanese residents and their economic activities in Singapore were greatly influenced by the political and economic changes that took place in the world as well as in these countries since then. Prior to World War I, *karayuki-san* (Japanese prostitutes abroad) and those who were connected with them such as pimps and drapers constituted a high proportion of the Japanese population, whereas in the inter-war period fishermen and those in commerce accounted for the large part of it. In the post-war period, it was employees of large Japanese companies and their dependents who constituted the large majority. In this study we have, therefore, examined in what ways Japan's economic advance took place in

Singapore from 1870 to 1965 in the light of the changing world economy, and have attempted to prove that some commonly held views on the economic advance are inaccurate.

We shall first describe briefly how we came to undertake this joint research. In July 1984, Shimizu took up a post of lecturer in economic history of Japan at the National University of Singapore (NUS), and, shortly afterward, began to supervise a fourth-year student's academic exercise (a graduation thesis) on the activities of *karayuki-san* in pre-war Singapore. With this as a turning point, he began to show much interest in the role of *karayuki-san* in Japan's economic advance, and while working on Japan's economic relations with Southeast Asia before World War II, came to find out other channels through which Japan made economic advances into the region.

As for Hirakawa, he was then an assistant professor at the Nagasaki Prefectural University of International Economics (the present Nagasaki Prefectural University), and was attached to the Institute of Southeast Asian Studies in Singapore as a visiting researcher for six months from 1985 to 1986. One day, he was invited to give a paper on the NIEs (newly industrialising economies) in the Department of Japanese Studies at the NUS. It was at the presentation room where we met each other. As Hirakawa lived and undertook research in the city state, he came to realise that there were only a few academic works on the activities of Japanese firms in Singapore, and on Japan's post-war economic relations with the country.

In 1989, Shimizu resigned from the NUS to take up a post at Nagoya Shoka University in Japan, while Hirakawa moved to Kanagawa prefecture to join the faculty of Bunkyo University. As a result, it became much easier for us to meet each other and exchange ideas about Japan's economic relations with Singapore. Eventually in the summer of 1990, we agreed to undertake joint research on the present theme, for we were both fully convinced that there ought to be an academic work on it. Taking our respective research interests into consideration, Shimizu was mainly put in charge of the pre-war period, and Hirakawa of the post-war period.

However, we have faced a number of problems in the course of our joint research, which have caused much delay in the completion of this work. First, Shimizu changed his place of work once, and Hirakawa twice. It meant that we needed some time to get used to new academic and social environments, and were also unable to meet each other for discussions as frequently as we wanted to, because of the geographical distance. Second, we were unable to devote ourselves only to our joint research, for we had not only heavy teaching loads at our respective universities but other research projects which we were undertaking individually or with other scholars. Third, as our research progressed, we realised that we had to restructure our work. For example, a few years after we started our joint research, we decided to include a chapter on the occupation period, for we considered it indispensable for the study. Moreover, although we initially planned to include the period after Singapore's independence in 1965, we became convinced that, if we covered it in our study, our work would not only become too voluminous but also take a long time before completion. Consequently, we decided to end the period at 1965, in the hope that we could write another book on the post-independence period in future. Nevertheless, in order to give the reader a bird's-eye view, we have included in the Conclusion a section on Japan's economic relations with Singapore since 1965. A final problem is related to the availability of relevant source materials. Although we have gathered a wide variety of source materials, both published and unpublished, in Japan, Singapore and Britain, we have had no choice but to skate over certain topics in this book lightly due to a dire lack of source materials. We have been, for example, unable to describe fully the financial aspect of Japanese brothels in pre-war Singapore, and the relationship between Japanese and Western firms in post-war Singapore.

During the long period of our research, we consulted source material mainly at the Singapore National Archives, the National University of Singapore Library, the National Library, Singapore, the library of the Institute of Southeast Asian Studies, Singapore, the Japanese Chamber of Commerce and Industry, Singapore, the Public Record Office, Richmond (England), the central library of the London School of Economics and Political Science (LSE), the Diplomatic Record Office, Tokyo, the National Diet Library, Tokyo, Kobe Central Library, Mitsui Bunko, Tokyo, the National Institute of Defence Studies (Boeicho Boei Kenkyujo), Tokyo, the Japan Singapore Association, Tokyo, the Immigration Resources Collection of the Wakayama City Library, Nagoya Chamber of Commerce and Industry, Aichi Prefectural Library, Nagoya City Tsurumai Library, Fujisawa City Shonandai Library and Yokohama Maritime Museum. We are grateful to the librarians of all these institutions.

We are indebted to large numbers of individuals. Mr Sakurai Kiyohiko, an ex-managing director of Jurong Shipyard Ltd, provided us with useful information and an invaluable photograph of the shipyard. Mr Lim How Seng, the director of Singapore National Museum, and Mr David K.Y. Chng of Trinity Theological College, Singapore, gave Shimizu advice on Chinese dialect groups. Professor Sugihara Kaoru of Osaka University took the trouble to advise Hirakawa on research materials kept at the library of the LSE in August 1994, when he was a senior lecturer at the School of Oriental and African Studies. Ms Béatrix Shimizu of Aichi Shukutoku University read the entire manuscript, and made constructive comments.

Thanks are also due, for their assistance in various ways, to Mr Katsu Yasuhiro, Mr Oe Masaaki, Dr Lee Cheuk Yin, Dr Paul H. Kratoska, Mr Leon Comber, Mr David Askew, Professor J.F. Warren, Dr Mak Lau Fong, Mr

Choo Yam Wai, Mr Chung Sang Hong, Mr Sugino Kazuo, Ms Ishii Yaeko, Ms Shiraishi Akiko, Professor Mikami Nobutaka, Mr Otaka Zenzaburo, Mr Yamashiro Masamichi, Mr Nukata Hiromitsu, Mr Maruyama Kyohei, Mr Hase Yasuo, Ms Yotsuya Asami, and to many other individuals and Japanese corporations. The staff of Routledge, especially Mr Craig Fowlie and Ms Liz Brown, have taken great pains in seeing through the publication. Obviously, we are alone responsible for the entire contents of this book.

Since 1990 we have frequently visited Singapore to gather source materials. Shimizu was granted financial assistance by Aichi Shukutoku University to undertake fieldwork in the country in 1996, 1997 and 1998, while Hirakawa's fieldwork in 1997 was financed by Tokyo Keizai University. We wish to express our gratitude to our respective universities.

Transcripts of Crown copyright records in the Public Record Office appear by permission of the Controller of Her Majesty's Stationery Office. Our thanks are also due to the Diplomatic Record Office (Tokyo), the National Institute of Defence Studies, Mitsui Bunko, the Singapore Subordinate Courts, and the National Archives of Singapore for their permission to draw on their unpublished materials for this study. We are grateful to Mr Takahashi Tadayuki, the Japanese Association, Singapore, and the Bridgestone Tire Co. Ltd for providing us with photographs, and to the Kobe Shipyard of the Mitsubishi Heavy Industries Ltd, and Cosmo Oil Co. Ltd for permitting us to use photographs which appeared in their company history books.

Parts of Chapters 2, 3, 4 and 5 appeared under the authorship of Shimizu Hiroshi in *Asian Studies Review* (vol. 20, no. 3, April 1997), *Asian Culture* (no. 21, June 1997), and *Journal of Southeast Asian Studies* (vol. 28, no. 2, September 1997). Moreover, Japanese versions of Chapters 6 and 7 in their earlier state have been published under the authorship of Hirakawa Hitoshi in *Ajia Keizai*, vol. 37, nos 9 and 10 respectively. We are grateful to the editors of these journals for their kind permission to re-use the material in this book.

The Japanese version of this book was published by Commons in Tokyo in April 1998 under the title of *Karayuki-san to Keizai Shinshutsu: Sekai Keizai no naka no Shingaporu Nihon Kankei-shi* (Karayuki-san and the Economic Advance: A History of Japan–Singapore Economic Relations in the World Economy). However, having English readers in mind, we have restructured it, rewriting certain chapters with fresh ideas and additional source materials. Consequently, this book has become very different in content and structure from the Japanese one, and cannot be regarded simply as a mere translation from the Japanese work.

As for the division of work, Shimizu has written the first to fifth chapters, and Hirakawa the sixth and seventh chapters, while the remainder have been jointly written. Shimizu has also undertaken the translation and editorial work for this English version.

Lastly, our heartfelt thanks go to our wives and children for their forbearance and moral support over many years.

Shimizu Hiroshi and Hirakawa Hitoshi

SEPTEMBER 1998

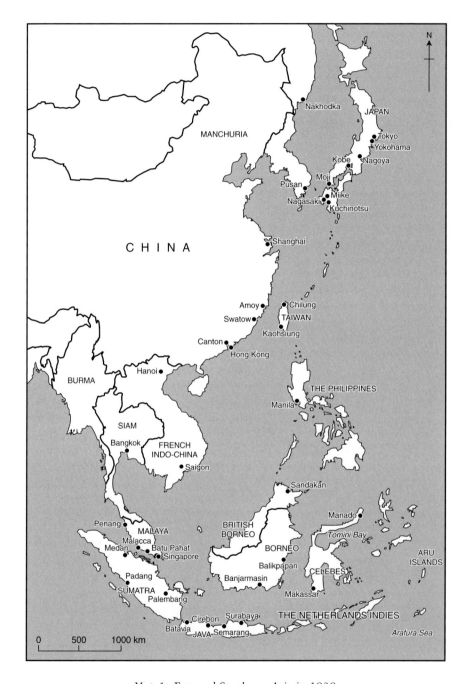

Map 1. East and Southeast Asia in 1938

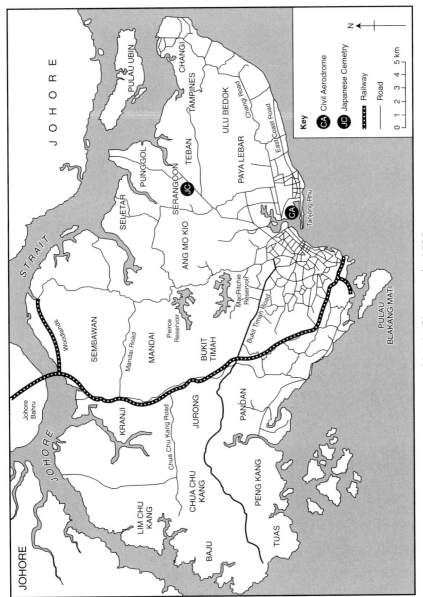

Map 2. Singapore in 1938

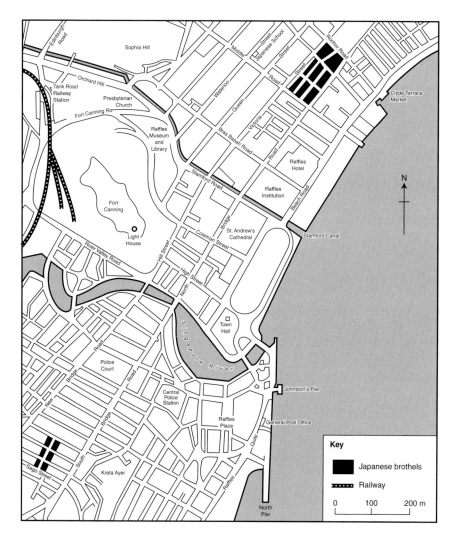

Map 3. Central Singapore in 1917

INTRODUCTION

Singapore is a small city state which has a land area of approximately 647.5 sq km and a population of just over three million, and is not well endowed with natural resources. Nevertheless, it has successfully attracted large numbers of Japanese and Western multinational corporations (MNCs) to invest in the manufacturing and finance/business services sectors, thanks largely to its locational advantages, and it enjoys the second largest per capita GNP (US$31,208 in 1996) in Asia after Japan (US$36,974) (Somucho Tokeikyoku 1998: 81).

Along with the US, Japan has played a leading role in Singapore's economic development. She has been the largest exporter to the country in recent years, and one of the leading importers from it. The Japanese share in Singapore's total imports rose from 11.1 per cent in 1965 to 16.9 per cent in 1975, 17.9 per cent in 1982, and 18.2 per cent in 1996. In the same years, her share in the country's total exports rose from 3.7 per cent to 8.7 per cent and 10.9 per cent, even though it then declined to 8.2 per cent (DSS 1983: 124–7; *idem* 1997: 130–1). Also, since the late 1970s, Japan has been the second largest investor in the country's manufacturing sector, coming after the US. There are now large numbers of Japanese firms operating there. At the end of 1996 there were 3,018 Japanese firms in Singapore, of which 701 were in the manufacturing sector, and the rest were in the services, commerce and other sectors (Kawada 1997: 115).[1] It is therefore not surprising that in 1996 Singapore had a Japanese population of 25,355, which was the fifth largest in the world, and the largest in Asia outside Japan (Somucho Tokeikyoku 1998: 36). The large majority of Japanese residents are company employees and their dependants, and this is reflected in the fact that Singapore boasts the largest Japanese primary school in the world outside Japan.[2]

In addition to the residents, there are numerous short-term Japanese visitors to the country. Their number rose sharply from 118,668 in 1975 to 287,395 in 1980, 377,686 in 1985, 971,637 in 1990, and since 1992 it has exceeded one million a year. In 1997, the total number of foreign visitors to Singapore amounted to 7,197,963, of whom 1,094,047 (or 15.2 per cent of total) were Japanese (STPB 1969, 1975, 1994; STB 1998a).

1

However, it would be wrong to assume that Japan has come to play an important role in the economic development of Singapore only in the past few decades or so, for Japan's economic activities in Singapore started as early as the last quarter of the nineteenth century. Indeed, in order to understand the reasons for Japan's economic presence in the city state today, one would need to examine the recent history of the economic relations between the two countries. This book therefore attempts to study various aspects of Japan's economic advance into Singapore, including the sex industry, foreign and domestic trades, fisheries, financial business and the manufacturing industry, from the 1870s until 1965 when Singapore was separated from Malaysia to become an independent state. The period is divided historically into three distinct sub-periods, namely the pre-war, occupation, and post-war periods. We shall try to shed light on the patterns and features of Japan's economic advance at each sub-period by making a critical study of popular views on the subject, and hope to find out whether or not there was any continuity in her economic advance from one sub-period to another. We shall also assess critically the response of the local inhabitants and the colonial power to the economic advance.

This book has a number of unique structural and other features. First, as far as we are aware, this is the first academic book to deal with the theme covering the entire period under study. It does not, obviously, mean that there are no specialist studies covering specific aspects of the period and the subject. For the pre-war period, there are individual works on Japanese emigration, foreign trade, fisheries and other aspects of the Japanese economic advance into Singapore or British Malaya. They include Kataoka Chikashi, *Senzenki Nanyo no Nihonjin Gyogyo* (Japanese Fisheries in the Pre-war South Seas) (1991), Kee Yeh Siew, 'The Japanese in Malaya before 1942' in *Journal of the South Seas Society*, vol. 20 (1966: 48–88), Koh, Denis Soo Jin and Tanaka Kyoko, 'Japanese Competition in the Trade of Malaya in the 1930s', in *Southeast Asian Studies*, vol. 21, no. 4 (1984: 374–99); Ian Brown, 'The British Merchant Community in Singapore and Japanese Commercial Expansion in the 1930s' in Sugiyama Shinya and Milagros C. Guerrero (eds), *International Commercial Rivalry in Southeast Asia in the Interwar Period* (1994: 111–32) .

There are also some comprehensive studies on the subject. Eric Robertson's *The Japanese File* (1986) deals with various aspects of Japanese economic activities mainly in pre-war British Malaya. Robertson has made extensive use of source materials from files prepared by the Special Branch of the Straits Settlements Police, but it should be noted that, in his book, there are occasional exaggerations and/or misunderstandings about the Japanese activities in British Malaya. Nanyo oyobi Nihonjinsha's *Shingaporu wo Chushin ni Doho Katsuyaku Nanyo no Gojunen* (The Activities of Our Compatriots in the South Seas in the Past Fifty Years: With Special Reference to Singapore) (1938), deals with the economic activities of the

Japanese mainly in Singapore from the Meiji era (1868–1912) to the mid-1930s, and is indispensable for those who are interested in the pre-war Japanese economic activities there.

As for the Pacific War years, quite a few works on the Japanese occupation of Singapore and other parts of Southeast Asia have been published, especially since the fiftieth anniversary in 1995 of the end of World War II. Such works include Paul H. Kratoska (ed.), *Malaya and Singapore during the Japanese Occupation* (1995) and Kurasawa Aiko (ed.), *Tonan Ajia-shi no naka no Nihon Senryo* (The Japanese Occupation in the Southeast Asian History) (1997). However, most of these works focus on the political, military, cultural and social aspects of the occupation, but not much on its economic aspect. It is true that Iwatake Teruhiko's *Nanpo Gunsei-ka no Keizai Shisetsu: Marai, Sumatora, Jawa no Kiroku* (The Economic Facilities under the Military Administration in the Southern Regions: Records of Malaya, Sumatra and Java) (Parts I and II, 1981) and Hikida Yasuyuki (ed.), *Nanpo Kyoeiken: Senji Nihon no Tonan Ajia Keizai Shihai* (The Southern Regions Co-prosperity Sphere: Japan's Economic Control over Southeast Asia during the War) (1995) do focus on the economic aspect of the Pacific War. But they contain no chapters devoted to the Japanese economic activities in Singapore, and are studies largely undertaken from Japan's point of view. It is therefore gratifying that Paul H. Kratoska's recent work, *The Japanese Occupation of Malaya 1941–1945: A Social and Economic History* (1998), deals partly with the economic aspect of Singapore.

Incidentally, most of those scholars who work on the recent economic history of Southeast Asia in general, or Singapore in particular, simply skip from the pre-war period to the post-war period, missing out the Japanese occupation period altogether, partly due to a paucity of relevant research materials.[3] One would naturally wonder how anyone could possibly talk of the twentieth-century economic history of the region without examining the occupation period. Indeed, although Japan ruled Southeast Asia for only three and half years, large numbers of Japanese firms were engaged in a wide range of economic activities there to meet the requirements of the Japanese Army. The experiences gained by these firms in Singapore and other parts of Southeast Asia are likely to have played some part in their return to the region in the post-war period. Moreover, it is possible that some future local leaders were much impressed by their economic activities, even though they experienced the cruel Japanese military rule which they would not forget. It should be noted that the British authorities had hardly taken any measures to encourage the development of the local manufacturing industry before World War II.

As for the period from the end of World War II until the end of the 1950s, there are virtually no specialist studies on Japan's economic relations with Singapore. It is commonly assumed that Japan resumed her economic activities in Southeast Asia only after the mid-1950s when the Japanese government began to pay war reparations to some Southeast Asian countries. Indeed, the period until this time is often called a 'void' period of the economic relations between Japan and the region. However, it was during this period that Japan resumed her economic relations with Singapore. Moreover, in the second half of the 1950s Singapore was eager to seek Japanese assistance in its industrialisation, with the main purposes of greatly improving the living standards of the inhabitants, and checking the spread of communism.

In the first half of the 1960s, there was a Japanese investment boom in Singapore, despite the fact that there was an anti-Japanese movement led by the Chinese Chamber of Commerce to demand war reparations from Japan. It is commonly assumed that during that period many Japanese firms made direct investment into Singapore in order to reap the benefit of the planned formation of Malaysia, which eventually came into being as a result of the merger involving Singapore, Sabah, Sarawak and the Federation of Malaya in September 1963. However, this explanation is not very convincing. This study examines carefully the special relationship between Japan and the Lee Kuan Yew regime, and sheds light on the Singapore government's policy towards Japanese firms.

Second, this book goes beyond the scope of the economic relations between the two countries, for Singapore and Japan were obviously not isolated from the rest of the world, and were subject to external influences. The position of Singapore as an international free port, in particular, needs to be taken into account when various aspects of Japan's economic advance into Singapore are examined. After the foundation of Singapore by the British in 1819, the island continued to develop as an international entrepôt, linking Asia with the West through inward and outward movements of people, money and merchandise. Moreover, their economic relations were greatly influenced by such international factors as wars and world-wide recessions. Therefore, this book tries as far as possible to deal with the theme in the context of the world economy.

Third, in this book we allocate a lot of space to the economic activities of *karayuki-san* (Japanese prostitutes abroad), for we want to make Japan's economic advance realistic. Indeed, we consider that the study of prostitution is indispensable to further our arguments in this work. This is not only because *karayuki-san* were the first Japanese immigrants in Singapore, and constituted a large proportion of the Japanese population before World War I, but also because, as we shall explain below, we try to criticise a popular view that they were instrumental in Japan's early economic advance into Singapore and other parts of Southeast Asia. We also describe how the *ryotei*[4] and comfort stations were organised and run in Singapore during the occupation period, and attempt to study what position Asian prostitutes and comfort women occupied in the wartime economy.

It should be noted that the study of prostitutes/prostitution has hitherto been undertaken mainly by women's historians and social historians. It is regretted that economists and economic historians have in general neglected an analytical study of the role of such a service sector as the sex industry in the economic development of a specific country. Apparently, most of them seem to consider that prostitution is outside the domain of economics or economic history, and it is therefore unworthy of a serious study. However, before World War II, prostitution was licensed in many countries, including Japan, and, putting aside the legal and moral questions, even today, there is hardly any country where there are no prostitutes. Actually, in the pre-war period, there were large numbers of male immigrants in British Malaya, causing a sex imbalance, and the *karayuki-san* and prostitutes of other nationalities were actively engaged in providing sexual services to Asian immigrant workers, the stationary troops of the colonial power, and others. One might therefore argue that prostitutes played an important role in the development of the colonial economy, though indirectly.

Fourth, this book attaches great importance to the role of overseas Chinese merchants and intra-Asian trade networks in Japan's economic advance into pre-war Southeast Asia in general and Singapore in particular, and criticises the *nanshin-ron* (views on Japan's southward advance).[5] Ever since the publication in 1975 of Yano Toru's book, *Nanshin no Keifu* (The Genealogy of the Southward Advance), where the author put forward an analytical framework for Japan's southward advance into Southeast Asia (*nanshin*), there has been remarkable progress in the historical study of Japan's relations with the region. In his book, Yano refers, first of all, to the Japanese advance into Singapore in the Meiji era, and maintains that, to relate the history of the Japanese advance, it is enough to trace the involvement of Japanese nationals in Southeast Asia from *karayuki-san* in the Meiji era (1868–1912) to *nanshin* in the pre-war years of the Showa era (1926–89). From this, it can be assumed that when he refers to the modern history of the relations between Japan and Southeast Asia, he regards Singapore as the focus of Japanese attention, and the keywords are *karayuki-san* and the advance of Japanese nationals (Yano 1975: 10).

Shimizu Hajime explains that Yano employed the term *nanpo kan'yo* (Japan's involvement in Southeast Asia) to skilfully describe the history of the relations between modern Japan and Southeast Asia. As he says, in the minds of Japanese, 'Southeast Asia was perceived as no more than a coveted object lying before Japan, the initiator of the relations', and modern Japan since the Meiji era has been one-sidedly concerned with Southeast Asia (Shimizu Hajime 1992: 141).

Various studies on the relations between Japan and Southeast Asia have been undertaken largely from the viewpoint of the involvement of Japanese in Southeast Asia. Indeed, one would not be far wrong to argue that Yano's work became a turning point for the study of Japan's pre-war relations with Southeast Asia (Shimizu Hajime 1992: 141; Hashiya 1993: 63).[6] Following the Yano tradition, Shimizu Hajime, Murayama Yoshitada, Mark R. Peattie and other Asia specialists have clearly shown in their works how Japanese nationals advanced into Southeast Asia (Shimizu Hajime 1987: 386–402; Murayama 1985: 52–69; Peattie 1996: 189–242). Moreover, it is often assumed that *karayuki-san* were the first Japanese to play a vital role in the early stage of Japan's economic advance into Southeast Asia in general, and Singapore in particular.

However, there were foreign merchants in Japan, notably overseas Chinese merchants, who were engaged in the cultivation of the Southeast Asian markets for Japanese goods, making use of overseas Chinese commercial networks, in the last quarter of the nineteenth century when *karayuki-san* began to ply their trade in the region. It was these non-Japanese merchants who laid the foundation of Japan's later trade expansion into the region. In our view, at the early stage of the Japanese economic advance into Southeast Asia, they played a far more crucial role in it than has previously been acknowledged. Curiously, Yano Toru and other scholars, who work on the *nanshin*, take hardly any notice of the role of non-Japanese in Japan's southward advance in their works. For this reason, the sub-title of this book is *Japan's Economic Advance into Singapore, 1870–1965*, not *The Economic Advance by the Japanese* or *by Japanese Companies into Singapore, 1870–1965*.

Finally, this work draws on a wide variety of both published and unpublished materials, including the archives kept at the Diplomatic Record Office of the Japanese Foreign Ministry, the National Institute of Defence Studies, Tokyo, the Mitsui Bunko (Mitsui Archives), Tokyo, the Singapore National Archives, Singapore, and the Public Record Office, Richmond (England). We also employ information obtained through oral history interviews. Based on diverse source materials, we try to study the subject from various angles critically, and put forward a new approach to Japan's economic advance into not only Singapore but also Southeast Asia as a whole.

1

EMERGENCE OF SINGAPORE AND JAPAN IN THE WORLD ECONOMY

Rise of Singapore as an international entrepôt

British control over Singapore and the Malay Peninsula

Britain acquired Penang in 1786, Singapore in 1819, and Malacca in 1824, and had them confirmed by the Dutch as British colonies under the Anglo-Dutch Treaty of 1824. In 1826, these three colonies were incorporated to form the Straits Settlements, and Singapore became the seat of the government in 1832.[1] By the mid-nineteenth century the British had come to recognise the Straits Settlements not only as ports of call for the trade route from India to China, but also as transit ports for Southeast Asian produce.

At that time, overseas Chinese traders were actively engaged in commerce everywhere in Southeast Asia, but, as far as the British were concerned, their major rivals were not these Chinese, but the Dutch merchants who were trying to maintain their monopoly over the Indonesian trade (Drabble and Drake 1981: 298). It was Thomas Stamford Raffles who was the first to recognise the immense potential of Singapore as an international port. He was of the view that by making Singapore a free port the British could not only seize the trade in Asian products from the Dutch, but cultivate a new market for their goods, notably cotton textile goods (*ibid*.: 301).[2]

When Singapore became a free port, the British merchants based in India and the overseas Chinese in Malacca settled in the island, which was well located on the southern tip of the Asian Continent, separating the Indian Ocean from the Pacific Ocean. By the mid-1830s, the port had overtaken Bangkok as the leading entrepôt for Southeast Asian products destined for China. The strategic and commercial position of Singapore was further enhanced when there was an increased British interest in China as a result of the Opium War of 1840–2 and the establishment of Hong Kong in 1841.

In 1840, the Peninsular and Oriental Steam Navigation Company (P & O) began to provide a regular shipping service for mail, cargoes and passengers between England and India, and extended its service to Penang, Singapore, Hong Kong and Shanghai in the 1840s, and to Sydney and Yokohama in the

1850s.[3] In the next two decades, other European shipping companies, including the Ocean Steamship Company (the Blue Funnel Line) which was managed by Alfred Holt & Co. of Liverpool, also started providing services between Europe and the Far East via Singapore (Allen and Donnithorne 1957: 210–11; Headrick 1988: 39–42).

In the second half of the nineteenth century, Singapore developed rapidly as the leading transit port for Southeast Asian trade and the strategic point for communications, thanks to the opening of the Suez Canal, the development of high-speed steamers, and the laying of ocean cables (Dixon 1991: 73)There was a huge expansion of British trade not only with China but also with Southeast Asia, increasing the demand for ocean-going shipping. As the European steamers equipped with high-power compound engines began to operate in 1873, coaling stations were established in various places on the coasts of the Arabian Peninsula and Southeast Asia, including Singapore. The British colony then became a leading strategic and economic base for foreign trade between Europe and the Pacific regions. Even after the Panama Canal was opened in 1914, the port remained very important, for the bulk of Straits products continued to be transported at a low cost from Asia to the Atlantic ports of the US via Singapore and the Suez Canal (Wong 1991: 52).[4]

The revolution in transport and communications technology coincided with a sharp increase in demand for rubber, tin, cotton, sugar, coffee and other primary commodities caused by the industrialisation of the Western nations, and this became a turning point for accelerating direct or indirect control by the Western powers over the developing world. Formerly, Britain, the workshop of the world, specialised in the production of industrial goods for export, while others were mainly agricultural countries, importing industrial goods from Britain, and exporting to her foodstuffs and raw materials. However, by the mid-nineteenth century, the industrial revolution had spread to France, Germany and the US, and in the second half of the century it also took place in such countries as Italy, Russia and Japan. These newly industrialised countries began to compete with Britain in seeking overseas markets for their industrial goods, and sources of raw materials and foodstuffs in developing parts of the world. It is therefore not surprising that in the late nineteenth and early twentieth centuries, various Western powers were engaged in the scramble for territories in Asia and Africa.

In Southeast Asia, the British had long been based in the Straits Settlements conducting foreign trade until the early 1870s, when they finally abandoned their non-interventionist policy in order to advance into the Malay Peninsula. Initially, they put under their control the three tin-producing states of Perak, Selangor and Sungei Ujong (the main part of Negri Sembilan whose remaining region was put under control in 1889) in 1874, and then in 1880 they took over Pahang in the eastern part of the peninsula, which was not endowed with rich tin deposits. In 1895–6, they began to rule these four Malay states as the Federated Malay States with the capital at Kuala Lumpur, and after 1909 ruled indirectly over the five states of Johore, Kedah, Perlis, Kelantan, and Trengganu as the Unfederated Malay States (Dixon 1991: 749). By World War I, Britain had come to control the whole of the Malay Peninsula.

The peninsula's principal export-oriented industries were tin-mining, which got into stride in the middle of the nineteenth century, and rubber, which became important in the early twentieth century. The rapid increase in the output of these industries, in turn, brought further prosperity to Singapore. The colony's annual average imports from the Malay Peninsula rose from $2,562,000 in 1871–3 (or 6 per cent of total imports) to $55,541,000 (15.6 per cent) in 1897–9 and $182,911,000 (18.4 per cent) in 1925–7. Its average annual exports to the peninsula also rose sharply from $1,681,000 (4.5 per cent of total exports) to $41,702,000 (16.2 per cent) and $108,517,000 (12.5 per cent) in the same years (Huff 1994: 50, 52, 81, 82).

Banking

The expansion of the trade between Southeast Asia and the West facilitated the development of Singapore as an international financial centre as well as an international transit port. From the mid-nineteenth century onward, Western banks were set up one after another in the British colony. The Union Bank of Calcutta, a British-controlled bank, was the first to set up a branch in 1840, but it was closed down a few years later. Then three British exchange banks, namely the Mercantile Bank of India (which was originally called the Mercantile Bank of India, London and China), the Chartered Bank of India, Australia and China (hereafter the Chartered Bank for short), and the Hong Kong Shanghai Banking Corporation established branches in Singapore and then in Malaya. In Singapore, the Merchant Bank of India and the Chartered Bank set up branches in 1855 and 1861 respectively, while the Hong Kong Shanghai Banking Corporation appointed Boustead & Co. as their agents in 1871, and subsequently established a branch in 1877. In the early twentieth century, Nederlandsche-Indische Handelsbank, Neder-landsche Handel Maatschappij, Banque de l'Indochine, and other Western banks established branches there (Makepeace et al. 1991b: 174–80).

All these banks operated in the British colony with their head offices in London, the Hague, Batavia, Hong Kong or elsewhere, and were commercial and exchange institutions. Prior to World War II, they were largely concerned with the provision of working capital and financing of international trade with associated foreign exchange business, and had little incentive to supply investment capital.[5] This was largely because the Europeans had hardly any interest in the development of manufacturing industry in the British colony, while the European concerns engaged in rubber-growing and tin-mining could borrow on the London capital market. In fact, there were no specialised agricultural or industrial banks in Singapore.

The Mercantile Bank of India, the Chartered Bank and the Hong Kong Shanghai Banking Corporation were able to issue banknotes in the early period, and continued to be very influential until the outbreak of the Pacific War in December 1941. Moreover, the second and third banks each played an additional and important role. The Chartered Bank had its head office in London, and acted as the cash office for the governments of those Malay States which were brought under British control after 1874. As for the Hong Kong Shanghai Banking Corporation, which had its head office in Hong Kong, it acted as the cash office for the Straits Settlements Government and became by far the most influential bank in British Malaya (Iwatake 1981a: 370).

Obviously, the Western banks were not the only financial institutions in Singapore. In 1903, the first Chinese bank, Kwong Yik Bank, was set up, but it was closed down in 1913. Branches were also set up by the Bank of China with its head office in Shanghai, and by several overseas Chinese banks, but the activities of their branches were fairly limited particularly in the face of competition from Western banks. It was three Hokkien banks which gave rise to the development of modern Chinese banks in Singapore in a real sense. In 1912, the Chinese Commercial Bank was formed, while the Ho Hong Bank and the Oversea Chinese Bank were established in 1917 and 1919 respectively. However, they all had great financial difficulties during the post-war recession of 1920–1 and the Great Depression of 1929–33, and therefore amalgamated to form the Oversea-Chinese Banking Corporation (OCBC) in 1932. Consequently, the new bank emerged as the largest Chinese bank outside China, and had a total of 16 branches in China and Southeast Asia at the end of the 1930s. In the inter-war period, other local Chinese banks, including the United Chinese Bank (the present United Overseas Bank) were founded.[6]

The Chinese banks kept deposits from overseas Chinese, and lent them to overseas Chinese merchants and entrepreneurs, while remitting foreign exchange to China for overseas Chinese in British Malaya. However, in comparison with the Western banks, their capital was very small and their financial standing was fairly low (Naito 1942: 319; Huff 1994: 230). Although the small Chinese traders made use of the facilities provided by the Chinese banks, which imposed less strict conditions on loans to them, the large Chinese firms continued to deal with the Western banks because they could obtain loans from them at lower interest rates (Allen and Donnithorne 1957: 206).

Besides the Chinese banks, there were large numbers of Chinese remittance shops and pawn shops, which had been active even before the Western banks began business in Singapore. The remittance shops were located everywhere in British Malaya,[7] and remitted money for overseas Chinese to China for a small charge. They maintained close relations with their counterparts in South China. They were also concerned with the provision of working capital to small local Chinese traders as well as undertaking foreign exchange business, postal services, and writing letters for overseas Chinese. When the remittance shops began to remit money by bank drafts after pooling small sums of money collected from many overseas Chinese, they became complementary with the Western banks. However, in the inter-war period, banks (particularly Chinese banks) themselves came to handle large amounts of remittances in direct competition with the remittance shops.

As for Indian banks, it was only in 1937 that the Indian Overseas Bank set up a branch in Singapore, to be followed by the Indian Bank in 1941. However, there were large numbers of Chettiars. They were Indians who belonged to a caste of bankers and money-lenders in Mysore state (present-day Karnataka) and the northern part of Madras state (present-day Tamil Nadu) in India, and had emigrated to Singapore, Penang, Burma and other parts of Southeast Asia. Singapore was in particular the main base for them in the region. They were largely concerned with usury but were also engaged in money exchange business. They made advances and loans to the small Indian and Chinese traders and cultivators whose credit-worthiness they were well acquainted with. They in turn obtained necessary funds from the influential Western banks such as the Chartered Bank and the Mercantile Bank of India (Allen and Donnithorne 1957: 204–5; Brown 1997: 45)

Immigration

Since the late nineteenth century Singapore also functioned as a major transit port for Asian immigrants to various parts of Southeast Asia. Large numbers of coolies were required in mines and plantations, and for infrastructural development particularly in Sumatra and the Malay Peninsula, but it was very difficult to draw labour from the traditional agricultural sector, for the population density was very low. Besides, the colonial officials from Europe in general tended to the view that local Malays were lazy and unproductive, and were therefore unsuitable to work in the modern sector of the economy (Dixon 1991: 109; Alatas 1977: *passim*). Therefore, workers were recruited mainly in South China and South India, and many of them landed first in Singapore to head for their destinations in Southeast Asia thereafter.[8] Since most of them were contracted labourers or 'free labourers who were similar to contracted labourers in character', they returned to their own countries via Singapore after a few years (Sugihara 1996: 308).

Both Chinese firms and European merchant houses in Singapore were engaged in the coolie trade, even though the latter were not directly in-volved in importing coolies from China. The European merchants normally obtained coolies from Chinese intermediaries, and then sent them to their clients in Southeast Asia. Apparently, they specialised in particular regions. For example, Paterson, Simons & Co. were engaged in sending mining coolies to the Malay Peninsula, Behn Meyer & Co. to Sumatra, and Mansfield & Co. to Sumatra and Borneo, while Guthrie & Co. dealt in coolies initially for Sumatra, but later for North Borneo (Edwin Lee 1991: 82).

Chartered steamers were used for the transport of coolies to Singapore. Until about the mid-nineteenth century, most intra-Asian shipping was provided by Asians, notably Chinese who used junks, schooners and other craft, plying between Southeast Asia and China/South Asia. However, since these craft were frequently attacked by pirates because of their slowness and since their cargoes were uninsured, they gave way to large European steamers, which provided both security and speed (Allen and Donnithorne 1957: 212–13). The number of British steamers arriving at Singapore with coolies rose from 147 (or 54.2 per cent of total) in 1878 to 216 (67.7 per cent) in 1884 and 242 (72 per cent) in 1888 (Edwin Lee 1991: 82). For example, by the late 1870s, the majority of passengers from Amoy to the Straits had been carried by the steamers owned by Alfred Holt & Co. The steamers carried European goods to Shanghai, and on their return voyage they picked up Chinese emigrants at Amoy for Singapore, even though they also loaded cargoes at the Chinese ports for Singapore and London. Similarly, the bulk of cargo and passengers from Swatow to Singapore and Siam was carried in Holt Line and other large European steamers (Allen and Donnithorne 1957: 213).

The sharp increase in the number of immigrants in the Malay Peninsula and the Netherlands East Indies produced a new type of foreign trade and financial business. Their movement, first of all, increased the demand for foodstuffs (especially rice) and such necessities of life as textile goods. Most of the goods required by immigrant workers were landed first in Singapore, and after being sorted out, they were then re-exported to these regions. Singapore imported large quantities of rice from Thailand, Burma and Indo-China, and re-exported the bulk of it to the Malay Peninsula and the Dutch colony. In 1911–13, for example, its re-export of rice on annual average amounted to 371,178 tons, of which 163,827 tons (or 44.1 per cent) was for the Malay Peninsula, and 151,738 tons (40.9 per cent) for the Netherlands East Indies (Huff 1994: 99).

Since Asian immigrants remitted the bulk of their earnings to their home countries, this gave rise to the emergence of a financial network between Singapore on the one hand and Hong Kong and India on the other. They initially remitted money through the Chinese remittance shops and the Chettiars, but when the Chinese and Indian banks started operations in British Malaya, some of them remitted it through these banks.

Commercial community

As Singapore continued to develop as an international port, the commercial community also grew in importance there. In the second half of the nineteenth century, it comprised, broadly speaking, two groups, namely

European and Asian merchants. These two groups of merchants were dependent upon each other. In the nineteenth century, the European merchants mainly imported industrial goods from the West, and exported Southeast Asian produce to the Western markets, controlling only the trade between Asia and the West. However, by the early twentieth century, they had diversified their activities into the management and running of rubber estates, and investment into rubber estates and tin mines, although they continued to attach importance to foreign trade (Drabble and Drake 1981).

Nevertheless, the Europeans accounted for a fairly small proportion of the total population in Singapore and other parts of Southeast Asia, and could not carry on their economic activities without the co-operation of overseas Chinese, Indians and other middlemen.[9] The European merchant houses incurred high running costs, for they normally kept offices in grand buildings in main cities, while their European employees were highly paid and lived in luxurious houses. Besides, most of the European employees, who seldom had command of local languages, did not stay in the region for many years, and were not well acquainted with local commercial conditions (Brown 1997: 43–5). It is therefore not surprising that they could not penetrate deep into the local markets on their own, and had to rely heavily on Asian intermediaries.

As for the Asian merchants such as Chinese, Indians and Arabs, they were engaged in traditional intra-Asian trade, but could not easily join the trade between Southeast Asia and the West through Singapore. Unlike the European merchants, they had hardly any connections with manufacturers, buyers, shippers, insurance companies and shipping companies in Europe (Drabble and Drake 1981: 300).[10] Nevertheless, the Asians were well acquainted with local languages and commercial practices, not only because they were long-term residents or settlers, but because many of them were married to local women. As a result, they could act as middlemen between the European merchants and the native inhabitants. The bulk of the industrial goods imported from the West by the European merchants was distributed through them in the Southeast Asian markets, while primary commodities, collected by the Asian merchants from local inhabitants, were taken to Singapore, and exported to the West by the European merchants. It should be borne in mind, however, that, although the European merchant houses were seldom involved in the internal distribution of Western goods in the Southeast Asian markets, they were nevertheless in a position to control the Asian merchants financially, for they often sold goods to them on credit (Allen and Donnithorne 1957: 240).

The Asian merchants such as Chinese and Indians, based in Singapore, conducted their businesses within the intra-Asian financial and commercial networks, linking Southeast Asia with India, China and Japan, and moved freely between Singapore and various Asian trade ports including Batavia, Surabaya, Hong Kong, Shanghai, Bombay and Kobe. In fact, quite a few of

13

them were in charge of the local branches of the trading and/or financial firms in their home countries, i.e. India or China (Brown 1997: 41–2, 44–5; OHI Sachdev).

Therefore, although the British had continued to control Singapore politically and economically since 1819, there was much interdependence between the Europeans (notably the British) and the Asians in commerce, financial business, and other fields. Obviously, we do not claim that their relationship was by any means on an equal basis, for it was the Europeans who played the leading role, whereas the Asians normally played the subordinate role.

RISE OF MODERN JAPAN AND JAPANESE EMIGRATION

Incorporation of Japan into the world economy

When Singapore became a British colony in 1819, Japan was under the Tokugawa feudal regime which lasted from 1603 until 1867. With a view to controlling foreign trade and enforcing a ban on Christianity, the Japanese government adopted a policy of Seclusion (*sakoku*) in the 1630s, issuing edicts to forbid Japanese to travel abroad, while nationals abroad were not allowed to return to their country. Also vessels were not allowed to go beyond coastal waters. In 1641 all the Dutch residents in Japan were moved to Dejima, an island in Nagasaki, through which Japan conducted the trade with China and the Netherlands. The Seclusion policy lasted until 1854 when Japan had to conclude friendship treaties with the US, and subsequently with Britain, France, the Netherlands and Russia, agreeing to open Shimoda and Hakodate to Western ships. Moreover, in 1858, she was obliged to conclude with these five powers commercial treaties under which she lost tariff autonomy, and agreed to open Kanagawa (Yokohama) and Nagasaki in July 1859, Niigata in January 1860, and Hyogo (Kobe) in January 1863, even though the opening of the last two ports was postponed until 1868. Now foreigners were permitted to live in Japan. Moreover, in May 1866, the government began to permit nationals to go abroad for studies or commercial business, while in June, seamen were allowed to work on foreign ships and employees of foreigners in Japan could go abroad with their employers (Suzuki Joji 1992: 12).

As a consequence of the commercial treaties, Japan was fully exposed to the world market, and was soon flooded with Western industrial goods, notably British cotton textiles, leading to the decline in the domestic textile industry, while exporting large quantities of raw silk and tea to the West. It was the large Western (especially British) merchant houses and banks, including Jardine Matheson & Co., David Sassoon & Co. and the Hong Kong and Shanghai Banking Corporation, which were actively engaged in

Japan's foreign trade by operating branches in Yokohama and other treaty ports. Also, the P & O established a regular shipping route between Shanghai and Nagasaki in 1859, while the French company Société des Services Maritimes des Messageries Nationales (renamed Société des Messageries Maritimes in 1871) began to provide a regular service between Yokohama and Shanghai in 1865. The Pacific Mail, an American shipping company, started operating a route (San Francisco–Yokohama–Hong Kong) and the Yokohama–Shanghai feeder route in 1867 (Katayama 1996: 16–17). These Western companies even seized a large part of Japanese coastal shipping.

Emergence of modern Japan

In 1867, the *ancien régime* was eventually overthrown, and the Meiji Restoration took place with the reinstatement of the Emperor as the *de facto* holder of power in 1868.

In the face of threats from the Western powers which had encroached upon China and other parts of Asia, the Meiji leaders were determined from the outset to modernise the country on Western lines. In the first years of the Meiji era, they carried out various social and political reforms to remove feudal institutions, and introduced unified currency and new land-tax systems. Since the private sector was not highly developed, the initiatives for industrialisation had to be taken by the state. Therefore, the government built railways, telegraphs and other infrastructure, while setting up model modern industries, including silk-filatures, cotton-spinning, glass-making, coal-mining and cement. The government also modernised the banking system. In 1880, the Yokohama Specie Bank, a semi-official bank, was set up with a capital of ¥3 million, and became the major foreign exchange bank in the country in 1897 when it revised its regulations. Moreover, in 1882 the Bank of Japan was established as the central bank, and began to issue convertible banknotes from 1885. The Japanese currency was given international standing in 1897, when Japan adopted the gold standard.

Nevertheless, in the 1880s it was the private sector that began to play a major role in the country's modernisation. In the first half of the 1880s, the government adopted a deflationary policy to deal with the country's hyper-inflation, and, as part of that policy, it sold most state-owned enterprises on very generous terms to a small number of private firms which subsequently grew into *zaibatsu* (family combines) such as Mitsui and Mitsubishi. These enterprises turned out to be more efficiently run in private hands.

In 1883, the Osaka Spinning Company (the present Toyo Spinning Co. Ltd) was founded with a capital of ¥250,000, and its success led to the establishment of many large-scale cotton spinning companies in the second half of the 1880s. From the mid-1880s to the mid-1890s, Japan went through an industrial revolution, beginning with light industries, notably cotton-spinning. She began to export large quantities of cotton yarn to China and

15

Korea after her victory over China in the Sino-Japanese War, while importing large quantities of raw cotton from China and India. The expansion of the import and export trade took place largely thanks to the role played by Mitsui & Co. (Mitsui Bussan), a major trading company,[11] and by the two Japanese shipping firms, the Nippon Yusen Kaisha and the Osaka Shosen Kaisha. By the early 1890s, Mitsui & Co. had set up branches at Shanghai, Hong Kong and Singapore.

The shipping industry had been under heavy government protection since the early Meiji period, because of its strategic importance. The Mitsubishi Company (the Mitsubishi Kaisha, originally called Tsukumo Shokai) was set up by Iwasaki Yataro in 1870 with the ships leased or purchased at low costs from the government, and grew rapidly. In 1875, it began to provide a weekly service between Yokohama and Shanghai via Kobe, Shimonoseki and Nagasaki under the orders of the Japanese government, and had successfully driven out the P & O and other Western shipping companies by the early 1880s. In 1885, it amalgamated with its rival, Kyodo Kaiun (the United Shipping Co. Ltd) to form the Nippon Yusen Kaisha, and started providing a service from Japan to Bombay via Hong Kong and Singapore. In 1884 another major shipping company, the Osaka Shosen Kaisha, was set up by ship-owners of the Setouchi region and merchants of Osaka. Both firms continued to receive annual shipping subventions from the government, and provided regular coastal shipping services. However, it was not until after the Sino-Japanese War that there was a great expansion of long-distance shipping services by Japanese companies. In 1896, the Nippon Yusen Kaisha opened a Europe route (Yokohama–Antwerp), a Seattle route (Hong Kong–Japan–San Francisco), and an Australia route (Yokohama–Australia). The Toyo Kisen Kaisha established a San Francisco route (Hong Kong–Japan–San Francisco) in 1897. When Taiwan became a Japanese colony after the Sino-Japanese War, the Osaka Shosen Kaisha started providing regular shipping services between Japan and Taiwan under the Taiwan government's heavy subventions, and then expanded its operations into South China and Southeast Asia also under its subventions (Katayama 1996: 129–30, 211–50). After Japan defeated Russia in the Russo-Japanese War of 1904–5, the Japanese shipping firms extended further the network of their overseas shipping routes.

It was apparent that by the turn of the twentieth century Japan had emerged as a major economic and political power in Asia, and was eager to join the industrial nations of the West. During World War I, although Japan joined on the side of the allies, she was not much involved in the war physically, and could therefore devote herself to the development of import-substitution and export-oriented industries. Consequently, the Japanese export trade went through a major structural change. This is clearly shown from the fact that the share of finished goods in total exports rose from 30.5 per cent in 1908–12 to 43.5 per cent in 1918–22, while that in total imports declined steeply from 24.1 per cent to 15 per cent in the same years (Allen 1981: 271 and 272). In the inter-war period, the Japanese manufacturing sector continued to develop, and large quantities of textiles and other consumer goods found their way to overseas markets.

Poverty and emigration

It should be pointed out that the Japanese population continued to grow steeply from 35,200,000 in 1873 to 46,100,000 in 1903, 56,000,000 in 1920, 64,500,000 in 1930, and 69,300,000 in 1935 (Allen 1981: 248). Much of the rapidly growing population was not sufficiently absorbed by the economy in which agriculture and small and medium-sized manufacturing industries continued to account for a large proportion of gainful employ- ment. Although the share of agriculture and forestry in the total labour force declined from 82.6 per cent (14,100,000 persons) in 1872 to 71.2 per cent (16,912,000 persons) in 1895 and 58.8 per cent (15,527,000 persons) in 1913, it was nevertheless as high as 52.4 per cent (14,287,000 persons) in 1920, and 47.7 per cent (14,131,000 persons) in 1930 (*ibid.*: 250).[12] Moreover, the percentage of cultivated land under tenancy rose from 35.9 per cent in 1883–4 to 39.6 per cent in 1887, 45.2 per cent in 1912, 46.2 per cent in 1922, and 46.3 per cent in 1937 (Nakamura 1983: 56). The rents for paddy-fields were as high as 50 per cent on average of total crop, and naturally imposed a heavy burden on the tenants. It is true that the peasant proprietors accounted for some two-fifths of the total agricultural population in 1910, but the majority of them cultivated fairly small plots of land. As for the share of the manufacturing sector in total labour force, it was 4.1 per cent (705,000 persons) in 1872 , 10.1 per cent (2,392,000 persons) in 1895, 15 per cent (3,957,000 persons) in 1913, 16 per cent (4,357,000 persons) in 1920, and 16.5 per cent (4,891,000 persons) in 1930 (Allen 1981: 250).

Prior to World War II, large numbers of impoverished Japanese sought better opportunities in foreign countries. For instance, in March 1868, van Reid, an American merchant of Dutch ancestry, who was a long-term resident in Japan, acted as an intermediary to send 153 Japanese workers to Hawaii and 42 to Guam, and this was the first mass Japanese emigration. However, it was not until the 1880s that large numbers of Japanese began to emigrate to North America, Latin America, Southeast Asia, Oceania and other parts of the world. The annual average number of Japanese who went abroad with valid passports was 2,045 in 1881–90, 11,672 in 1891–1900, 14,729 in 1901–10, 16,727 in 1911–20, 16,000 in 1921–30 and 27,413 in 1931–40 (Kokusai Kyoryoku Jigyodan 1979: 326–7).

However, Australia passed an Immigration Restriction Act in February 1902 which virtually excluded further immigration from Japan. Also, under the Gentleman's Agreement of 1907–8, Japan agreed to restrict the number of Japanese immigrants into the US. In 1924 the American government passed an Immigration Act which in effect barred Japanese from migrating into the country until 1952. However, such Southeast Asian countries as British Malaya and the Netherlands Indies placed hardly any restriction on immigration, at least until the Great Depression. As noted earlier, from the late nineteenth century the colonial powers continued to bring in cheap foreign labour on a large scale, especially from China and India, for the development of mines, plantations and infrastructure with a view to maintaining minimum capital outlay. The total number of Japanese emigrants to Southeast Asia was 1,148 in 1900, 1,192 in 1905, 1,934 in 1910, 936 in 1915, and 1,107 in 1920, to reach the peak of 6,009 in 1929.[13] Moreover, after the Manchurian Incident of 1931, many Japanese peasants migrated, under the auspices of the Japanese government, to Manchuria, which took, for example, 3,539 Japanese in 1935, 7,788 in 1937, and 40,423 in 1939 (Kokusai Kyoryoku Jigyodan 1979: 326–7).

2

KARAYUKI-SAN AND JAPAN'S
ECONOMIC ADVANCE
INTO SINGAPORE

Karayuki-san were Japanese women who were engaged in prostitution abroad before World War II.[1] According to Morisaki Kazue, the term *karayuki* was used in western and northern parts of Kyushu from the Meiji era (1868–1912) to the late 1930s. *Kara* meant 'China' or 'foreign countries', and after the Meiji Restoration, 'working abroad' and 'the people who worked abroad' were called *karayuki* or *karankuni-yuki*. There were not many jobs available for Japanese men in foreign countries, and women began to account for the large majority of those going abroad, for they could be employed at Japanese brothels. Therefore, *karayuki* came to mean 'Japanese who went abroad to work as prostitutes'. At the beginning of the Taisho era (1912–26), *karayuki* began to be differentiated by name according to their destinations, including *amerika-yuki* (those heading for the US), *shina-yuki* (those heading for China), *shiberia-yuki* (those heading for Siberia), *chosen-yuki* (those heading for Korea), and others. Eventually, *karayuki* came to mean *nanyo-yuki* (those heading for Southeast Asia) (Morisaki 1976: 17–18).

Prior to World War II the term *karayuki-san* was, however, not employed in the consular reports and published works, and in its place a variety of terms were used, including *inbai* (an obscene seller), *shugyofu* (a woman in an ugly trade), *sengyofu* (a woman of a dishonourable calling), *joshigun* (Amazonian troops), *shogi* (a licensed prostitute), and *baishofu* (a woman seller of laughter). It was only in the post-war period, particularly after Yamazaki Tomoko and Morisaki Kazue employed this word in their books in the 1970s (Yamazaki 1975; Morisaki 1976), that Japanese prostitutes in foreign countries began to be called *karayuki-san*.

Broadly speaking, there were two types of *karayuki-san* in Southeast Asia, prostitutes and concubines. Whereas the former generally plied their trade in urban areas, the latter were mainly kept by Caucasians, overseas Chinese, Malays and other men living in the countryside. Normally, *karayuki-san* started their careers first as prostitutes, and then some of them became concubines. However, there were quite a few cases where Japanese concubines were discarded by their 'masters', and returned to their former trade.

In the late nineteenth and the early twentieth centuries, there were large numbers of *karayuki-san* in Southeast Asia. It is said that there were some 6,000 Japanese prostitutes in the region in their heyday around the Russo-Japanese War of 1904–5, of whom some 600 were in Singapore alone. Prior to the First World War, most of the early Japanese immigrants, particularly in British Malaya and the Netherlands East Indies, were those in 'improper trades' such as *karayuki-san*, brothel-keepers, ruffians and sundry-goods store keepers (some of whom were also engaged in flesh trade).[2] In the Straits Settlements, for example, there were 1,835 Japanese residents in 1906, of whom 852 were prostitutes and 113 were brothel keepers (*Tsusho Isan*, 3 February 1907: 11–12). It is also said that the bulk of the huge earnings made by the *karayuki-san* in Southeast Asia were partly remitted to Japan, and partly invested in rubber estates and other Japanese ventures (Nanyo oyobi Nihonjinsha 1938: 146–50, 155–65; Warren 1993: 62–3).

Apparently because of the large numbers and supposedly huge earnings of the *karayuki-san*, quite a few authors claimed in their books or articles on Southeast Asia published before or during World War II that the *karayuki-san* were instrumental in laying foundations for the early Japanese economic advance into the region. Tsukuda Koji and Kato Michinori, for example, wrote in 1919 that:

> it is true that five-*shaku* men followed the Japanese prostitutes, and then spread everywhere [in Southeast Asia].[3] . . . They [the Japanese prostitutes] needed Japanese foods, Japanese beverages, Japanese clothes, and many other Japanese goods. Their demand was met by the queer Japanese sundry-goods stores which dealt in a wide variety of goods, ranging from Japanese clothing to tinned foods. As the Japanese goods were also sold to non-Japanese customers by such stores, they became widely known. The prosperity of [Japan's] Southeast Asian trade today is not thanks to Mitsui & Co. and some other large merchants. But the trade was in fact developed by these sundry-goods retailers, behind whom there was a shadow of the Japanese prostitutes.
>
> (Tsukuda and Kato 1919: 101–2)

In this book, we shall employ the term, 'the *karayuki*-led economic advance', to denote the pattern of the Japanese economic advance into Singapore and other parts of Southeast Asia led initially by Japanese prostitutes. Figure 2.1 shows how the economic advance took place in Southeast Asia. First, many young women from impoverished Japanese villages were smuggled out of Japan and taken to Southeast Asia by procurers to work in Japanese brothels. Second, as the brothels and their inmates increased in number, sundry-goods stores, drapers' shops, photo-graphers, hair-dressers, doctors and other businesses sprang up. They catered initially to the requirements of the *karayuki-san*, but later to other Japanese and non-Japanese as well. Third, the *karayuki-san* and brothel-keepers used part of their earnings to provide loans to other Japanese residents, invest in rubber and other plantations, or remit to their families in Japan. In the meantime, as the Japanese community developed, Japanese consulates were established. Finally, in response to an increase in demand for Japanese goods, trading and shipping companies, banks and other large Japanese companies set up branches/representative offices in the region (Nanyo Dantai Rengokai 1942: 346–9; Nanyo oyobi Nihonjinsha 1938: 134–65; Irie 1942a: 231–8; *idem* 1942b: 227–33).

Even today some Southeast Asia researchers talk about the *karayuki-san*'s initial role in Japan's economic advance, even though they do not make explicit reference to the complete pattern. Sone Sachiko, for example, argues that:

> The *karayuki-san*, as 'beautiful merchandise', were a valuable commodity to export, as there were so few Japanese goods to retail in Southeast Asia in the first fifty years after 1868. . . . In a very real sense, as migrants, Japanese prostitutes were early pioneers in the history of Japanese economic expansion in Southeast Asia, especially in the period before 1920.
>
> (Sone 1992: 48)

Shigeru Ikuta also writes in *Tonan Ajia wo shiru Jiten* (*Encyclopedia of Southeast Asia*) that:

> The relations between Japan and Singapore began with the so-called *karayuki-san*. . . . Following the *karayuki-san*, the Japanese in Singapore were active in various trades in the services industry, including drapers, haberdashery, sundry-goods stores, inns, photo-graphers, doctors, laundry and others. . .
>
> (Ishii *et al.* 1986: 434)

Other scholars such as J.F. Warren, Yano Toru and Shimizu Hajime also take a similar position in their works (Warren 1993: 59–63; Yano 1975: 10–46, 80–9; Shimizu Hajime: 1982: 194–7; *idem* 1994a: 256–8).

This chapter examines the main factors behind the emergence of *karayuki-san* in Singapore, and sheds light on their economic activities. It includes a critical analysis of the popular view about their role in Japan's economic advance into Singapore, arguing that *karayuki-san* were by no means the only channel through which Japan's early economic advance took place into Singapore and other parts of Southeast Asia.

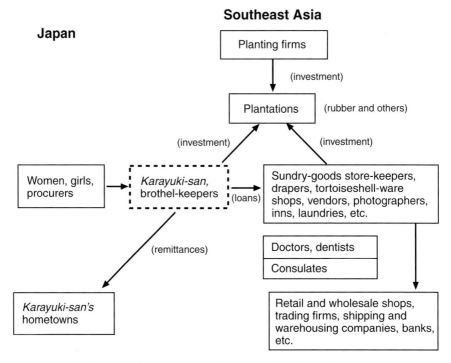

Figure 2.1 The *karayuki*-led economic advance into Southeast Asia.

BACKGROUND TO THE EMERGENCE OF PROSTITUTION IN BRITISH MALAYA

Sex disparity and the colonial policy for prostitution

As Table 2.1 shows, in the early part of the twentieth century there was a much higher proportion of males than females in the Straits Settlements (Singapore, Penang and Malacca), as well as in the Federated and Unfederated Malay States. This gender imbalance was strikingly large among the immigrant populations, notably Chinese, Indians and Europeans (see Table 2.2). It was caused largely by the development of the colonial economy in British Malaya.

In the second half of the nineteenth century, the developing world was closely linked to Europe and the US, thanks to the opening in 1869 of the Suez Canal, the replacement of sailing-ships by steam-ships and the laying of submarine cables for telegraphic communication (Ashworth 1975: 61–79). Southeast Asian produce could now be shipped to the West at a low cost in a shorter period than ever before. As for the Malay Peninsula, tin production increased in the second half of the nineteenth century, while at the turn of

Table 2.1 The number of females to 1,000 males in 1911 and 1921 in towns over 10,000 inhabitants in British Malaya

	Singapore	Penang	Malacca	FMS[a]	UMS[b]
1911	406	563	602	382	698
1921	479	617	587	460	679

Source: Constructed from Nathan 1921: 51.
Notes
[a] Federated Malay States.
[b] Unfederated Malay States.

Table 2.2 Population by race and sex in Singapore

| | 1881 | | 1901 | | 1911 | |
Race	Male	Female	Male	Female	Male	Female
Japanese	8	14	188	578	513	896
Chinese	72,571	14,195	130,367	33,674	161,648	57,929
Indians	9,674	2,464	14,345	3,478	23,069	4,701
Malays	18,627	14,475	20,260	15,820	22,638	19,294
Europeans[a]	2,207	562	2,619	1,205	4,091	1,620
Total[b]	105,423	33,785	170,875	57,680	215,489	87,832

Sources: Constructed from Census of Returns, 1881, 1901, 1911.
Notes
[a] Includes all whites.
[b] Includes others.

the century rubber plantations became increasingly important. Large numbers of workers were recruited in India and China and brought to the peninsula, where they were employed in tin-mining and rubber estates as well as in the construction of peninsular infrastructure. This was partly because there was a shortage of local labour, and partly because the colonial authorities regarded the native Malays as lazy and not very productive.[4]

Singapore, surrounded by the hinterlands of the Malay Peninsula, Thailand and the Dutch East Indies, became a tremendously important entrepôt with the increasing export of Southeast Asian produce to the West and the import of Western industrial goods. Indian and Chinese immigrants, their foodstuffs and other necessities were also brought into the peninsula through the port of Singapore. As a result, Asian immigrants found employment in the construction of its infrastructure and in commerce and other industries, while Caucasians were mainly engaged in administration, the armed forces, foreign trade and other non-menial works. In addition, there were many foreign visitors to the British colony, including seamen, tourists, transit-visitors and so on.

23

In 1911 there was a total population of 303,321 in Singapore, of whom 215,489 were males and 87,832 were females. To make the gender imbalance even worse, the majority of immigrants were young unmarried males, creating a large demand for prostitutes. Males in their twenties and thirties (the sexually most active age group) accounted for 58 per cent of the total male population, whereas females in the same age group constituted 35.6 per cent of the female population (DSS 1983: 7). This simply meant that there was a critical shortage of young women in the British colony. In the Malay Peninsula, the sexual situation was similar to that of Singapore.

As Table 2.3 shows, there were prostitutes of different races in Singapore. In 1885, for example, there were 1,005 licensed prostitutes, of whom over 90 per cent were Chinese, the remainder comprising Europeans, Malays, Japanese and Indians. The colonial authorities were fully aware of the gender imbalance in British Malaya, and of the need for prostitution as a kind of a 'safety-valve' particularly for Asian immigrant workers and British soldiers. Therefore in 1870 the Contagious Disease Ordinance (CDO) was introduced, stipulating that licensed prostitutes were to be registered with the colonial authorities and to undergo regular medical check-ups at the Lock hospital (a hospital established for the treatment of venereal disease) (Lai 1986: 33–4; Edwin Lee 1991: 86–90).

In 1888, however, the Straits Settlements government under the pressure of the British government abolished the CDO, and introduced in its place a new decree, the Women and Girls Protection Ordinance. The administration of licensed prostitution was then transferred to the Chinese Protectorate, which had been established in 1877. The Chinese Protectorate was not empowered under the new ordinance to compel licensed prostitutes to undergo regular medical check-ups, although, since it was given a free hand to close any brothel, it could do so indirectly (Warren 1993: 116–18).

After the abolition of the CDO in 1888, the number of Chinese and Japanese prostitutes increased greatly. European prostitutes, though not shown in the table, continued to ply their trade even after 1888. According to a British Colonial Office document, there were ten European brothels in Singapore in 1900 (PRO, Report by Capper, Acting Protector, 24 July 1900CO 273/25.). It would appear that the colonial authorities did not wish to publicise the existence of white prostitutes.

Of the prostitutes of various races, the *karayuki-san* were most popular among customers. The reasons for it are not difficult to find. Although the Japanese brothels were set up mostly after the abolition of the CDO, they were all licensed. As the Japanese brothels were patronised by many Europeans, the Chinese Protectorate made sure that the Japanese prostitutes were clean. Actually, it made an unofficial list of the Japanese brothel-keepers and their inmates, and kept a close watch over the activities of the Japanese brothels. It even interviewed new Japanese prostitutes, and could compel any brothel-keeper, with the threat of closing her brothel, to send

Table 2.3 Licensed brothels and prostitutes by race in Singapore (annual average)

Year	Brothels	Prostitutes by race					
		Europeans	Japanese	Malays	Indians	Chinese	Total
1885	101	9	16	8	32	940	1,005
1887	225	25	59	13	29	1,668	1,794
1889	227	–	134	22	28	1,880	2,064
1890	410	–	148	20	27	1,911	2,108[a]

Source: Constructed from *Government Gazette*, 12 February 1886:138; 27 April 1888: 924; 24
April 1890: 864; 12 June 1891: 1,110.

Note
[a] Includes two Thais.

her inmates to a private doctor for medical check-ups twice a week (Warren
1993: 149). There were other reasons for the popularity of Japanese prostitutes. They entertained any customers irrespective of race or nationality,
quickly acquired some knowledge of English, and acted as excellent
companions for their customers. Also, they were generally considered to be
honest, as they hardly ever cheated their customers of money or valuables
(Kobayashi and Nonaka 1985: 166; Butcher 1979: 197).[5]

Although Chinese prostitutes were most numerous,[6] they catered mainly
for Chinese customers (Butcher 1979: 196; Warren 1993: 257–62).[7] There
were also Indians and Malays, but most were clandestine prostitutes. As for
the European prostitutes, they went through regular medical check-ups, and
were considered as clean as their Japanese rivals, but they were few in
number, and entertained mainly Caucasian men as customers (Warren 1993:
87–8). It should be noted that they were mostly from France, Central Europe
and Russia, but not from Britain. The colonial authorities banned the
activities of any British prostitute in British Malaya, because, in their view,
such women would tarnish the British prestige (Lockhart 1936: 122–3).
Although there was a tacit agreement among British men that Asian women
should be kept at a distance in public, it was considered acceptable for them
to visit Japanese and other Asian brothels (Warren 1993: 270–1).

Number of *karayuki-san* in British Malaya

The first Japanese prostitute in Singapore is said to have appeared in 1870 or
1871 (Inoue 1915: 76). By about 1878, two Japanese brothels had been set
up in Malay Street . The number of prostitutes then rose steeply, from 16 in
1885 to 134 in 1889, and continued to increase thereafter (Yoshioka 1942:
117; *Government Gazette*, 12 February 1886: 138, and 24 April 1890: 864).
At the end of the nineteenth century, *karayuki-san* and others in the sex
industry constituted a high proportion of the Japanese population in

Southeast Asia. In November 1895, the then Japanese Consul in Singapore, Fujita Toshiro reported to Tokyo that:

> in this port [Singapore] there are approximately 450 to 460 Japanese residents, of whom only 4 out of every 100, i.e. less than 20 in total, are in the respectable trades, and over 400 are prostitutes or those men and women related to them. There are also 200 to 300 Japanese each in Penang, the Malay Peninsula, Java and Sumatra, who are either engaged in prostitution or kept as concubines by non-Japanese men. And, there is an air that no Japanese has a respectable occupation.
>
> (DRO, 4.2.2.27, 16 November 1895).

As Table 2.4 shows, there was a high proportion of women in the Japanese population in Singapore, Malaya and Java in June 1897. In 1897 there were an interpreter for the colonial administration, two medical doctors, and several inn-keepers, while most of the remainder were prostitutes and those connected with them. Moreover, as Table 2.5 shows, in 1901 Japanese women in their teens and twenties accounted for over 80 per cent of the female population, and these age groups were suitable for prostitution. As for men, those in their twenties and thirties accounted for nearly 70 per cent of the male population

In Penang, Malacca and the Malay Peninsula, almost all the Japanese women were prostitutes in 1897. There were some 300 to 400 Japanese prostitutes in Sumatra, over 200 in French Indo-China, and over 100 in Borneo and its nearby islands. It was said that *karayuki-san* could be seen even in a remote place and an isolated island, which were hardly known to ordinary people (DRO 4.2.2.99, 29 July 1897).

Table 2.4 Japanese population by sex and occupation in regions under the jurisdiction of the Japanese Consulate in Singapore (as of 30 June 1897)

Region	Officials M	F	Students M	F	Merchants M	F	Others M	F	Total M	F
Singapore	2	0	11	0	24	2	100[a]	450[a]	137[a]	452[a]
Penang	–	–	–	–	–	–	30	120	30	120
Malacca	–	–	–	–	–	–	10	30	10	30
Malay Peninsula	–	–	–	–	25[b]	–	80	350	105	350
Java	–	–	–	–	6	–	20	150	26	150
Total	2	0	11	0	55	2	240	1,100	308	1,102

Source: Constructed from DRO 4.2.2.99, 29 July 1897.
Notes
[a] Approximate.
[b] Settlers.

As Table 2.6 shows, there were even more *karayuki-san* in Singapore in the early twentieth century. Their number is said to have been well over 600 at the peak around the Russo-Japanese War of 1904–5 (Nanyo oyobi Nihonjinsha 1938: 160). In Penang and Malacca, there were also many Japanese prostitutes (see Table 2.6). And, although we have not obtained any figures for the *karayuki-san* in the Malay Peninsula before World War I, there must have been many. Ronald Hyam writes that 'every village in the Federated Malay States, if it was big enough to have a post office, had its brothel. Most of them were Japanese' (Hyam 1986: 63).

However, as will be studied later, in 1914 most of the Japanese pimps in Singapore were banished from Singapore by the colonial authorities (DRO, 4.2.2.27, 30 May 1914), and restriction on the entry into the British colony of new *karayuki-san* was imposed. As a consequence, the number of Japanese brothels and their inmates declined sharply. As Table 2.6 shows, in 1919 there were 37 brothel-keepers, 138 licensed prostitutes, and nine concubines in Singapore, while in the rest of British Malaya there were 191 brothels, 724 prostitutes and 263 concubines.[8] Finally, in 1920 the Acting Japanese Consul-General, Yamazaki Heikichi took a bold step to abolish the licensed prostitution of *karayuki-san* in British Malaya, with the result that the number of Japanese prostitutes declined sharply thereafter.

Table 2.5 The age composition of the Japanese population in Singapore in 1901

Age	Under 10	10–15	15–20	20–30	30–40	40–50	Over 50	Total
Males	6	9	24	76	52	19	2	188
Females	7	8	145	341	55	20	2	578

Source: Blue Book 1904: 42.

Table 2.6 Number of Japanese brothels and *karayuki-san* in British Malaya

Region	1903 bro.	inm.	con.	1907 bro.	inm.	con.	1910 bro.	inm.	con.	1919 bro.	inm.	con.
Singapore	99	585	–	93	516	–	80	303	52	37	138	9
Penang	32	127	–	39	191	–	28	126	–	–	–	24
Malacca	2	9	–	6	41	–	10	45	–	7	15	4
Malay Peninsula	n.a.	n.a.	n.a.	n.a.	n.a.	n.a.	n.a.	n.a.	n.a.	184	709	235
Total	133	721	–	138	748	–	118	474	52	228	862	272

Source: Constructed from DRO, 7.1.5.4, 21 August 1903, 31 May 1908, and 30 October 1911; DRO, 4.2.2.27, undated.

Notes
bro. is brothels; inm. is inmates; and con. is concubines.

Networks of the flesh traffic

One would wonder why so many young women were 'pushed out' of Japan to become prostitutes in Southeast Asia. There were several factors, including poverty, tradition of working away from home, and the existence of a licensed prostitution system in Japan. The majority of the *karayuki-san* in the region came from impoverished villages in Kyushu, Shikoku and the western part of mainland Japan. As Table 2.7 shows, in December 1889 there were 144 *karayuki-san* in Singapore, of whom nearly 80 per cent came from Nagasaki prefecture, and over 10 per cent from Kumamoto prefecture. By 1902 the total number of *karayuki-san* had risen to 611, and although their birthplaces in Japan also became varied, the two prefectures were still responsible for nearly 50 per cent of the total.

It should be noted, moreover, that there were many *karayuki-san* in Southeast Asia from the Shimabara district of Nagasaki prefecture, and the Amakusa district of Kumamoto prefecture. There were many impoverished villages in these districts which were characterised by over-population, a lack of modern industries, limited cultivable land, which in any case had poor soil, and long traditions of migration into other parts of Japan for employment.[9] Nevertheless, it should be noted that there were similarly many poor agricultural and fishing villages in Tohoku (northern Japan) at that time, but there is no evidence to suggest that large numbers of young women left these villages to work as prostitutes in Southeast Asia. Therefore, it is necessary to explore other factors for the emigration.

Some might suggest a geographical factor. However, although Okinawa was much closer geographically to the region than was Kyushu, there were hardly any *karayuki-san* from the former. As a matter of fact, as of late June 1897, there were 471 Japanese prostitutes in the eastern part of Siberia, but the majority of them were from Kyushu and Chugoku regions (particularly from Nagasaki and Kumamoto prefectures), not from Tohoku and Hokuriku which were closer to Siberia (DRO, 4.2.2.99, 11 August 1897). A more convincing explanation would be the historical relationship between Kyushu

Table 2.7 Birthplaces (prefectures) of Singapore's *karayuki-san*

Dec. 1889	Nagasaki	Kumamoto	Hyogo	Shizuoka	Okayama	Other	Total
	112	19	4	3	2	4	144
Aug. 1902	Nagasaki	Kumamoto	Yamaguchi	Fukuoka	Saga	Other	Total
	187	96	29	22	19	258	611

Source: Compiled from DRO, 4.2.2.27, 4 January 1890, and 5 September 1902.
Note
The totals include brothel-keepers, some of whom also worked as prostitutes. According to a Straits Settlement document, as of December 1889 the number of *karayuki-san* registered with the Chinese Protectorate was 150 (*Government Gazette*, 24 April 1890: 864).

and foreign countries. After the mid-Tokugawa era, many Amakusa and Shimabara people continued to work in other regions, especially in Nagasaki, which prospered as the only port permitted to conduct foreign trade with China and the Netherlands during the period of Japan's closed door policy (Mori Katsumi 1959: 22, 50; Irie 1943: 172–3). The Dutch and the Chinese residents in Dejima, Nagasaki, employed Japanese women and girls as maids, wet nurses, and babysitters, while the men were entertained by Japanese prostitutes and *geisha* (Kobayashi and Nonaka 1985: 76). Besides, as will be studied in detail shortly, in the Meiji era there were sea-routes through which Kyushu women could stow away to China and Southeast Asia.

The existence of licensed prostitution in Japan also played a part in encouraging Japanese women to work as prostitutes in Southeast Asia. In the Meiji and the Taisho eras, there were brothels in almost every part of the country, creating great demand for young women, and many daughters from poverty-stricken families were traded by procurers. As Table 2.8 shows, there were nearly 49,000 licensed prostitutes, but since geisha and barmaids were more often than not engaged in prostitution, they also need to be included in the category of 'prostitutes'. In addition, there were many more women who were not included in the official statistics.

It is true that, as early as April 1896, the Emigrants Protection Act was passed, forbidding prostitutes and vice racketeers to go abroad. But, since it was not applied to Korea and China, procurers were able to take Japanese women to other parts of the world via these countries (Morisaki 1976: 46, 116). Indeed, it was only in 1956 that an anti-prostitution law was passed in Japan, with effect from April 1958.

How did Japanese women then go to Southeast Asia as stowaways? Prior to World War I, there existed highly organised flesh trade networks, linking Japan with Asia, Australia and Africa (including Zanzibar and the Cape of Good Hope), which were controlled by several kingpins[10] (DRO, 4.2.2.27, 16 November 1895). The kingpins were the bosses for kidnappers and procurers of young women in Japan, and were men of influence in the red-light districts and the early Japanese communities abroad. Around 1900 and 1901 there were some 4,000 Japanese prostitutes in the area stretching from the Malay Peninsula to the Medan district in Sumatra, and it was the kingpins who were responsible for supplying some 500 to 600 new Japanese women a year (Nanyo oyobi Nihonjinsha 1938: 152).

Table 2.8 Numbers of *geisha*, barmaids, and licensed prostitutes (end of 1910)

Geisha	Barmaids	Licensed prostitutes	Total
37,038	23,956	48,769	109,763

Source: *Kakushin*, vol. 2, no. 2, February 1912: 6–7.

It would be wrong to assume that all the *karayuki-san* were kidnapped in Japan, and taken to Southeast Asia. Although in the early period many women were deceived with honeyed words by flesh dealers and kidnapped by them, there were also large numbers of those who were impressed by former *karayuki-san*, and became *karayuki-san* of their own free will. Besides, many women were sold by their poverty-stricken families into bondage to work for brothels in Southeast Asia and other parts of the world (DRO, B.9.10.0/1–1–1, 10 June 1930).

At any rate, one cannot imagine that young women could stow away to Southeast Asia alone, for it was extremely difficult to travel abroad at that time. In fact they were normally accompanied by procurers through Kuchinotsu, Moji, Nagasaki and other Japanese ports. This is shown in Figure 2.2. The port of Kuchinotsu, used for shipping Miike coal, was particularly important. Generally, they first landed at Shanghai and Hong Kong, and then some of them were taken to Singapore. Those unsold in Singapore were once again taken to other destinations (DRO, 4.2.2.27, 5 September 1902 and 14 June 1922). Kuchinotsu became less important in the late Meiji era when Miike coal was increasingly shipped through the Miike port which was opened in 1908. By this time, Moji and Nagasaki had become the main ports for illegal emigration (Morisaki 1976: 46).

In the 1870s and 1880s Shanghai and Hong Kong were the two leading centres for prostitution in Asia and the redistribution of Japanese women (Warren 1989: 53–4). Since the late sixteenth century there had been no formal diplomatic relations between Japan and China, but in 1871 the Sino-Japanese Friendship Treaty (the first Sino-Japanese Commercial and Navigation Treaty) was concluded, re-establishing diplomatic relations between the two countries. This enabled the Japanese to travel to Shanghai, from where they could move on to Hong Kong and Southeast Asia.

In the late nineteenth century foreign ships chartered by large Japanese companies for the transportation of coal were used by procurers for the purpose of stowing away. At the end of the 1880s, for example, the steamer *Marcia*, which was chartered by the Takashima Coal Mining Company for the transport of coal from Nagasaki to Hong Kong, carried Japanese women to Hong Kong at each sailing. Women were rarely taken on board when the ship was at anchor, for they were normally picked up in the offing. On 31 December 1887, Captain Mackintosh picked up three men and 36 women at Nagasaki, and carried them in the steamer to Hong Kong, charging HK$9 per woman. At Hong Kong, women were hidden in the passageways and store-rooms when the port authorities came on board for inspection (DRO, 4.2.2.34, 24 January 1888).

By the end of the nineteenth century, Singapore had emerged as the leading transit port for redistribution of Japanese women to other parts of Southeast Asia, outstripping Shanghai and Hong Kong (Warren 1989: 53–4). This was largely because there was an increase in the number of

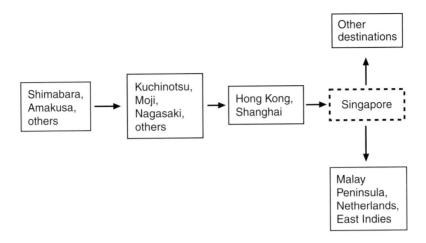

Figure 2.2 Stowing-away routes for Japanese women at the end of the nineteenth century.

Japanese ships calling at the port, while the demand for prostitutes grew enormously with the development of the colonial economies in the Southeast Asian region. There was also a restriction on the number of Japanese brothels and inmates in Hong Kong after 1885 (DRO, 4.2.2.99, 29 February 1912; Taiwan Sotokufu Nettai Sangyo 1937: 306–7).

In the late nineteenth century, four or five Japanese women without passports arrived at Singapore by the Nippon Yusen Kaisha's ships every week, and 80 to 90 per cent of them were from poverty-stricken families in Japan (DRO, 4.2.2.27, 16 November 1895). In early September, 1902, William Evans, the director of the Chinese Protectorate, visited the Japanese Consulate, and informed the Consul that:

> Recently there are many Japanese women without passports, who land in Singapore with the main purpose of prostitution. Each ship brings some 20 to 30 women. Although the Chinese Protectorate examines these women very strictly, it cannot refuse legally to issue licences to them in Singapore, if they insist on becoming prostitutes out of their own free will.
>
> (DRO, 4.2.2.27, 5 September 1902)

He therefore asked the Consul for co-operation in dealing with them (*ibid.*). However, the number of Japanese women who landed in Singapore did not decline, as there were more than 1,000 of them in 1905 (DRO, 4.2.2.27, 13 June 1906).

The flesh traffic in women was very lucrative. According to Nanyo oyobi Nihonjinsha, the average price for a Japanese woman was $250 ex Hong

31

Kong, $300–350 ex Singapore. It was said that, even after deducting travelling and other miscellaneous expenses, the procurer could make some $200 per woman (Nanyo oyobi Nihonjinsha 1938: 155). However, Fujita Tenmin, a journalist based in the Malay Peninsula, wrote in 1913 that Japanese women were even more expensive, costing ¥600 to ¥700 ($510 to $595) per head in Singapore (*Kakushin*, vol. 3, no. 12, December 1913: 24).

Those who remained unsold by auction in Singapore were sent to other parts of Southeast Asia, including Penang, Kuala Lumpur, Ipoh and the main port cities in the Netherlands East Indies (*ibid.*). There were those who were transferred to other countries after working in the British colony for some time, while there were also those who moved to other parts of Southeast Asia of their own volition after the end of their bondage period. The first destination for those sent to the Dutch colony was normally Medan. They were then taken by pimps to Java, Palembang, the Celebes and elsewhere (Ishii 1978: 17–18). Makassar and Surabaya were two leading redistribution centres for the Celebes and Java respectively. From the port of Surabaya, *karayuki-san* were then redistributed to the neighbouring islands, while those who were gathered in Makassar were also sent eastwards, eventually to Australia (DRO, 4.2.2.27, 14 March 1912).

Some European men who resided in other parts of Southeast Asia visited Singapore to procure Japanese women. For example, some of the Caucasian men working in plantations in Sumatra visited Singapore during holidays, bought *karayuki-san* from brothel-keepers, and returned with them to Sumatra (Irie 1942a: 231). According to John Butcher, some 90 per cent of the Caucasian men in the Malay Peninsula kept Asian concubines at the beginning of the twentieth century (Butcher 1979: 200–1). It is possible that some of them visited Singapore, and brought *karayuki-san* back to the peninsula. Although he does not give the racial composition of the women, it is highly likely that there were many *karayuki-san* among them. Indeed, according to a Japanese Foreign Office document, as of late December 1919 there were 272 Japanese concubines kept by non-Japanese men in British Malaya, of whom the large majority were in the Malay Peninsula (DRO, 4.2.2.27, undated). Unfortunately, there is no available information to show how many of these women were the concubines of Caucasian men.

The *karayuki-san* were very popular among Caucasian men in Malaya and the Netherlands East Indies, for they were very clean, and were generally devoted and submissive to them. When their 'masters' decided to marry white women, or when their wives were about to return from Europe to live with them, the *karayuki-san* would simply leave them after getting a considerable sum of alimony. However, Malay and Indonesian women were often not ready to leave their 'masters', with the result that they were considered a nuisance when the white men wanted to take wives from their mother countries (Shimizu Hiroshi 1991: 27–8; Kobayashi and Nonaka 1985: 166; Butcher 1979: 194–216; Maugham 1985: 157–201).

THE ROLE OF *KARAYUKI-SAN* IN JAPAN'S ECONOMIC ADVANCE

Organisation and management of the brothels

In the pre-World War II period, there were two distinct groups of Japanese residents in Singapore, namely the *shitamachi-zoku* (downtown people) and the *gudang zoku* (the '*élite*' class). The *shitamachi-zoku* lived mainly in the Japanese town around High Street and Middle Road, comprising the long term settlers, such as *karayuki-san*, brothel-keepers and proprietors of retail shops. It is true that most of the *karayuki-san* initially intended to stay in Singapore or other parts of Southeast Asia for only a few years, but in fact resided there for many years due to illness, increasing debts to brothel-keepers and for other reasons. Indeed even if they wanted to go back to Japan, they could not easily do so, for most of them were illiterate and therefore had hardly any prospect of finding alternative employment in their country.

The *gudang zoku* resided in the colony for a short period (probably two or three years), and comprised the employees of trading companies, banks and other large Japanese firms located in the commercial centre around Raffles Place and Battery Road (Yano 1975: 124–9; Shimizu Hajime 1982: 204–6). Their life-style was probably similar to that of the Europeans working for the banks, merchant houses and other large Western institutions in Singapore. Besides the employees of Japanese firms, there were also dentists and doctors who belonged to the elite class. However, most of them resided in the Japanese town for many years, and treated all classes of Japanese patients, while some of them were active in taking care of non-Japanese patients as well.

As we shall see shortly, *karayuki-san* and other members of the *shitamachi-zoku* were mutually dependent. In 1905, there were 109 Japanese brothels with 633 *karayuki-san* in Singapore. They were mainly located in Hylam Street, Malabar Street, Malay Street and Bugis Street, even though some were in Sago Street, Banda Street and Spring Street (Warren 1993: 49). Around these streets there were large numbers of *shitamachi-zoku*, including sundry-goods storekeepers, drapers, photographers and other self-employed Japanese residents, who were all closely connected to the *karayuki-san* for their living.[11]

Each brothel kept an average of five to seven inmates, and was managed by a Japanese mistress. As men were not permitted to manage any brothels openly in British Malaya, Japanese pimps had no choice but to register their brothels under the names of their legal or common-law wives as *de jure* brothel-keepers. They then kept sundry-goods stores or other shops as fronts, while controlling their brothels behind the scenes.

As noted earlier, the majority of *karayuki-san* in Singapore were from Kyushu, and this was equally true of Japanese pimps. Indeed, as Table 2.9 shows, in 1914 most pimps were also from the same island in Japan. In the early twentieth century, there were several well-known pimps, including Futaki Tagajiro, a certain Yonei, Shibya Ginji and Kobayashi Chiyomatsu. Futaki and Yonei were said to be particularly influential, commanding many followers, and vying against each other for the extension of their respective territories at the expense of the other (Nishimura Tekeshiro 1941: 97 and 148). It would be wrong, however, to simply assume that all the pimps were scoundrels. Although they were actively engaged in the flesh trade, they were at the same time prepared to make large contributions to the development of the early Japanese community in Singapore. In 1891, for example, Futaki Tagajiro together with Shibuya Ginji and Nakagawa Kikuzo built a Japanese cemetery in Yio Chu Kang as the burial ground for deceased *karayuki-san* and other Japanese. Six acres of land owned by Futaki and two acres of public land were used for this purpose (Shingaporu Nihonjinkai 1983: 8–9).[12]

One of the main jobs for the pimps was to procure young and attractive women to replace the old and the dead, whenever necessary. As noted earlier, young Japanese women were 'precious commodities' and were very expensive. The Japanese brothels therefore had to outlay considerable sums of money to procure them, which they did by reinvesting their profits and obtaining loans from local money-lenders.[13] It is said that, although local money lenders were, in general, unwilling to lend money to individual Japanese on account of the high risks involved, they made an exception for the highly profitable brothels. According to Murakami Shoichi, the cost of procuring more than 1,000 Japanese women in British Malaya were met by loans from Chinese money lenders (Murakami 1916: 74).

Karayuki-san also earned a lot of money. Japanese brothels normally operated on a shift basis for 24 hours a day, seven days a week, in order to cater for their customers at any time (Warren 1993: 65 and 68). How much did the *karayuki-san* charge their customers? Nishijima Masanobu, who lived in Singapore from 1912 to 1924, said that the fee was $5, and Nanyo oyobi Nihonjinsha also wrote that just before the outbreak of the First World War, the fee was usually $5 (Mori Katsumi 1959: 116; Nanyo oyobi Nihonjinsha 1938: 162). Although neither of them makes it clear whether it was a charge for one encounter or an overnight stay, it seems to have been the latter, as $5 was a good sum of money at that time.

Table 2.9 Birthplaces of Japanese pimps by prefecture (as of May 1914)

Nagasaki	Kumamoto	Saga	Fukuoka	Hyogo	Other[a]	Total
14	7	3	2	2	9	37

Source: DRO, 4.2.2.27, 30 May 1914.
Note
[a] One each from Aichi, Gunma, Tokyo, Hiroshima, Kanagawa, Oita, Ehime and Kyoto. The birthplace of one pimp is unknown.

Prior to the First World War, a *karayuki-san*'s average earnings were $75–$150 per month; those who made more than $150 were given special allowances by their brothel-keepers (*Kakushin*, vol. 3, no. 12, December 1913: 25). In comparison, the average daily pay of female workers in the Japanese manufacturing industry was a mere ¥0.20 (about 18 cents) in 1900, and ¥0.30 (about 27 cents) in 1910 (Ando 1975: 12). In Singapore in 1913, the daily pay of carpenters, joiners, blacksmiths and bricklayers was 45–75 cents, while the annual earnings of domestic servants were $72–$180 with food (*Blue Book* 1913: W3).

It is often said that the *karayuki-san* remitted huge amounts of foreign exchange to their hometowns in Japan. Kimura Masutaro, the director of the Singapore Commercial Museum, wrote in the May 1919 issue of *Nanyo Kyokai Zasshi* (Journal of the South Seas Association) that, 'there are at least 1,000 [Japanese] prostitutes in and around Singapore and the Malay Peninsula. . . . I hear the total remittances to Japan by these prostitutes amount to about half a million yen a year' (*Nanyo Kyokai Zasshi*, vol. 5, no. 5, May 1919: 33).

However, there is another view on the question of remittances. Fujita Tenmin argued that 'if all the earnings were remitted to Japan, they must have amounted to a huge amount, but the amount actually remitted to their parents in Japan is less than one-tenth of the total' (*Kakushin*, vol. 3, no. 12, December 1913: 25). We are inclined to think that Fujita's comment is exaggerated, but it is true that as soon as Japanese women began their careers as prostitutes they usually incurred a heavy debt of $500–$600, and were bonded to their brothels for four to five years on average (DRO, 4.2.2.27, 5 September 1902). The composition of the debts differed from one *karayuki-san* to another, but in general they comprised pre-payment to parents by procurers, travel expenses from Japan to Singapore, costs of bedding and furniture, etc. (Nanyo oyobi Nihonjinsha 1938: 161–2). As the debts were deducted from their daily earnings which were shared on a fifty–fifty basis with their brothel-keepers, the *karayuki-san* had little money left at least during the period of bondage.

Additionally, the *karayuki-san* had to pay for the full cost of regular medical check-ups at private clinics (*ibid.*: 163). If and when they fell ill, their debts would be multiplied, extending the bondage period. There were also large numbers of *karayuki-san* who died of illness or committed suicide. Indeed, even today, many unnamed gravestones belonging to *karayuki-san* stand desolately in the Japanese cemetery in Singapore.

It is however true that, unlike prostitutes in Japan, the *karayuki-san* in British Malaya were free to go out, and were seldom punished even if they could not get any customers for a whole day (*ibid.*: 161–2). Moreover, although they were issued with licences by the colonial authorities, they were entirely free to quit their trade at any time. And as soon as they ceased to work as prostitutes, their debts to brothel-keepers would be written off unconditionally. For this reason, the brothel-keepers did not normally inform the inmates of their legal entitlements. However, since most of the *karayuki-san* were honest and loyal to their brothel-keepers, they did nothing to cause any nuisance to the latter (*Kakushin*, vol. 3, no. 12, December 1913: 24). At any rate, as pointed out earlier, most of the *karayuki-san* were illiterate, and were fully aware that if they returned to Japan, they would have great difficulty in finding an alternative job. It was the same in British Malaya. Indeed, some of the *karayuki-san* who dared to quit their trade could not find a decent job, and most ended up as concubines to Europeans, Chinese or other men (DRO, 4.2.2.27, 5 September 1902). Under these circumstances, very few of the *karayuki-san* could wash their hands of their trade.

The *karayuki-san's* economic relations with the Japanese community

As Table 2.10 shows, in 1903 there were 948 Japanese residents in Singapore, of whom 666 persons (or over 70 per cent of the total) were engaged directly in the sex industry. Most of the remainder were initially dependent heavily upon the *karayuki-san* and brothel-keepers as customers, and included sundry-goods store-keepers, drapers, doctors, shop-keepers selling tortoiseshell ware, photographers, and the like. We shall take the drapers and doctors as case studies, in order to show the readers how some trades were much involved with the sex industry.

Japanese drapers' shops were indispensable in the red-light districts of Singapore and other parts of Southeast Asia, for the *karayuki-san* usually wore kimono. Before World War I, the drapers catering to the *karayuki-san* in Singapore included Takahashi Chubei's Echigoya Gofukuten and Koyama Shinnosuke's Shin-Koyama Shoten in Middle Road, Koyama Yoshimatsu's Koyama Shoten in Malabar Street, Shirono Shozo's Nihon Shokai in North Bridge Road, and Ishii Inosuke's Maruju Gofukuten (Yano 1975: 87). Although the names of all these drapers are listed in *Nanyo no Shin-Nihonjinmura* (The New Japanese Villages in the South Seas), published in January 1919, the owner of Maruju Gofukuten was not actually Mr Ishii Inosuke, but Ms Yamada Miyo (Tsukuda and Kato 1919: 108–23). There is no information about their relationship, but it is known that Ishii, also a pimp, had been banished from Singapore by the colonial authorities in 1914 (DRO, 4.2.2.27, 30 May 1914).

Of the above-mentioned drapers, Echigoya Gofukuten was the most successful. Its owner, Takahashi Chubei set up a draper's shop in the Japanese red-light district in Hong Kong in 1904. But, as it did not prosper, he moved to Singapore in 1908, where he opened a small draper's shop in Middle Road, catering to the *karayuki-san*. He sold kimono and related goods to them on a cash basis, and continued to extend his business with sound management (Nakane 1976: 119; Yano 1975: 84–9). In 1915, he acquired a 79–acre rubber estate in Johore (Tsukuda and Kato 1919: 225).

Table 2.10 Japanese residents in Singapore by sex and occupation (as of late June 1903)

Occupation	No. of households	Males	Females	Total
Officials	2	3	3	6
Traders	1	6	–	6
Sundry-goods store-keepers	12	43	19	62
Travellers' inns	6	10	8	18
Eating houses	4	10	7	17
Coffee shops	14	14	26	40
Hairdressers	1	5	3	8
Laundries	5	19	4	23
Doctors	3	11	7	18
Monks	1	7	3	10
Tortoiseshell-makers	1	2	1	3
Dart-game shops	3	1	4	5
Drapers	3	8	2	10
Tailors	1	–	2	2
Carpenters	1	4	2	6
Animal husbandry	1	3	1	4
Brothels	99	1	80	81
Prostitutes	–	–	585	585
Others[a]	18	32	12	44
Total	176	179	769	948

Source: DRO, 7.1.5.4, 21 August 1903.

Note

[a] Includes dependants and the unemployed.

When licensed Japanese prostitution was abolished in British Malaya in 1920, he swiftly switched to dealing in the type of clothes required by his Caucasian customers, even though he initially had some difficulties. In 1923, there was the Kanto Earthquake in Japan, and he made large profits by organising a relief bazaar, and sending large quantities of textiles to Japan. In the meantime, in 1916 Fukuda Kurahachi, who had just graduated from a primary school, was brought to Singapore by Takahashi to work for Echigoya Gofukuten. In 1933, Takahashi Chubei died, and in the following year, his widow, Sawa, reorganised the draper's shop into a company with Fukuda as the manager. Sawa kept 50 per cent of the shares, while the remaining 50 per cent was owned by the employees including Fukuda. As the company then continued to prosper under Fukuda's management, it could build a three-storeyed shop with a lift installation in the Middle Road in 1937 (*ibid.* 1976: 119–20; Shingaporu Nihonjinkai 1978: 183).

It would be wrong to assume, however, that there were many successful cases like Echigoya Gofukuten. As a matter of fact, only a few of the Japanese retailers, including the drapers, who relied heavily on the custom of the *karayuki-san* had a thriving trade. As the Commercial Bureau of the Japanese Foreign Ministry explained in January 1896:

> Many of the shop keepers [in Singapore] had previously been sailors, shell-fish collectors, gamblers, or prostitutes/brothel keepers. . . . There are also those who came [to Singapore] with few articles for sale, after hearing a rumour about the [prosperous] business. Very few of them come with firm determination to engage in commerce from the beginning.
>
> (*Tsusho Isan*, 4 January 1896: 33)

Next, we shall examine the relationship between the *karayuki-san* and medical doctors. As mentioned earlier, the *karayuki-san* were required to attend clinics for medical check-ups twice a week, and underwent treatment if they had contracted VD. As the number of *karayuki-san* continued to increase sharply from the late nineteenth century, the demand for Japanese doctors rose correspondingly.

In British Malaya, Japanese doctors could practise medicine freely, for Japanese medical qualifications were recognised by the colonial authorities.[14] In consequence, by 1903 three Japanese clinics had been opened, with the fourth one being established in 1910. Nakano Kozo from Nagasaki was the first Japanese doctor to open a clinic in Singapore in 1894, and he continued to practise medicine there until his death in 1923. He practised under the auspices of the Singapore branch of Mitsui & Co., and was, along with such influential pimps as Futaki Tagajiro and Kobayashi Chiyomatsu, one of the leading figures in the Japanese red-light district before World War I. It was said that, 'had any new arrival not paid his respects to Nakano, he would have been in trouble' (Nishimura Takeshiro 1941: 148).

Although the Japanese clinics were originally opened to cater mainly to the *karayuki-san*, one of the doctors, Nishimura Takeshiro was very active in providing medical services to both Japanese and non-Japanese patients. Nishimura opened a clinic in September 1902 in Bras Basah Road, and then moved to Beach Road. After he moved again to Middle Road in November 1903, he gave medical treatment to Osman, a member of the Jambi royalty in Sumatra. Soon afterward, many other Malays began to visit his clinic, as his reputation spread widely by word of mouth (*ibid.*: 46). After he moved to Hill Street, a Chinese residential area, in August 1906, his outpatients were mainly Chinese. At first, most of the Japanese residents regarded him as a rather peculiar doctor who specialised in non-Japanese patients, and kept aloof from himHowever, when it became known that he was favoured by the Malay royalty and influential Chinese merchants, he began to be highly respected by the Japanese community (*ibid.*: 68 and 145). He was eventually appointed to the post of president of the Japanese Association in December 1934.

Prior to World War II, almost all Japanese doctors were fairly successful, for they provided medical services to both Japanese and non-Japanese patients, and continued to practise medicine in Singapore for many years. This is equally true of Japanese dentists.

At this point, we shall consider how the *karayuki-san* and brothel-keepers made use of part of their earnings. As noted earlier, some of it was remitted to their families in Japan. It is possible that the Singapore branches of the Japanese banks made certain profits out of the remittance arrangements, but, in view of the paucity of the relevant statistical data, it is impossible to determine accurately the total remittances made in any year before 1920. It is highly likely that some, if not a large part, of the foreign exchange earned by the *karayuki-san* was squandered by their pimps and the like. At any rate, it was not until 1912 that the Bank of Taiwan set up the first branch of a Japanese bank in Singapore, while two other Japanese banks, the Yokohama Specie Bank and the China and Southern Bank opened their branches in 1916 and 1919 respectively. These branches were set up largely to provide credit and foreign exchange facilities to merchants, plantation companies and other credit-worthy Japanese, mainly in British Malaya.

The *karayuki-san* and brothel-keepers/pimps also used part of their earnings to invest in rubber plantations and to make loans to other Japanese residents. In 1902, Kasada Naokichi and Nakagawa Kikuzo, who were said to be pimps, jointly purchased a 150–acre rubber estate in Seremban, Negri Sembilan in the Malay Peninsula. It was the first time that a Japanese in British Malaya had purchased a rubber estate (Kobayashi and Nonaka 1985: 96–7; Hara 1978: 257).[15] And, from 1909 onward, prostitutes, brothel-keepers, sundry-goods store keepers, doctors and other Japanese began to buy small-sized rubber estates in Johore or elsewhere in the peninsula (Kobayashi and Nonaka: 96–7). In Johore, for example, Futaki Tagajiro, a pimp, bought an estate of 500 acres (with a planted area of 200 acres) in December 1909, while Nakano Kozo, a medical doctor, bought, jointly with two other Japanese, a 1,000–acre rubber estate (with a planted area of 400 acres) in July 1910. There were also many women among the Japanese owners of rubber estates, most of whom seem to have been *karayuki-san* or former *karayuki-san* (Gaimusho Tsushokyoku 1918: 114–15).[16] Some of the Japanese drapers also invested in rubber estates in Johore. In 1910, Koyama Yoshimatsu acquired a 413–acre rubber estate (with a planted area of 370 acres), and Shirono Shozo a 215–acre rubber estate (planted area 85 acres), while in 1915 Takahashi Chubei bought a 79–acre rubber estate (planted area 79 acres). Koyama's rubber estate was large for a privately owned one, as it produced 1,800 kg of raw rubber per month, and, as of March 1917, employed seven Japanese workers and 150 coolies (Tsukuda and Kato 1919: 224–5). It should be borne in mind, however, that many of the privately owned rubber estates frequently changed hands as early as the 1910s, largely on account of a lack of funds. When the price of rubber collapsed in 1920, it dealt a fatal blow to many individual investors (Hara 1978: 262).

As for loans, the *karayuki-san* and brothel-keepers seemed to have given fairly large amounts to other Japanese residents. There were 28 mutual-aid societies in various parts of the Malay Peninsula before the abolition of licensed Japanese prostitution in 1920. It is said that *karayuki-san* contributed $10,000 out of the total monthly contributions of $26,000. Also, loans advanced to Japanese residents by local money lenders at an interest rate of 40 per cent per annum amounted to some $1 million in 1919. Of this amount, some 30 per cent is said to have been lent to Japanese residents under the names of credit-worthy *karayuki-san* and brothel-keepers (DRO, 4.2.2.27, 29 December 1920).

From the above, it can be safely assumed that the sex industry had a considerable financial impact on the Japanese community. But there was also the risk of bad debts, for brothel-keepers often used part of their inmates' savings to extend loans to a variety of Japanese residents. When the post-World War I recession occurred, the brothel-keepers experienced great difficulties in recovering the principals of their loans from their debtors. For this reason, even if the *karayuki-san* wanted to quit their trade when licensed prostitution was abolished, they could not do so. Indeed, many of them had no choice but to become 'sly' (i.e. illicit) prostitutes because of their financial problems (*ibid.*).

It should be noted at this point that there were some positive effects of the brothel business on Japan's economic advance into British Malaya. Japanese brothels, for example, increased the demand for the Japanese beers imported by Mitsui & Co. and other trading companies, as the *karayuki-san* encouraged their customers to drink. Indeed, R.H. Lockhart, a Scotsman, who worked as a planter in British Malaya after 1908, recalls in his book that he and his colleagues visited Japanese brothels after playing football, and had a nice time there, drinking a lot of Japanese beer (Lockhart 1932: 5; *idem* 1936: 124). More importantly, it was partly through the customers that the brand names of the Japanese beers became established in British Malaya and other parts of Southeast Asia. In 1905, the volume of imported Japanese beer amounted to 2,748 dozens ($7,568), some of which were drunk by the customers at the brothels (*Tsusho Isan*, 23 September 1908: 19). When Caucasian and Chinese men visited Japanese brothels, they often used rickshaw transport, increasing the demand for Japanese rickshaws: up till about 1920, most of the rickshaws in use in British Malaya were Japanese made (Shingaporu Shohin Chinretsukan 1920: 450).

DECLINE AND ABOLITION OF JAPANESE PROSTITUTION

Movements for the abolition of prostitution

In the late nineteenth century, public opinion became increasingly critical of the traffic in women and girls in Western Europe, and in 1899, an international conference was held in London to ban it. In 1904 an agreement was concluded in Paris by the European countries, including Britain and the Netherlands, on the control over the traffic in women and girls for prostitution purposes. Moreover, in 1910, another agreement was signed at an international conference in Paris to ban it, and contained two main points. First, if anyone lured or enticed a female minor to engage in prostitution, even if it was with her consent, and in a foreign country, he should be punished. Second, anyone who forced an adult woman to engage in prostitution even in a foreign country should be punished (Mori Katsumi 1959: 226–7).

Movements for the abolition of prostitution spread into the European colonies in Asia. It was the Netherlands East Indies which was the first country in Southeast Asia to abolish licensed prostitution. As the Netherlands was one of the signatories of the 1904 agreement at the international conference in Paris, in March 1908 the Dutch government at the Hague asked the Japanese government, through the Colonial Administration at Batavia, to understand the importance of the agreement with reference to the Netherlands East Indies where there were large numbers of *karayuki-san* (DRO, 4.2.2.27, 15 April 1915). As soon as A.W.F. Idenburg, a staunch Calvinist, was appointed as Governor-General at Batavia in 1909, he declared that within three years prostitution ought to be eliminated for the sake of improving public morals in the Dutch colony. Also the priests in various parts of the Netherlands East Indies came to co-operate with the National Committee for Opposing the Trade in Women in the Netherlands to press the Dutch government to do something about the traffic in Japanese women in the Dutch colony (*ibid.*, 14 March 1912; *Bataviasch Nieuwsblad*, 12 March 1912).

On 1 April 1912, the Batavia government put into effect an immigration control law with a view to preventing prostitutes and vice racketeers from entering Java and Madura, and in mid-August of the following year ordered Japanese brothel-keepers in Batavia to close their brothels by the end of the month. Also, the Batavia government decided to provide financial assistance to those *karayuki-san* who needed travel expenses for returning to Japan (DRO, 4.2.2.27, 17 August 1913). Moreover, on 1 September 1913, the Netherlands East Indies' amended penal code came into effect. Clause 250b of Article 1 read that 'anyone who makes a profession or a habit of intentionally causing or promoting fornication by others with third persons, shall be punished with imprisonment from one month to one year or a fine of 100 guilders to 1000 guilders', and Clause 250c stipulated that 'anyone, who is engaged in the trade in women shall be punished with imprisonment from two to five years'. Clause 208a of Article 2 stipulated that 'anyone, who makes a profit out of women's fornication as a brothel-keeper shall be punished with imprisonment from one to three years' (*Java Gazette*, Resolution no. 33, Proclamation no. 265).

41

It is likely that the British colonial policy on prostitution was influenced, to a certain extent, by the measures taken by the Dutch Colonial Administration at Batavia. In Singapore various individuals and organisations worked hard to achieve the abolition of licensed prostitution. A Moral Improvement Committee, organised by the local Christian association, for example, gave a series of lectures on public morals for a week, while appealing to the Governor-General for the abolition of licensed prostitution (DRO, 4.2.2.27, 30 May 1914). On 9 June 1913, after the last session of the Malaya Conference of the church held in Singapore, the Reverend William E. Horley of the Methodist Episcopal Church in Ipoh, Perak, sent a letter to the Japanese Consul to draw his attention 'to the frightful immorality existing in the Straits Settlements, and the Federated Malay States', and to ask him:

> to take steps to [abolish] it, on the same lines as the English Government, who have just passed new laws to stop the 'Hotel Slave Traffic'. The fair name of Japan is disgraced in these lands because of this traffic . . . We urge your Government to punish all procurers by flogging and imprisonment and to prevent any ship from leaving Japan with unmarried girls, destined for immoral purposes.
>
> (DRO, 4.2.2.27, 30 June 1913)

Mr Miles, a British priest at St Andrew's Cathedral, who had previously lived in Japan, also appealed strongly to the Japanese Consul for the abolition of prostitution (DRO, 4.2.2.27, undated).

However, in Singapore it was the European pimps, rather than the Japanese ones, who were the first to be imprisoned and subsequently banished under the 1912 amendment to the Women and Girls Protection Ordinance, as the colonial authorities wanted to alleviate criticism against licensed prostitution by public opinion in Western Europe.

In the meantime, just before World War I, there had been a major change in the Japanese community, as the bosses who had controlled the red-light district in Singapore passed away. Futaki Tagajiro died in the British colony in 1912, and Shibuya Ginji in Yokohama at the end of the Meiji era.[17] Moreover, in 1914 the Japanese red-light district underwent a major setback, when most of the Japanese pimps were banished by the colonial authorities. In the early 1910s, some Japanese pimps opened disreputable coffee shops in North Bridge Road, taking away customers. As the proprietors of the five or six existing coffee shops began to suffer from severe competition from them, they informed the colonial authorities of the illegal activities of the pimps, and this eventually led to the 'hunting out of Japanese pimps' (Nanyo oyobi Nihonjinsha 1938: 147).

On 31 March 1914, R.J. Wilkinson, the Colonial Secretary of the Straits Settlements government, visited the Japanese Consul Fujii Minoru and informed him that the Colonial Administration had decided to banish 37

42

Japanese pimps. Fujii was apprehensive of the fact that the banishment of so many Japanese pimps might give the world the wrong impression that Japanese were causing harm to public security, while advocates for an anti-Japanese policy in various countries might make use of it as a pretext for placing obstacles in the way of Japan's overseas expansion. Therefore, he visited Wilkinson to explain that, although twelve pimps were directly engaged in running the harlot business, the other 25 were not directly involved in it, for their wives or common-law wives ran the brothels. He then asked the Colonial Secretary that they should be told to leave the colony voluntarily (DRO, 4.2.2.27, 30 May 1914).

On 28 April 1914, the Chinese Protectorate arrested three Japanese pimps and imprisoned them as an exemplary punishment.[18] However, they were released on 21 May, thanks largely to Fujii's tough negotiation with the colonial authorities, and returned to Japan 'voluntarily' a week later by the Nippon Yusen Kaisha ship, *Kita no Maru*, (*ibid.*). Through the mutual aid society of the Japanese red-light district, Fujii ordered the remaining pimps to present themselves at the Consulate, and he persuaded them one by one to return to Japan. As a consequence, by late May 1914, all these 37 pimps had left the British colony. In addition, nine pimps, who were as villainous as the 37 men or even worse than them, were also persuaded to return to Japan by 15 June (DRO, 4.2.2.27, 30 May 1914). In the meantime, the Japanese Consul and the colonial authorities agreed not to issue licences to new Japanese prostitutes, and this agreement was kept by Fujii's successor. Nevertheless, Japanese prostitution was far from disappearing in Singapore.

It is worth noting that according to Kobayashi Kazuhiko and Nonaka Masataka, Consul Fujii worked upon the Straits Settlements government to take measures for a large-scale hunt for the pimps in 1914 (Kobayashi and Nonaka 1985: 167). It was, however, the colonial authorities which took the initiative in this matter, while the Japanese Consulate simply co-operated with it out of fear of international criticism against Japan. The colonial authorities decided to banish the 37 Japanese pimps apparently on the pretext that they had found out their names under the category of brothel-keepers in the account book of the mutual aid society (DRO, 4.2.2.27, 30 May 1914). However, the true reason behind the banishment was the fact that, as noted earlier, the priests of the Methodist Episcopal churches were pressing the Colonial Administration to ban the traffic in Japanese women and girls in British Malaya. Indeed, they were actively engaged in writing letters to local newspapers, and giving anti-prostitution talks (*ibid.*).

During World War I, the movement against the traffic in women and licensed prostitution became even more active. In Britain, the National Council for Combating Venereal Disease and women's organisations, including the Association for Moral and Social Hygiene, pressed the

Colonial Office to abolish licensed prostitution in British Malaya. In 1916, John Cowen, a social reformer in Asia investigated the red-light districts around Malay Street and Smith Street in Singapore and made a report, describing in detail the misery of prostitutes and the indecency of their activities. Making use of Cowen's statements, various women's associations in London put even greater pressure on the Colonial Office to reform the law concerning licensed prostitution in Singapore (Warren 1993: 155–7). However, Sir Arthur Young, the Governor-General was of the view that the licensed prostitution system was indispensable for, *inter alia*, the economic development of the colony, and the colonial labour policy, and therefore appealed to the Colonial Office to keep the law intact (*ibid.*: 157–8).

Shortly after the outbreak of the war, the colonial authorities in Singapore banned prostitution by white women, with the result that, although over 20 white brothels existed in the British colony in June 1914, they all disappeared by 1916 (Nanyo oyobi Nihonjinsha 1938: 216; Warren 1993: 155). Consequently, Japanese brothels in Singapore began to face harsher criticism from every quarter. A campaign for the abolition of licensed prostitution began to be conducted by the Japanese side too. Japanese priests who were connected with the Salvation Army were actively engaged in appealing for the closure of Japanese brothels and the salvation of *karayuki-san* in Singapore. In particular, Umemori Hideo with his wife Ikumi frequently visited Malay Street where he went around the brothels, remonstrating with *karayuki-san* against prostitution (Yamazaki 1977: 73–4). Moreover, in September 1915, the Japanese residents in foreign trade, finance and other 'proper trades' set up a Japanese Association with its office in Wilkie Road, in rivalry with the mutual aid society which consisted mainly of those in the *shitamachi-zoku* (downtown Japanese), and started campaigning for the abolition of Japanese prostitution (Mori Katsumi 1959: 232). The president of the Japanese Association was Suzuki Shigemichi, a medical doctor, and its 22 directors comprised mainly professionals such as medical doctors and dentists, and branch managers of large Japanese firms, including Mitsui & Co., the Nippon Yusen Kaisha, and the Bank of Taiwan (Nanyo oyobi Nihonjinsha 1938: 496).

The Japanese Consulate wanted to improve public morals in the Japanese community in co-operation with the directors of the Japanese Association and other influential Japanese residents, and therefore watched Japanese prostitutes closely from 1918 onwards. Eventually, in December 1919, Yamazaki Heikichi, the Acting Consul-General decided to abolish licensed Japanese prostitution.[19] On New Year's Day in 1920, he gathered the presidents of the Japanese Associations in various parts of British Malaya, and informed them that all the Japanese prostitutes in Singapore and Malaya should be banished within the year.[20]

Karayuki-san after the abolition of Japanese prostitution

The preservation of Japan's dignity and morality were two reasons behind the abolition of Japanese prostitution. But, there was possibly another and far more important one, namely Japan's successful economic expansion into British Malaya. In other words, by this time the Japanese as first-class nationals

> had set up offices in a dignified manner in the *gudang* area, and managed large numbers of rubber estates in the Malay Peninsula. And, it was beyond doubt that they could not ignore their compatriot women, being the playthings of bare footed non-Japanese men.
>
> (Nanyo oyobi Nihonjinsha 1938: 153)

As a matter of fact, there was a major transformation of Japan's industrial structure thanks to the rapid growth of the Japanese economy during World War I. This was also reflected in a significant change in the occupational and sexual structure of the Japanese population in Singapore. Indeed, a sharp rise in the value of Japanese exports to Singapore was accompanied by a large increase in the number of importers, retailers, employees of shipping companies, banks and trading companies, and others in the 'proper trades' and their dependants, while those in the 'improper trades' declined in number. As a consequence, the percentage of males in the total Japanese population rose sharply.

The Colonial Administration welcomed the abolition of Japanese prostitution, and did not grudge its support. Those *karayuki-san* who decided to quit their trade were issued with a certificate by the Japanese Consulate-General. If they wanted to stay on in the British colony, they needed to be accompanied to the Consulate-General by their guarantors who were their common-law husbands or new employers, and they could be granted permission to stay provided that they were considered suitable. However, such women, together with 42 *geisha* and 18 Japanese restaurants (including *ryotei*), were under the close watch of the Japanese Consulate and the colonial authorities. For instance, in June 1920, a moral committee was formed by the directors of the Japanese Association with a view to watching over the Japanese residents and the restaurants especially in the Malay Street area (DRO, 4.2.2.27, 29 December 1920).

As Table 2.11 shows, by late 1920 all the *karayuki-san* had quit their trade in Singapore and Malacca. However, there remained as many as 575 prostitutes in the Malay Peninsula. Taking British Malaya as a whole, over 40 per cent of those who quit their trade returned to Japan. As noted earlier, they simply had little prospect for finding alternative employment in their hometowns in Japan where only poverty-stricken families awaited them. Actually, many of the remaining *karayuki-san* in Singapore feigned to have changed their jobs, but continued to work as 'sly' (clandestine) prostitutes. Some of them moved to remote places in the Malay Peninsula where they resumed their former trade (Irie 1942a: 227–8). It is also said that some *karayuki-san* went to the territories under Japanese control, including the Korean Peninsula, Manchuria and Sakhalin to engage in prostitution (Morisaki 1976: 233).

Some of the *karayuki-san* who had moved to the Malay Peninsula from Singapore after the abolition of Japanese prostitution returned to the British colony when the peninsula suffered post-war recession due to a fall in the price of rubber. Also, large numbers of *karayuki-san* in Borneo, Sumatra, Java and other parts of Southeast Asia moved to Singapore at this time. As a consequence, the numbers of 'sly' Japanese prostitutes in the British colony rose greatly for a while. When Ukita Kyoji was appointed to the post of Consul-General at Singapore in August 1921, he reported to Tokyo that there were over 200 former licensed Japanese prostitutes in the Malay Street area, of whom some 100 were said to be actively engaged in prostitution (DRO, 4.2.2.27, 24 January 1924).

It should be noted that many *karayuki-san* were married to Japanese, Indian (especially Tamil), Malay and other men, or became their concubines, after licensed Japanese prostitution was abolished. Those who were married to Indians were particularly large in numbers, for *karayuki-san* actively took Indian men as their customers when overseas Chinese boycotted anything Japanese including the brothels, in relation to the May Fourth Movement in China in 1919. As a matter of fact, some 70 per cent of the old Japanese women (former *karayuki-san*) whom Imamura Shohei, a film director, interviewed in Malaysia in the post-World War II period, were the wives or concubines of Indian men (Warren 1993: 328–9).

Table 2.11 The courses of action taken by the *karayuki-san* who quit their trade in British Malaya (as of late November 1920)

Region	Returned to Japan	New jobs	Common-law wives	Maids	Concu-bines	Un-decided	Total
Singapore	97	11	36	28	5	7	184
Malacca	9	1	2	1	1	2	16
Malay Peninsula	132	3	83	39	35	6	298
Total	238	15	121	68	41	15	498

Source: DRO, 4.2.2.27, 29 December 1920.
Note
In addition to the total of 298, there were still 575 Japanese prostitutes in the Malay Peninsula. 'Undecided' means that although they had quit their trade, they were undecided as to what courses of action they should take.

One effect of the abolition of licensed Japanese prostitution was the wide spread of venereal diseases among men of all races in Singapore. As noted earlier, under the licensed prostitution system, the *karayuki-san* went through regular medical check-ups, and kept themselves as clean as possible. But, when the licensed Japanese prostitutes disappeared, there was a sudden increase in the number of 'sly' prostitutes who were not medically checked. On 10 January 1924, the Chinese Protectorate made a raid on the Japanese inns in the Malay Street area, which superficially ran ice shops, but were brothels in disguise. On the following day, 21 Japanese prostitutes were questioned by the colonial authorities in the presence of the Japanese Consul-General. When they were medically checked by a female doctor, it was found that seven of them were suffering from gonorrhoea, one from both gonorrhoea and syphilis, and four from some other illness (DRO, 4.2.2.27, 24 January 1924).

Caucasian men had previously visited the European or Japanese brothels in the Malay Street area, but when these were closed down, they began to go to Chinese, Eurasian and other prostitutes. Some of them even bought Muslim prostitutes. As for the Singapore-born Chinese, they had formerly visited comparatively high-class brothels, but they began to visit unclean prostitutes after the abolition of the Japanese prostitution (*ibid.*). It was also found that there was a high rate of venereal diseases among the British soldiers in Singapore, for 12 per cent of the men were suffering from gonorrhoea, and 4.2 per cent from syphilis in 1922 (*Kakushin*, vol. 22, no. 11, November 1932: 4–5). As a consequence, in 1926 the Colonial Administration set up several free clinics, put a ban on the entry into Singapore of foreign women who had the intention of prostituting themselves for money, and restricted the number of brothels. Thanks to these measures, the number of brothels in the British colony fell from 221 with a total of 1,804 inmates in 1926 to 176 with 1,189 inmates in 1928 (*ibid.*).

However, it was not until 1930 that the licensed prostitution system was totally abolished in British Malaya. In that year, the Women and Girls Protection Ordinance was amended, cancelling the licences to prostitutes and banning the harlot business. From October 1930 to April 1931, some 50 per cent of the brothels were closed down step by step, and the closure continued thereafter. Although there had been 15 white prostitutes before the amendment of the ordinance, there was none after it. However, after the closure of Asian brothels, there was a sudden increase in the number of Japanese and Chinese inns where prostitution was resumed. As of September 1931, there were several Japanese brothels with a total of some 50 'old' prostitutes, offering services to European residents, Japanese sailors and other men. Indeed, even after the abolition of the licensed prostitution system, prostitutes did not disappear entirely from Singapore and other parts of British Malaya (*Kakushin*, vol. 23, no. 7, July 1933: 4–5).

CONCLUDING REMARKS

The colonial power recognised the existence of prostitutes as a 'necessary evil' in British Malaya where there was a large gender imbalance, and therefore introduced a system of licensed prostitution. Prostitutes, for example, helped to alleviate, to a certain extent, cultural and political friction among the different races. The *karayuki-san*, in particular, took all kinds of customers while some of them were kept as concubines, or were married to non-Japanese men. Through the *karayuki-san* and prostitutes of other nationalities, opportunities could be provided for men of different cultures and political ideas to meet with each other at brothels (Warren 1993: 258). Setting aside the moral and humanitarian issues with regard to prostitution, it is very difficult to ignore entirely the fact that prostitutes of various nationalities made large contributions to the prosperity of Singapore and the rest of British Malaya, albeit indirectly.

It should, however, be noted that there are several moot points concerning the *karayuki*-led advance. First, it is wrong to deny that at an early stage the *karayuki-san* played a role in Japan's economic advance into Singapore and other parts of Southeast Asia. It is true that drapers, photographers, doctors, sundry-goods store-keepers, and other early Japanese immigrants were attracted to Singapore by the custom of the *karayuki-san* and brothel keepers, but it should nevertheless be pointed out that apart from Echigoya Gofukuten, and some professionals such as doctors and dentists, very few were successful in their trades. Moreover, although many of the early Japanese immigrants invested in rubber estates, they made huge losses in the post-World War I recession when rubber prices plummeted, and were obliged to sell them.

Second, one should bear in mind that the *karayuki*-led advance was merely one type of Japan's economic advance into Southeast Asia, and was by no means the only one. As we shall study in the next chapter in detail, at a time when *karayuki-san* began to move into Southeast Asia in the 1870s, the overseas Chinese merchants in Japan had already been incorporated into the intra-Asian overseas Chinese networks, and began to cultivate Southeast Asian markets for Japanese goods. We shall employ the term, 'advance through overseas Chinese merchants' to denote this pattern of Japan's economic advance into Singapore and other parts of Southeast Asia.

Third, when Nanyo Dantai Rengokai (the Federation of the South Seas Associations), and Nanyo oyobi Nihonjinsha talk about the *karayuki*-led advance before World War II, they do not refer specifically to Singapore, but to Southeast Asia in general (Nanyo Dantai Rengokai 1942: 346–9; Nanyo oyobi Nihonjinsha 1938: 134–65). However, within Southeast Asia there were different countries and regions, and obviously one cannot generalise the pattern of Japan's economic advance. Although *karayuki-san* were undoubtedly the first Japanese immigrants in Singapore and Malaya, this does not necessarily mean that they were also the first Japanese immigrants in other parts of Southeast Asia.

Unlike most of the Southeast Asian countries, there was a very high proportion of men in the Japanese population in the pre-war Philippines where a sharp rise in the number of male Japanese was followed by that of females, but not vice versa. In 1915, for example, males accounted for 83 per cent of the population in the Philippines as compared to 62 per cent in Southeast Asia as a whole. Even in the Meiji era, males constituted the bulk of the population, for there were many employment opportunities for them in agriculture and the construction industry. Evidently, their occupations were not related to *karayuki-san* and Japanese brothels (Hashiya 1985: 33, 37–8).

Moreover, one would find another type of Japanese economic advance, the 'diver-led advance' in the Netherlands East Indies, which was very different from the '*karayuki*-led advance' or the 'advance through overseas Chinese merchants'. In Dobo, Aru Islands, for example, the first Japanese immigrants were pearl-divers, not *karayuki-san*. The sea between Aru Islands and the south-west coast of New Guinea was widely known for pearl-oyster fishing. In 1893, over ten Japanese divers were brought to Dobo by a certain Briton, and they were apparently the first Japanese immigrants. The number of Japanese then continued to rise thereafter. In 1908, the Celebes Trading Company under Australian ownership acquired a ten-year pearling right at 350,000 guilders from the Dutch East Indies government, and established its operating base at Dobo. It employed some 500 Japanese divers (Shimizu Hiroshi 1992: 30; Inoue 1915: 87–9; Okayagura 1911: 76).

Whether they worked as divers or operators of boats assisting the former, the Japanese had to put up not only with heavy labour but with insipid foods and lack of social activities for eight or nine months a year. Besides, as divers had to undertake pearling at the depth of some 45.5 metres, they faced constant danger, and, in fact, many of them died of accidents or illness (Hosaka 1916: 890). Nevertheless, they could normally earn ¥500 to ¥600 by the end of the season (Hosaka 1916: 890).[21] They enjoyed holidays in Dobo during the period from late May to late August when no pearling was done due to the monsoons. As soon as they went ashore, they began to spend their earnings on women, alcohol and gambling. When they had used up their money, they could still obtain an advance payment from the Celebes Trading Company

As Fig. 2.3 shows, a Japanese town was formed around the Dobo harbour, with Japanese divers as its core. As of 1913, there were ten inns, three sundry-goods stores, two barbers' shops, one bathhouse, and eight restaurants. Moreover, there were nine brothels with 22 inmates. But, since the demand for sexual needs far exceeded the supply, some 100 migrant Japanese prostitutes moved to Dobo from Singapore, Merauke, Ambon and Makassar at the off-season for pearling every year (Inoue 1915: 87–9).[22] It is therefore

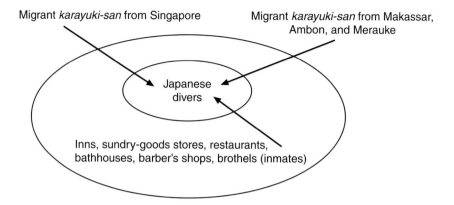

Figure 2.3 The Japanese community in Dobo, Aru Islands, in the early twentieth century.

clear that Japan's economic advance into Aru islands was 'divers-led', not '*karayuki*-led'.

Lastly, we shall put forward topics for further discussion. In the Dutch East Indies before World War I, the Japanese Consul Someya Shigeaki actively supported Governor Idenburg's policy for the abolition of licensed prostitution and the Acting Japanese Consul-General Yamazaki Heikichi abolished licensed Japanese prostitution in British Malaya in 1920. However, the system of licensed prostitution was maintained in the Japanese colonies and protectorates until the end of World War II, and in Japan until April 1958. One would naturally wonder why it was that the Japanese government took one policy for licensed prostitution in Japan proper and the territories under Japanese control, and another for foreign countries under Western control including British Malaya and the Dutch East Indies. The Japanese authorities were probably concerned with their own dignity and prestige in foreign countries, but one would need to further study the reasons for the different policies.

Incidentally, as Ronald Hyam points out, the British empire-builders forbade their own women to work as prostitutes in their colonies, whereas as soon as their French counterparts acquired a new colony, they brought French prostitutes there (Hyam 1986: 67). Like the French, the Japanese instituted a system of licensed prostitution in their colonies and protectorates, and Japanese brothels were set up keeping many Japanese prostitutes to provide sexual services to Japanese men (Peattie 1988: 206–9, 338; Kurahashi 1989: 97–183). It is also a subject for further discussion to find out why it was that there was such a difference in prostitution policy between Britain on the one hand, and France and Japan on the other hand.

3

JAPAN'S TRADE EXPANSION
INTO BRITISH MALAYA

With special reference to Singapore

In the second half of the nineteenth century and the early twentieth century there was an enormous expansion of the trade between Asia and the West, thanks to the reduction in transport costs on the sea routes between Europe and the East, caused by the opening of the Suez Canal in 1869 and by major technological advances in shipbuilding.[1] Communications, improved greatly by the laying of the submarine telegraph cables, also contributed immensely to commercial expansion. In Southeast Asia, with the development of the colonial economies, large quantities of tin, rubber, coffee, sugar and other primary commodities could now be shipped to the West at a low cost in a shorter period than ever before, while large quantities of Western industrial goods found their way into the Southeast Asian markets.

It should be noted that the intra-Asian trade was also growing rapidly at this time. According to Sugihara Kaoru, during the period from 1883 to 1913, it grew at 5.5 per cent on average per year, whereas the annual average growth rates of Asia's trade with the West were 3.2 per cent for export, and 4.3 per cent for import (Sugihara 1991: 243–59; *idem* 1996: 22). Unlike Asia's import trade with the West, industrial goods did not play a central role in the intra-Asian trade especially in the early years. In 1883, India's exports to China, for example, consisted mainly of opium (80 per cent of total) and cotton yarn (over 10 per cent). However, with the development of the modern spinning industry in India and Japan, cotton yarn and piece goods began to play an increasingly important role in the intra-Asian trade in the late nineteenth century. In 1913 India's exports to China, Hong Kong and the Straits Settlements comprised mainly cotton yarn and piece goods, and gunny bags, even though opium remained an important export item. In the same year, Japan exported large quantities of cotton yarn and piece goods to China, Korea, Hong Kong and other Asian countries, and imported the bulk of raw cotton from India (Sugihara 1996: 22–9).

British, German and other Western merchants largely controlled the trade between Southeast Asia and the West; however it was not these merchants but the Asian traders, notably Chinese, Indians and Arabs, who mainly conducted the intra-Asian trade. As for Japan's trade with Asia before World War I, the overseas Chinese merchants based at Kobe, Yokohama and other large Japanese port cities, were particularly active, making use of intra-Asian Chinese commercial networks (Kagotani 1989: 205–21; Post 1995: 157–63; Shimizu Hiroshi 1997b: 1–8). Indeed, they were largely responsible for cultivating various Southeast Asian markets for Japanese goods, including British Malaya, but, as far as we are aware, there is hardly any major work on their commercial activities, specifically with regard to the Southeast Asian region.[2]

In this chapter we shall study in what ways Japan began to trade with British Malaya in the late nineteenth century, and how she emerged as one of the leading suppliers of industrial goods during and after World War I. In so doing, we shall shed light on the role of the overseas Chinese merchants and overseas Chinese commercial networks in Japan's Southeast Asian trade, and show that the overseas Chinese merchants were largely responsible for laying the foundations for Japan's early economic advance into British Malaya and other parts of Southeast Asia before World War II.

THE OVERSEAS CHINESE AND THE DEVELOPMENT OF JAPAN'S TRADE WITH BRITISH MALAYA

The European merchant houses and overseas Chinese merchants

In the pre-World War II period, Singapore prospered as an entrepôt not only for the Malay Peninsula, but also for other parts of Southeast Asia such as Thailand and the Netherlands East Indies. The bulk of primary commodities, including rubber and tin, produced in the Southeast Asian region were exported to Japan and the West through the port,[3] while large quantities of industrial goods used in the region were imported from them also through it. Moreover, rice and other foodstuffs were imported into Singapore from Thailand, Burma and French Indo-China, and were re-exported mainly to the Malay Peninsula and the Netherlands East Indies.

As Table 3.1 shows, the colonial power was responsible for about 50 per cent of all the goods imported into Singapore from Japan and the West before World War II. Moreover, both the import and export trades between Singapore and the West were largely in the hands of the European merchants based in the British colony. Prior to World War I, there were very influential British merchant houses including Boustead & Co., Guthrie & Co., Sime Darby & Co., Paterson Simons & Co. and McAlister & Co., but they faced severe competition from the German merchant houses such as Behn Meyer,

Table 3.1 Imports into Singapore by Japan and Western countries, 1900/02–
1937/39 (annual average)

	Total ($1,000)	Britain (%)	Continental Europe (%)	U.S. (%)	Canada (%)	Japan (%)
1900/02	49,111	55.0	27.0	3.1	0.0	14.9
1911/13	65,382	53.0	24.7	7.4	0.2	14.7
1925/27	184,419	48.5	19.4	16.7	1.3	14.1
1929	172,817	49.3	23.0	14.0	1.1	12.6
1932/34	81,837	46.4	16.1	6.4	1.6	29.5
1937/39	112,238	48.5	20.7	10.6	4.0	16.2

Source: Huff 1994: 258.

Katz Brothers and Brinkmann & Co. However, the Germans had to withdraw from the British colony during World War I, and no longer posed any
serious threat to the British merchant houses, even though some German
merchants returned to Singapore after the war (Huff 1994: 258–9). Unexpectedly, it was the Japanese merchants and Japanese goods which
challenged Britain's supreme position in the British Malayan market in the
inter-war period.

One would then wonder how the influential European merchant houses
emerged in Singapore. Around 1750, some sailors of the East India Company
were granted licences by the company, and became private traders to conduct
the trade between the main ports in Africa and Asia. This was known as 'the
country trade' (Wong 1991: 44–6; Tsurumi 1982: 23–4). Moreover, in 1813
the monopoly trading right held by the East India Company for India was
abolished, and British traders moved to India, where they acquired licences,
and kept a trading base to conduct the country trade (Wong 1991: 42–8).
When the company's monopoly over the China trade was abolished in 1834,
the trading activities of the private traders became even more energetic.
These traders accumulated capital, settled in Penang and Singapore, and
became influential merchants. Other European (particularly German)
merchants also moved to these islands later on.

The European merchants initially bought European goods at their own
risk, and sold them in the Straits Settlements. Although they had high credit
standing, they required the co-operation of local Asian retailers and wholesale
merchants, who were well acquainted with local conditions. They therefore
chose overseas Chinese merchants in Malacca as their trading partners
(Tsurumi 1982: 23–4). This was the beginning of the 'symbiotic' relationship
between the Europeans and overseas Chinese merchants. When Singapore was
developed as a free port, the overseas Chinese merchants in Malacca set up
branches, or moved their head offices there. Obviously, there were also many
Chinese who migrated to Singapore direct from mainland China.

In the early years of British rule over Singapore, both the European merchants and overseas Chinese merchants established themselves around Boat Quay at Singapore River, but the harbour was too small and shallow to accommodate international liners. When docking facilities were built at New Harbour (renamed Keppel Harbour in 1900) which was large and deep, a growing number of steamers began to call at the harbour instead of Boat Quay. Then the established European firms relocated their offices to Raffles Place which soon became a banking and commercial centre, while overseas Chinese traders remained in the Boat Quay area to conduct the wholesale trade in Straits produce and the intra-Asian trade (Wong 1991: 57; Turnbull 1977: 48).[4]

In 1846 there were 43 merchant houses in Singapore, of which 20 were British, six Jewish, five Arab, five Chinese, two German and five other nationalities (*ibid.*: 40). At that time, most European merchant houses received goods from European manufacturers and/or exporters, and sold them on commission through Chinese middlemen. However, some of them soon acquired specialised knowledge, accumulated capital, kept purchasing offices or affiliated companies in London and other European cities, and began to trade directly with European manufacturers at their own risks (Wong 1991: 57–8; Huff 1994: 258–9)

The industrial goods imported into Singapore by the European merchants were partly consumed in the Straits Settlements, and were partly re-exported to the neighbouring countries. However, the European merchants sold these goods to Asian merchants, notably overseas Chinese wholesalers on generous credit terms for 60 days or 90 days, and exceptionally 120 days D/A (documents against acceptance) (Mantetsu 1941: 259), and were likely to have a high risk of bad debts. Besides, there were many overseas Chinese who intentionally went bankrupt to evade the payment of debts. In 1870 the law stipulating the imprisonment of those who went bankrupt, was repealed. But it was re-introduced in 1895, simply because there were many fraudulent Chinese merchants (SICC 1979: 19–20).

In 1905 a bill was brought in to oblige all overseas Chinese traders to register with the authorities, with a view to facilitating the arrest of dishonest Chinese merchants. However, the bill fell through due to strong opposition from the well-established European merchant houses, which were primarily concerned with the exclusion of new entrants rather than checking dishonest Chinese merchants: they were financially sound and able to withstand bad debts, and had certain knowledge about the credit standing of their Chinese customers (*ibid.*: 20). Had the bill been passed, it would have greatly assisted new European entrants in the trading business, for they were not familiar with the local commercial practices and the credit standing of local Chinese traders. Indeed, in the inter-war period, hardly any new European merchant could become successfully established in British Malaya.

Now let us examine what was the 'symbiotic' relationship between the leading European merchant houses and local overseas Chinese wholesale merchants, taking as a case study cotton piece goods which constituted a main British export item. Prior to World War II, British Malaya relied heavily on foreign countries for almost all textile goods, which were necessities of life. There was no textile mill in Singapore, while in the Malay Peninsula there was merely a cottage-type weaving industry in the eastern coastal states of Pahang, Trengganu and Kelantan, producing sarong of cotton-silk fabric (Shokosho Shomukyoku 1925: 311). As a result, British Malaya continued to import the bulk of cotton piece goods from Britain until the late 1920s, when Japan began to supply large quantities of cotton textiles. In 1909, for example, Singapore imported $1,6647,000 worth of the goods, of which Britain was responsible for 68.3 per cent (*Return of Imports and Exports* 1909).

The importers of British cotton piece goods in Singapore were largely British, and included Guthrie & Co., Paterson Simons & Co., McAlister & Co., Boustead & Co. and Sime Darby & Co. Some German houses such as Behn Meyer, and those with German connections such as Katz Brothers and Brinkmann & Co., were also engaged in the import trade. The British and German merchants houses sold cotton piece goods through overseas Chinese wholesale merchants (mainly Teochius) of Circular Road in Singapore, and re-exported them, also through them, to the neighbouring countries (Huff 1994: 258–9; Nishimura Takeshiro 1941: 83–4, 190).

At the turn of the twentieth century, more than 50 influential Chinese wholesale merchants existed in Circular Road, specialising in British cotton piece goods, and they set up the Singapore Piece-goods Traders' Guild, with the purpose of protecting members' interests. Since they dealt only in Lancashire goods, showing no interest in any other cotton piece goods, the European merchant houses treasured them, and sold goods to them on credit with D/A 60 days or 90 days (Huff 1994: 264–5). The Chinese merchants in turn sold goods to retailers on credit for a shorter period, and could therefore make large profits by rotating their capital several times before paying the debts to the European merchants. The leading Chinese merchants, in particular, made full use of the credit facilities provided by the European merchants to sell Lancashire goods through their branches in the Netherlands East Indies, Thailand and the Malay Peninsula, and to purchase local produce through them in these countries (Nishimura Takeshiro 1941: 83–4, 190).

The established European merchant houses could also expand their trading activities by undertaking agency works for rubber estates when the rubber-plantation industry in the Malay Peninsula began to grow at the turn of the century. The merchant houses acted as the intermediaries between investors in Britain and local planters, since many rubber-growing firms offered shares for subscription in London. Besides, they themselves launched out into running rubber estates. They managed a number of estates in different parts of the Malay Peninsula on behalf of investors in London, and undertook the sorting out, drying and export of rubber. They also supplied the rubber estates with foodstuffs, machinery and other necessary goods, and undertook other agency works for them (Huff 1994: 259).

As large manufacturers in the West tended to choose as their agencies established European merchant houses in Asia, it was not rare for the same merchant houses to act as agencies for several manufacturers. Guthrie & Co., for example, acted as agencies for Francis Shaw & Co., a manufacturer of plantation rubber machinery, and Tyneside Engineering Co., a manufacturer of drying machines for copra and rubber (*ibid.* 1994: 260). Similarly, Western shipping and insurance companies entered an agency agreement with the established merchant houses, and encouraged them to use their ships and marine insurance services (Wong 1991: 57–8).

Therefore, the leading merchant houses could make a large profit on various agency works. They invested it in rubber estates and tin mining, and/or used it to subscribe for the shares of the rubber estate firms listed in London.

RISE OF THE OVERSEAS CHINESE MERCHANTS AT KOBE AND JAPAN'S FOREIGN TRADE

In Chapter 2 we suggested that it was the overseas Chinese merchants in Japan, rather than *karayuki-san*, who played a major role in Japan's economic advance into Southeast Asia at an early stage. Actually, until the turn of the twentieth century, the bulk of Japan's export trade with foreign countries was conducted by overseas Chinese and Western merchants in Japan (Shokosho Boekikyoku 1938: 139–40). Apart from Mitsui & Co. and few others who were engaged in foreign trade, Japanese merchants acted mainly as middlemen between Japanese manufacturers and foreign merchants in Japan.

It was, indeed, not the Japanese merchants but the overseas Chinese merchants in Japan who were instrumental in cultivating Southeast Asian markets for marine products, lacquer ware, rickshaws, textile goods and other Japanese goods in the last quarter of the nineteenth century and the early twentieth century, by making use of their intra-Asian trade networks (Nihon Keizai Kenkyukai 1941: 41; Kikakuin 1939: 344; Watanabe Takeshi1 942: 81–8).[5] It is, however, true that the export to Southeast Asia of Japanese bunker coal was largely undertaken by Mitsui & Co. and the branches of the Western merchant houses in Japan. In 1896, for example, Japan exported to Singapore 156,710 metric tons of coal, of which the Japanese firm was responsible for 50,225 metric tons, Paterson, Simons & Co. 32,553 metric tons, Mansfield Company 19,568 metric tons, and Borneo Company 20,003 metric tons (*Tsusho Isan*, 15 September 1897: 9).

Of the overseas Chinese merchants in Japan, those at Kobe are particularly important in this study for two main reasons. First, prior to World War II, Kobe had the largest number of overseas Chinese in Japan. In 1936, for example, there were a total of 20,654 overseas Chinese in Japan, of whom 6,263 (30.3 per cent of total) were in Kobe, 5,507 (26.7 per cent) in Tokyo, 3,873 (18.8 per cent) in Yokohama, 3,747 (18.1 per cent) in Osaka, and 1,264 (6.1 per cent) in Nagasaki (Kobe Shoko Kaigisho 1936: 9). Second, Kobe's overseas Chinese merchants played a very important role in the development of Japan's export trade with Southeast Asia particularly before World War I. Although the overseas Chinese merchants resided largely in Kobe, Osaka and Yokohama, it was those at Kobe who virtually monopolised the Southeast Asian trade conducted by the overseas Chinese in Japan. The overseas Chinese at Kobe also traded with Taiwan, Amoy, South China and South America. As for Yokohama's Chinese merchants, their trading regions were mainly China, North America and Latin America, while Osaka's Chinese merchants principally traded with Manchuria, Kwangtung Leased Territory and North and Central China. There were not many Chinese merchants at Osaka or Yokohama who specialised in the Southeast Asian trade (Kikakuin 1939: 339).

There is little information available about statistical figures for Japan's Southeast Asian trade conducted by Kobe's Chinese merchants in the Meiji era (1868–1912). But there is little doubt that they were responsible for the bulk of the trade at least until World War I (Kikakuin 1939: 344; Watanabe Takeshi1 942: 81–8; Post 1995: 158–63). Indeed, in 1910 the overseas Chinese were responsible for 97.6 per cent of Kobe's marine products exports to the world market, 71.9 per cent of its textiles, 34.6 per cent of its clothes, and 57.4 per cent of its matches (Post 1995: 162).[6] Moreover, although the period is a bit later, in the second half of the 1920s they exported annually some ¥50 million worth of cotton textiles, and some ¥30 million worth of sundry goods and marine products. By region, the annual value of their exports was some ¥30 million for Southeast Asia, some ¥25 million for Hong Kong, and some ¥25 million for South China and India (Toa Keizai Chosakyoku 1938: 22). Even in the years before the outbreak of the Sino-Japanese War in July 1937, they exported to Southeast Asia some ¥30 million worth of goods annually, and were responsible for some 20 per cent of Kobe's total exports to the world market, and slightly less than 10 per cent of Japan's total exports to Southeast Asia (Kikakuin 1939: 362). Indeed, as Table 3.2 shows, the overseas Chinese merchants in Japan, most of whom were apparently at Kobe, held fairly large shares in the export of underwear, socks and rubber shoes in 1936.

Despite the importance of Kobe's Chinese merchants, those scholars who work, in part or in whole, on Japan's economic advance into Southeast Asia before World War II hardly mention anything about their role. Moreover, works on the history of the Kobe port or the foreign trade make only passing

Table 3.2 Japanese exports to Southeast Asia by nationalities of merchants in 1936 (in dozens)

	Japanese	*Chinese*	*Dutch*	*Other*	*Total*
Underwear	639,407	951,193	168,802	65,487	1,824,889
(%)	35.0	52.0	9.0	3.6	99.6
Socks	126,961	69,136	12,912	9,364	218,373
(%)	58.0	32.0	6.0	4.0	100
Rubber shoes	192,992	116,044	32,844	1,328	343,208
(%)	56.1	33.8	9.6	0.5	100

Source: Constructed with some modifications from Shokosho Boekikyoku 1938: 176–7, 188–9.
Notes
Rubber shoes are for the first half of 1937. The total of export shares by nationalities of merchants for underwear is less than 100 per cent due to roundings.

references to the overseas Chinese merchants, even though a lot of space is allocated to Japanese trading companies.[7]

How did overseas Chinese merchants come to settle in Kobe? It was shortly after the opening of Kobe in 1868 that eleven or twelve overseas Chinese moved to Kobe from Nagasaki, and settled down in an area along the coast which later developed into a China town centering around Sakae-machi, Uradori and Kaigandori.[8] Using their Nagasaki experiences as foreign traders, they began to export sea- and land-products to China.

After the conclusion of the Sino-Japanese Amity Treaty in 1871, the number of Chinese immigrants in Kobe and other Japanese cities began to increase rapidly. They came first from Fukien province, then from Kwangtung province, and finally from San Kiang provinces (Kiangsu, Chekiang and Kiangsi). The overseas Chinese also moved to Kobe from Osaka and Yokohama. The port of Osaka was opened at about the same time as that of Kobe, and the Kawaguchi district of Osaka became a Chinese settlement. However, as Osaka's port facilities were not well developed, international liners called at Kobe instead of Osaka. As a result, imports were first unloaded at Kobe, and were then transported by lighters to Osaka. Similarly, export goods had to be transported by the same means to Kobe for trans-shipment (Koyama 1979: 156). In 1895, the transport system between the two ports was greatly improved when the Osaka–Kobe railway was built. Despite this, around 1896 all the Cantonese merchants, including those of Yee Woo and Yue Ching Cheong, and the Shanghai merchants dealing in marine products moved to Kobe (Koyama 1979: 38; Kikakuin 1939: 343). Apparently, Osaka's Japanese entrepreneurs failed to persuade them from staying on there (Kobe Boeki Kyokai 1968: 86). Moreover, after the Kanto Earthquake of 1923, Yokohama's overseas Chinese moved to Kobe and Osaka in large numbers (Koyama 1979: 59).

Besides the individual Chinese merchants, there were many compradores (native agents) in Kobe, who had previously been employed by the branches of the Western merchant houses located at the Chinese treaty ports. When Kobe was opened as a treaty port in 1868, they were brought there by Western merchants, largely because they had good command of the Japanese language and were well acquainted with Japanese commercial practices (Beasley 1987: 27). Although many Chinese residents fled the country in 1894 when the Sino-Japanese War broke out, most of them returned to Kobe shortly after the war. However, by this time the Western merchants had realised that the Japanese monetary and trading systems were much simpler than those of China, and did not re-employ all the compradores (Shokosho Boekikyoku 1938: 140). Then some of the unemployed compradores set up their own trading companies.

In this way, the number of the overseas Chinese in Kobe rose from 619 in 1878 to 988 in 1895, 2,887 in 1917 and 5,814 in 1928. At the end of 1936, there were 5,144 overseas Chinese. They accounted for over 60 per cent of the foreign population in Kobe in most of these years (Kobe Boeki Kyokai 1968: 82–7; Shokosho Boekikyoku 1938: 148). In the early Meiji era, the Hokkiens were most numerous, but at the turn of the twentieth century the number of Cantonese rapidly increased. As for the number of overseas Chinese merchants engaged in foreign trade, there were 59 Cantonese, 19 Hokkiens and five Sankiangs just before the outbreak of the Sino-Japanese War in 1937 (Shokosho Boekikyoku 1938: 216).

The overseas Chinese of these dialect groups established their respective associations which functioned as a kind of a chamber of commerce and friendship/mutual help organisation. The Hokkien Association, the oldest of the three, came into existence in the early Meiji era. As for the Sankiang Association, it already existed in 1871, and was consolidated around 1896 when many of Osaka's Chinese moved to Kobe. Its membership comprised not only merchants but some tailors and money-changers. The Cantonese Association is said to have been set up as early as 1876, but there is no strong evidence to support it. At any rate, in 1896 it was formally set up by Kobe's Cantonese merchants together with those who moved there from Osaka (*ibid*. 1938: 154–5).

Most of the Chinese merchants at Kobe brought with them their families, and kept imposing shops and warehouses. In the late Meiji era and the Taisho era, some of the influential Chinese merchants in Kobe, including Liu Dou Ming, the proprietor of Kwong Hing Cheong, acquired Japanese nationality (Koyama 1979: 42, 156). One should not assume, however, that most of Kobe's overseas Chinese merchants were in the trading business for many years. In 1937, for example, there were 83 overseas Chinese merchants at Kobe, of whom only 15 had been in the trade for more than 20 years. In the same year, there were 59 members of the Cantonese Association, over half of whom had been in the trading business for less than five years (Shokosho Boekikyoku 1938:144).

The reasons for it are not far to seek. As already noted, when the Sino-Japanese War broke out in 1894, many overseas Chinese left Japan for China. When the Tatsumaru Incident took place in February 1910, the Chinese boycotted Japanese goods in China and Southeast Asia. Thereafter, Chinese boycotts took place from time to time. With each incident, large numbers of Chinese merchants closed their commercial houses and returned to their country, even though many of them subsequently came back to Japan. On the other hand, employees of Chinese or Western commercial houses set up business on their own, and many new arrivals from China joined the foreign trade (*ibid.*: 148).

The capital ownership of Chinese trading companies at Kobe was largely in the form of partnership. The proprietor of each firm was in general the largest investor, and acted as the representative partner. Other partners consisted mainly of overseas Chinese residents in Kobe. But they could also include his or her trading partners in Southeast Asia, as well as the Japanese manufacturers in Osaka who sold goods to the firm. In this way, the owner could strengthen their ties with them in Japan and abroad. But the managerial system was similar to that of a private shop, where the proprietor runs his or her business personally.

In sharp contrast with the Japanese merchants who exported goods mainly on their own account, almost all the overseas Chinese merchants at Kobe handled goods on a commission basis, selling and buying for the principals. It naturally helped them avoid the risk of over-stocking (Kikakuin 1939: 386–7).

Annual sales ranged from ¥2 to ¥3 million for a large trading company to just over ¥100,000 for a small one. As the expenses were kept to a minimum, amounting to only ¥3,500 to ¥4,000 per company a year, most of them made large profits. This was done partly by keeping a small number of employees. It was fairly common for a Chinese trading company with sales of a few million yen to employ not more than ten employees (*ibid.*: 349).

The Chinese merchants at Kobe bought textiles and sundry goods mainly in Osaka, while stocking rubber goods in Kobe and ceramics in Nagoya (Kikakuin 1939: 387). Moreover, they bought marine products (such as cod sticks, dried scallops, dried sea tangles, dried abalone, etc.) largely from Japanese brokers in Kobe either by spot trading or by samples (*ibid.*: 390). They normally received a commission of 3 to 3.5 per cent for the purchase of cotton yarn and piece goods, and 2.5 to 3 per cent for that of sundry goods (Toa Keizai Chosakyoku 1938: 13). Commissions constituted the main source of their income. As for the methods of payment, in Japan the overseas Chinese merchants bought various goods normally by cash, whereas they drew documentary bills on Southeast Asia's overseas Chinese merchants usually at 30 days or 60 days after sight (Kikakuin 1939: 390, 392–3).

CHINESE COMMERCIAL NETWORKS

Kobe's overseas Chinese merchants and intra-Asian trade networks

As Table 3.3 shows, Japanese exports to the Straits Settlements (largely to Singapore) rose steeply from $3,662,000 in 1894 to $6,384,000 in 1905, $12,898,000 in 1913, and to $50,399,000 in 1918. As for the Japanese share in Singapore's total imports, it was fairly small up to the turn of the century, but reached 7 per cent in 1913. During the war years Japan's share rose steeply from 7.5 per cent in 1914 to 9.8 per cent in 1916 and 18.3 per cent in 1918, whereas Britain's share declined from 22.3 per cent to 18.8 per cent and 18 per cent in the same years (*Return of Imports and Exports*, 1914, 1915, 1917, 1919). There was also a considerable change in the commodity structure of Japan's export trade with the Straits Settlements before 1920 (see Table 3.3). Although coal accounted for over 40 per cent of total exports before World War I, its share continued to decline reaching 34.4 per cent in 1919. On the other hand, the share of industrial goods, notably cotton textiles, rose considerably during the same period.

The overseas Chinese merchants at Kobe were actively engaged in Japan's trade with Singapore and other parts of Southeast Asia. However, one should not assume that, from the very beginning, they exported large quantities of Japanese goods direct to the British colony, for they were initially concerned with export to South and Central China because of a lack of Japanese

Table 3.3 Value and commodity composition of the Straits Settlements' imports from Japan, 1894–1919 (in $1,000)

Item	1894	1905	1913	1915	1918	1919
Coal	1,616	2,624	5,300	4,404	19,009	11,533
Cotton textiles	396	457	346	374	1,482	3,017
Matches	495	1,241	851	1,152	2,488	2,268
Chemicals	–	57	–	235	6,925	1,597
Knitwear	192	b	606	681	1,737	1,213
Ceramics	73	b	192	387	797	892
Dry & salted fish	26	100	1,175	847	762	352
Rickshaws[a]	51	240	261	b	427	292
Lacquer ware	216	612	b	b	b	b
Other	623	1,053	4,167	6,838	16,772	12,360
Total	3,662	6,384	12,898	14,918	50,399	33,524

Source: Constructed from *Tsusho Isan*, 4 January 1896: 35–7, and 23 September 1908: 18–24; *Naigai Shoko Jiho*, vol. 6, No. 10, October 1919: 68; Nanyo oyobi Nihonjinsha 1938: 235, 238–9.

Notes

[a] Includes parts.

[b] Included in Other.

shipping to Southeast Asia (Kikakuin 1939: 363). It was in 1879 that the Mitsubishi Company (which became the Nippon Yusen Kaisha after its amalgamation with the Kyodo Unyu Kaisha in 1885) established a direct Japan–Hong Kong shipping route, facilitating the trading relationship between the overseas Chinese merchants at Kobe and those at Hong Kong. During the period from about 1890 to the early twentieth century, Kobe's Chinese merchants energetically exported marine products, matches, ceramics and other Japanese goods to Southeast Asia through Hong Kong and imported through it sugar from Java, rice from Thailand and French Indo-China, tin from the Malay Peninsula, and some other Southeast Asian produce (Shokosho Boekikyoku 1938: 142). As the Nippon Yusen Kaisha and other Japanese shipping firms began increasingly to establish long-distance routes via Singapore in the late nineteenth century, the overseas Chinese merchants started exporting large quantities of Japanese goods direct to the British colony for redistribution in Southeast Asia.

As Figure 3.1 shows, Kobe's Chinese merchants exported Japanese goods to Singapore and other parts of Southeast Asia, making use of the overseas Chinese commercial networks. They took orders from Singapore's Chinese importers, stocked goods from wholesale merchants or manufacturers in Japan, and shipped them to their Singapore clients. It should be noted that some of Kobe's Cantonese merchants exported goods to Singapore through the Nam bak hang, which consisted of tens of influential Chinese merchant houses in Hong Kong (Watanabe Takeshi 1942: 84–5; Shokosho Boekikyoku 1938: 141–2).[9] The Nam bak hang could easily re-export Japanese goods to Singapore where many of them had branches. Heng Lee, which imported large quantities of marine products from Japan, was, for example, a Singapore branch of a Nam bak hang commercial house (Shokosho Boekikyoku 1930: 102–3).

In general, the overseas Chinese merchant in one country traded only with overseas Chinese of their own dialect group in other countries, largely because they were familiar with the spoken Chinese and credit standing of their trading partners. For example, Hokkien merchants virtually monopolised the trade between Japan and the Philippines, while Cantonese controlled the Japan–Batavia trade. As for the trade between Japan and Surabaya, Hokkiens traded largely in cotton piece goods, and Cantonese in sundry goods (Kikakuin 1939: 345, 347–8).

We shall now examine which dialect group of overseas Chinese merchants were involved in the Japan–Singapore trade. As Table 3.4 shows, there were 16 Chinese merchant houses at Kobe exporting goods to Singapore as of January 1929, of which eleven were Cantonese, four were Hokkiens and one was Taiwanese. There was not much difference in the type of goods handled by the merchants of different dialect groups. In Singapore, there were 421,821 Chinese in 1931, of whom 181,287 were Hokkiens, 95,114 Cantonese, and 82,516 Teochius (Mantetsu 1941: 63–4). In addition to these

Japan   **Southeast Asia**

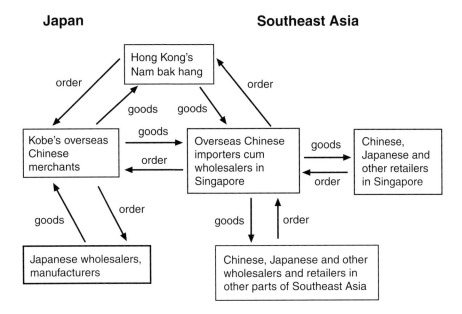

Figure 3.1 Japan's export trade with Singapore through Kobe's overseas Chinese merchants before World War II.

three largest dialect groups, there were also Hainanese, Hakkas, Hockchius and others. The Hokkiens were prominent in 'overseas Chinese commerce', including banking and rubber trade. The Teochius were actively engaged in trade in cotton piece goods, tropical products, rice and other foodstuffs, and were also influential in fresh fish trade. Indeed, the Hokkiens and the Teochius are said to have dominated foreign trade and finance. As for the Cantonese, it is often argued that they were mainly engaged in shoe-making, carpentry, smithery, and other traditional occupations, and were not prominent in the field of foreign trade (Yamashita 1988: 73–6; Mak 1995: 62–70). Did they really not play an important role in foreign trade?

Since Table 3.4 does not give the trading partners in Singapore of Kobe's overseas Chinese merchants, we look at Figure 3.2 for this information. Although Figure 3.2 dates back to 1919, it nevertheless does indicate the trading relationships between the overseas Chinese merchants in Japan and Singapore. Singapore's overseas Chinese merchants had their premises in High Street or North Bridge Road, and were engaged in the import of cotton yarn, cotton piece goods, and sundry goods through the overseas Chinese merchants at Kobe and/or Yokohama (Kobe Shoko Kaigisho 1929: 1–50). Him Woo & Co. of High Street had branches at Kobe and Yokohama, while Tong Joo Heng of North Bridge Road kept a resident representative at Yokohama, who was actively engaged in the purchase of Japanese goods. We

Table 3.4 Kobe's overseas Chinese merchant houses which traded with Singapore's
Chinese importers (as of January 1929)

Firm	Trading goods
Hokkiens	
Loong Shun & Co.[a]	Textiles, marine products, sundry goods, matches
Hoo Gwan Tjan	Sundry goods
Yue Hing & Co.	Textiles, marine products, sundry goods
Ban An Leong & Co.	Textiles, marine products, sundry goods, others
Cantonese	
Tung Nam & Co.	Textiles, marine products, sundry goods
Cheong Fat & Co.	Textiles, marine products, sundry goods, others
Kwong Hin Cheong & Co.	Textiles, marine products, ceramics, matches
Yuen Cheong Tai	Marine products, sundry goods
Yue Ching Cheong[b]	Textiles, marine products, sundry goods, others
Kwong Yick & Co.	Textiles, sundry goods
Hoo Loong & Co.	Textiles, marine products, sundry goods, ceramics
Yun Woo & Co.	Textiles, marine products, sundry goods
Tuck Wo[c]	Textiles, marine products, others
Ming Hing & Co.	Marine products, sundry goods
Kwong Wing On	Marine products, sundry goods
Taiwanese	
Chuang Yü P'o & Co.	Marine products, sundry goods, matches, others

Source: Constructed from Kobe Shoko Kaigisho (1929: 1–50).
Notes
[a] It was set up as a Kobe branch by Loong Shun & Co. of Amoy in 1909, and had a trading
relationship with Tai Yick & Co. of Nagasaki (Shu 1997: 108–9).
[b] Kobe branch of a merchant house in Hong Kong.
[c] Kobe branch of a Yokohama-based Chinese commercial house.

also learn from Figure 3.2 that several Chinese merchants in Singapore had a
trading relationship with Tung Nam & Co., an influential merchant house at
Kobe.

As for their dialect groups, Kwong Hing Loong, Him Woo and Hiap
Loong must have been Cantonese, because they were included in the 1908
membership of the Chinese Chamber of Commerce under the Cantonese
section (Singapore Chinese Chamber of Commerce 1908: 6–7). Moreover,
Kong Kee must also have been Cantonese, for its owner was the same as Him
Woo's. There is no information about the dialect groups of the other
merchant houses in Singapore. But assuming that they traded with the
Chinese merchants in Japan of the same dialect group, then most of them
would have been Cantonese.

In fact, according to the Trade Bureau of the Japanese Ministry of Trade
and Industry, those Chinese who imported Japanese silk and rayon goods

Table 3.5 Overseas Chinese merchants in Japan and their trading partners in Singapore (as of 1919)

Japan		Singapore	
Firm	*Location*	*Firm*	*Location*
Tong Joo Heng[a]	(Yokohama)	Tong Joo Heng	(North Bridge Rd)
Wing Shing Ho	(Yokohama)	Eng Heng Leong	(High St)
Kwong Hin Cheong	(Kobe)	Goh Hock Heng	(High St)
Tung Nam & Co.	(Kobe)	Ng Sing Hing	(North Bridge Rd)
Sin Yee Cheong	(Yokohama)	Lee Sang Yion	(High St)
Him Woo[b]	(Yokohama)	Ng Hong Hing	(High St)
Him Woo[b]	(Kobe)	Him Woo	(High St)
Ming Hing	(Kobe)	Kong Kee	(n.a.)
Kwong Cheong Loong	(Kobe)	Hiap Loong	(High St)
Gwan Tai	(Kobe)	Chup Yick	(Hih St)
Kwong Yuen Sang	(Kobe)	Kwong Hing Loong	(High St)
Lee Hing Shing	(Kobe)	Ban Lee Hing	(n.a.)

Source: Shimizu Hiroshi 1997b: 11.

Notes

[a] A purchasing office

[b] A branch.

were Cantonese and Teochius, while there were hardly any Hokkiens in this trade (Shokosho Boekikyoku 1932: 58–9). Also, W.G. Huff claims that the Chinese merchants who bought Japanese cotton piece goods from the Japanese importers in Singapore were mainly Cantonese, keeping their shops in North Bridge Road, South Bridge Road and Arab Street, and were known as 'High Street' dealers (Huff 1994 : 267–8). However, he does not refer to the Chinese merchants who imported textiles direct from Japan.

Furthermore, Nishimura Takeshiro, a Japanese medical doctor, who resided in pre-war Singapore for many years, wrote in his book that Chinese merchants in High Street began to deal in Japanese cotton textiles during the First World War, and rapidly increased their market share (Nishimura Takeshiro 1941: 84, 190). Although he does not make reference to their dialect group, they were definitely not the Teochiu textile merchants of Circular Road who were closely associated with the British merchant houses.

Incidentally, as Table 3.4 reveals, most of the Cantonese and Hokkien merchants at Kobe handled marine products. Then were their trading partners in Singapore the overseas Chinese of the same dialect groups? In the Straits Settlements, the merchants who dealt in marine products belonged to the three dialect groups, i.e. Hokkien, Teochiu and Cantonese. Each group set up an association of marine products merchants, in order to strengthen the co-operation among the members. The Cantonese, for example, founded the Toh Yan Club at 75 New Bridge Road. As of the end of the 1920s, its membership comprised about 100 merchants, many of whom handled, at least in part, Japanese marine products (Shokosho Boekikyoku 1930b: 110, 114). Moreover, as of 1915, Sasaki Tanetaro, a Japanese marine products exporter at Kobe, had a trading relationship with Heng Seng & Co. of Circular Road, whose owner was Cantonese, specialising in marine products (*Boeki Jiho*, vol. 2, no. 3, March 1915: 78).

In brief, although it is often said that Singapore's Cantonese did not play a significant role in foreign trade, as far as the trade with Japan is concerned, they were actively engaged in the import of textile goods and marine products. Besides, most of the Chinese merchants at Kobe were Cantonese, and it is highly likely that the trading relationship between the Chinese merchants at Kobe and those in Singapore was based on the traditional pattern that the Chinese merchants of one dialect group in one country preferred to trade with those of the same dialect group in another country.

JAPAN'S TRADE WITH BRITISH MALAYA DURING WORLD WAR I AND THE 1920s

Rise of Japanese merchants in Singapore

As noted earlier, prior to World War I the overseas Chinese merchants in Japan endeavoured to cultivate Singapore and other Southeast Asian markets for Japanese goods by making use of intra-Asian Chinese commercial networks, and Japanese merchants followed their footsteps by joining Japan's trade with the region. In this section, we shall therefore consider how Japanese trading companies and individual merchants advanced commercially into British Malaya in competition with the overseas Chinese merchants.[10]

In the last quarter of the nineteenth century and the early twentieth century there were some Japanese retailers and foreign traders in Singapore. Around 1878, Ogawa Shino opened a sundry goods shop with her Chinese husband who had previously lived in Kobe (Nanyo oyobi Nihonjinsha 1938: 136–7, 142, 227). This was apparently the first Japanese shop in the British colony. However, since the Japanese population comprised only eight males and 14 females in 1881 (Makepeace, *et al.* 1991a: 358), it is highly likely that their shop catered to both Japanese residents and non-Japanese customers.

Subsequently, sundry-goods shops, drapers' shops and other Japanese retail businesses were opened to cater initially to the Japanese prostitutes whose number rose sharply from 16 in 1885 to 585 in 1903, and later to other Japanese residents and non-Japanese customers as well (*Government Gazette*, 12 February 1886: 138; DRO, 7.1.5.4, 21 August 1903). But most of them were not successful. According to the January 1896 issue of *Tsusho Isan* (*Trade Compilation*), many of those who opened shops in Singapore had formerly been sailors, pearl divers, prostitutes, brothel-keepers or gamblers, and very few Japanese came to Singapore with the firm determination of running a business from the start (*Tsusho Isan*, 4 January 1896: 33). Actually, the Commercial Bureau of the Japanese Foreign Ministry wrote in May 1909 that:

> Although the Japanese population in this port [Singapore] is not small, the Japanese are not active industrially or commercially. This is because the unproductive women [i.e. prostitutes] are numerous, while the Japanese in the legitimate trades, especially those of powerful retail shops and companies, are few.
>
> (*Tsusho Isan*, 5 May 1909: 11–12)

As for the Japanese merchants in Singapore, apart from Mitsui & Co. and Otomune Shoten, few were engaged in trade with Japan before World War I. Mitsui & Co.'s branch was set up in 1891, and was engaged in the import of such bulky Japanese goods as coal, ingot copper, matches and beer. As for Otomune Shoten which was based in Osaka, its branch was opened in 1905, and was concerned with the import of cotton textile goods, ceramics, fancy mats and other articles. Although Nakagawa Shoten, Yamato Shokai and some others were wholesalers-cum-retailers, they also imported small quantities of Japanese goods similar to the ones handled by Otomune Shoten (Nanyo oyobi Nihonjinsha 1938: 227).

On the other hand, Singapore's Chinese merchants could import Japanese goods at low costs, because they 'keep branches or purchasing agencies in Osaka, Kobe or Yokohama, and make purchases at a right moment through them, making [Japanese] manufacturers compete in price'(*Tsusho Isan*, 5 May 1909: 32). Indeed, as of late December 1910, there were 178 Japanese in commerce, but many of them obtained Japanese goods mainly from the Chinese wholesale merchants (DRO, 7.1.5.4, 30 October 1911). Moreover, Japanese retailers in the Malay Peninsula, Sumatra and West Borneo occasionally visited Singapore to stock goods from the Chinese wholesalers (Nanyo oyobi Nihonjinsha 1938: 227).

However, the First World War witnessed a major change in the position of the Japanese merchants in both Singapore and Japan. During the war, the major European powers had to devote themselves to war efforts, and were therefore unable to supply large quantities of goods to Singapore and other countries in the world. Taking advantage of this situation, Japan was able not only to develop her own manufacturing industry greatly, but also to get a firm foothold in overseas markets. Her exports to Singapore rose from $11,503,000 in 1913 to $19,388,000 in 1916 and $44,530,000 in 1918. Similarly, her imports increased from $5,006,000 to $11,218,000 and $25,672,000 during the same years (Nanyo oyobi Nihonjinsha 1938: 235).

There was also a major change in the commodity composition of Japanese imports. Although coal accounted for 41.1 per cent of total imports in 1913, its share declined to 37.7 per cent in 1918, and 34.4 per cent in 1919.[11] During the war years, one could also witness a marked increase in the import of cotton textiles, wooden boxes for raw rubber, matches, ceramics and other Japanese goods. In particular, the share of cotton textiles in total imports from Japan rose slightly from 2.7 per cent in 1913 to 2.9 per cent in 1918, but then jumped to 9 per cent in 1919. This was clearly a presage for Japan's trade expansion from the late 1920s onwards when Japan began to compete fiercely with Lancashire in the British Malayan market. Also, the import of Japanese rickshaws and spare parts rose sharply from $261,000 in 1913 to $427,000 in 1918. Although Japanese cars hold a large market share in Singapore today, at that time Japan virtually monopolised the Malayan market for rickshaws, because Japanese rickshaws were durable, and very popular among rickshaw-pullers in the region (Shingaporu Shohin Chinretsukan 1927: 450).[12]

As the demand for Japanese goods increased greatly, the number of Singapore-based Japanese merchants also rose sharply. During the three years from 1916 to 1918, more than 20 Japanese trading companies and individual merchants set up branches or representative offices in the *gudang* area around Raffles Place. Also many Japanese retail shops were opened in the downtown area centering on High Street and Middle Road. Indeed, during the war years, a combined total of 78 retail shops and branches/ representative offices of trading companies were opened. By the end of 1918, the total number of existing Japanese trading firms and retail shops (including brokers' offices) was over 110, which was thrice as many as that of the pre-war period (Nanyo oyobi Nihonjinsha 1938: 225–6).

As Table 3.5 shows, the large majority of Japanese trading companies and individual foreign traders started their businesses in Singapore in 1916 or 1917. In May 1917, the trade department of the Mitsubishi Goshi Kaisha, which became an independent company under the name of Mitsubishi Corporation (Mitsubishi Shoji) in 1918, made preparations for setting up an office in the British colony, because, according to the company, 'irrespective of how much it would cost, we ought to keep a base of business operations in Singapore for our company's advance into the Malay Peninsula, the Nether-lands Indies, and India'. It therefore established a representative office at Raffles Place in September of that year (Mitsubishi Shashi Kankokai 1980: 3754; *idem* 1981a: 3938).[13] Moreover, those Japanese retailers who had launched their retail businesses before World War I took the advantage of the war-time boom to engage in foreign trade and in the wholesale trade in Japanese goods to overseas Chinese and Indian retail shops.

It should be noted at this juncture that most of the Japanese merchants in Singapore imported Japanese goods directly from their head offices, Japanese exporters or manufacturers in Japan, not through overseas Chinese merchants at Kobe. In order to confirm this point, we shall take Choya Shokai as a case study of the activities of a Japanese trading company in Singapore.[14] Choya

Table 3.6 Japanese trading companies in Singapore

Company	Location	Line of business	Start of Operation
Mitsui & Co.[a]	1 Battery Road	Import and export trade	1891
Nakagawa Shoten	7–8 High Street	Import and sale of sundry goods and foodstuffs	1895
Yamato Shokai	41 High Street	Import and export trade	1898
Otomune Shoten[a]	1 Raffles Place	Import and export of Southeast Asian produce, sale of Japanese sundry goods	1905
Nippon Baiyaku[a]	North Bridge Road	Import and sale of chemicals and medicines	1907
Choya Shokai[a]	2 Change Alley	Import and sale of chemicals and medicines	1916
Sakabe Shokai	17 Change Alley	Export of Southeast Asian produce, import of rubber goods, sundry goods, etc.	1916
Murata Koshi	29 High Street	Import of leather goods and sundry goods, export of local produce	1916
Tomota Goshi Kaisha[a]	43 High Street	Import of leather goods and sundry goods, export of local produce	1916
Kawahara Shoten[a]	7 D'Almaida Street	Export of Southeast Asian produce, import of Japanese sundry goods	1916
Kato Shokai[a]	100–1 Robinson Road	Import and export trade	1916
Arisaka Shoten	96 North Bridge Road	Import and export trade, commission sale	1916
Komai Shoten[a]	16 Collyer Quay	Import and export trade	1916
Mitsubishi Goshi Kaisha[a]	Raffles Place	Import and export trade	1917
Chuo Bussan[b]	27 Robinson Road	Import and export trade	1917
Masuda Boeki[a]	6 Battery Road	Import and export trade	1917
Osaka Seiyaku[a]	40 Vaton Street	Import and export trade	1917
Ogura Boekibu[a]	16 Collyer Quay	Import of Japanese sundry goods	1917
Suzuki Shoten's Agency	6 Battery Road	Import of Japanese sundry goods	1917
Mukaigasa Shoten[b]	16 Collyer Quay	Import of sundry goods, export of sheep skin, ox-hide, and Southeast Asian produce	1917
Ikeda Shoten[b]	6 Battery Road	Import and sale of ceramics and sundry goods	1917
Yamamoto Shokai	176 Middle Road	Import and wholesale trade in Japanese cotton textiles	1917
Nagai Shoten	High Street	Import and export of general merchandise, sale of Japanese goods	Not available

Source: Constructed from Gaimusho Tsushokyoku 1918: 165–7, and Nanyo oyobi Nihonjinsha 1938: 689.
Notes
[a] A branch.
[b] A representative office.

Shokai set up a branch at Surabaya in Java in 1902, and then branches at Semarang in 1907 and Batavia in 1909. In December 1911, Arai Ensaku, an executive director of the company, visited Southeast Asia and made preparations for the purchase of a rubber estate and the establishment of a branch in Singapore. In early 1912, he managed to buy a 200–acre rubber estate at ¥200,000 from a certain overseas Chinese in Lim Chu Kang, and named it the Chitose-en (Choya Hyakunen-shi 1986: 33). According to Choya Shokai's financial statements, the company invested in the rubber estate ¥21,817.59 in each of the first and the second half of 1918, and the first half of 1919, and ¥59,811.45 in the second half of 1919 (Choya Shokai, 'the 12th to 15th Financial Statements', 1 August 1918 to 1 February 1920). In 1919, the rubber estate produced 35,000 lb of crude rubber (Nanyo oyobi Nihonjinsha 1938: 190).

As for the establishment of a branch, Choya Shokai made good preparations. Arai Ensaku hired Kawabuchi Keisuke away from Yamato Shokai as a staff member for the head office in Japan. Kobayashi Kichiji, who later became a general manager of the company in charge of the Java region, worked as an accountant at the Chitose-en for three years, and during that period he was frequently engaged in sales activities for the company's brand goods, 'Choya shirts', not only in Singapore, but in the Malay Peninsula, Penang and British Borneo (Choya Hyakunen-shi 1986: 33).

In December, the company eventually set up a Singapore branch in Change Alley, with Kawabuchi Keisuke (the first branch manager) and another Japanese. However, with the expansion of its business, three Japanese staff members and two local employees joined them afterwards (*ibid.*: 34). The branch tried to promote the sales of Choya shirts in co-operation with Takeshita Shokai, a sundry-goods store at North Bridge Road, by means of offering free cinema tickets, and subsequently expanded its sales activities into the Malay Peninsula and the neighbouring countries (Choya Shatsu 1974: 44). When it succeeded in making shirts for Caucasians in co-operation with its head office in Japan, it concluded a sales agreement with J.L. Campbell & Co., Singapore-based British tailors, of Raffles Place (Choya Hyakunen-shi 1986: 35).

Choya Shokai's branch acted as an agency for the Morinaga Confectionery Company, and attempted to expand its sales network through its sub-agent, Lim Wo Cheong, a Chinese merchant, in Singapore, the Malay Peninsula and Sumatra. Also, it imported from Japan unbleached and striped cotton piece goods and *Ashikaga* cotton crêpe, and sold them in Southeast Asian markets, while also exporting them to Europe through Yamato Shokai of High Street. However, as it expanded its business rapidly, it began to trade cotton piece goods on speculation (Choya Shatsu 1974: 44; Choya Hyakunen-shi 1986: 36).

In addition to the above, the Singapore branch became an exclusive agency for the Matsuzaki Kaban Kaisha (bags), the Ideal Cosmetics Company, the

Azumi Shoten (pharmaceuticals) of Osaka and the Sasaki Glass Company, and an agency for the Matsumura Toki Gomei Kaisha (ceramics). Also it imported straw hats, silk stockings and other Japanese goods (Choya Hyakunen-shi 1986: 35–6; Choya Shatsu 1974: 44). There is little available information about the Singapore branch's export trade. According to Choya Shokai's company history book, *Choya: Isseiki no Ayumi* (*Choya: A Hundred-year History*), the branch was engaged in the export of Southeast Asian produce to Japan (Choya Hyakunen-shi 1986: 36).

It is worth noting that the employees of Choya Shokai were encouraged to hold their company's own shares with the purpose of increasing their loyalty to the company. As of 1 February 1920, for example, Tsutsumi Yoichi owned 37 shares, Kawabuchi Keisuke 15 shares, Tamura Kichiro 7 shares, Yamamoto Arajiro 5 shares, and Fuji Ryoji 5 shares. At that time, one share cost ¥100 (Choya Shokai, 1 February 1920). In this way, their interests could be identified with those of their company.

During the war years, like Choya Shokai, other Japanese trading companies based in Singapore diversified their activities. One should not simply assume, however, that the expansion of their trading activities in the war time and then in the inter-war period were due to their own efforts alone. Indeed, we need to take into account institutional factors for their success. First, the South Seas Association (Nanyo Kyokai) set up a commercial museum in Singapore in April 1918, using a subsidy of ¥112,000 from the Japanese Ministry of Commerce and Industry.[15] The functions of the commercial museum included surveys of the British Malayan market, exhibitions of Japanese goods and sales of sample goods. It also published a monthly journal, *Nanyo Keizai Jiho* (Review of the South Seas Economies), to provide manufacturers and exporters in Japan with the latest information on Southeast Asian markets (DRO, E.2.7.0/1–1, 7 and 14 May 1937).

Second, Japanese banks set up branches in Singapore and other major cities in Southeast Asia to assist trading companies and other Japanese firms financially. Western banks in the region were not certain about the credit standing of Japanese firms, and did not give loans to them unless the latter had large assets and high credit standing. There were three Japanese banks which set up branches in Singapore before World War II. These were the Yokohama Specie Bank, the Bank of Taiwan,[16] and the China and Southern Bank (Kanan Ginko). The Bank of Taiwan set up its first Southeast Asian branch in Singapore in September 1912, and subsequently established branches in Thailand and the Netherlands East Indies (Taiwan Ginko 1919: 431–2). The Singapore branch provided loans for a maximum period of one year. The maximum amount of a loan was $2,000, while the total amount of loans in the British colony as a whole was limited to $250,000 per year. Those who wanted to obtain loans from it were required to have a guarantor. Moreover, although the interest rate was not fixed, it was kept at a rate 5 per cent lower than the average rate prevailing in British Malaya (Robertson 1986: 16).

The China and Southern Bank was a Chinese–Japanese joint venture bank, and it was a subsidiary of the Bank of Taiwan. It was established on 29 January 1919 in Taipei, and within the year it set up branches in Semarang, Singapore, Canton and other large cities. Whereas the Bank of Taiwan made loans mainly to large Japanese companies, the China and Southern Bank targeted small and medium-sized Japanese firms. However, in the 1920s both banks suffered a financial crisis, and were obliged to cut down the amount of their capital.[17] Consequently, the Bank of Taiwan began to concern itself with foreign exchange business in the main, while the other bank had to trim down the total amount of loans drastically (DRO, E.1.1.0/8, undated, January 1930).

As for the Yokohama Specie Bank, it set up a representative office (which was promoted to a branch later on) in Singapore in September 1916, in response to the huge increase in Japanese exports to Southeast Asia (Tokyo Ginko 1981: 162). According to its research section:

The main task of our Singapore branch is, after all, to act as a subsidiary organ for obtaining handling charges by foreign exchange transactions, and our direct role in financing the development of foreign trade will be very small even in the future.

(Yokohama Shokin 1922: 42)

However, in the inter-war period, the branch came to give huge loans to certain Japanese firms.[18]

Third, the Japanese shipping companies also played an important role in Japan's trade expansion into British Malaya and other parts of Southeast Asia. During World War I, the number of Japanese ships on Japan–Southeast Asia routes increased enormously, largely because of the sharp decline in the number of European ships on Europe–Far East routes. Indeed, the tonnage of Japanese ships on Japan–Southeast Asia routes via Singapore, for example, rose from 30,000 tons to 130,000 tons (Nanyo oyobi Nihonjinsha 1938: 226). Japanese ships on other routes linking Japan with Southeast Asia also increased greatly. Both the Osaka Shosen Kaisha and the Nippon Yusen Kaisha set up branches in the British colony, largely in response to a sudden increase in demand for Japanese shipping.

Formerly, the Osaka Shosen Kaisha used Guthrie & Co. as its agency. But when it opened the Japan–Bombay route in 1913, and the Southeast Asia and South America routes in 1916, the number of its ships which called at Singapore, began to increase greatly. In February 1918 the company sent its staff member, Takeuchi San'ichi, to the British colony to work as its resident representative at Guthrie & Co., and it set up a branch in Souza Street shortly afterward. The branch began to undertake shipping business under the branch manager, Yamauchi Shinobu, after dissolving an agency agreement with Guthrie & Co. in June of that year (Osaka Shosen 1934: 766). As for the other major Japanese shipping company, the Nippon Yusen Kaisha, it had an agency agreement with Paterson, Simons, & Co., but it set up a representative office in December 1918, which was promoted to a branch in January 1920 (Nanyo oyobi Nihonjinsha 1938: 225). The Yamashita Kisen Kaisha and other Japanese shipping companies also opened up Southeast Asian routes one after another, while the Nanyo Soko Kaisha (The South Seas Warehousing Company) set up a branch in Singapore in June 1921.

The transport cost from Japan to Singapore was much lower than it was from Britain to Singapore, thanks to Japan's low operating costs and geographical proximity to the British colony, and this also helped the Japanese trading companies to be very competitive. In the middle of 1921, for example, the freight rate for a ton of cotton piece goods was ¥12 from Kobe to Singapore as compared to 90 shillings (some ¥47.12) from London or Liverpool to Singapore (*Naigai Shoko Jiho*, vol. 8, no. 6, June 1921: 31).

Kobe's overseas Chinese merchants and Japanese competition

Obviously, the emergence of the Japanese merchants constituted a threat to the supreme position of the overseas Chinese merchants at Kobe and their intra-Asian trade networks. Indeed, the share of the overseas Chinese merchants in Japan's export trade with Singapore and other parts of Southeast Asia declined considerably. Nevertheless, since there was a huge increase in both the value and range of Japanese exports during World War I, they also benefited greatly from the Japanese trade expansion. Indeed, such influential Chinese firms as Sin Sui Hing, Tung Nam & Co. and Yue Ching Cheong made huge profits (Shimizu Hiroshi 1997b: 9).

It should be noted that the Chinese merchants could find a niche in the Japanese trade with Southeast Asia. As small and medium-sized Japanese middlemen and manufacturers found it risky to export goods direct to their foreign customers whose credit standing was hardly known to non-Chinese, many of them preferred to rely on Kobe's Chinese merchants for export. Besides, they were paid in cash for their goods, and did not have the trouble of shipping and other arrangements, even though they had to give the Chinese merchants a commission (Kikakuin 1939: 388–9). Moreover, as a means of quick export, some small and medium-sized manufacturers in the Kobe–Osaka region sent their salesmen with sample goods to Southeast Asia at regular intervals, and took orders from local Chinese merchants there. However, they turned these orders into ones involving the overseas Chinese merchants at Kobe (*ibid*.: 388). In other words, they exported the goods on order through them. According to the then Japanese Consul-General at Batavia, Miyake Tetsusaburo, the Japanese manufacturers chose to do so for distinct advantages. They were paid normally in cash for their goods by Kobe's Chinese merchants. And since they did not need to draw documentary bills on Southeast Asia's Chinese merchants, they were free from the risk of non-payment by their overseas customers (DRO, E.3.2.0/J3, 27 December 1929).

As noted earlier, European merchant houses, particularly new entrants, had great difficulties in obtaining information on the credit standing of Chinese merchants in Singapore. It was certainly risky to trade with Chinese merchants in Singapore. Chinese merchants often set up a commercial business with a few hundred dollars, and yet undertook the trade value of 10 to 15 times its capital. Indeed, there were many cases of bankruptcy among them. Moreover, they would refuse to accept goods on order, if and when such goods had fallen in price on delivery. There was no reliable organisation to provide information about their credit standing (Mantetsu 1941: 261; SICC 1979: 19–20). Obviously, it is wrong to argue that all the Chinese merchants were fraudulent, for there were also many reliable and honest ones.

In view of the risk involved, Kobe's overseas Chinese merchants could still play an important role in Japan's foreign trade, and continued to export large quantities of goods to Singapore and other parts of Southeast Asia. As of 1920, the Chinese importers of Japanese cotton textiles in Singapore were Chup Yick, Ng Hong Hing, Ng Hock Hing, Hiap Loong, Ban Lee Hing and some others. As they could import cotton textiles through the Chinese commission merchants at Kobe, they did not need to rely on the Japanese exporters in Japan, or the Japanese trading companies in Singapore. Indeed, in the British Malayan market, Mitsui & Co. increased its sales of the goods tremendously, but Choya Shokai, Masuda Boeki, Suzuki Shoten and other Japanese trading companies were not very successful (*Naigai Shoko Jiho*, vol. 8, no. 6, June 1921: 30) .

However, the share of the Japanese merchants in the ceramics trade increased enormously at the expense of the overseas Chinese merchants. Although prior to the First World War the bulk of ceramics had been exported to Southeast Asia by Kobe's overseas Chinese merchants, during and after the war the number of Japanese merchants trading with the region increased, while in Singapore there was also a rise in the number of Japanese merchants in the import trade. In 1924, there were nine main importers of Japanese ceramics, of whom seven (Nanyo Shoko, Otomune Shoten, Ikeda Shoten, Nichiran Boeki, Tosa Shoten, Komoto Shoten and Ebata Yoko) were Japanese, and only two (Chup Yick and Ng Hong Hing, both of High Street) were Chinese (*Nanyo Keizai Jiho,* vol. 6, no. 4, April 1924: 36–7; *Nagoya Shoko Kaigisho Geppo*, no. 214, May 1925: 65). Ikeda Shoten and two Chinese firms imported ceramics from Kobe, while the remaining Japanese trading companies imported them directly from manufacturers in Nagoya and its outskirts (*Nanyo Keizai Jiho,* vol. 6, no. 5, May 1924: 11–12). Nevertheless, even as late as 1936, the Chinese merchants at Kobe were responsible for slightly more than 10 per cent (191 metric tons) of Japan's ceramics exports to the Straits Settlements (Shokosho Boekikyoku 1938: 174).

Lastly, we examine the export of marine products, of which the overseas Chinese merchants in Japan had handled the bulk of exports before World War I. Japanese marine products were exported mainly to Hong Kong, China and Southeast Asia through Kobe, Hakodate, Moji and Nagasaki. But Kobe was by far the most important among these, not only because it was the starting point for the China and Southeast Asia shipping routes, but also because there were many influential overseas Chinese merchants handling marine products there. During World War I, Kobe's overseas Chinese merchants were hardly challenged by Japanese merchants in this trade, and continued to enjoy their predominant position in the inter-war period. Kobe's share in Japan's total exports of marine products was 48.1 per cent in 1925, and 61 per cent in 1927 (Shokosho Boekikyoku 1930a: 39). As Table 3.6 shows, in 1927 the Straits Settlements (largely Singapore) took ¥1,853,238 worth of marine products from Kobe (15.1 per cent), and ranked the third largest customer for it after Hong Kong and China (Shokosho Boekikyoku 1930a: Foldout Table 7). As the Cantonese merchants at Kobe exported large quantities of marine products to Singapore through Hong Kong, the value of exports to the Straits Settlements would have been much larger than the above figure. In the market, there was particularly a large demand for dried cuttlefish which accounted for nearly 45 per cent of total exports in 1927.

In the late 1920s there were about 50 overseas Chinese merchants in the export trade in marine products in Kobe, most of whom were also engaged in the export of other products. In the same city, there were 57 Japanese wholesale merchants specialising in marine products, twelve of whom were also engaged in the export trade as well. Almost all of them had commercial relations with the overseas Chinese merchants there. The Japanese and overseas Chinese merchants had their premises in the vicinity of each other, and had dealings principally on a cash basis at either of their shops. The overseas Chinese merchants took stocks of marine products for cash probably in order to get a large discount, just like today's discount stores which buy goods in large quantities for cash. However, in the late 1920s, overseas Chinese merchants suffered a sharp fall in profits, and consequently it became a common practice for them to make a lump-sum cash payment

Table 3.7 Exports of Japanese marine products to the Straits Settlements through Kobe in 1927 (in yen)

Dried cuttlefish	Dried trepang	Dried codfish	Dried scallops	Dried abalone	Tangle	Other	Total
827,600	321,280	218,675	196,293	134,419	9,363	145,608	1,853,238
(44.7%)	(17.3%)	(11.8%)	(10.6%)	(7.3%)	(0.5%)	(7.9%)	(100.1%)

Source: Constructed from Shokosho Boekikyoku 1930a: Foldout Table 7.

to the wholesale merchants within a week after the purchase (Shokosho Boekikyoku 1930a: 108).

In the Straits Settlements the bulk of foreign marine products were imported through the overseas Chinese merchants who maintained branches and/or representative offices in the main exporting countries. As for Japanese products, they were imported into Singapore either directly from Japan or indirectly via the Nam bak hang in Hong Kong. In both cases, the overseas Chinese merchants in Japan were involved in the trade. In the late 1920s there were 36 Chinese merchants in Singapore, who were engaged in the import of both Japanese and other foreign products (Shokosho Boekikyoku 1930b: 101–2). Also, there were four Japanese firms importing marine products from Japan, namely Mitsui & Co., the Taichong Kongsi, the Shimota Koshi and Asano Shoten. In the late 1920s the combined value of their imports amounted merely to $60,000 (some 100 metric tons) (*ibid.*: 91, 94).

In short, Kobe's Chinese merchants witnessed a steep decline in their shares of the export trade in cotton textiles and ceramics due to the emergence of Japanese competitors. But it should be noted that they could continue to maintain a large share of the trade in certain Japanese exports, notably marine products. Indeed, as late as 1921, even all-powerful Mitsui & Co. felt that Yee Wo & Co. was posing a major threat, for it exported large quantities of matches to Singapore (Mitsui Bunko, Bussan 357/1, April 1921: 61). Moreover, some of the influential merchants including Tung Nam & Co., Yue Ching Cheong and Sin Sui Hing took the advantage of the war-time boom, and made huge profits by exporting large quantities of cotton textiles, sundry goods, and other Japanese goods to Singapore and other parts of Southeast Asia (Koyama 1979: 47).

Japan's trade with British Malaya in the post-World War I period

Japan witnessed a sharp increase in her exports to British Malaya during World War I, but she then suffered a sharp fall during the post-war years. Indeed, the value of her exports declined sharply from $44,052,000 (or 4.1 per cent of British Malaya's total imports) in 1920 to $18,147,000 (3.9 per cent) in 1922 and $16,556,000 (2.5 per cent) in 1924 (Shokosho Boekikyoku 1931: 11). There are several reasons for the fall. First of all, the European countries resumed their export trade with Singapore and other countries, competing with Japan. Formerly, the major strength of Japanese goods was cheapness. However, in the post-war period, the exchange value of the pound sterling declined considerably from 2s. 2d. per ¥1 in 1918 to 2s. 8d. per ¥1 in 1920 (Seki 1956: 408), and since the Straits dollar was linked to the British currency, its value also declined against the yen. This simply meant that the Japanese imports were now much more expensive in the British Malayan market, and were therefore less attractive to local

consumers. Besides, the quality of Japanese goods was in general inferior to
competing European goods. According to the Commercial Bureau of the
Japanese Commerce and Industry, the hairs of Japanese cotton flannel

> easily fall out, when the cloth is washed, and yet its price is not low
> at all. In comparison, European cloth was not cheap, but as it is of
> high quality, there is a large demand for it among the middle-class
> consumers.
>
> (Shokosho Shomukyoku 1925: 314)

Besides, as noted earlier, European merchant houses sold goods to Chinese
wholesale merchants on generous credit terms. In sharp contrast, since
Japanese import merchants in Singapore normally sold goods by cash or on
short-term credit, they could not easily compete with their European rivals
(*Nagoya Shoko Kaigisho Geppo*, no. 193, August 1923: 81). The boycotts of
Japanese goods by the overseas Chinese in British Malaya, related to the May
Fourth Movement in 1919 and the Movement for the Return of Lüshun and
Dalien in 1923, both of which took place in mainland China, also seriously
affected the sales of Japanese goods in the British Malayan market (*ibid.*:
84–5).

Furthermore, the average price of rubber declined sharply from 2s. $\frac{3}{4}$d. per
pound in 1919 to 1s. $\frac{1}{10}$d. per pound in 1920 and $9\frac{9}{16}$d. per pound in 1921
(Drabble 1991: 306) with the result that the Malayan economy, based
heavily on rubber, suffered a major setback. The local consumers, whose
purchasing power was greatly curtailed, now bought fewer imported goods,
while substituting domestically produced goods for imports (Nanyo oyobi
Nihonjinsha 1938: 243).

The post-war recession gave rise to a growth of import-substitution
industries in British Malaya. Rickshaws are a case in point. As already noted,
until the end of World War I, the majority of the rickshaws in use in British
Malaya were Japanese made. However, in the post-war recession, they were
so expensive that ordinary rickshaw-pullers could simply not afford them.
Since the locally made rickshaws were manufactured from old wooden boxes
and Southeast Asian timber, they cost merely a third to a quarter of
Japanese-made rickshaws, and soon began to hold a large market share at the
expense of the Japanese imports. Consequently, the value of imports of
Japanese rickshaws and parts in the Straits Settlements declined sharply from
$427,439 in 1918 to $189,552 in 1920 and $150,264 in 1922 (Shingaporu
Shohin Chinretsukan 1927: 447–8). However, the Japanese rickshaws did
not disappear completely from the local market, as they were kept for private
use or were used by comparatively rich rickshaw-pullers (*ibid.*: 448–50).

The post-war recession also saw the bankruptcies of many small and
medium-sized Japanese trading companies, including Mogi Shoten, Choya
Shokai, Masuda Boeki, Chuo Bussan, Komai Shoten, Sakabe Shokai and

Nanyo Boeki (Nanyo oyobi Nihonjinsha 1938: 243). Almost all these trading companies moved into Singapore during the war years, and expanded their business activities rapidly.[19] When the war-time boom came to an abrupt end, they were burdened with huge stocks of Japanese goods which they had earlier imported at high costs.

Even Kawahara Shoten and Otomune Shoten, whose owners had both been awarded the Dark-blue Ribbon Medals by the Japanese government for their pioneering work in cultivating the Singapore and other Southeast Asian markets for Japanese goods, went bankrupt because of financial difficulties (Taiwan Ginko-shi 19644: 13). Also, Sakabe Shokai could not withstand the recession, and went bankrupt in December 1919, even though it had a turnover of between ¥6 and ¥7 million in 1918, and was financially backed up by an influential overseas Chinese. As the Yokohama Specie Bank had given the trading company a large amount of loans in foreign exchange, it suffered a loss of over $300,000 as a bad debt (Tokyo Ginko 1981: 213–14).

However, the markets for Japanese goods, which had been cultivated by the now bankrupt small and medium-sized companies, were taken over by such large Japanese trading companies as Mitsui & Co. and Mitsubishi Corporation, while many of their former employees embarked on their own retail businesses in various parts of Southeast Asia with financial assistance from the Taiwan Bank and other Japanese banks (Taiwan Ginko-shi 1964: 413).

In the mid-1920s, the economy of British Malaya began to show signs of recovery, and the value of imports from Japan rose to $34,900,000 in 1926.

Table 3.8 British Malaya's imports from Japan, 1920–29 (in $1,000 and percentages of total)

	1920 Value	%	1923 Value	%	1926 Value	%	1929 Value	%
Coal	16,101	36.5	2,942	16.2	2,729	7.8	2,648	11.4
Cotton piece goods	6,028	13.7	3,178	17.5	6,235	17.9	5,397	23.3
Rayon goods	1,080	2.5	527	2.9	1,937	5.6	4,626	19.9
Hosiery	1,873	4.3	833	4.6	1,020	2.9	673	2.9
Matches	1,916	4.3	1,122	6.2	1,065	3.1	156	0.6
Salted and dry fish	185	0.4	565	3.1	2,704	7.7	191	0.8
Rubber boxes	4,322	9.8	1,578	8.7	2,602	7.5	941	4.1
Ceramics	676	1.5	838	4.6	1,566	4.5	512	2.2
Cement	686	1.6	2	0	953	2.7	855	3.7
Other	11,185	25.4	6,558	36.1	14,089	40.4	7,192	31.0
Total	44,052	100.0	18,143	99.9	34,900	100.1	23,191	99.9

Source: Constructed from Shokosho Boekikyoku 1931.

However, in 1928 a general recession set in, while overseas Chinese resorted to the boycott of Japanese goods in response to the Chi'nan Incident in Shantung province in May. As a consequence, the Japanese imports declined to $20,147,000 once again in that year (Shokosho Boekikyoku 1931: 11).

In this way, the value of Japan's trade with British Malaya fluctuated in the 1920s. Moreover, one saw a major change in the composition of imports from Japan throughout the decade. As Table 3.7 shows, the share of coal declined sharply from 36.5 per cent of total imports in 1920 to 11.4 per cent in 1929, whereas a combined share of cotton piece goods and rayon goods rose steeply from 16 per cent to 42.2 per cent during the same years, showing the progress in industrialisation in Japan.[20]

JAPAN'S TRADE WITH BRITISH MALAYA IN THE 1930s

Japanese trade expansion and the response of the colonial power

Japan's exports to British Malaya went through 'the second boom' in the first half of the 1930s, after experiencing 'the first boom' during the First World War. This was because Japan managed to overcome the temporary difficulties in her export trade which were due not only to the world-wide recession in the wake of the Great Depression of 1929, but also to the Chinese boycotts of Japanese goods triggered by the Manchurian Incident in 1931. As Table 3.8 shows, the share of Japan in British Malaya's imports rose steeply from 2.6 per cent in 1929 to 3.9 per cent in 1931, and 7.4 per cent in 1933. If we refer only to industrial goods, then the Japanese share jumped from 6.2 per cent in 1930 to 13.6 per cent in 1933 (Nanyo oyobi Nihonjinsha 1938: 96).

As for the commodity structure of the Japanese imports, there was a large increase in cotton piece goods (see Table 3.9). Since Britain was the major supplier of these goods, Japanese commercial expansion affected her trade directly.[21] The imports of British cotton piece goods declined sharply from

Table 3.9 British Malaya's imports from Britain and Japan (in $1,000)

Year	Britain	Japan	Others	Total
1929	147,978 (16.5%)	23,190 (2.6%)	727,400	898,568
1930	98,076 (13.7%)	24,935 (3.5%)	593,105	716,116
1931	62,485 (13.7%)	17,895 (3.9%)	413,027	493,407
1933	51,016 (14.2%)	26,593 (7.4%)	280,606	358,215
1935	75,118 (15.8%)	30,405 (6.4%)	369,965	475,488
1937	108,175 (15.6%)	40,482 (5.8%)	543,508	692,165
1938	102,332 (18.4%)	12,426 (2.2%)	440,235	554,993

Source: Constructed from *Foreign Imports and Exports*, 1930–9.

Table 3.10 British Malaya's imports from Japan, 1920–38 (in $1,000)

	1920	1929	1931	1933	1935	1937	1938
Cotton							
textiles	6,028	5,397	5,335	8,952	5,076	5,943	2,787
Rayon piece							
goods	1,080	4,626	1,762	1,984	1,149	2,253	1,524
Yarn	–	–	802	870	1,688	1,998	611
Coal	16,101	2,648	1,461	1,556	1,432	2,138	1,570
Cement	686	855	1,272	356	775	715	237
Dry and							
salted fish	185	191	673	546	1,318	1,201	27
Other	19,972	9,472	6,590	12,329	18,967	26,234	5,670
Total	44,052	23,189	17,895	26,593	30,405	40,482	12,426

Source: Constructed from Shokosho Boekikyoku 1931: Foldout Table 3; Mantetsu 1941: 379.

Table 3.11 Cotton piece goods imports into British Malaya (in thousands of yards)

	1929	1931	1933	1934	1935	1937	1938
Britain	86,013	21,577	25,886	29,008	33,364	53,253	46,597
Japan	34,720	49,777	99,466	99,239	53,759	51,113	26,588
India	4,103	1,497	851	920	4,156	19,011	20,956
China	18,128	15,628	12,032	9,721	7,533	10,113	8,076
Others	23,543	11,447	7,668	5,516	4,837	8,311	12,776
Total	166,507	99,926	145,903	144,404	103,649	141,801	114,993

Source: Constructed from Nanyo Kyokai 1943: 160–1.

86,013,000 yd (51.7 per cent of total) in 1929 to 25,886,000 yd (17.7 per cent) in 1933, whereas those of Japan rose sharply from 34,720,000 yd (20.9 per cent of total) to 99,466,000 yd (68.2 per cent) in the same years (Table 3.10).

Also, there was a large demand even for those Japanese goods which had hitherto been unable to compete with similar Western goods in the British Malayan market. For example, Japanese-made tinned sardines were formerly of low quality, and unpopular among local consumers. For instance, the July 1916 issue of *Suisankai*, a Japanese journal of fisheries, described that, 'as [fish] oil was mixed with various inferior oils in Japanese tinned sardines, there is inevitably a criticism against the use of inferior oils' (*Suisankai*, no. 406, July 1916: 71). On the other hand, American tinned sardines under the brand name of Chap Ayam virtually monopolised the market, largely because they were of high quality, full of tomato juice, and palatable to consumers' taste. However, by the early 1930s Japanese producers of tinned sardines had managed to improve their quality tremendously, and had begun to drive out the American product from the market. Indeed, they became a cheap source of nutrition for workers in tin mining and rubber estates in the Malay Peninsula. Consequently, the American imports fell sharply from 4,140 tons in 1930 (97.2 per cent of total) to 156 tons (4.4 per cent) in 1934, whereas the Japanese imports rose steeply from a mere 28 tons (0.7 per cent) to 3,329 tons (93 per cent) (*Naigai Shoko Jiho*, vol. 23, no. 1, January 1936:11).

The main reason for Japan's success in her export trade can be explained by the fall in prices of various Japanese goods. In the case of the textile industry, rationalisation took place in the late 1920s and early 1930s, with the result that productivity was greatly raised (Seki 1954: 83–124; Howe 1996: 201–31). Moreover, Japan left the gold standard in December 1931, and subsequently the exchange value of the yen fell sharply from $87.4 per ¥100 in 1930 to $51.5 in 1933 and $49.9 in 1934 (Nanyo Kyokai 1943: 338–9).

Cheap Japanese goods became even cheaper in the British Malayan market. In 1933, the average cost of British cotton piece goods was 18 to 19 cents per yard, and that of Japan 10 cents. Also, Japanese rubber shoes cost only 30 to 35 cents a pair, as compared to 65 cents for local products and $1.10 for European imports (Mills 1942: 139, 150).[22]

In the Depression years, the local consumers saw a sharp reduction in their purchasing power as a result of the steep fall in the prices of rubber and tin in the world market, and substituted cheap Japanese goods for expensive European imports (*Nanyo*, vol. 25, no. 7, 1 July 1939: 26). This is reflected in the fact that, although there was a sharp decline in British Malaya's total imports from $898,568,000 in 1929 to $358,215,000 in 1933, the value of imports from Japan rose from $23,190,000 to $26,593,000 in the same years (Table 3.8).

British commercial strategy and Japan

How did the colonial power then respond to the sharp increase in imports from Japan? Since the mid-nineteenth century, Britain had continued to advocate free trade, and in the British Empire she firmly maintained a free-trade policy. However, after the Great Depression of 1929, other industrialised nations protected their own industries by raising tariff walls against imports, while intensifying their export drive into British Empire markets. At that time, the cotton textile industry in Lancashire was still Britain's leading export industry, even though it was in decline. Eventually, in February 1932 Britain abandoned the free trade policy, and put into practice a protectionist policy in the colonies and protectorates in accordance with the decision made at the Ottawa Conference held in July and August.[23]

In British Malaya, customs duties were formerly designed largely for revenue purposes, and almost all goods were imported fairly freely, irrespective of the origins of the goods imported. However, once Britain decided to introduce a protectionist policy there, this free trade principle could no longer be maintained. Therefore, at the Legislative Assembly on 26 September 1932, Sir Cecil Clementi, the Governor of the Straits Settlements, emphasised the need to change the free trade policy on the basis of the agreements at the Ottawa Conference (DRO, E.3.1.2/X1–B9, 15 October 1932). However, the British, Chinese and Indian Chambers of Commerce were all opposed to it on the grounds that if the Straits Settlements adopted the same protective tariff policy as that of the Federated Malay States, it would be detrimental to the entrepôt trade of the colonies (*ibid.*, 14 December 1932). In addition, the Singapore and Penang Chambers of Commerce were equally against it, arguing that free trade was essential for the continual prosperity of the Straits Settlements (Legislative Council, 18 January 1932: 36–7).

On 27 September 1932, John Bagnall, the president of the Singapore Chamber of Commerce, also expressed his opposition to the Governor's view at the general meeting for the first half-year. However, there were some European merchants who did not share his view. Indeed, some accused Japan of dumping goods, and asked for the imposition of prohibitive duties on Japanese imports (DRO, E3.2.0/J3, 10 October 1932).

In the Federated Malay States, Imperial Preference was established in March 1932, imposing a lower rate of tariffs on imports from British Empire countries. For example, the tariff rate for foreign cement was subject to $12 per ton, as compared to the tariff rate of $6 for British cement (DRO, E.3.1.2/X1–B9, 14 December 1932). On 1 June 1932 the Federated Malay States raised import duties on certain goods, while the number of British Empire goods which could enjoy preferential rates was greatly increased. The customs duty on foreign bicycle parts (excluding tyres and tubes) was raised from 10 per cent *ad valorem* to 20 per cent *ad valorem*, while it was kept intact for British Empire goods (*ibid.*, 2 June 1932). In October 1932 the customs duty on imported textiles and garments was also raised from 10 per cent to 20 per cent, while a 10 per cent preferential duty was newly introduced for British Empire goods. Similar measures were taken for many other goods.

A sort of Imperial Preference was also introduced in the Unfederated Malay States, apparently under British pressure. For example, as from 1 July 1933, the Johore State government began to impose customs duties on foreign goods, whereas imports from the British Empire remained free of duty. The import duties were 20 per cent *ad valorem* on cotton piece goods, 50 cents on a pair of rubber shoes, $5 on condensed milk per 100 lb and 20 per cent *ad valorem* on tinned and bottled foods (DRO, E.3.1.2/X1–B9, 30 June 1933).

Incidentally, Japan obviously did not stand idle when Imperial Preference was established in the Federated Malay States. On 15 May 1933, the Egyptian government increased the tariff on cotton piece goods by some 30 per cent, something which mainly affected the lower-grade cottons Japan was supplying in large quantities. Moreover, Australia decided to impose special import duties on cotton piece goods, towels, ceramics and electric bulbs on 19 June (PRO, Minutes by John Simon, 22 June 1933, FO371/17154). All these measures were taken primarily against severe Japanese competition, and naturally helped increase the suspicion on the part of the Japanese that they were taken by these countries, under British pressure, to save Lancashire. Indeed, the Japanese government feared that the measures would lead to a decline in Japan's bargaining position at the Anglo-Japanese commercial talks, which were planned to be held in London in September 1933 (DRO, E.3.1.2/X1–B9, 24 July 1933).[24] Therefore, the Japanese Ambassador at London, Matsudaira Tsuneo, strongly protested to the British Foreign Secretary, Sir John Simon, that the new tariff in Malaya had been imposed on foreign goods without being submitted to the Legislative Body. Simon then simply replied to him that 'this appears to be a matter of internal Government and if what has been done was validly done, it did not concern other Powers.' (PRO, Minute by Simon, 27 June 1933, FO371/17154).

In March 1934, the Anglo-Japanese commercial talks ended in failure. On 7 May of the same year, the British government announced the introduction of a quota system for imports of cotton and rayon piece goods in most of the colonies and dependencies, and ordered the governments of the Straits Settlements and other British territories to take necessary legal measures.[25] Although Britain was not a large exporter of rayon piece goods, since the Japanese goods competed fiercely with British cotton piece goods in the world market, she decided to include rayon piece goods in the quota system (Shimizu Hiroshi 1986: 47, 50–1).

Not surprisingly, the British protectionist policy was unacceptable to most merchants in Singapore. At the extraordinary general meeting of the Singapore Chamber of Commerce on 1 June 1934, some of the members argued that, although the quota system would benefit the industrialists and workers in Lancashire, it would be harmful to the impoverished consumers in British Malaya, who were forced to buy expensive British cotton piece goods. They went on to argue that, if the Lancashire cotton interests wanted to recapture the market from Japan, they ought to do so, not at the expense of the local consumers, but by cutting down the costs of production (Mills 1942: 148). However, when L.A. Davies of Henry Waugh & Co., which imported Lancashire cotton piece goods, talked persuasively in favour of the import restriction against Japanese goods, quite a few merchants moved onto his side unexpectedly. In the end, nine out of 23 members were in support of the resolution (Brown 1994: 120). The Association of British Malaya and the British Association of Straits Merchants in London were also opposed to the quota system on the grounds that it would affect Singapore's entrepôt trade (DRO, E.3.1.2/X1–B9, 18 January 1935).

At any rate, on 11 June 1934, the Importation of Textiles (Quotas) Ordinance was passed at the Straits Settlements Legislative Council. Seven unofficial representatives, consisting of merchants and others, were all against the quota system. But, since the official members constituted the majority (twelve), it was nevertheless passed without any difficulty (Mills 1942: 150). Consequently, the quotas for supplying countries were decided on the basis of actual imports of cotton and rayon piece goods (plus cotton-rayon fabric) during the period from 1927 to 1931, and the institution of the quota system was backdated to 7 May 1934.[26] Moreover, in December 1937, the Straits Settlements government decided to include cotton and rayon garments in the quota system, giving a further blow to Japan.

We shall now examine the effects of the quota system on British and Japanese textile imports, the importers of Japanese textile goods, and on Singapore's entrepôt trade. It was only in the early 1930s that the imports of Japanese cotton piece goods began to increase rapidly in British Malaya and other British Empire markets, and it is beyond doubt that the British quota system was designed specifically against Japanese competition. As a matter of fact, although the average Japanese shares in British Malaya's total imports of cotton and rayon piece goods were 30 per cent and 73.8 per cent during the period from 1927 to 1931, they were 62.6 per cent and 92.5 per cent during the period from 1932 to 1933 (Nomura 1941: 249–50).

As a result of the fall in imports of cheap Japanese cotton piece goods, local consumers bought larger quantities of Lancashire goods and low-priced Indian goods, both of which were free from the quota restriction. The imports of Japanese cotton piece goods declined sharply from 99,23,000 yd in 1934 to 53,759,000 in 1935, and 26,588,000 yd in 1938. On the other hand, the imports of Lancashire goods rose from 29,008,000 yd in 1934 to 33,364,000 in 1935 and 46,597,000 yd in 1938, and those from India from 920,000 yd in 1934 to 19,010,000 yd in 1937, and 2,0960,000 yd in 1938 (Table 3.10).

Unlike cotton piece goods, the import of Japanese rayon piece goods was not much affected by the quota system, for there was no major competitor in the market. The volume of the imports declined from 13,538,000 yd (91.8 per cent of British Malaya's total imports) in 1934 to 7,635,000 yd (90 per cent) in 1935 due to a sudden fall in British Malaya's total imports of rayon piece goods, but it then rose steeply to 15,103,000 yd (87.9 per cent) in 1937 (*Foreign Imports and Exports,* 1936 and 1938). However, thereafter it fell sharply due to the Chinese boycotts which took place after the outbreak of the Sino-Japanese War in July 1937.

What, then, were the effects of the quota system on the importers of Japanese cotton piece goods? After the institution of the quota system, merchants in the Straits Settlements had to obtain restricted import licences to import cotton piece goods from foreign countries, which had more than 2.5 per cent share in the import of the textiles during the period from 1927 to 1931: these countries were Japan, China, the Netherlands Indies, Italy and Holland. Merchants were permitted to import textiles in the quantities based on their actual imports from these countries during the period from 1 January 1933 to 7 May 1934 (Mills 1942: 151). As for the racial composition of those merchants who were granted the licences to import Japanese textiles, 20 per cent were Japanese, 35 per cent Indians, 40 per cent Chinese and 5 per cent were others (mainly European merchants) (*Nanyo*, vol. 25, no. 9, September 1939: 18–19).

Although the leading Japanese trading companies suffered from a decline in the import of Japanese cotton piece goods due to the introduction of the quota system, they could make up for the loss to a certain extent, thanks to a sharp rise in the prices caused by the shortage in the market. In fact, as no import duty was imposed on the textile imports in the Straits Settlements, it was said that the importers who obtained licences to import Japanese goods were able to reap huge profits. It should also be noted that small and medium-sized firms sold their import licences to the large trading companies at a high price, and devoted themselves to importing sundry goods and other Japanese goods (Nanyo oyobi Nihonjinsha 1938: 328). Incidentally, five major Japanese importers of cotton piece goods, namely Mitsui & Co., Mitsubishi Corporation, Katsura Shokai, Kato Yoko and Shimota Koshi, set up the Japanese Association of Textile Importers in Singapore in September 1934, with a view to protecting their mutual interests. Its office was kept at the Japanese commercial museum in High Street (DRO, E.3.1.1/4-10, 24 September 1934).

Was the re-export trade of Singapore greatly affected as a result of the institution of the quota system? With a view to protecting the entrepôt trade, the colonial authorities did not include in the quota system the textiles imported for re-export, and therefore set up bonded warehouses for re-export in Singapore and Penang. At first, many merchants expressed concern over the fact that such warehouses would not be well managed because of complicated procedures, high warehousing charges and other expenses. However, there was hardly any problem as far as the re-export of textiles for Malaya was concerned, especially since the re-export warehousing system, introduced in May 1934, turned out to function fairly well.

Lastly, it should be noted that, when the volume of Japanese textile imports was restricted by the quota system, smuggling became widespread among overseas Chinese merchants. Since the Straits Settlements was surrounded by the sea, it was impossible to keep a constant eye on smugglers. At any rate, as the methods of smuggling are described in detail by Mills, Koh and Tanaka, we do not need to dwell on them here (Mills 1942: 158–60; Koh and Tanaka 1984).

Chinese boycotts and their effects on Japan's trade

In the 1930s, Japan's trade expansion was interrupted not only by the change in the colonial power's commercial policy, but also by the large-scale Chinese boycotts. The Chinese boycott triggered by the Manchurian Incident lasted from September to December 1931. However, when it came to an end in British Malaya, there was a sharp increase in demand for inexpensive Japanese goods thanks to a steep fall in prices of the goods and also in the purchasing power of local consumers. As in the First World War, the number of Japanese trading companies, wholesalers and retailers rose greatly to take advantage of the great demand for Japanese goods (Nanyo oyobi Nihonjinsha 1938: 289). Even the existing Japanese retailers and the branches of the Japanese trading companies which had hitherto acted as brokers of rubber also joined the import trade, and began to supply Japanese goods to overseas Chinese, Indian and other traders not only in Singapore, but in the Malay Peninsula, southern part of Thailand, Sumatra and Borneo. At the same time, the Chinese and Indian merchants came to Singapore from the neighbouring countries to purchase Japanese goods from the Japanese merchants (*ibid.*: 289).

Japanese commercial trainees

Japan suffered from Chinese boycotts of Japanese goods in Southeast Asia from time to time. Although the number of Japanese firms and retail shops increased immensely after World War I, the overseas Chinese merchants continued to control the domestic distribution system in the region, and without their co-operation, Japanese goods could not be easily sold. As a measure to counter Chinese boycotts, the Japanese government introduced a commercial training scheme with the co-operation of the South Seas Association in 1931, and attempted to increase the number of Japanese retailers in Southeast Asia.

Commercial trainees were selected from Japanese youths of around 20 years old with secondary or professional school education (under the old education system), who were not the eldest sons and were sound in mind and body. In 1931, there were 200 applicants, of whom ten were accepted (DRO, I.1.10.0/2–4, 17 June 1931). The new recruits studied Malay and other relevant subjects at the head office of the South Seas Association in Tokyo. They were then sent to Japanese trading companies in Southeast Asia where they went through practical training for a period of five years. Those trainees who were considered to be excellent received an interest-free loan of ¥1,500 to ¥2,000 as an initial capital for setting up their own retail shops, and were also lent ¥500 worth of goods from the trading companies where they had been trained (*Ibid.*, 7 December 1936).

The South Seas Association sent ten trainees to Southeast Asia at public expenses every year from the first time in 1929 to the third time in 1931, and, from the fourth time onwards, it increased the number to dozens of them a year. The Japanese government provided the association with an annual subsidy of ¥20,000 for this purpose. Initially, the Foreign Ministry and the Colonial Ministry contributed ¥15,000 and ¥5,000 respectively, but from 1937 onwards, it was entirely financed by the former which also became solely responsible for supervision (*ibid.*, 17 June 1931).

The first and second batches of trainees were all sent to Java, but, beginning with the third one, trainees headed for other parts of Southeast Asia, including Singapore. The total number of young men sent to the region in the first eleven cohorts was 393. Of these, as of 1 March 1940, 44 owned retail shops, ten were dead, 64 had gone back to Japan, and 275 were still under apprenticeship. As for British Malaya, six trainees in Singapore and two in the Malay Peninsula set up their own retail stores successfully (Konno 1978: 172). The commercial training scheme produced some results, but it was far from controlling the distribution system dominated by the numerous overseas Chinese merchants.

Rise of Indian merchants

In the meantime, beside Japanese merchants, Indian and European merchants also expanded their shares of the import trade with Japan by taking advantage of the Chinese boycotts in the early 1930s. Prior to the Depression, some of the local Indian merchants had imported silk and rayon piece goods through Indian and other merchant houses in Japan.[27] When the Chinese merchants were engaged in the boycott of Japanese goods in the last quarter of 1931, their Indian and Arab counterparts seized the opportunity to re-export Japanese goods to Sumatra and Thailand, where overseas Chinese did not constitute a large part of the population. Consequently, the negative effect of the boycotts on Japanese imports diminished somewhat (PRO, Trade Commissioner to Comptroller, Despatch, 31 May 1932, CO 273/583).

By the mid-1930s, the number of Indian merchants engaged in the import of Japanese goods had risen to some 60 (Nanyo oyobi Nihonjinsha 1938: 327). The Indians kept shops mainly in North Bridge Road and Middle Road, and retailed the bulk of their imports at their own premises, even though they wholesaled some to Indian retailers in Arab Street (Shokosho Boekikyoku 1932: 58–9). Moreover, in the 1930s many of the Indian merchants in Singapore set up purchasing offices in Japan to import Japanese goods actively. For example, Maganlal Nagindas & Co. had established a branch in Japan by 1933, and begun to import large quantities of textile goods through it. The Singapore branch of B.H.T. Doulatram & Co. in Penang imported silk piece goods, cotton textiles, curios, paper screens and other items through its Kobe office in the 1920s (Shingaporu Shohin Chinretsukan 1927: 468; Kobe Shoko Kaigisho 1929: 40, 49). Although there is no further information about its commercial activities, it is likely that the branch continued this trade in the 1930s.

The Indian merchants had a large share particularly in the import of silk and rayon textiles. Although Mitsui & Co., the Shimota Koshi, other Japanese trading companies and overseas Chinese merchants of High Street and Circular Road were also engaged in this trade, they lagged far behind them (Shokosho Boekikyoku 1932: 33, 59). Indeed, in 1930 the Straits Settlements imported ¥3,685,743 worth of rayon textiles from Japan, of which Mitsui & Co. was responsible for a mere 1.1 per cent of the total (Mitsui Bunko, Bussan 394/1–7, July 1931).

European merchant houses and the Japanese trade

As noted earlier, some European merchants were already in competition with Mitsui & Co. in the import of Japanese coal to Singapore in the late nineteenth century (*Tsusho Isan*, 15 September 1897: 9). Thereafter, they began to import various kinds of goods directly from Japan as the industrialisation of the country progressed. In the 1920s, for example, Guthrie & Co. imported cement, the Straits Trading Company imported fir and veneer boxes, cups for receiving rubber latex and other goods used in rubber estates, and the United Engineer Company and the Borneo Company imported industrial chemicals, including alum and sulphuric acid (Shingaporu Shohin Chinretsukan 1927: 465, 475, 478). What is noteworthy is the fact that a British company in Kobe, the Dunlop Rubber Co. Ltd, set up a business office in Robinson Road, and sold tyres, tubes, belts and other rubber products in Singapore and the neighbouring countries through it (*ibid*. 1927: 450; Kobe Shoko Kaigisho 1929: 43). Nevertheless, in the 1920s the value of imports from Japan by the European merchant houses in Singapore was fairly small as compared to that by Asian merchants (notably Chinese and Japanese). At that time, most of the European merchants were, at any rate, satisfied with the trade with the West, and did not feel a strong need to import Japanese goods.

However, as the boycott stemming from the Manchurian Incident came to an end, there was a large increase in demand for cheap Japanese goods, and even those European merchants who had hitherto handled no Japanese goods began to import goods from Japan. In the second half of 1934, the number of European merchant houses importing Japanese goods rose greatly to reach about 30. It was said that some 80 per cent of the European merchant houses in Singapore handled Japanese goods in some ways (*Nanyo Kyokai Zasshi*, vol. 21, no. 5, May 1935: 62–63; Nanyo oyobi Nihonjinsha 1938: 327).

Such leading European merchant houses as Guthrie & Co. and Boustead Co. bought wire, nails, galvanised iron sheets and other goods in bulk at low costs from wholesale merchants or manufacturers in Japan, imported them to Singapore, and wholesaled them to retailers in the British colony or elsewhere in Southeast Asia (Nanyo oyobi Nihonjinsha 1938: 292). Other large European merchant houses also imported various Japanese goods. For example, William Jacks & Co. handled ceramics, enamel ware, and woollen textiles, Borneo Sumatra Trading Co. alum, East Asiatic & Co. tyres for motor vehicles, Paterson, Simons & Co. woollen textiles and nails and Singapore Cold Storage Co. tinned salmon (*Nanyo Kyokai Zasshi*, vol. 21, no. 5, May 1935: 62–63). It is obvious that most of the European merchant houses began to import goods from Japan, largely because they saw a sharp decline in demand for European goods, and had no choice but to handle them; as the old saying goes, 'if you can't beat them, join them'.

Chinese boycotts and overseas Chinese merchants

As already noted, in the 1930s an increasing number of Japanese trading companies and individual merchants joined British Malaya's trade with Japan, and they strengthened their commercial relations with local overseas Chinese wholesalers and retailers. The Indian and European merchants also began to actively import goods from Japan. What were the effects of this new development on the commercial networks involving the overseas Chinese merchants at Kobe and Singapore? When the Manchurian Incident took place in 1931, many overseas Chinese merchants at Kobe returned to China, but, shortly after it, most of them came back to Kobe to resume their commercial activities. As Table 3.11 shows, 15 overseas Chinese merchants at Kobe had trading relations with Singapore in 1935, but, apart from Kwen Yick Co., Sen Cheong & Co. and Sam Sing & Co., they all traded with other parts of Southeast Asia as well. As Japanese trading companies and individual exporters joined the trade, the share of Kobe's overseas Chinese merchants in the export trade with Southeast Asia continued to decline. But they nevertheless exported to the Straits Settlements 191 metric tons out of a total of 1,826 metric tons of Japan's total ceramics exports in 1936 (Shokosho Boekikyoku 1938:174), while, as already mentioned, they virtually monopolised the export of marine products even at the end of the 1930s.

At this juncture, we shall examine the effects on the Chinese and Japanese merchants in Singapore of the Chinese boycotts which began to take place in British Malaya and other parts of Southeast Asia after the outbreak of the Sino-Japanese War in July 1937. They inflicted losses not only on Japanese trade with the Southeast Asian region but also on Chinese importers of Japanese goods. In Singapore, the Chinese importers had great difficulties in selling Japanese goods to Chinese retailers, while they had to pay high charges to warehousing companies for the large stocks of unsold Japanese goods. Moreover, they could not easily collect the debts from their Chinese clients (*Naigai Shoko Jiho*, vol. 26, no. 5, May 1939: 43). In these circumstances, several Chinese commercial houses, including Tai Lee & Co., Sam

Table 3.12 Kobe's Chinese merchant houses trading with Singapore (as of 1935)

Firm	Trading items
Sam Sing & Co.	Cotton piece goods, silk/rayon textiles, marine products, sundry goods
Chiwan Tai & Co.	Marine products, foodstuffs, tinned foods, onions, sundry goods
Yue Fat & Co.	Cotton piece goods, silk textiles, marine products, sundry goods
Lee Wah & Co.	Cotton piece goods, marine products, sundry goods
Tung Nam & Co.	Silk/rayon/woollen textiles, marine products, metal goods, sundry goods
Sin Sui Hing	Cotton piece goods/yarn, silk/rayon textiles, marine products, sundry goods
Lai Hing & Co.	Cotton piece goods, rayon textiles, ceramics, marine products, etc.
Seng Wo & Co.	Cotton textiles, towels, toys, matches, sundry goods
Men Lee & Co.	Cotton piece goods/yarn, sundry goods
Kwen Yick Co.	Cotton piece goods, sundry goods, rubber shoes, aluminium ware, etc.
Jing Kee & Co.	Cotton piece goods, sundry goods, marine products, etc.
Sui Fong & Co.	Ceramics, glassware, matches, etc.
Sen Cheong & Co.	Cotton piece goods, sundry goods
Hing Loong & Co.	Canvas shoes
Kwong Yu Seng	Ceramics, glassware, cotton hosiery, toys, etc.

Source: Constructed with some modifications from Kobe Shoko Kaigisho, 1936: 16–18.

Yeo & Co. and Hiap Fung & Co., were closed down in September and October 1937 (Kikakuin 1939: 267–8). Finally, Him Woo & Co. of High Street, the largest Chinese importer of Japanese goods, went bankrupt (Nanyo oyobi Nihonjinsha 1938: 304).

It goes without saying that the Japanese foreign traders and retailers in Singapore also suffered a blow from the Chinese boycotts. Chinese landlords raised the rents for houses occupied by Japanese residents, or demanded that the Japanese retailers should vacate premises where they had been in business for many years (PRO, Governor, Singapore to Gore, Despatch, 6 October 1937, CO 273/634). With the growing financial difficulties, the Japanese merchants asked the Singapore branch of the Taiwan Bank to give them loans against the deposit of their stocks of goods, but the branch turned it down, apparently on the grounds of the high risks involved (*ibid.*).

As the Japanese merchants could no longer depend on the overseas Chinese for distribution, they attempted to persuade the members of the Indian Chamber of Commerce to handle larger quantities of Japanese goods, and actually invited its president to Japan (Robertson 1986: 33). Partly thanks to these measures, the Indian retailers and wholesalers in Arab Street increased the handling of Japanese goods to a certain extent (*Naigai Shoko Jiho*, vol. 26, no. 5, May 1939: 43). However, although there were 4,257

Indians in commerce in the Straits Settlements, they were too few to replace their Chinese rivals. At any rate, the majority of the consumers were overseas Chinese (Kikakuin 1939: 268–9).

The Sino-Japanese War also had adverse effects on the overseas Chinese merchants at Kobe. In 1935 there were 54 Chinese merchant houses engaged in foreign trade (Kobe Shoko Kaigisho 1936: 16–18). As Table 3.11 shows, 15 of them traded with Singapore, handling mainly marine products, textiles and sundry goods. However, after the outbreak of the war, the number of Chinese merchant houses began to decline rapidly (Kikakuin 1939: 352–3). Their commercial activities were made even more difficult when the Japanese government started exercising strict control over the country's foreign trade (Koyama 1979: 60). Under these circumstances, the president of the Overseas Chinese Exporters' Association of Kobe[28] wrote to the Japanese Foreign Minister Arita Hachiro, saying:

> The overseas Chinese [in Japan] recognise the fair attitude of the Japanese government, and wish to support the formation of a new East Asia in the wake of the China Incident of 1937. As the boycotting of Japanese goods is carried out feverishly by the anti-Japanese elements in Southeast Asia, the export trade of the Kobe Chinese merchants has been seriously affected. Their commercial houses have been closed down one after another due to financial difficulties. In Kobe, there were about 5,000 overseas Chinese, most of whom are dependent either directly or indirectly on the export trade. The association has sent 13,000 letters to overseas Chinese in Southeast Asia, urging them to stop harmful and unprofitable boycotts and to co-operate [with Japan] for the object of building a new East Asia.
>
> (DRO, F.1.6.0/7, 18 May 1939)

His letter did not seem to do much to lessen the plight of the overseas Chinese merchants at Kobe, for the Sino-Japanese War continued to deteriorate. After the outbreak of the Pacific War in December 1941, the Japanese government further tightened its control over foreign trade. As the overseas Chinese merchants were virtually excluded from it, most of them had no choice but to return to China (Koyama 1979: 59).

CONCLUDING REMARKS

Prior to World War I, the Western countries virtually monopolised the British Malayan market for industrial goods. The European merchant houses in the Straits Settlements were largely responsible for the import trade, while the internal distribution system was controlled by Asian merchants, notably overseas Chinese wholesalers and retailers. However, as A.G. Frank and I. Wallerstein argue, developing countries were in a position to foster nascent industries during World War I and the Depression years of the 1930s when their economic relations with the West became much weakened (Frank 1969: 62–3, 102–3 and *passim*; Wallerstein 1979: Chapter 4). Indeed, this was the case for British Malaya, to a certain extent, as its new-born industries such as rubber shoes and tyres for rickshaws were fostered during these periods.[29] However, what was far more important was the fact that Japan, which had achieved industrial revolution in the late nineteenth century and emerged as a newly industrialised nation, began to supply large quantities of cotton textiles and other industrial goods, and captured a large share of the market at the expense of the Western suppliers, notably Britain.

As for Japan's trade relations with British Malaya, the overseas Chinese merchants in Japan started cultivating the British Malayan market for Japanese goods in the last quarter of the nineteenth century, when large numbers of young Japanese women began to travel to Singapore to work as prostitutes. Making use of the overseas Chinese commercial networks, they pioneered the export of traditional Japanese goods such as ceramics, lacquer ware and marine products, and industrial goods such as cotton piece goods, and played an important role particularly in the development of Japan's trade with British Malaya in the pre-World War I period. During World War I and the inter-war period, large numbers of Japanese trading companies and individual merchants followed in the footsteps of the overseas Chinese merchants, and increased their share in the Japanese export trade at the expense of the pioneers. But the overseas Chinese could nevertheless continue to play an important role as commission merchants until the end of the 1930s. They based themselves at Kobe, and managed to continue their trading activities for many years, for they were able not only to respond appropriately to the changes in the industrial structure of Japan, but to find a niche in Japan's trade with British Malaya and other parts of Southeast Asia.

Beside the overseas Chinese and Japanese merchants, in the 1930s many Indian and European merchants also actively joined the Japan–British Malayan trade, and they took advantage of the Chinese boycotts to increase their shares in the import of Japanese goods. Even those European merchant houses, which had previously imported only European goods, showing hardly any interest in Japanese goods, began to import goods direct from Japan, when there was a growing demand for cheap Japanese goods.

In this way, Japan successfully penetrated into the British Malayan market for industrial goods, the market which had been virtually monopolised by the Western countries, and this could also mean that there was a large crack in the 'symbiotic relationship' between the European merchants and overseas Chinese merchants in the West–British Malaya trade. Moreover, Japan's entry into the British Malayan market not only provided local Asian merchants with the possibility of reaping large profits by trading directly with Japan, but brought about an opportunity to move away from their heavy dependence upon the Western countries for the first time in modern Asian history. One could argue that this experience became invaluable and useful to local Asians in the post-war period when they achieved independence from Britain.

Finally, it would be wrong to assume simply that there was always a clash of interests between Japan and the colonial power. Prior to the Depression, some British merchant houses in Singapore were on good terms with Japan, importing Japanese goods and serving as agencies for Japanese shipping companies. Also, in the Depression years of the 1930s, large quantities of cheap textiles, tinned sardines, dry and salted fish and other goods were imported from Japan. These imports enabled the Asian workers to cut down the cost of living greatly, and British-owned rubber estates and tin-mining companies could, in turn, keep the wages of their workers low. Wooden boxes for rubber and rubber latex-receiving cups imported from Japan were also widely used in rubber estates in the Malay Peninsula, and contributed to the development of the rubber-growing industry, albeit indirectly.

However, when Lancashire's cotton textile industry, the leading export industry in Britain, lost competitiveness on the world market, the colonial power attempted to eliminate Japanese competition by 'imperialistic' means in British Malaya and other parts of the British Empire markets, disregarding the interests of local inhabitants.

4

THE RISE AND FALL OF THE
JAPANESE FISHERIES BASED
IN SINGAPORE

In the pre-war period Japanese fishermen occupied a very important position in the fishing industry in Singapore where fish constituted a major source of protein for the Chinese, Malays and Indians.[1] As Table 4.1 shows, large numbers of local Chinese and Malay fishermen were engaged in fishing; but, since their catch was not significant, the British colony had been heavily dependent upon imports of seafood before the Japanese fishermen began to supply large quantities of fresh fish in the second half of the 1920s. In 1924, for example, the fresh fish landed in Singapore amounted to 6,400 tons, of which 17 per cent came from the local waters (including the catch by the Japanese), 6 per cent from Johore, and 73 per cent from the Netherlands Indies' various islands (Firth 1966: 11). In 1937 it amounted to 13,000 tons, of which the local fishermen were responsible for 17 per cent, the Japanese 41 per cent, and the remaining 42 per cent brought largely from the Netherlands Indies (*Malayan Year Book*, 1937: 92; *Blue Book* 1938: 761).

It should be noted that, as Table 4.1 shows, the number of Japanese fishermen rose greatly, from 200 in 1920 to 688 in 1929 and 903 in 1933, finally reaching a peak of 1,752 in 1936. Moreover, in the 1930s the fishermen accounted for a quarter to one-third of the total Japanese population in Singapore. As of 1 October 1934, for example, there were 3,287 Japanese residents, of whom 971 were directly engaged in the fishing industry, and 189 were their dependents (DRO, K.3.7.0/5, 27 November 1934).[2] Together, they accounted for over 35 per cent of the population.

In what follows we shall study the factors behind the rise and fall of the Japanese fisheries based in Singapore before the Pacific War, examine the activities of the Japanese and local fishermen during the Japanese occupation period, and evaluate the economic contributions made by the Japanese fisheries to Singapore and Japan.

94

Table 4.1 Number of fishermen by race in Singapore

Year	Japanese (A)	Chinese	Malay	Other	Total (B)	A÷B (%)
1920	200	2,100	450	0	2,750	7.3
1923	180	2,100	950	0	3,230	5.6
1927	490	1,840	1,543	0	3,873	12.7
1929	688	2,027	1,088	1[a]	3,804	18.1
1930	718	2,122	1,018	0	3,858	18.6
1931	950	2,189	1,036	0	4,175	22.8
1932	907	2,096	1,048	0	4,051	22.4
1933	903	2,091	1,236	0	4,230	21.3
1934	1,050	1,635	1,532	0	4,217	24.9
1935	1,063	1,800	1,265	0	4,128	25.8
1936	1,752	1,773	1,230	0	4,755	36.8
1937	1,478	1,757	1,180	0	4,415	33.5
1938	1,083	1,797	1,215	4[b]	4,099	26.4

Sources: Constructed from *Blue Book*, various issues.

Notes

[a] One Indian.

[b] Two Indians and two Portuguese descendants.

RISE AND GROWTH OF JAPANESE FISHERIES

Local fishermen and Japanese fishermen

The local fishermen used various fishing methods including *kelong* (fish trap) fishing, drift netting and line-fishing, but were not productive compared to the Japanese fishermen. In the early 1930s, the Malay or the Chinese drift netter caught on average 4 to 8 *katis* of fish a day, whereas his Japanese counterpart caught 150 *katis* (Birtwistle 1933: 7–8). The reasons for the former's low productivity are not hard to find. He used:

> either a sampan or *Koleh* from 18 to 25 feet long, a drift net from 60 to 220 fathom long and either sails or rows from home early in the evening for his fishing grounds which may be from two to six miles away. . . . Generally speaking he has no choice of fishing grounds: he simply depends on luck as to which fish came his way . . .[3]
>
> (*ibid.*: 7)

In sharp contrast with the local fishermen, the Japanese fishermen employed large power boats as well as modern fishing gear, and engaged in large-scale fishing. They used drift nets, *muro ami* (bream net),[4] handlining, shell-fishing and other methods. Drift netting, used to catch Spanish mackerel, shad, pomfret and dorab, was initially conducted by fishermen from Kagawa prefecture in Japan and was the most important technique until about the mid-1920s.[5] The Japanese drift netter 'uses a boat 38 feet long and a net from 486 to 500 fathom long. He goes in search of good fishing grounds and he has a good many to choose from. His farthest ground may be 300 miles away' (Birtwistle 1933: 8).

The *muro ami* fishing was conducted almost exclusively by Okinawan fishermen. A *muro ami* fleet normally consisted of two powered parent ships and four non-powered fishing boats each of which accommodated about ten fishermen. One of the parent ships tugged the boats to the coral-reefed fishing ground where naked divers drove a shoal of fish, mainly caesio (*delah* in Malay), into a large net bag, and then closed and hauled it in. Since the fishermen did not draw a large fishing net over the sea bottom, the *muro ami* system did not cause major damage to their nets or coral. The length of the fishermen's stay on each fishing ground ranged from a few hours to two days, depending on the quantity of fish available (*ibid.*: 6). The fishermen could continue fishing for about six months, because the two parent ships in turn plied between the fishing ground and Singapore, bringing ice, stores and provisions, and taking away the iced fish.[6] As the fish caught by Japanese drift nets and *muro ami* were immediately iced in the charcoal-insulated fish-hold of the parent ship, they were still fresh when they were landed in Singapore (Takumusho: 1931: 89–90; Green 1927: 11).

The formation of Japanese fishing companies

The Japanese fisheries based in Singapore did not suddenly develop. In the late nineteenth century, many Japanese were already attempting to fish in the region, but without success. During the period from 1892 to 1895, 70 Japanese fishermen are known to have travelled to Singapore. Of these, ten were from Chiba prefecture, and they fished in the waters of Singapore in 1895. However, after about three months they had to quit when most of them became ill owing to the heavy work of fishing at night and the tropical climate to which they were not accustomed (Hara 1987: 144–5). In the years before World War I, large numbers of divers from Wakayama prefecture went to Broome, Australia, for pearl fishing. They travelled to Singapore where they signed employment contracts with Guthrie & Co., McAlister, Katz Bros and other European merchant houses acting as agencies for Australia-based pearling companies. However, some of them changed their minds and stayed in Singapore to engage in fishing (Takayama 1914: 306).

It was only in 1912 that a Japanese line-fisherman, Sakamoto Sojiro, achieved success. In the following year the Japanese Ministry of Agriculture and Commerce, which had taken an interest in Southeast Asian fisheries for the past few years, sent a fisheries expert, Takayama Itaro, to Singapore to investigate the viability of Japanese fisheries and the conditions of local fish markets. As Takayama found that fishing licences were easily obtained, and that there was a large demand for fresh fish with efficient and well-organised fish markets, he recommended to the ministry labour-intensive and small-scale fisheries based in Singapore (PRO, Colonial Office to Foreign Office, 18 September 1924, FO371/10299; Kataoka 1991: 49–50).

The ministry commissioned two fishermen, Yoshino Nobuyoshi and Someya Hamashichi, to carry out experimental fishing in the waters of Singapore, Riau and the Straits of Malacca for two years from June 1914, employing five fishing boats and 20 fishermen. The undertaking was supervised by two pelagic fishery trainees from the Fisheries Training College (Suisan Koshujo) in Tokyo, Eifuku Tora and Ishii Teiji. This experimental fishing showed that drift-net and line-fishing were most suitable for Japanese fishermen (Aichiken Suisan Shikenjo 1932: 32). It should be noted that at that time no mention was made of the *muro ami* system which was to become the driving force in the rapid growth of Japanese fisheries from the second half of the 1920s onwards.

In 1917, Nakamura Itaro and Ishizu Tojiro, both from Kyushu, embarked on line-fishing and drift netting, operating from Singapore, and employing 15 Japanese fishermen. In the following year, Nakamura used the *muro ami* method for the first time, and in June 1920 he set up the Nanmei Fishing Company with other Japanese when Ishizu quit. As for Ishizu, he founded the Ishizu Fishing Company in January 1921, and engaged in *muro ami* and drift-net fishing, employing ten Okinawan fishermen at first in the waters around Sumatra, but later around Singapore (*ibid.*).

In the meantime, Eifuku Tora decided to stay on in Singapore after the fishing experiment. In 1917, he set up the Taisei Fishing Company with loans from his relatives and acquaintances as well as from a local Indian Chettiar. He embarked on drift-net fishing, employing fishermen from Kagawa prefecture. In 1920, the company was reorganised as a joint stock company with authorized capital of ¥1 million, and paid-up capital of ¥250,000 (Kee 1966: 85; Kataoka 1991: 53, 58, 86).

From 1919 to 1923 the Japanese Ministry of Agriculture and Commerce provided the Taisei Fishing Company with an annual subvention of ¥10,000 under the pretext of meeting the expenses for research on fisheries. The real motive behind the financial assistance was to make sure that the company would be a success, for its failure would have a devastating impact on Japanese fisheries in Southeast Asia. However, the company continued to make losses due to the fall in fish prices and fishing output in the post-World War I period, and was obliged to scale down its operations. In the end, it was taken over by the Mihashi Fishing Company (Kataoka 1991: 58).

Eifuku resigned from the Taisei Fishing Company in 1922, as he did not see much prospect for the company. He then took over the Nanmei Fishing Company in financial difficulty, and renamed it the Taichong Kongsi. He adopted *muro ami* fishing, in addition to drift-net fishing, employing many

Table 4.2 Value of catch by Japanese companies (in dollars)[a]

Year	Taichong	Ishizu	Oshiro	Shinzato	Kinjo	Other	Total
1928	234,214	256,835	77,566	16,757	[b]	192,847	778,219
1929	435,902	290,121	18,730	41,103	[b]	151,511	937,367
1931	357,154	231,280	47,673	39,256	46,202	12,771	734,336
1932	333,015	196,836	12,245	56,393	30,196	30,341	659,026
1933	376,483	96,745	21,993	49,221	42,390	18,615	605,447
1934	465,922	116,571	40,255	58,764	68,492	16,151	766,155
1935	647,593	29,231	81,498	89,511	94,087	10,600	952,520

Sources: Suisankai, no. 589, October 1931: 24–5; Takumusho, 1938: 85.
Notes
[a] Value of catches is given after deduction of 5% municipal tax and 5% commission.
[b] Included in others.

Okinawan fishermen. The company prospered and began to operate from Batavia and Penang, while also embarking upon purchases of fresh fish and shrimps from Chinese and Malay fishermen at sea. Moreover, it engaged in shell-fishing in the waters off the Andaman and Nicobar Islands (Kataoka 1991: 58). In May 1929, Eifuku expanded the company by absorbing the Mihashi Fishing Company, which had just gone bankrupt largely because of the adverse effects of the Chinese boycott of the previous year (*Suisan Iho*, no. 3, March 1931: 50).

In the second half of the 1920s the Taichong Kongsi and the Ishizu Fishing Company emerged as the leading Japanese fishing companies based in Singapore. As Table 4.2 shows, the catch by all the Japanese companies amounted to $778,219 in 1928, and these two companies were responsible for $491,049 (63.1 per cent) of the total. Both firms owed their rapid growth to *muro ami* fishing which they adopted by employing large numbers of Okinawan fishermen. Indeed, by the mid-1920s the *muro ami* system had taken the place of drift netting as the most important fishing method. In 1929 there were 600 *muro ami* fishermen, accounting for some 75 per cent of the Japanese fishing population, and this method accounted for some 90 per cent of the total catch (Aichiken Suisan Shikenjo 1932: 36–7; *Suisan Iho*, no. 5, November 1932: 188).

Okinawans and the growth of local Japanese fisheries

Muro ami fishing and Itoman fishermen

Between 1912 and 1938 a total of 2,751 Okinawans obtained passports for Singapore. In 1912 the first batch of 25 travelled to the British colony, but there was then a seven-year hiatus. It was actually in the mid-1920s that the number of Okinawans began to increase rapidly in the British colony owing largely to the growing importance of *muro ami* fishing, and Okinawans came to account for the majority of Japanese fishermen there (Azato 1941: Appendix). As Table 4.3 shows, the number of Okinawan males in Singapore rose steeply from 292 in 1926 to 774 in 1930 and 1,035 in 1937.

A majority of the Okinawan fishermen, 571 out of the 1,070 Japanese fishermen in Singapore in 1935, came from the town of Itoman (Okinawaken Kyoiku Iinkai 1974: 26–9, Appendix Table 15). Itoman had become the leading fishing town in Okinawa, not only because it was surrounded by excellent fishing grounds, but also because it was close to Naha, which provided a huge market for fresh fish (Hiroyoshi 1987: 140). It was actually in Itoman where the *muro ami* method was born, and, as Table 4.4 shows, a large majority of Itoman people overseas were found in Singapore and other parts of Southeast Asia where *muro ami* fishing was actively conducted.

Non-Itoman fishermen also used *muro ami* methods when fishing in the waters of Japan and Southeast Asia. The reason is not hard to find. In Itoman, each fisherman kept a number of *yatoigo* (apprentices), and formed *muro ami* fishing teams together with other fishermen who also brought their *yatoigo*. As *muro ami* fishing required a high level of diving skills and

Table 4.3 Number of Okinawans in Singapore and amount of remittances to Japan

Year	Male	Female	Total (A)	Remittance (in yen) (B)	Remittance per head (in yen) (B ÷ A)
1926	292	15	307	36,686	119.50
1927	501	34	535	80,528	150.52
1928	577	33	610	71,873	117.82
1929	587	28	615	56,761	92.29
1930	774	55	829	44,851	54.10
1931	755	83	838	54,498	65.03
1932	566	37	603	22,924	38.02
1933	802	86	888	90,157	101.53
1934	904	82	986	92,434	93.75
1935	972	98	1,070	93,822	87.68
1937	1,035	217	1,252	101,893	81.38

Sources: Constructed from DRO, J1.2.0/J8–2, 1927–38.
Note: Relevant figures for 1936 are not available.

Table 4.4 Number of Itomans overseas by region (as of 1935)

Singapore	Philippines	Borneo	Celebes	Batavia	Sumatra	Other	Total
571	414	53	69	16	26	300	1,449

Source: Okinawaken Kyoiku Iinkai 1974: 26–9.

teamwork, boys aged around 10 were recruited locally, to undergo rigorous training in diving techniques, and at the same time to do heavy work such as collecting seaweed and shell-fish. While they became skilled divers, they were employed in *muro ami* fishing, but most of their earnings went to their respective masters. The apprenticeship lasted for about ten years (Ueda Fujio 1987: 67–9, 145). Because the fishing method became very popular, the demand for boys exceeded the supply, and the Itoman fishermen began recruiting boys from other parts of Okinawa. In the inter-war period, such impoverished Okinawan islands as Izena Jima and Iheya Jima as well as Motobu-cho in Kunigami district of mainland Okinawa constituted the main sources of supply (Masuda 1987: 28). Poor parents sent their sons to the Itoman fishermen for apprenticeship, and received advance payment of ¥50 to ¥100 per head (Hiroyoshi 1987: 145). However, as soon as the apprenticeship was over, many of the boys returned to their hometowns and began to conduct *muro ami* fishing in the Okinawan waters, or elsewhere. In this way, the *muro ami* method was adopted by non-Itoman fishermen (Masuda 1987: 28–9).

Muro ami fishing was highly productive but required extensive fishing grounds as it had to change location each time it was used. By about 1920 the fishing resources around Okinawa had become depleted, and many fishermen had to migrate to other parts of Japan and to Southeast Asia.

The process of migration was accelerated by economic recession in Okinawa. Prior to World War II, the Okinawan economy was heavily dependent on agriculture, notably cultivation of sweet potatoes for human consumption and sugar cane as a cash crop. Although sugar prices shot up during World War I, they plummeted after the mid-1920s, due to severe competition from imported sugar from Taiwan and elsewhere. As a consequence, the prefecture experienced the period of a chronic economic slump, and large numbers of Okinawans migrated to other parts of Japan and to foreign countries in search of employment (Okinawaken Kyoiku Iinkai 1972: 173–88).

Those who went to various parts of mainland Japan were unable to conduct fishing at will, as local authorities imposed strict control over the activities of Okinawan fishermen, who were highly productive. In certain regions, Itoman fishermen had to pay exorbitant licence fees, or were obliged to work in partnership with local fish wholesalers or other influential figures in return for the use of the licences granted to these local partners (Ueda Fujio 1987: 70–2). For example, they had to give to the local authorities as licence fees 15 to 20 per cent of the catch in Iyo, Ehime prefecture, and 40 per cent of the catch in Ojika Jima (Goto Retto), Nagasaki prefecture (Hiroyoshi 1987: 143–4). To make matters worse for Okinwan fishermen, the costs of fishing boats rose to the point that most fishermen simply could not afford them. At the end of the Meiji era (1868–1912), for example, a fishing boat made of cedar cost as much as ¥150 to ¥200 (Ide 1987: 47–8).

For several reasons, it was easy for Okinawan fishermen to fish in the waters of Southeast Asia. First, like Okinawa, Southeast Asia had a tropical climate, and was full of coral-reefed fishing grounds. Second, they could fish without restrictions, provided that they did not intrude into territorial waters and paid fees for registration of boats and certain fishing gear, fees which were imposed on all fishermen irrespective of nationality. In the 1930s, the annual registration fee was 50 cents per boat, and the licensing fee for a drift net was $2 (Taiwan Sotokufu Gaijibu 1942: 943). Finally, Okinawan fishermen could easily find employment with the Japanese fishing companies, which provided them with fishing gear and other equipment. Such fishing companies also recruited fishermen directly in Okinawa, and gave them advances to cover travel and other expenses. This made it fairly easy even for impoverished fishermen to migrate to Singapore. In July 1937, for example, Eifuku Tora, the owner of the Taichong Kongsi, had Higa Kawajiro and Yonashiro Zen'ei come to Singapore from Kunigami village in mainland Okinawa (Kunigami Mura 1992b: 31–2). As a consequence, a *muro ami* group in Singapore often consisted of fishermen who came from different parts of Okinawa and spoke varied dialects.[7] Nevertheless, once the fishing company chose a leader, this man was responsible for co-ordinating the entire *muro ami* operation (Kataoka 1991: 67).

Remittances by Japanese fishermen and fatal accidents

Pastimes and earnings of Japanese fishermen

Prior to World War I, Japanese fishermen/divers in certain parts of Southeast Asia were known for spending their earnings lavishly on gambling, drinking and women. As already noted in Chapter 2, some 500 Japanese divers were employed by the Celebes Trading Company for pearl-fishing in the sea between Aru island and the south-west coast of New Guinea. During the pearling season which ended in late May, they made large amounts of money. However, during the off-season from late May to late August, they normally squandered the bulk of their earnings on prostitutes, alcohol and gambling in Dobo, and remitted little, if anything, to their families in Japan. Similarly, there were large numbers of Japanese divers and fishermen based in Australia's Thursday Island. As of February 1906, this community numbered 713 Japanese, including 230 seamen, 140 pearling divers, 125 assistant pearling divers working on boats, ten trepang fishermen, seven ordinary fishermen, and 30 *karayuki-san* (*Tsusho Isan*, 23 July 1906: 35–7). It is likely that most of the divers, fishermen and other Japanese men spent their earnings lavishly as the divers in Dobo did.

In contrast with the divers/fishermen at Dobo or on Thursday Island, the Okinawan fishermen, based in Singapore spent most of their time at sea, and had little opportunity to squander their earnings on land. Nevertheless, they seem to have made use of valuable time to enjoy their life in Singapore. Kinjo Yasuichi of Kunigami village in mainland Okinawa, who worked as a fisherman for Eifuku Tora in the 1930s and during the occupation period, recalls that:

> [In pre-war Singapore], many Okinawans resided in a district which resembled Itoman town. When groups of *muro ami* fishermen returned [to Singapore] from fishing, the streets were flooded with Okinawans. I felt as if I had been in Itoman, for the fishermen enjoyed gambling, while there were sounds of *shamisen*.
>
> (Kunigami Mura 1992a: 506)

As seen in Chapter 2, there were large numbers of *karayuki-san* in the British colony in the late nineteenth and the early twentieth centuries, but licensed Japanese prostitution was abolished by the Acting Japanese Consulate-General, Yamazaki Heikichi, in 1920. Some *karayuki-san* stayed on in Singapore, plying their trade illegally, but they had grown rather old by the mid-1920s when Japanese fishermen began to arrive there in large numbers. Moreover, since it was not until the early 1930s that licensed prostitution was formally abolished by the colonial authorities in British Malaya, the fishermen could also have gone to non-Japanese brothels.

At any rate, the Japanese fishermen, based in Singapore, did save a great deal of money, and remitted it to their families in Japan. As Table 4.3 shows, remittances by the Okinawans (mainly fishermen) amounted to ¥36,686 in 1926, ¥56,761 in 1929, ¥22,924 in 1932, and ¥101,893 in 1937. The average remittances per head in these years were ¥119.50, ¥92.29, ¥38.02 and ¥81.38 respectively. Besides those in Singapore, there were many Okinawans in the Philippines, Borneo, the Netherlands Indies, and elsewhere in Southeast Asia, who also remitted a large part of their earnings to Okinawa. In 1927, for example, remittances by the Okinawans in Southeast Asia, many of whom were fishermen, amounted to ¥387,520.90 (DRO, J1.2.0/J8-2, 12 June 1928), and this money must have been a great help in alleviating the effects of the chronic economic recession in Okinawa.

Deaths of Japanese fishermen abroad

Fishermen had a difficult existence, and many lost their lives while working. As Table 4.5 shows, at least 16 Japanese fishermen based in Singapore died of fatal accidents between 1920 and 1937. They were mainly in their twenties, as divers were young men. Although we have not been able to obtain any information about the birth places of the deceased, judging from their names most of them seem to have been Okinawans.

Since Japanese fishermen did not go through medical check-ups before going fishing, some could have been in poor health, or suffering from chronic

Table 4.5 Accidental deaths of Japanese fishermen based in Singapore, 1920–37

Name	Age	Place of accident	Cause of death	Date of death
W. Okada	35	Siglap	Murdered	Dec. 1920
K. Kaneshiro	26	Sea off Trengganu	Drowned while fishing	Apr. 1928
K. Oshiro[a]	40	Geylang Rd	Traffic accident	Jun. 1928
K. Shinzato[b]	36	Open sea	Accident while repairing a motor boat	Sep. 1929
A. Tsuikawa	33	Open sea	Attacked by shark	Apr. 1930
Fujiwara	60	Telok Blangah Rd	Fatally wounded by a Chinese	Aug. 1930
G. Tamashiro	20	Sea off Pahang	Drowned while fishing	July 1932
S. Sakehama	27	Pulau Dumia	Fatal accident	July 1932
K. Masukado	20	Off South Brothers Islands	Suicide on boat	Jan. 1933
J. Shimabukuro	29	Sea off Siam	Drowned while fishing	May 1933
K. Oshiro	19	Sea off Siam	Drowned while fishing	May 1933
S. Gabe	26	Not known	Fatal accident	Dec. 1933
S. Nakama	22	China Sea	Attacked by shark	May 1935
A. Ikehara	23	Tokong Kembang	Attacked by shark	Sep. 1935
C. Urasaki	22	Pulau Tioman	Drowned while fishing	July 1937
S. Tamashiro	24	Rhio Straits	Drowned while fishing	Sep. 1937

Sources: Constructed from Singapore Subordinate Courts, AD-006 to AD-060, 1904–39.
Notes
[a] Technician.
[b] Engineer.

illness. For example, Uragaki Chukusei, aged 22, was an excellent diver, but he drowned at Pulau Tioman on 1 July 1937 while driving fish into a net bag with other fishermen. On that day he had been in the water for six hours and was probably exhausted. Attacks of malaria fever he had suffered in September 1936 might have contributed to his sudden death (Singapore Subordinate Courts, AD-049, 399/1937, 3 July 1937). In the event of an accident, fishermen could not take an injured person to a hospital within a short period of time, as their fishing grounds were far away from Singapore.

THE DEPRESSION AND THE SUPREMACY OF THE TAICHONG KONGSI

Fall in fish prices and rise in fishing expenses

In the early 1930s, most of the Japanese fishing companies experienced financial difficulty caused by a sharp fall in the demand for fresh fish and a rise in the costs of fishing. The demand for fish declined not only because the Depression reduced the purchasing power of local consumers, but also because Chinese boycotted Japanese goods after the Manchurian Incident in September 1931. Since caesio were caught only by the Japanese at that time, they were an easy target for the Chinese, and suffered particularly sharp falls in price. Their price was now a mere quarter of that prevailing in the pre-Depression period (DRO, E.4.9.0/7-7, 16 November 1931), and the monthly average income of the *muro ami* fisherman declined accordingly, from $70 in the late 1920s to $25 in 1932 (Birtwistle 1933: 6). Many fishermen switched from *muro ami* to drift-net fishing to catch Spanish mackerel whose price declined much less steeply. Indeed, the number of Japanese engaged in drift-net fishing rose from 60 in 1929 to 262 in 1936, whereas the number in *muro ami* fishing fell from 600 to 460 in the same years (Kataoka 1991: 69), although there was a recovery later on.

The rise in fishing expenses was caused by the high cost of oil and ice. As the Southeast Asian fisheries became widely known in Japan, more and more Japanese fishermen migrated to Singapore. With the increase in the number of Japanese fishermen and fishing companies, the fishing resources in the nearby waters of British Malaya became depleted, and the fishermen had to sail to increasingly distant fishing grounds (DRO, E.4.9.0/7-7, 16 November 1931). Since the fishing grounds were now located in the waters some 100 to 800 miles away from Singapore, large quantities of oil and ice had to be consumed, thereby increasing the cost of fishing (*ibid*.). In 1932, a 65-gallon drum of oil cost $13.20, and a ton of ice $13.25 (Birtwistle 1933: 6). In 1933, the fishing expenses of the Taichong Kongsi (including those of the Batavia branch) amounted to $211,355, of which ice and oil accounted for 43 per cent and 22 per cent respectively (DRO, E.4.9.0/7-7, 25 June 1934).

In Singapore, ice prices were particularly high due to an oligopoly practised by three major ice manufacturers, the Singapore Cold Storage Co. Ltd, the New Singapore Ice Works and the Atlas Ice Co. Ltd. In 1916, ice was sold to large purchasers at $20 per ton (*Suisankai*, no. 407, August 1916: 70). However, the price jumped between $30 and $40 owing to increased demand in the immediate post-war period, and all three manu-facturers made immense profits, prompting them to expand production facilities greatly. There was then over-production, leading to cut-throat competition. The price subsequently declined to $8 per ton. The manu-facturers therefore entered a cartel, fixing the price at $12 to $15 per ton. However, the Atlas Ice Co. Ltd expanded its production capacity greatly in the early 1930s, again causing an over-supply of ice in the market. Then one of the three companies began to sell ice below the agreed prices, in effect causing the cartel to collapse. As each firm tried to outsell its rivals, the price fell to as low as $5 (*Nanyo Suisan*, vol. 3, no. 2, February 1937: 21–2). In 1933, the three agreed on the prices of $14.25 ex factory, and $15 ex pier. They also divided the market among themselves. The Cold Storage got the largest share of 50 per cent of the total, while the New Singapore Ice Works and the Atlas Ice Co. Ltd were given 32 per cent and 18 per cent respectively (*Suisankai*, no. 614, January 1934: 83).

The Japanese fishing companies faced hard times. Arrears of pay owed to fishermen amounted to about $30,000, and they owed local money lenders and banks more than $30,000. Furthermore, they were in urgent need of some $40,000 working capital for oil, ice and other supplies (DRO, E.4.9.0/7-7, 16 November 1931).

In order to deal with the mounting problems, through the good offices of Ito Kenzo, the Acting Consul-General, and Sakai Rikita, a Consulate-General employee, the Japanese Fisheries Association of Singapore was formed in 1931. Sakai was appointed to the post of advisor, while four fishing company owners, including Eifuku Tora and Ishizu Tojiro, were appointed members of the board of directors. The association negotiated with the Singapore branches of the Japanese banks for three-year loans, for which all the members were jointly liable (*ibid.*). It also attempted to prevent members from over-fishing and dumping fresh fish at local markets. Nevertheless, the association did not function effectively, since it did not have effective means to overcome differences among its members (Kataoka 1991: 69–70).

Reorganisation of Japanese fishing companies under the Taichong Kongsi

The Depression years brought the ascendancy of the Taichong Kongsi. In 1931, there were 889 Japanese fishermen, of whom 393 (44.2 per cent of total) were employed by the Taichong Kongsi, and 290 (32.6 per cent) by the Ishizu Fishing Company (Kataoka 1991: 76). In 1936, as Table 4.6 shows, the total number of fishermen was 1,038, with 671 (64.6 per cent of total) employed by the Taichong Kongsi, and only 56 employed by the Ishizu Fishing Company. In that year, the Ishizu Fishing Company and the Shinzato Company went bankrupt, as they were unable to repay debts they owed to Chettiars and other financial organisations (*ibid.*: 75). In the meantime, the Taichong Kongsi continued to expand by buying up transports and fishing boats from the companies in financial difficulty.

In 1937, the Taichong Kongsi was reorganised as a joint-stock company under the name of the Eifuku Sangyo Koshi (The Eifuku Enterprise Ltd). Eifuku Tora and his wife owned 41 per cent of the shares, and their relatives and several executive staff held the rest. The new company consisted of the Taichong Kongsi (fisheries), the New Taichong Kongsi (foreign and domestic trade), the Taihock Kongsi (ice manufacturing and cold storage), Taihin Kongsi (iron works and ship-chandlering) and the Taichong Farm. Moreover, Eifuku constructed a pier at Tanjong Rhu, and installed oil tanks there (Robertson 1986: 56; Kataoka 1991: 83–4).

Table 4.6 Japanese fishing fleet based in Singapore (as of 1936)

Company	Fish carriers	Power boats	Fishing boats	Fishermen	Capital investment($)
Taichong[a]	33	18	49	671	915,000
Oshiro	4	2	6	90	50,000
Kinjo	5	2	9	107	80,000
Ishizu	2	3	4	56	150,000
Others	10	1	26	114	105,000
Total	54	26	94	1,038	1,300,000

Source: DRO, E.4.9.0/7-8, 7 November 1936.
Note
[a] Includes two groups of *muro ami* fishermen operating from Batavia.

Why was the Taichong Kongsi so successful at a time when most of the other Japanese fishing companies were either closing down or scaling down their fishing operations? According to Eric Robertson, the firm 'was founded in 1924, with a capital of $6,000, and by dint of bank advances and subsidies advanced to a leading position in the [fishing] industry' (Robertson 1986: 55). It is true that the Taichong Kongsi received, from time to time, subsidies from the Japanese government under the pretext of conducting research on Southeast Asian fisheries and training Japanese fishermen (*Suisan Iho*, no. 3, March 1931: 46). In 1934, for example, the Japanese Ministry of Colonies provided a subsidy of ¥5,376 to train 14 or 15 drift-net fishermen from Kagawa prefecture.

However, what deserves special attention is the ministry's subvention granted to the company in 1935. In the early 1930s Eifuku managed to acquire 1,257 sq m of land at Tanjong Rhu for $13,000, and he obtained permission from the municipal authorities to construct an ice factory and refrigeration plant. However, as he did not have sufficient funds to buy equipment and carry out construction work, he applied to the Japanese Ministry of Colonies for a fisheries subvention on grounds that, since his company and the fishermen bore the costs of ice equally, lower ice prices would benefit both sides, and that, with a refrigeration plant, his company could regulate the supply of fish, and help stabilise fish prices (DRO, E.4.9.0/7-7, 25 June 1934). The ministry was well aware that the oligopolistic agreement involving the three ice manufacturing companies was causing difficulties for the Japanese fishing companies. Therefore, it decided to grant Eifuku a subvention of ¥25,000 (DRO, E.4.9.0/7-7, 17 April 1935). It might also have taken into consideration the Taichong Kongsi's relationship with the Kyodo Gyogyo Co. Ltd, which we shall discuss later.

Eifuku Sangyo became a general fishing company both in name and reality after constructing its ice factory and refrigeration plant. The factory was capable of producing 27 tons of ice a day while the refrigeration plant had 600 tons of cold storage capacity (Nanyo oyobi Nihonjinsha 1938: 414). Although there are no figures for ice production, the company may have sold part of its output to other fishing companies, provided that the factory operated at its full capacity, because in 1933 the Taichong Kongsi had been purchasing an average of just 12.7 tons of ice per day (a total of 4,621 tons for the year) (DRO, E.4.9.0/7-7, 25 June 1934). In any case, the three existing companies, which together produced a total of 200 to 240 tons of ice per day, not only lost a good customer, but faced competition from the new Japanese rival. As a result, ice prices declined sharply to a mere $4 a ton in November 1936 (DRO, E.4.9.0/7-7, 7 November 1936).

Bank loans played an important role in Eifuku's success. Prior to World War II, three semi-official Japanese banks – namely the Bank of Taiwan, the China and Southern Bank, and the Yokohama Specie Bank – had branches in Singapore. Eifuku must have been on good terms with these institutions, for Eifuku Sangyo's outstanding liabilities to them amounted to $2 million in the late 1930s: $1 million owed to the Yokohama Specie Bank, and $500,000 owed each of the other two banks. The company had obtained the bank loans mainly to finance its new ventures, including ice production (Kataoka 1991: 82–4).

Eifuku Sangyo was not the only Japanese fishing company which received large loans from the Japanese banks. Robertson claims that the Yokohama Specie Bank granted a loan of $150,000 to the Ishizu Fishing Company, even though he does not say when this took place (Robertson 1986: 16). Moreover, it would be wrong to assume simply that the bank loans and government subsidies were the only factors behind Eifuku Sangyo's success. Eifuku's managerial skills and his company's relationship with the Kyodo Gyogyo Co. Ltd, a huge fisheries company based in Japan (renamed the Nihon Suisan Co. Ltd. in 1937), contributed greatly to his success.[8]

Unlike the owners of the other Japanese fishing companies, Eifuku was a graduate of the Fisheries Training College in Tokyo, and was equipped with a knowledge of fisheries management and Southeast Asian fisheries. At the end of the 1920s he began to secure capable men by recruiting graduates from his alma mater, other fisheries schools and commercial schools. At the same time, he appointed his relatives to key posts, and attempted to enhance the loyalty of his executive staff, for example, by offering them shares in the company (Kataoka 1991: 79).

Eifuku's method of profit-sharing between the company and the fishermen worked to the company's advantage. In the case of his Taichong Kongsi's *muro ami* fishing, after deducting fishing expenses from sales, the profit-sharing was done on the basis of 40 per cent to the company, and 60 per cent to the fishermen. For drift-net fishing, the company was responsible for fishing expenses, and the sales value was equally divided between them. By way of contrast, the Ishizu Fishing Company bore all the fishing costs of *muro ami* fishing, and shared the proceeds equally, whereas for its drift-net fishing the company provided fishermen with food, basic salaries according to grades of fishermen, and a percentage of the turnover. The Oshiro Company took 15 per cent of gross sales, and the balance remaining after various fishing expenses were deducted was given to the fishermen (Takumusho 1931: 64–6; *Nanyo Suisan*, vol. 2, no. 19, December 1936: 22). Thus, the method of profit-sharing was different from one company to another, but in the 1920s the average monthly income of the skilled fisherman was virtually the same, being about $50 (Aichiken Suisan Shikenjo 1932: 35). However, as the proceeds of the fishing companies declined sharply in the early 1930s, the Taichong Kongsi's method became advantageous to the company. In addition, Eifuku revised the ratio of profit-sharing in favour of the company.

The Taichong Kongsi and the Kyodo Gyogyo Co. Ltd

What was the relationship between the Taichong Kongsi and the Kyodo Gyogyo Co. Ltd? In 1935, Kyodo Gyogyo sent a trawler, the *Shinkyo Maru* (473 tons), to Southeast Asia to conduct trawling operations in the waters of northern Australia, Siam Bay and Java, and in the open sea facing the Indian Ocean.[9] It chose Singapore as its operating base, and concluded an agency agreement with the Taichong Kongsi. Kyodo Gyogyo planned to trans-ship most of the catch at Singapore onto mail steamers bound for Japan and other countries, and sell some in Singapore through the Taichong Kongsi (DRO, E.4.9.0/7-7, 14 September 1935).

In October 1935, the *Shinkyo Maru* began trawling in the waters of Southeast Asia. It seemed very difficult at first sight to sell frozen fish in Singapore's fish markets, for large quantities of fresh fish were regularly supplied there. However, it happened that there was a large demand for deep-sea fish which could only be caught by trawling. As a result, 50 per cent of the catch was sold locally, while the remainder was transferred at Singapore onto a mail steamer bound for Japan (DRO, E.4.9.0/7-8, 7 November 1936).

The volume of the *Shinkyo Maru*'s catch landed at Singapore was fairly large, amounting, for example, to 17.4 metric tons in December 1935, 38.6 metric tons in March and 54.2 metric tons in August 1936 (*ibid.*). However, after the outbreak of the Sino-Japanese War in July 1937, the Chinese in British Malaya boycotted Japanese products, including Japanese-caught fish, and Chinese coolies refused to unload the catch from the trawler in Singapore. Under these circumstances, the *Shinkyo Maru* was obliged to abandon its Singapore base, and established a temporary base at Kaohsiung in Taiwan (DRO, E.4.9.0/7-8, 10 January 1938).

Although the Taichong Kongsi's relationship with Kyodo Gyogyo only lasted for slightly more than two years, it helped to raise the company's standing greatly. The Japanese Ministry of Colonies may have decided to give the subvention to Eifuku in 1935 for construction of the ice factory and the refrigeration plant, in anticipation of future co-operation between the two companies, and Eric Robertson claims that the Taichong Kongsi 'built a large cold-storage plant at Tanjong Rhu *largely* for the benefit of the Kyodo Gyogyo' (emphasis added) (Robertson 1986: 57). Although he seems to have overstated the case, there is some truth in the assertion. It is also likely that in the 1930s Eifuku was able to get large loans from the Japanese banks partly thanks to his relations with the major fishery company in Japan. Incidentally, the managing director of Kyodo Gyogyo, Kunishi Kosuke, was, like Eifuku, a graduate of the Fisheries Training College, and he was the person in charge of trawling.

THE JAPANESE FISHERIES ON THE DECLINE IN THE LATE 1930S

In the late 1930s there were two main factors which caused a sudden decline of the Japanese fisheries. They were Chinese boycotts, and a change in the colonial fisheries policy.

When the Sino-Japanese War broke out in July 1937, the Chinese could not entirely boycott Japanese-caught fish in Singapore, because as much as 40 to 50 per cent of the fresh fish traded at the local market came from the Japanese. In the Malay Peninsula the Chinese boycotted most Japanese imports, but could not easily do so in the case of fish, for it was difficult to distinguish Japanese-caught fish from those caught by Malays or Chinese. When the war intensified in mainland China, however, the Chinese in the peninsula decided to boycott all fish brought in from Singapore (*Nanyo Suisan*, vol. 5, no. 5, 1938: 49–50). This decision dealt a blow to the Japanese fishing companies since some 30 to 40 per cent of their catches had been sent to the peninsula via Singapore before the outbreak of the war. Consequently, there was an over-supply of fresh fish in Singapore, which in turn led to a sharp fall in fish prices. The price of the fish caught by the *muro ami* method declined between one-third and one-half of the figure before the Sino-Japanese War, while the prices of drift-net catches by the Japanese and by the local fishermen fell by some 30 to 40 per cent (*ibid.*).

To make matters worse for the Japanese fishing companies, the colonial authorities changed their fisheries policy in the late 1930s. The British Colonial Office had been suspicious about the activities of the Japanese fishermen ever since the early 1920s. In September 1924, for example, it reported to the British Foreign Office that:

> The expansion of the Japanese fishing fleet in Malaya and neigh-bouring waters has become on a large scale during the past ten years

and it may not be unjustifiable to point out that a fleet of this nature might in a case of war prove of great utility to the Japanese navy and a source of danger to ourselves.

(PRO, Colonial Office to Foreign Office, 18 September 1924,
FO371/10299)

Moreover, Robertson writes:

> In order to play a part in time of war, it is necessary in naval matters to do so in time of peace. This precept was undoubtedly followed by both the Kyodo Gyogyo trawlers such as the *Shinkyo Maru* and by many of the Japanese fishing boats operating from Singapore . . . There were so many cases of poaching by these boats within the three-mile limit, when frequently there was insufficient evidence of the presence of the shoals of fish to justify running the risk of detection, that it was accepted as a matter of course by the British authorities at the time that in most of these cases the vessels were acting as Japanese naval intelligence units.

(Robertson 1986: 59)

The British suspected Eifuku Tora, in particular, of having close relations with the Japanese military. This is largely because, whenever a Japanese officer visited Singapore, Eifuku personally showed him around the fortified zone. Eifuku was never issued with a fishing licence for the territorial waters of Sarawak and Burma, no matter how many times he applied to the British colonial authorities for it (DRO, E.4.9.0/7-7, 14 May 1936).

Eventually, in 1937 the colonial authorities set about restricting the Japanese fishing activities, on the pretext of preserving the fishing grounds for local fishermen. To begin with, in February 1937 they decided not to issue fishing licences to any new Japanese fishing boats. Then, in 1938 they revoked the licences for 30 out of the 150 Japanese-owned fishing boats, thereby forcing most of the small fishing companies to cease operations. In February 1939 they informed the Japanese Consul-General that they would not renew the licences for the 20 power boats and three sailing boats owned by Eifuku Sangyo and seven other Japanese companies (DRO, E.4.9.0/7-7, 10 February 1939). Furthermore, the Director of the Fisheries in the Straits Settlements gave advance notice to the Japanese Fisheries Association that there would be no more renewal, after three months' grace, of the licences for the fishing boats due to expire in July 1939, and this would equally apply to those which were to expire thereafter. In 1940, only three Japanese fishing companies remained, namely, the Taichong Kongsi, the Oshiro Company and the Kinjo Company, even though 30 had been in operation in 1938 (Watanabe Haruo 1942: 211).

The rapid decline in the Japanese fisheries resulted in massive unemployment among Japanese fishermen. Many of these men had no choice but to move to the Malay Peninsula to seek work. It happened that the Nippon Mining Company was anxious to employ them together with local Malays and Indians at the Bukit Besi Iron Mine at Dungun in Trengganu to replace some 2,300 Chinese coolies who had just quit in protest against the Japanese invasion of China (Kee 1966: 61). By late 1938 more than 500 Japanese fishermen had found employment with this and other Japanese mining companies in the peninsula (DRO, E.4.8.0/X4-B1, 3 December 1938, and E.4.9.0/7-7, 10 July 1939).

The restrictive measures against Japanese fisheries also resulted in a steep fall in supplies of fresh fish in Singapore. Total landings in Singapore declined from 13,044 tons in 1937 to 10,726 tons in 1939 and 10,116 tons in 1940. The Japanese fishermen's share of these quantities also fell from almost 60 per cent to 45 per cent over the same period (Le Mare 1950: 98). As the local Malay and Chinese fishermen were unable to take the place of the highly productive Japanese, Singapore had to rely heavily on landings from Moro, Cucub, Karimun and Rhio (Birtwistle 1939: 3; Robertson 1986: 61).

CONCLUDING REMARKS

The economic contributions made by the Japanese fisheries were substantial. Japanese fishing companies employed Japanese fishermen, who spent most of their time at sea, and remitted large part of their earnings to their families in Japan, thus contributing little to the local economy. Nevertheless, it would be wrong to conclude that the Japanese fisheries constituted an economic enclave in Singapore. Japanese fishermen supplied some 40 to 50 per cent of the fresh fish traded in the local fish markets, thereby helping to lower fish prices for local consumers, and reducing greatly the British colony's dependence upon the import of fresh fish. Moreover, although all the equipment used by the Japanese such as fishing nets and boats were initially imported from Japan, they began to be produced locally during World War I (*Suisan Iho*, no. 3, June 1931: 51; Kataoka 1991: 54). Japanese fishermen were the first to supply large quantities of caesio to the local fish markets. As this fish was fairly inexpensive, it soon became very popular among the local consumers. In fact, they brought about a major change in the food culture of British Malaya, for caesio replaced dorab and Spanish mackerel as a main ingredient for fish balls, an indispensable ingredient in soup and vermicelli dishes (Green 1927: 11).

The economic impact of the Japanese fisheries was not confined to British Malaya alone, for Japanese fisheries in Singapore and other parts of Southeast Asia made large economic contributions to Okinawa. After World War I, the Okinawan economy was in decline, and local marine resources were decreasing due to over-fishing. The massive migration of the fishermen to Southeast

Asia helped to cut down the unemployment rate in the prefecture, while the remittances they sent helped improve economic conditions.

The relationship between the overseas Chinese and the Japanese in pre-war Southeast Asia is often described in terms of the conflict between the two racial groups, for the overseas Chinese boycotted Japanese goods to protest against Japanese military aggression in China. It is important, therefore, to note their symbiotic relationship. This is largely because the bulk of Japanese goods including the Japanese-caught fish were sold through the overseas Chinese who controlled wholesale and retail trade in the region. No matter how much fish the Japanese caught, they could not have easily reached local markets without the co-operation of Chinese merchants.

It should also be noted that the Japanese and local fishermen were not always rivals, since the Japanese fishing companies provided a sales outlet for the local fishermen's catch. The Taichong Kongsi, for example, purchased fresh fish and shrimps from Chinese and Malay fishermen in Tanjong Datoh, Ketaman and other remote islands of the Netherlands Indies to sell in Singapore, and supplied them a variety of goods including fishing gear, fuel and foodstuffs. The fishermen in these islands had formerly either dried or salted their catch for preservation, but they could now obtain ready cash for fresh fish and had access to a wide range of goods thanks to the company (Green 1927: 11; *Suisan Iho*, no. 5, November 1932: 194–200).

5

JAPAN'S ECONOMIC ACTIVITIES IN SYONAN

Singapore was under Japanese rule for three and a half years from February 1942 to August 1945. However, as already noted in the Introduction, Japanese economic activities during the period have been little studied by scholars. It is true that the occupation period was comparatively short with a limited achievement in the economic field, while in addition relevant source materials are not easy to obtain. Nevertheless, one cannot possibly miss out the period simply on the pretext of a dire lack of source materials. This is not only because it constitutes an important part of the twentieth-century economic history of Singapore/Southeast Asia, but also because there is a possibility that Japanese economic policy and activities of Japanese firms then may have had a considerable impact on the economic development of Singapore in the post-war period.

Prior to World War II, Singapore prospered as an international free trade port, thanks largely to its close link with Asia and the industrial nations of the West. Two days after the commencement of the occupation, the Japanese Army renamed the island Syonan or Light of the South,[1] and then made it the military and economic capital for Southeast Asia within the Greater East Asia Co-prosperity Sphere (self-sufficient economic area). The army abolished the *laissez-faire* policy, and imposed in its place stringent direct economic controls over manufacturing, transport, finance and other sectors of the economy. Selected Japanese companies were commissioned by the Japanese military government to run industrial and other undertakings in Syonan. According to the National Institute of Defence Studies, as of 1 May 1944 the Japanese companies in Syonan numbered 130, headed by those owned by Mitsui and Mitsubishi family combines (Boei Kenkyujo Senshibu 1985: 202–5).[2] It should be noted that, in addition to manufacturing firms, hotels, restaurants, and others also moved into Syonan one after another from mid-1942 onwards, and operated, more often than not, under the auspices of the military authorities. There were also those Japanese businessmen and entrepreneurs who wanted to make a fortune by devious means.

The Japanese authorities emphasised that all Asians were equal in a Greater East Asia New Order. However, racial equality among Asians turned out to be empty words, for priority was given to the military personnel and Japanese civilians in Syonan throughout the occupation period. For example, first- and second-class train seats, lifts in public buildings, and imported goods were exclusively reserved for the Japanese (Turnbull 1977: 207; Thio 1991: 96). Since Japanese civilians such as clerical staff of the Syonan Special Municipality were also given a ration of the goods confiscated from the 'enemies', they were well provided with foodstuffs, beer, Johnnie Walker whisky, tinned tabacco and others, which were considered luxuries by local citizens (OHI Negishi *et al.*).

There are numerous episodes involving the high-handedness of the Japanese. Turnbull says:

> While the new Japanese masters preached a doctrine of Asian equality and an anti-materialistic, anti-western sacrifice for Singaporeans, they themselves showed a predilection for big British and American cars, lording it in former colonial mansions, enjoying tennis, golf, and horse racing.
>
> (Turnbull 1977: 207)

As a matter of fact, it was General Kuroda Shigenori, the Chief of the General Staff of the Southern Regions Japanese Army, who restored the golf course near Bukit Timah Hill, for he was extremely fond of that sport. However, an ex-official of the Syonan Special Municipality recalls with displeasure:

> General Kuroda used to assert his authority, yelling at others during play. Although influential local people were also permitted to play the golf there, they returned home, the moment they saw a car with a yellow flag parked in front of the gate.[3]
>
> (Shingaporu Shiseikai 1986: 367–9)

While Syonan was 'a soft posting for Japanese far from the rigour of the battle front', the Japanese occupation period was a period of 'hell' for the local inhabitants (Turnbull 1977: 194, 207). As the war situation moved against Japan, the living standards of local citizens deteriorated with grave shortages of foodstuffs and hyper inflation. It was in fact the overseas Chinese among the various ethnic groups in Syonan who suffered most at the hand of the Japanese. Since there are many works describing the cruelty of the Japanese military rule, here we refer only briefly to the massacre of overseas Chinese, and the extraction of $50 million 'gift money' from the Chinese community. The massacre was carried out by the Japanese army shortly after the occupation began. However, it is not clear how many overseas Chinese were massacred by the Japanese army at that time. The Japanese side says that the number was about 5,000, whereas the Singapore side claims that it was at least 25,000 (Shü and Chua 1986: 63–7). At any rate, the massacre was kept secret until the early 1960s when numerous human remains were unearthed at a work site on the east coast. As we shall see in Chapter 7, it became the so-called 'blood-debt issue' which eventually grew into a major political issue between Japan and Singapore.

As for the issue of 'gift money', in March 1942 Watanabe Wataru, the chief military administrator of the Military Administration, demanded that Chinese leaders raise $50 million in Singapore and Malaya. This was because he wanted to obtain necessary funds for the Military Administration, and to make the overseas Chinese atone for their past anti-Japanese activities. An Overseas Chinese Association, which was created under the auspices of the Japanese, decided that $10 million was to be raised in Syonan, and the remainder to be collected in the Malay states. By June, the assigned amount had been collected in Syonan, but in the Malay states only $18 million had been raised. As a result, the Military Administration obtained the full amount of $50 million from the Chinese community by arranging for a loan of $22 million from the Yokohama Specie Bank to the Overseas Chinese Association at an annual interest rate of 6 per cent (Shinozaki 1982: 48).

We shall now examine in what ways the 'Japanese masters' undertook a wide range of economic activities in Syonan where they exercised cruel rule over the local inhabitants, notably overseas Chinese, using their military might from the beginning of the occupation.

THE OUTBREAK OF THE PACIFIC WAR AND THE JAPANESE IN SYONAN

In the early 1940s Anglo-Japanese relations deteriorated steadily, and many Japanese company employees and their families returned to Japan or took temporary shelter in Thailand. The Japanese residents who stayed in Singapore were, mostly *shitamachi-zoku* (the downtown people), including over 400 fishermen, proprietors of retail shops, dentists, former *karayuki-san* and the like (Kataoka 1991: 85; Shinozaki 1978a: 55).

When the Pacific War broke out on 8 December 1941, the colonial authorities detained some 1,000 Japanese and sent them to prison camps in the suburbs of New Delhi in India. In the internment camps in India there was a total of some 3,000 Japanese internees who were brought not only from Singapore but also from other parts of Asia (Ueda Kiyoji 1972: 54). However, as the British and Japanese governments agreed to exchange their respective internees at Lourenço Marques (present-day Maputo in Mozambique), over 700 Japanese were able to return to Japan in September 1942 (Taiwan Ginko-shi Hensanshitsu 1964: 960–1; Ueda Kiyoji 1972: 54–7). The Japanese internees selected for exchange by the Japanese government were largely those who were indispensable in the Japan-occupied territories, i.e. professionals such as doctors, and employees of the Japanese companies, plus their dependents (*ibid*.: 57). Consequently, the majority of the former *shitamachi-zoku* had to stay behind in India until after the Pacific War in 1945.

At the beginning of the occupation, the military authorities apparently did not have any intention of permitting the return to Syonan of the former Japanese residents who had been shop-owners and the other self-employed. However, by late August they had changed their policy, for they decided to make use of the Japanese who had close relations with local residents, and had good command of Malay and other foreign languages. As a result, over 200 former Japanese residents were allowed to return to Syonan, and were asked to act as a link between the Military Administration and local inhabitants, even though they were forbidden to re-open their own retail shops. The young Japanese were employed as interpreters for the military and municipal governments, while the older ones were put in charge of a newly created commodities ration association (Shinozaki 1978b: 68). Thus, the former residents were employed in those works which were indispensable for the military rule and the war-time economy.

CURRENCY AND BANKS UNDER JAPANESE RULE

Well before the invasion of Malaya by Japan on 8 December 1941, the Japanese government had begun to print unnumbered military yen notes denominated in dollars for Singapore, Malaya and North Borneo, in guilders for the Dutch East Indies, and in pesos for the Philippines. When the Pacific War broke out, the Japanese Army started invading Southeast Asia, carrying them. In January 1942, it was decided that military notes denominated in Southeast Asian currencies should be at par with the yen. Moreover, as soon as the Military Administration was established in various parts of the region, these notes were declared legal tender, and were valued at par with the local currencies. Since Sumatra, Syonan and Malaya[4] were ruled by the Twenty-Fifth Army until April 1943, the military notes denominated in guilders and Straits dollars circulated concurrently with the original Straits dollars and guilders. However, since the pre-war exchange value of the three currencies (the yen, the guilder and the Straits dollar) had been different, there was much confusion among local inhabitants in these Japanese-occupied territories (Kobayashi 1993: 110–13).[5]

On 27 April 1942 the Military Administration at Syonan ordered the requisition of the Straits Settlements Currency Board, the Chartered Bank of India Australia and China, the Hong Kong and Shanghai Banking Corporation, Nederlandsche-Indische Handelsbank, Nederlandsche Handel Maatschappij, and other Western banks. However, it permitted the re-opening of five Chinese banks (Lee Wah Bank, Ban Hin Lee Bank, Sze Hai

116

Tong, United Chinese Bank and Oversea-Chinese Banking Corporation) in April 1942, another Chinese bank (Kong Yik Bank) in September, and three Indian banks (the Indian Bank, the Indian Overseas Bank and the Oriental Bank of Malaya) later on, for it needed their co-operation in ruling Syonan and Malaya. Also, the Indian banks were able to re-open, partly because they were in support of the independence of India from Britain. However, the Bank of China and the Bank of Canton were liquidated on the grounds that Japan was at war with China (Tokyo Ginko 1983: 163).

As for Japanese banks, the Yokohama Specie Bank and the Taiwan Bank re-opened their branches in Singapore and Malaya in March 1942, while a Southern Regions Development Bank (Nanpo Kaihatsu Kinko) was established with a capital of ¥100 million in Tokyo on 30 March 1942 as a Southeast Asian agency for the Bank of Japan. Moreover, the China and Southern Bank re-opened in June. The Yokohama Specie Bank served as the cash office of the Japanese Military Administration in Syonan and Malaya. Its Syonan branch was located at the former building of the Hong Kong and Shanghai Banking Corporation. As of May 1943, the bank had twelve branches/offices in the Syonan-Malay region (Shimazaki 1989: 310–11). The Taiwan Bank took over the Singapore branch of Nederlandsche Handel-Maatschappij NV, and resumed its work on 20 March. Its Syonan branch had a history of 30 years in operation, and for this reason it continued to undertake banking activities, including deposits, loans and remittances for the Japanese Navy and some Japanese companies (Taiwan Ginko-shi Hensanshitsu 1964: 969). Nevertheless, the Yokohama Specie Bank far exceeded the bank in the total amounts of deposits and loans. In late June 1943, for example, the former's deposits amounted to $167,763,000 and its loans to $120,754,000, whereas the latter's respective amounts were a mere $13,620,000 and $6,939,000 (Shimazaki 1989: 313).

The Southern Regions Development Bank started operations on 1 April 1942, and set up a branch each in Syonan, Jakarta and Manila. Thereafter, it established branches or representative offices in the main cities of Southeast Asia. The ordinary banks, i.e. the Yokohama Specie Bank, the Bank of Taiwan and the China and Southern Bank were concerned with commercial loans short-term development loans, and local finances, whereas the Southern Regions Development Bank was mainly responsible for giving long-term development loans, and special loans to Japanese firms (*ibid.*: 312). Moreover, although surplus money in the Military Administration's account was supposed to be kept at the Southern Regions Development Bank, the Yokohama Specie Bank was in charge of it on its behalf, largely because it had an extensive network of branches and representative offices in Southeast Asia (*ibid.*: 325). However, when the Southern Regions Development Bank began to issue notes, friction arose between it and the ordinary banks. For example, the Military Administration transferred its account from the Yokohama Specie Bank to the Southern Regions Development Bank in

Syonan at the beginning of 1943 (in the case of Malaya from July onward). In other words, the Bank of Japan's agency work was transferred from the former to the latter in accordance with the original arrangement. Also, in the field of loans, the Southern Regions Development Bank had abundant funds, and began to give short-term loans to Japanese companies in competition with the Yokohama Specie Bank.

In the early days of the occupation, the financial requirements of the Military Administration were met largely by the 'gift money' and the seizure of local currency, but with the intensification of the war, the amount of the military budget expanded so much that the Japanese government authorised the Southern Regions Development Bank to issue notes (*nanpo kaihatsu kinko ken* or *nanpatsu ken* for short) as from 1 April 1941 (*ibid.*). The new notes were not different from the existing military notes, as they merely succeeded the latter with a different name (Tokyo Ginko 1984: 145).[6] As the Japanese continued to printed military notes, it gave rise to hyper-inflation. In Syonan, the wholesale price index rose from 100 (base year) in December 1941 to 900 in June 1943, 5,765 in September 1944, and 185,648 in August 1945 (Shimazaki 1989: 382–3). Actually, the Military Administration introduced some measures to control inflation. The first government lottery was held in August 1943, and at the end of the year gambling was legalised. There were some 300 gambling houses in operation in Syonan (Kratoska 1998: 211). In February 1944, savings campaigns were launched, and the value of savings amounted to $281,546,000 at the end of the war (Turnbull 1977: 204). However, these measures turned out to be ineffective, 'since too much money was chasing too few goods'.

FISHERIES AND THE EIFUKU SANGYO KOSHI

When the Pacific War broke out on 8 December 1941, the local fishermen were prohibited by the British from conducting fishing in the territorial waters for security reasons. But, since the supply of fresh fish was of critical importance to the Japanese military, about one month after the Japanese occupation of Singapore began, the military authorities permitted them to resume it. Then, in the autumn of 1942 they ordered Sako Noboru, the fisheries chief of the Syonan Special Municipality, to exercise the control of fishing equipment and other necessities, so as to give priority to their own fish requirements. However, as Sako was fully aware of the difficulty in controlling the local fishermen, he persuaded them to adopt the following: the local fishermen were ordered to take all their catches to the fish markets in Orchard Road for auction, and were provided with fishing equipment, ice, fuel and foodstuffs according to the amount of their fresh fish. However, they had to supply 10 per cent of their catches to the military at a fixed price (Shingaporu Shiseikai 1986: 173).

According to Sako, the volume of fresh fish brought to the markets by the local fishermen increased from some 100 tons per day in the pre-occupation period to some 200 tons per day in the early occupation period, thanks to the system of control (*ibid.*). However, since the total output of fresh fish by the local fishermen was 2,210 tons in the whole of 1937 (*Malayan Year Book* 1937: 92; *Blue Book* 1937: 761), the figures quoted by him do not seem to be accurate.

Incidentally, in October 1943, six British and Australian sailors and soldiers infiltrated the Singapore harbour, and successfully blew up seven ships after attaching limpet mines to the Japanese ships (Turnbull 1977: 210). At that time, there were 15 to 16 *kelongs* (fish traps) in the offshore area some 500 metres away from the beach. As the Japanese military authorities assumed that the special unit reached the Singapore harbour by going along one *kelong* after another, they ordered the removal of all the *kelongs* (Shingaporu Shiseikai 1986: 173–4). This resulted in a steep fall in the output by local fishermen, although the *kelong* fishing was obviously not the only method employed by them.

As for the Japanese fisheries, in 1942 the Cabinet Planning Board at Tokyo decided to grant fishing licences mainly to those fishing companies which had been in operation in the region in the pre-war period. In Syonan, the Eifuku Sangyo Koshi, the Oshiro Company and the Kinjo Company were commissioned to conduct fishing, while the Nihon Suisan Co. Ltd was ordered to undertake ice-manufacturing and cold storage business jointly with Eifuku Sangyo (Kikakuin Dairoku Iinkai 1942: 193–4).[7]

However, there were not many Japanese fishermen left in Syonan, for the British had interned 1,000 Japanese residents in Singapore after the outbreak of the Pacific War, and had then transported them to internment camps in India. Among them were 475 fishermen: 329 from Eifuku Sangyo including Eifuku Tora and his wife, 87 from the Kinjo Company, 51 from the Oshiro Company and 18 from others (Kataoka 1991: 85). In addition, some fishermen were engaged in fishing at sea when the war broke out, and were taken to Australia.

Shortly after the fall of Singapore into the hands of the Japanese military in February 1942, there was an outcry among the alumni of the Fisheries Training College in Tokyo (Suisan Koshujo) that 'the efforts and achievement made by Eifuku Tora in the past thirty years ought not be wasted'. As we have seen in Chapter 4, Eifuku was a graduate of that school. The Nihon Suisan Co. Ltd, which had used Eifuku Sangyo as its agency for its trawl-fishing in the 1930s, decided to provide ¥2 million for the reconstruction of his company (Hashimoto 1964: 70). Moreover, Hashimoto Tokuju, a former lecturer in wooden ship-building at the Fisheries Training College, volunteered to join the staff of Eifuku Sangyo as ship-building manager in August 1942 (*ibid.*: 590).

When Hashimoto arrived in the Japanese-occupied island, there were only four Eifuku Sangyo employees who had returned there from Japan. However, on 17 September 1942, Tora Eifuku and his family landed at Singapore from a Japan-bound ship which was carrying exchanged prisoners of war (*ibid.*: 69). Then Eifuku set out to reconstruct Eifuku Sangyo with the assistance of Hashimoto. The main activities of his company were the fishing in the waters of Syonan, the Malay Peninsula and Western Java, and the building of wooden fishing boats in Syonan and the Malay Peninsula (Kataoka 1991: 86).

As of 3 December 1943, it had a fleet of 27 fishing boats, and employed 200 Japanese fishermen and roughly the same number of local Malays and Chinese. As for the volume of the catch, it amounted to 4 to 5 metric tons per day (*The Syonan Times*, 3 December 1942). As the Japanese fishermen later increased in number, the volume of the catch also rose considerably, reaching some 10 metric tons a day in May 1943 , even though it was much smaller than its pre-war output of 20 to 30 metric tons (*ibid.*; Hashimoto 1964: 152). The Japanese military exclusively bought all the catches from the company at fixed prices. According to Hashimoto Tokuju, Eifuku Sangyo supplied fresh fish to the military at ¥1,600 to ¥2,000 per metric ton in February 1944, whereas fresh fish was traded in the black market at ¥6.42 per kilo (Hashimoto 1964: 208). As the military authorities purchased fresh fish at a very low price, some Japanese fishermen sold part of their catch on the black market (Kunigami Mura 1992a: 505). As a sideline, a certain Japanese officer even purchased fresh fish from local fishermen and, using the employees and vehicle of the Nam Poh Kaisha, a Japanese company, sold them on the black market, making a large profit (OHI Soo).

When the position of Japan in the war began to weaken in 1943, the military authorities conscripted all Japanese men under the age of 40 in Syonan. Thus there was a decreasing number of Japanese fishermen available to Eifuku Sangyo. Moreover, although the military ordered Eifuku to increase the catch greatly, his company was always short of fishing boats. Indeed, the moment it repaired an old boat or built a new one, the army or the navy requisitioned it (Hashimoto 1964: 152). Fishing gear was also in short supply. However, in early 1944, fishing nets and rope were successfully made from coconut husks by two employees of Senda Shokai (Senda Trading Company), and some of them were sold in the local market (*Syonan Shimbun*, 21 January 1944). It is not clear if Eifuku Sangyo made extensive use of such products. At any rate the fishing output must have continued to fall steeply as the war progressed. When the war ended in August 1945, Eifuku Tora was interned by the British, and was not able to return to Japan until February 1946 (Kataoka 1991: 86). As for Kinjo Yasuichi, he became a prisoner of war around Banka Island in January 1945, and was subsequently transported to Australia. It was in January 1946 that he eventually returned to Japan from Sydney (Kunigami Mura 1992a: 503–4).

COMMERCIAL ACTIVITIES

Mitsubishi Corporation and Mitsui & Co.

When the Japanese Army occupied Singapore, they began to exercise strict control over the distribution system, while allowing large Japanese trading companies to monopolise the trade between Japan and the Southeast Asian region. Tables 5.1 and 5.2 list the Japanese companies which were commissioned to undertake the trade with Japan. Prior to World War II, most of them had set up branches or representative offices in Singapore to conduct foreign trade in competition with overseas Chinese merchants, European merchant houses and other traders. However, during the occupation period, Mitsui & Co., Mitsubishi Corporation and other Japanese firms were able to enjoy a virtual monopoly of the domestic and foreign trades in the absence of their Chinese and European rivals.

Mitsubishi Corporation was the first Japanese firm to resume operations in Syonan in February 1942. The company had been obliged to close its Singapore branch in December 1941 when the Pacific War was approaching. As soon as Singapore fell into Japanese hands, it wanted to pick the first opportunity to return there. However, since the military authorities did not permit the entry of Japanese civilians into the island in the early days of the occupation, the company sent staff to Singapore on the pretext of investigating the whereabout of the Egyptian cotton on its ship, the *Awa Maru*, which had been seized by the British military shortly before the outbreak of the Pacific War, and managed to re-open its branch there (Mitsubishi Shoji 1986: 482–3, 594). The Japanese Military Administration granted it a monopoly over the import of rice into Malaya and Syonan as from July 1942.[8] Subsequently, it was placed in charge of the collection of rubber and other primary commodities, the management of various factories, and the building of wooden ships (*ibid.*: 594–5).

Similarly, Mitsui & Co. secured a monopoly of the trade in salt and sugar, and was engaged in manufacturing activities. The rapid expansion in its economic activities in Syonan is evident from the fact that the number of its Syonan branch employees rose from eighr (all Japanese) as of 30 September 1940 to 86 (including some local employees) as of 31 October 1942, and 136 (including some local employees) as of 1 April 1943 (Mitsui Bunko, Bussan 51/38, September 1941: 41; Bussan 51/40, October1942: 56–7; Bussan 51/44, April 1943: 52–3).

Although the Japanese trading companies in Syonan were able to monopolise the trade with Japan and other parts of Asia, they found it increasingly difficult to secure means of transport, notably shipping. Indeed, the Japanese Navy lost four aircraft carriers in the sea battle of Midway in June 1942, and thereafter Japanese war-ships were sunk one after another. Moreover, an increasing number of Japanese commercial ships were either

Table 5.1 Japanese firms in the import trade in Syonan (as of July 1942)

Firm	Trading items	Type of offices
Iseya Shoten	Textile goods, leather goods	Head office
Shimota Koshi	Textile goods, paper, dyestuffs, and others	Head office
Kato Yoko	Textile goods, pyrethrum	Head office
Daido Yoko	Textile goods	Head office
Mitsubishi Corporation	Textile goods, vegetable oil, tinned foods, tea, tobacco, beer, cosmetics, paints, matches, sheet glass, industrial chemicals, beverages and foodstuffs	Branch
Nippon Baiyaku Koshi	Textile goods, large bottles, pharmaceuticals, sundry goods	Head office
Senda Shokai	Textiles, plywood, industrial chemicals, paints, cosmetics, tools for artisans, and other	Head office
Mitsui & Co.	Textile goods, farm products, vegetable oil, tinned foods, beverages and foodstuffs, matches, dyestuffs, industrial chemicals, paints, cosmetics, paper	Branch
Kobe Kairikusan Boeki	Farm products, tea, marine goods	Representative office
Nippon Yakubo	Pyrethrum	Head office
Yamanaka Shoten	Tinned foods	Head office
Nishiyama Shokai[a]	Plywood	Branch
Kasho	Plywood	Branch
Nanyo Shoko	Ceramics, glassware, metal goods, electrical machinery and appliances, sundry goods	Branch
Asano Bussan[a]	Cement	Representative
Sakura Shokai	Celluloid goods, leather goods, toys	Head office
Santei Shokai	Bicycles and parts	Head office
Nissan Motors Co. Ltd[a]	Motor vehicles, auto parts	Branch[c]
Ebata Yoko	Brushes	Head office
Sakamoto Shoten	Brushes	Head office
Omiya Shoten	Accessories (excluding celluloid goods)	Representative office[d]
Nomura Higashi Indo Shokusan[b]	Electrical machinery and appliances	Branch
Pairotto Mannenhitsu[a]	Stationery	Representative office

Source: Constructed from Kikakuin Dairoku Iinkai 1942: 135–7.

Notes

[a] These companies had not done business in pre-war Singapore.

[b] There was Nomura Shoten instead of Nomura Higashi Indo Shokusan in the pre-war period.

[c] To be set up in the near future.

[d] Already withdrawn from Syonan.

Table 5.2 Japanese exporters of Southeast Asian commodities in Syonan and Malaya

Commodity	Exporter in Syonan and Malaya	Importer in Japan	Relationship between exporter and importer
Crude rubber	Mitsui & Co.	Mitsui & Co.	Branch and head office
Crude rubber	Nomura Higashi Indo Shokusan	Nomura Higashi Indo Shokusan	Branch and head office
Crude rubber	Senda Shokai	Senda Shokai	
Crude rubber	Koei Shokai		
Crude rubber	Kasho		
Crude rubber	Mitsubishi Corporation		
Copra	Mitsui & Co.	Mitsui & Co.	Branch and head office
Resin	Nomura Higashi Indo Shokusan	Nomura Higashi Indo Shokusan	Branch and head office
Derris roots	Konan Yoko	Konan Yoko	Branch and head office
Hides and skins	Nippon Genpi	Nippon Genpi	Branch and head office
Tannin	Nippon Tannin Shoji	Nippon Tannin Shoji	Branch and head office
Scrap iron	Nampo Scrap Iron Yunyu Tosei Kumiai	Nampo Scrap Iron Yunyu Tosei Kumiai	Same company
Other commodities	Most suitable companies among the above	Most suitable companies among the above	

Source: Constructed from Kikakuin Dairoku Iinkai 1942: 101–2.

requisitioned by the Navy for military purposes, or sunk by the Allies' submarines (see Table 5.3). The critical shortage of shipping obliged the trading companies to cut down their activities.

Advance of Japanese Department Stores into Syonan

In the Japanese-occupied territories in Asia, Japanese department stores were given the special privilege of controlling the internal distribution system for the Japanese Army. In Syonan, although the Military Administration placed a restriction on the commercial activities of small Japanese retail stores, it permitted three large department stores, Daimaru, Matsuzakaya and Shirakiya (the present Tokyu Department Store) to move into Syonan, and engage in retail business at the former premises of John Little, Robinson and Whiteway respectively. They were also commissioned to run dormitories for Japanese soldiers and procure military goods for the army. According to Turnbull, these department stores aimed only at Japanese customers (Turnbull 1977: 207). However, Choo Yam Wai, an ex-library staff member

Table 5.3 Japanese shipping tonnage during the Pacific War (in 1,000 gross tons)

Year	New ships and other additions	Loss of ships	Total tonnage	Index
8 Dec. 1941	–	–	6,384.0	100
1942	661.8	1,095.8	5,942.6	93
1943	1,067.1	2,065.7	4,944.0	77
1944	1,735.1	4,115.1	2,564.0	40
1945[a]	465.0	1,502.1	1,526.9	24

Source: Constructed from Ando (1975: 139) with some modifications.
Note
[a] Until August.

at the National University of Singapore, recalls that as a primary school boy living in Kuala Lumpur during the occupation period, he used to go with his family to a Japanese department store in the city, which had previously been the Whiteway department store, even though there were not many goods kept there (OHI Choo). At that time, local people could shop in the store comparatively freely, and it is likely that they could have done the same in Syonan.

How did these department stores then come to do business in Syonan? Daimaru advanced into China in the mid-1930s, where they mainly supplied military goods to the Japanese Army. During the Pacific War, it greatly expanded its activities by setting up branches at Mukden in Manchuria, Canton in China, Syonan and Rangoon, and kept representative offices in many parts of China and Southeast Asia (Daimaru 1967: 436). When the Japanese Army was stationed in Hanoi in September 1940, the Canton branch of Daimaru set up representative offices in Hanoi, Hyphon and Saigon to run dormitories for Japanese soldiers.

About two months after the fall of Singapore, Daimaru together with Matsuzakaya and Shirakiya submitted to the Japanese Military Administration an application for permission to run department stores and dormitories for non-commissioned officers, and also to engage in the trade in rice for military use in Syonan and Malaya. In late April 1942, Daimaru set up a representative office, and it managed to obtain a permission for embarking on retail business in early 1943. It then moved its office into the premises of John Little, and promoted it to a branch on 1 July 1943 (*ibid.*: 469).

As Table 5.4 shows, the activities of the Syonan branch were closely related to the Japanese Army. The dormitory for non-commissioned officers was opened after Nakatani Sukeo of Daimaru took up the post of general manager for the Southeast Asian region on 15 February 1942. Daimaru also embarked on civil engineering works for the army. It, for example, built an office for the Southern Region's fuel storage installations, and residential houses for officers (Daimaru 1967: 469).

124

Table 5.4 Daimaru's activities in Syonan

Military dormitory	Manufacturing	Commerce and other
First Syonan military dormitory	Furniture factory	Department store
Kiosk in Middle Barracks	Toothbrush factory	Restaurant
Kiosk in South Barracks	Paper-making factory	Procurement for military goods
	Needlework factory	Transport
	Button-making factory	Civil engineering works for the military
	Iron foundry	

Source: Constructed from Daimaru 1967: 470.

Initially, Daimaru sold the goods requisitioned from the British, but since supplies of such goods did not last long, it had no choice but to cater mainly for military requirements the more so as it became increasingly difficult to import goods from Japan. In view of shortages of goods, it began to manufacture toothbrushes, paper and buttons, but had great difficulties because it had not been engaged in any industrial production in the past (*ibid.*: 463, 469).

As for Matsuzakaya, in the Southeast Asian region it ran department stores, hotels, confectionery factories, farms and other concerns in Syonan, the Malay Peninsula, Java, and Sumatra. As Table 5.5 shows, like Daimaru, it diversified its activities widely.[9] As Matsuzakaya was very interested in Robinson's building (basement and three floors) at Raffles Place, it negotiated with the military authorities for two months, and was finally given permission to use it. As the building had been damaged by British and Japanese bombings, the repair cost some ¥92,000, of which the Military Administration financed some ¥72,000. This clearly reveals Matsuzakaya's close relationship with the army.

Matsuzakaya's department store was opened on 21 March 1943, making use of two-thirds of the ground floor of Robinson's building as a display room, with the remaining space used as its office. At the time of the opening, there were some 20 employees, including Japanese, Chinese, Malays and Indians (Takenaka 1964: 511). Although toys and ceramics were imported from Japan, the bulk of the goods sold there were locally procured. The production of socks, furniture, candies and other goods were contracted to Chinese-owned firms in Syonan (*ibid.*). The only exception was a brand of toothpowder called 'Kulene'. Matsuzakaya purchased the production and sales rights from F.A.C. Oehlers, a student of dentistry who had originally developed it. It converted a room in a house in Tomlinson Road into a workshop, and secured several workers and the necessary raw materials, while Oehlers was employed in his capacity as a production supervisor (OHI Oehlers).

Table 5.5 Matsuzakaya's activities in Syonan

Undertaking	Date of establishment	Location	Details of activities
Department store	March 1943	In Robinson Department Store building, Raffles Place	Sales of furniture, stationery, confectionery, leather goods, ceramics, sundry goods, and other
Business office	June 1943	In Robinson Department Store building, Raffles Place	
First seamen's home	Dec. 1943	Beach Road	Accommodation for sailors, and running a restaurant and kiosk
Second seamen's home	Dec. 1943	Bras Basah Road	Accommodation for the quarter-deck, and running a restaurant
Farm	Dec. 1943	Paya Lebar	Raising domestic animals and growing vegetables for seamen's homes
Restaurant for substitute food	July 1944	On third floor of Robinson Department Store building	Sales of tapioca noodles, and tapioca dumplings covered with bean jam

Source: Constructed from Matsuzakaya 1981: 67; Takenaka 1964: 513.

Matsuzakaya was also engaged in various activities in the Malay Peninsula. As from 1 October 1943, it ran, for example, the Perak Highlands Hotel (the former Cameron Highlands Hotel) in Cameron Highlands. As tea was grown widely in Tanah Rata village near the hotel, Matsuzakaya obtained an exclusive right for tea distribution from a tea-processing factory with the purpose of wholesaling tea in the Malay Peninsula and retailing it at its Syonan office (Takenaka 1964 : 514).[10]

As for Shirakiya, its overseas activities started when it began, together with Daimaru and Matsuzakaya, to cater for military requirements in China at the instance of the Japanese Ministry of Commerce and Industry in the 1930s (Shirakiya 1957: 517). During the occupation period, Shirakiya moved into Syonan and Sumatra. Although it opened a department store in the building of Whiteway in Syonan, there is no information available about its retail business. It also opened a canteen for the army, and ran soap and leather-goods factories (Shinozaki 1976: 80; Shirakiya 1957: 522). It is worth noting that Shirakiya was a kind of a 'purveyor' to the Japanese Army (OHI Nukata), for it even manufactured military swords at Shirakiya Token Seisakujo (Shirakiya Sword Manufacturing Works) at Ichigaya, Ushigome

Ward (part of present-day Shinjuku Ward) in Tokyo, to meet military requirements (Shirakiya 1957: 530). In Syonan, military swords were sold at Shirakiya's department store (OHI Nukata). There is not much information about its activities in Sumatra, but, according to its company history book, it ran a military canteen, and manufactured crockery (Shirakiya 1957: 522).

Distribution control system

The Department of Commerce and Industry of the Syonan Special Municipality organised *haikyu kumiai* (ration associations) of local retailers. There were *haikyu kumiai* for rice, dried fish, vegetables, sugar and many other daily necessities, and rationed commodities were supplied to local consumers through them (Shingaporu Shiseikai 1986: 171). The department also set up Syonan Busshi Haikyu Kumiai (the Syonan Commodities Ration Association) with the purpose of controlling various *haikyu kumiai*, and put pre-war Japanese residents in charge of it. Sugiyama Shozo, the president of Nanyo Shoko, took office as the managing director, while Uchida Takeo of Baba Shoten, Satake Toshio of Satake Shokai, and others were appointed as directors.[11] Moreover, Fukuda Kurahachi of Echigoya Gofukuten was put in charge of procuring commodities, for he could make use of his long-time experience as a sales manager in pre-war Singapore.[12] The Japanese were assisted by local overseas Chinese to carry out the duties of the association, and some of the overseas Chinese made use of their working experiences to launch new business with Japan in the post-war period. Hsieh K'ai Kuo was a case in point. He set up the Singapore Tancho (Chikku) Company to trade in Tancho cosmetic products (Shinozaki 1982: 54; *idem* 1978a: 56).

The Japanese stated in public that the main purpose of *haikyu kumiai* was to stabilise prices and improve the efficiency of the internal distribution system, but this was not entirely true. In fact, through *haikyu kumiai* they tried to collect as much essential materials as possible, and only after they had got hold of sufficient stocks for military purposes was the remainder rationed out to local people (Hung 1986: 200).

One would then wonder if the distribution control system functioned well. Rice, which was the staple food, began to be rationed in April 1942, and, in order to make the system more effective, ration cards were issued to local people from August of that year onwards. Syonan and the Malay Peninsula imported rice mainly from Burma and Thailand by ship, but it became increasingly difficult to do so owing to the Allies' submarine attacks on Japanese ships. From the autumn of 1943 onwards, it became virtually impossible to transport rice by large ships from Burma to Syonan and Malaya, and small sailing and wooden vessels had to be used. As for Thai rice, it was transported more and more by rail, when ships carrying rice were increasingly attacked by the Allies' submarines off the east coast of the Malay Peninsula. Actually, the volume of rice imports into Syonan declined sharply from 21,500 metric tons during the period from October 1942 to March 1943 to 5,250 metric tons during the period from October 1944 to March 1945 (Kurasawa 1997: 155). Besides, as the Japanese kept rice in stock for future battles, the staple food became increasingly scarce for local inhabitants. Indeed, with the deterioration of the war, the monthly rice ration for a local male was cut down from 20 *katis* on 10 March 1942 to 12 *katis* on 1 September 1943, and 8 *katis* on 11 February 1944. As for the ration for a local woman, it was reduced from 20 *katis* to 9 *katis* and then 6 *katis*. However, the Japanese were treated differently, as the ration for them was reduced from 20 *katis* per person to 14 *katis* and 12 *katis* (Kratoska 1998: 253). It is highly likely that, in addition to their rations, the Japanese were in a position to get extra rice by various means including bribery, thanks to their position as the 'rulers'.

It seems that other daily necessities were not well rationed out to local people. The controlled distribution system did not function well, partly because, often under the auspices of the Japanese, black markets flourished in different parts of Syonan. The Japanese, mostly in collaboration with overseas Chinese merchants, bought up linen, furniture, cutlery, electrical appliances, watches, jewellery and many other goods, and it was said that the moment a *haikyu kumiai* for a specific commodity was set up, that commodity disappeared from the market, causing prices to rise sharply (Thio 1991: 103–6). Actually, large numbers of hawkers sold goods in the streets, while there were those who visited houses for sales of goods (OHI Cheah). Although the number of hawkers was 6,000 in 1941, it had risen to between 20,000 and 30,000 by the end of the Japanese occupation (Thio 1991: 104).[13]

The local people suffered doubly from critical food shortage and hyperinflation. Prices of goods shot up, not only because of the over-issuing of military notes, but also because of the grave shortage of all types of goods on the open market. The price of an electric bulb, for example, rose from 45 cents in December 1941 to over $210 in August 1945, and that of rice per *pikul* (about 133.3 lb) from $5 in December 1941 to $4,000 in June 1945 (*ibid.*: 103).

In order to deal with the food shortage, the Japanese military authorities offered technical and financial assistance to the local people to grow their own foods. But since there was not much progress, in 1944 they threatened them with a stern warning that those who did not co-operate in the self-sufficiency programme would be punished. Most of the local inhabitants then started growing vegetables, tapioca, sweet potatoes and other edible crops, and kept domestic animals such as hens in their front gardens to supplement their food. Children also dug school grounds for planting. Consequently, the critical food situation was somewhat alleviated, but it was nevertheless far from solved (Turnbull 1977: 204–5; OHI Lee).

However, one should not assume that there was no meat or fish available during the occupation period. A local Chinese recalls that 'the poor could

Table 5.6 Numbers of births and deaths in Singapore

Year	Births	Deaths	Balance
1935	25,880	13,920	11,960
1939	34,613	14,197	20,416
1941	34,421	15,975	18,446
1942	27,635	29,833	−2,198
1943	31,266	21,936	9,330
1944	31,722	42,751	−11,029
1945	24,441	35,330	−10,889
1946	38,654	15,287	23,367

Source: Constructed from DSS 1983: 10.

not buy fresh fish and decent ingredients for two years. . . . However, there were plentiful supplies of huge fish and lumps of meat in restaurants, *ryotei*, and stalls' (Hung 1986: 202). Tan Cheng Hwee who worked for the Japanese-controlled Cold Storage Company, recalls that, in the Cold Storage warehouse with 26 cold storage rooms in Orchard Road, there were huge quantities of pork, which had been put in stock before the Japanese occupation and which amounted to over two and half years' supplies. However, it was distributed only to hospitals and the Japanese Army. There were also large stocks of deep-frozen mutton there, but since the Japanese were not in the habit of eating mutton, they remained intact (OHI Tan).

As Table 5.6 shows, deaths far exceeded births in the Syonan years. The number of deaths rose greatly, especially in 1944 and 1945, even though fighting did not really take place between the Allied forces and the Japanese Army in Syonan. It was largely because all the hospitals gave priority to the Japanese, while, even if there were general practitioners, patients themselves had to procure the necessary medicines at high cost on the black market (OHI Ang). These statistical figures reveal clearly the appalling living conditions of local inhabitants, which were exacerbated by the food shortage and the lack of medical facilities.

MANUFACTURING SECTOR

In pre-war Singapore there was no major Japanese manufacturing firm, with the notable exception of Eifuku Sangyo, which was engaged in fisheries, commerce and manufacturing (including ice production). However, as Table 5.7 shows, there were large numbers of Japanese companies engaged in manufacturing activities in Syonan at the instance of the Japanese Ministry of Army. Most of these companies were there for the first time, while quite a few workshops were newly set up for military purposes. Shortly after the fall

129

of Singapore in February 1942, the Japanese military authorities sequestered the production facilities, mostly owned by the Europeans and Americans, and commissioned Japanese companies to manage them. Moreover, some Japanese companies attempted to seize factories from local Chinese owners without permission from the military authorities (Shingaporu Shiseikai 1986: 171–2; Shinozaki 1982: 49). The Nihon Chisso Kaisha (Japan Nitrogen Company), for example, took over the Ho Hong Oil Mills by force to produce soap. In response, Lim Peng Mau, the president of the company, made a petition to the Syonan Special Municipality. Eventually, through the intervention of its official, Shinozaki Mamoru, Lim agreed to lease out the factory to the Japanese firm for three years, provided that all his employees would be kept (Shinozaki 1982: 49–50).[14] There were other cases like this, including the Johore Pineapple Factory. It is also said that certain high-ranking officers in the army and officials of the Special Municipality acted as directors of the sequestered Western companies, or took over Chinese-owned companies (Thio 1991: 105).

Table 5.7 lists Japanese manufacturing companies and the production capacity of their workshops/plants in Syonan. However, since we have no production figures, we are not in a position to know how much was actually produced at these workshops. As the shipping tonnage declined rapidly owing to the sinking of Japanese transport ships by the Allies' submarines, it became increasingly difficult to obtain machinery, parts and raw materials, while there was a grave shortage of Japanese engineers and skilled workers. Consequently, most factories were obliged to operate far below their production capacity.

It should be borne in mind that various military production figures were much exaggerated during the occupation period. Hashimoto Tokuju, who worked as an engineer building wooden ships for both the Eifuku Sangyo Koshi and the Japanese Army, recalls:

> Conferences on shipbuilding for the whole of Southeast Asian region were frequently held. . . . As the shipyard at Kuantan was still under construction, not more than 10 ships could be built in 1943. At a shipbuilding meeting, it was decided that 10 ships would be built. However, in a document to be submitted by a staff officer to the general headquarters [in Syonan], it was unilaterally changed to 40 ships. . . . It was really shocking that in all cases figures were falsified like this, and were reported to the Imperial Headquarters [in Tokyo], which in turn made a military plan based on such far-fetched figures.
>
> (Hashimoto 1952: 350)

Incidentally, for the purpose of the future economic construction of Syonan, the Japanese Military Administration attempted to replace the

British education system with the Japanese one.[15] There is a controversy about the merit of the replacement. Although the British had placed much emphasis on learning, the Japanese stressed the technical and practical aspects of education, simply because they were in need of skilled and semi-skilled workers for military production. They therefore replaced secondary schools with vocational and technical schools to provide technical education to teenagers who were recruited locally. According to Eunice Thio, those youths who received technical education during the occupation period played a useful role in the economic reconstruction of Singapore in the post-war period. Indeed, the establishment of the Polytechnic in 1954 was partly a result of the war-time education of that segment of the population (Thio 1991: 104–5).

However, there is a negative view about the Japanese education policy. Chou Chu Chi who worked as a mechanic at the Seletar naval station during the occupation period, recalls:

> At the beginning of the occupation, the Japanese forces recruited large numbers of Chinese workers' children, and put them in the training school for young workers at the Navy's Engineering Work Section. Children of up to 14–15 years old were all put there. . . . They were taught Japanese, and were given lectures and military training in the ratio of two to three. They graduated from the school after 6 months, and then undertook work practices at each machine factory. But, many of them escaped from the naval camp, because of low wages, hard work, and under-nourishment. . . . As the Japanese forces could not recruit juvenile workers in the Syonan city or at the naval station, they had to send men to the countryside to recruit them. . . . During the period of over three years, more than 1,000 juvenile workers applied, but some 80 per cent of them escaped one after another.
>
> (Chou 1986: 112–13)

Although Chou is highly critical of the treatment of local workers at the naval station, and may have overstated the case, there must have been some truth in his description. At any rate, what and how Japanese education contributed to the economic development of Singapore in the post-war period is a topic for further discussions.

Manufacturing activities by Japanese firms

We shall make three case studies of manufacturing industry, namely assembling and repairing of motor vehicles, ship-building and ship-repairing, and beer-brewing, in order to show how Japanese companies re-opened and ran the sequestered Western factories and other production facilities in Syonan.

Table 5.7 Production facilities under the jurisdiction of the Japanese Army in
Syonan at the end of World War II

Name of workshop or type of work	Company in charge	Main products	Monthly production capacity	Remarks
Syonan Smeltery	Mitsui Kozan	Tin, copper, lead, zinc, antimony	800 tons of tin, 23 tons of copper, 800 tons of other	Pulau Brani
Furukawa Kogyosho	Furukawa Kogyosho	Bauxite	80,000 tons	Pulau Bintan
Machinery and appliances	Tokyo Shibaura Denki	Nails	80 tons	Enemy property
Machinery and appliances	Tokyo Shibaura Denki	Electric bulbs	¥100,000 worth of electric bulbs	Newly established
Machinery and appliances	Nichinan Zosen Zoki	Nails, steel bar	100 tons	
	Ishii Seimitsu Kikai	Repair of machinery, parts production	100 machine tools	Newly established
	Sakaguchi Kosan	Rolled steel	450 tons of primary product, 160 tons of secondary products	Newly established
	Osaka Teppan	Manufacture and repair of drums	Manufacturing: 35,000 drums; repairing: 40,000 drums	Mostly 'enemy' property
Factory for submarine cables	Nippon Kaitei Densen	Submarine cables and other	47 workers	Mostly 'enemy' property
Communica -tions workshop	Tokyo Shibaura Denki	Repair of wireless	37 workers	
Syonan Denseikyoku's Workshop	Syonan Denseikyoku	Assembly of telephonic equipment, and other	270 workers	'Enemy' property
Machinery and appliances	Kokusai Denki Tsushin	Repair of wireless communications related equipment	30 workers	Mostly newly established
	Furukawa Kogyo	Repairing of machinery and small boats	300 workers, 80 machine tools, can-manufacturing facilities	Pulau Bintan, newly established
Chemical industry	Nippon Rika	Oxygen	25,000 m^3	'Enemy' property
	Yokohama Gomu	Rubber products	About 450 workers	Mostly 'enemy' property
	Chuo Gomu	Rubber products		'Enemy' property

Table 5.7 (Continued)

Name of workshop or type of work	Company in charge	Main products	Monthly production capacity	Remarks
	Dai Nippon Toryo	Paints	70,000 tons	'Enemy' property
	Nissan Kagaku	Paints	100,000 tons	Newly established
	Nippon Gikaku	Imitation leather	Under construction	Newly established
	Oji Seishi	Paper	20 tons	Newly established
	Kurosaki Yogyo	Bricks	¥1 million worth of bricks	Mostly 'enemy' property
	Kurosaki Yogyo	Firebricks	¥100,000 worth of firebricks	Newly established
	Yokohama Gomu	Tyres for motor vehicles	4,000 tyres	Newly established
Repair of motor vehicles	Nissan Motors Co. Ltd	Repair of motor vehicles	300 skilled and semi-skilled workers	Three factories
Rikuo Syonan workshop	Rikuo Jidosha	Repair of motor vehicles	110 skilled and semi-skilled workers	Two factories
Syonan Workshop of Teikoku Jidosha	Teikoku Jidosha	Repair of motor vehicles	75 skilled and semi-skilled workers	
Diesel automobile workshop	Diesel Jidosha Kogyo	Repair of motor vehicles	150 skilled and semi-skilled workers	Two factories
Sawmill	Kaijikyoku Zosenjo	Sawing	1,300[a]	Newly established
	Takegoshi Seizaisho	Sawing	800[a]	Newly established
	Ataka Sangyo	Sawing	500[a]	Newly established
	Oji Seishi	Sawing	700[a]	Newly established
	Takasu Shokai	Wooden barrels	2,000 barrels	Newly established
	Nosaki Sangyo	Wooden barrels	4,000 barrels	Newly established
	Nisshin Beniya	Wood veneer	60,000 pieces	Newly established
Others	Kimura Seiyaku	Pharmaceuticals		'Enemy' property
	Syonan Seiyaku	Pharmaceuticals		Newly established
	Nippon Hassoden	Electric power	20,000 kilo watts	'Enemy' property
	Kokusai Denki Tsushin	Broadcasting		

Source: NIDS, no. 97, June 1946.
Note
[a] The original military document does not give any unit.

133

The Nissan Motors Co. Ltd

The Japanese Military Administration was in need of large numbers of motor vehicles for the exploitation of natural resources and the restoration of security in Syonan and Malaya. It therefore decided to repair the vehicles seized from the 'enemies', most of which were in Syonan, and redistribute them to other parts of the region. In late March 1942, repair work began at the requisitioned garages, with the co-operation of overseas Chinese-owned repair workshops, and the Administration managed to complete the first stage of redistribution, despite the grave shortage of spare parts and the poor conditions of the garages (NIDS, no. 17, October 1943).

The Military Administration was initially in charge of repairing automobiles, but it then ordered the Nissan Motors Co. Ltd to undertake the following four types of works in the Syonan–Malaya region: (a) import and export trade in motor vehicles and parts, (b) manufacturing and assembling of motor vehicles and parts (only in Syonan), (c) distribution of motor vehicles and parts, (d) maintenance and repairing of motor vehicles and parts. It was on 21 October 1942 that Nissan began operations (*ibid.*). Incidentally, according to Nissan's company history book, in June 1942 the company set up a Southeast Asia office in Syonan, and established representative offices in Bangkok, Rangoon, Hanoi and Saigon. This meant that Nissan had moved into Syonan several months before the Military Administration ordered the company to be in charge of the motor vehicle-related works in October 1942 (Nissan Jidosha Chosabu 1983: 66).

Nissan's major work in the Syonan–Malaya region was the assembling of motor vehicles at Ford's assembly plant in Syonan. Ford was locally incorporated in November 1926, and at the end of 1941 it built a modern car assembly factory in Upper Bukit Timah Road. However, after the fall of Singapore, it was requisitioned by the Japanese Army, and was run by the Japanese company for the assembly of lorries (SICC 1979: 134). In January 1943 the preparations for the re-opening of the assembly factory began to be made by eight Japanese from Nissan and 130 local workers. In the meantime, assembly parts for 300 knockdown lorries for military use and those for 120 knockdown vehicles for civilian use were landed at Syonan in mid-May and mid-June respectively. The assembling of the first lorry was completed on 3 July 1943.

As of late October 1943, six Japanese and 188 local workers were employed at the factory with a monthly production capacity of 150 vehicles (NIDS, no. 17, October 1943).[16] Aziz bin Rahim Khan Surattee, a Malay who worked as an assembly worker there for a year from 1943 to 1944, recalls that about ten lorries were assembled a day. There were four Japanese (the factory head and three engineers), and between 200 and 300 local workers (Chinese, Malays and Indians). Although he did heavy work from eight to five o'clock six days a week (with one hour lunch-time break), he was paid a mere $10 per week with one *kati* of rice, which was obviously not sufficient for living (OHI Aziz).

It is not clear how long this mass production lasted, but, since Japanese ships were sunk one after another by the Allied powers' submarines after the middle of 1943, the plant must have found it increasingly difficult to obtain necessary parts from Japan. Nevertheless, Japanese officials and high-ranking officers continued to drive new cars in Syonan until the end of the war (Corners 1981: 56). It is possible that the assembly of new cars continued albeit with increasing difficulties. Also, with repair work, vehicles were apparently available in sufficient numbers so that the daily life of the Japanese was not much affected.

Nissan was also commissioned to run a number of repair workshops. For example, on 21 October 1942 it began to undertake work at the former workshops of the Malayan Motors and the Universal Motors. These had a combined repairing capacity of 150 vehicles a month, employing 112 local workers. On the same day, it also embarked on repair work at the Borneo Motors workshop with 176 workers, which was capable of repairing 100 vehicles a month (NIDS, no. 17, October 1943).

Ship-building

The ship-building and ship-repairing industry was indispensable for the Japanese, not only because they required a huge amount of shipping for transportation of goods and people between Japan and Southeast Asia, but also because war-damaged ships had to be repaired quickly. Indeed, Syonan was designated by the Japanese Navy as the leading base for ship-repairing and building wooden ships for the Southeast Asian region.

When the Malayan operations began on 8 December 1941, the Japanese Navy informed the Mitsubishi Heavy Industries Ltd that in the event of the fall of Singapore, the reconstruction and management of the dockyards at Keppel Harbour and Tanjong Rhu would be entrusted to the company. For that task, Mitsubishi then chose its Kobe Shipyard which was well experienced in repairing war-ships.

The first batch of eleven clerical staff and 83 workers left Kobe in late January 1942, and, after staying in Saigon for some time, they arrived at the Seletar harbour in Syonan on 2 March (Mitsubishi Jukogyo 1956: 320; Minamikai 1968: 2–3). A few days before the fall of Singapore, the British Army had begun to destroy the shipyard, but they failed to render it beyond repair, because the occupation of the island by the Japanese Army was unexpectedly fast. Shortly after the Japanese sequestered it, many of the former local workers were brought back by the four former local executives of the shipyard. As a result, the Kobe Shipyard could embark on the reconstruction work fairly smoothly. The first task was to restore the docks to the former state as soon as possible so that they could be used for repairing war-ships. However, since it was very dangerous for anyone to check the various facilities, local workers were used for this purpose when the shipyard was re-opened. One of the workers from the Kobe Shipyard who worked at the shipyard in Syonan recalls:

> There would be no danger, if there was pressure after igniting in the boiler room. All the Japanese evacuated from there, after ordering some local workers to ignite. We told them to report to us when the pressure reached 5 pounds, and watched their work from a distance. During that time, we had a terrible feeling beyond description, and felt as if it took a very long time.
>
> (Asano 1968: 44)

When the third dock had been restored to its former state by 21 March, the workers began to repair a special service vessel, *Tsurumi*, which had been damaged by a torpedo. By June, all the dockyards had been repaired, and in July the shipyard was given a new name, the Mitsubishi Heavy Industries' Syonan Shipyard, which consisted of the First Shipyard at Keppel Harbour and the Second Shipyard at Tanjong Rhu (see Table 5.8) (Mitsubishi Jukogyo 1956: 317–18; Minamikai 1968: 3–4).

After the Kobe Shipyard had begun to undertake ship-repairing at Syonan, other Japanese ship-building companies began operations there, competing for skilled workers. In order to alleviate the labour shortage, a worker-training scheme was introduced at the Syonan Shipyard to secure local workers, while youths were brought from Java and other parts of Southeast Asia to the shipyard for training (Minamikai 1968: 11).

The Syonan Shipyard was mainly engaged in repairing damaged ships in the Southeast Asian region, and constantly kept over 30 ships under repair in its docks. Its rate of operation was close to 100 per cent. During the period of three years and five months from March 1942 to August 1945, the number of vessels repaired at the shipyard was 2,364 (or a total of 5.2 million gross tons). However, it had great difficulties in building new ships

Table 5.8 The facilities at the Syonan Shipyard

	Land area (sq. yards)	Building area (sq. yards)	Size of five dry docks (in feet)		
			Length	Width	Depth
First shipyard at Keppel Harbour	177,930	47,448	377	47	15
			430	62	17
			852	95	33
Second shipyard at Tanjong Rhu	59,310	11,862	458	63	20
			460	56	21

Source: Constructed from Mitsubishi Jukogyo 1956: 317–18.

due to the shortage of raw materials and machinery. In fact, apart from the completion in December 1942 of two steel tugboats (140 gross tons each) which had been under construction by a British ship-building company, only two high-speed wooden vessels and five others (lighters and motor launches) were built there (Minamikai 1968: 11–12).

By September 1944 nine teams totalling 287 employees of the Kobe Shipyard had been sent to Syonan, but some of them died or returned to Japan due to illness or other reasons. As a result, at the end of 1944, there were 243 Japanese working at the Syonan Shipyard, of whom 87 were clerical staff and 156 were workers. The number of local workers rose from 425 at the beginning of the operations to 1,500 in May 1942 and 3,200 in May 1943. As for their racial composition, Chinese accounted for 60 per cent, and the remainder comprised Indians and Malays in a more or less equal ratio.

Now we shall examine the building of wooden ships. Table 5.7 does not show any Japanese ship-building company building wooden ships in Syonan, because it covers only those companies under the control of the Ministry of the Army. However, large numbers of wooden ships were constructed by some Japanese firms there. As a matter of fact, Prime Minister Tojo Hideki visited Singapore on 5 July 1943 to give words of encouragement to Japanese soldiers in the Southeast Asian battle lines. He stayed about one hour at the Syonan general headquarters where he spent about half an hour, urging the construction of wooden ships (Hashimoto 1952: 330).

When Hashimoto Tokuju landed at Syonan on 8 August 1942, there was already a Japanese ship-building company, called the Nippon Giso Kaisha, building wooden vessels at a site on reclaimed land. There were many engineers and shipwrights working there, but, since there was no one dependable, Hashimoto was asked to become a technical advisor to them. At the work site the company began to build its first ship on 20 October 1942, and managed to launch it on 30 March 1943. It was a 150-ton wartime standard freight vessel which was curved and semi-Western in shape. It was said that, as this was the first ship to be built in Southeast Asia, the launching ceremony was filmed and was shown in Japan. However, there was constant disagreement about personnel matters at the shipyard, causing much delay in completing ships. Eventually, the shipyard was requisitioned by the military authorities in the middle of June 1943 to become the shipyard of the Maritime Department of the Military Administration at Syonan. It continued to build wooden ships until the end of the war (Hashimoto 1952: 343).

Eifuku Sangyo also built various types of wooden ships under orders from the military authorities. For example, in 1943 the company built 60 large motor launches measuring 39.76 ft in length, 14.91 ft in width, and 4.47 ft in depth in preparation for the India landing operations. In Southeast Asia, thousands of such motor launches were built by various Japanese ship-building companies, but they were all wasted, for the plan for the operations was called off due to the deterioration of the war. Eifuku Sangyo then built surface suicide (*kamikaze*) boats (Hashimoto 1952: 354). Although there is no accurate figure for the total tonnage of the wooden vessels built in Southeast Asia during the occupation, it has been estimated at 100,000 gross tons, including wartime standard freight vessels, lighters, fishing boats and other vessels (*ibid.*: 355).

Breweries

Large quantities of Japanese beer were imported into British Malaya until the early 1930s when the colonial authorities began to impose restrictions on imported beers with a view to protecting the two new local breweries, namely the Malayan Breweries Ltd and the Archipelago Breweries Ltd. The Malayan Breweries Ltd was set up by Fraser & Neave Ltd in 1931 as a joint venture with the Netherlands' Heineken to produce Tiger-brand beer, while the Archipelago Breweries Ltd was established by German capital in 1932 to produce Anchor-brand beer. When World War II broke out, the Straits Settlements government sequestered the Archipelago Breweries Ltd as an enemy property, and sold it to Fraser & Neave Ltd in 1941, which then began to monopolise beer production in the whole of British Malaya (Iwasaki 1990: 120–1). However, when the Japanese occupied Singapore in February 1942, they in turn sequestered the two breweries.

In November 1942 the Kirin Breweries Ltd was ordered by the Military Administration to run the Malayan Breweries Ltd in Alexandra Road, and began its operation in the following month (NIDS, no. 29, March 1943). It produced beer for civilian and military consumption, using locally obtained raw materials as well as raw materials and necessary equipment brought from Kirin's factories in Japan (Kirin Biru 1957: 150–1). The Malayan Breweries factory was very modern. The Military Administration stated that 'the building and machines are new, and well-maintained. For example, the transport of yeast from a storage to a tank is done by an air-conveyor method, while cleaning of bottles, bottling, and labelling are all done automatically' (NIDS, no. 29, March 1943).[17]

The factory was capable of producing 200,000 boxes (4 dozen bottles per box) per year, employing 100 male and 50 female workers. It required some 1,000 tons of yeast a year, and initially made use of what was in stock. However, by March 1943 it had used it up, and had to import it from Japan. As for hops, the factory had sufficient quantities in stock. There were 1.2 million bottles, as of March 1943, which were sufficient for beer production. Old bottles were collected at 3 cents per bottle (*ibid.*). There was also a plan to manufacture bottles locally, and although technicians were brought from Japan to prepare for it, it was not realised owing to the end of the war (Kirin Biru 1957: 150–1).

Besides the Kirin Breweries Ltd the Dai-Nippon Breweries Ltd (which was to split into two companies, Asahi and Sapporo in the post-war period) took over the Archipelago Breweries Ltd in Alexandra Road. As of February 1943, its monthly beer production amounted to about 80,000 bottles, catering exclusively for the army. The factory was occasionally short of bottles, and had to cease production temporarily. As a result, it offered to buy empty bottles at 5 cents each. The brewing facilities were excellent, whereas the storing and bottling facilities were rather outdated. The storing tanks were, for example, made of wood. One brew amounted to about 9,000 litres, which was much smaller than the average quantity in Japan. The factory at first made use of the Australian yeast of the pre-war period, but when it ran out of stock, it brought yeast from Japan. There was a two-year supply of Tasmanian hops, although the quality was considered to be low (NIDS, no. 29, March 1943).

KARAYUKI-SAN, RYOTEI AND COMFORT STATIONS

Revival of prostitution

As noted in Chapter 2, the Acting Japanese Consul-General, Yamazaki Heikichi, repealed licensed Japanese prostitution in Singapore in 1920, while the licensed prostitution system in British Malaya was finally abolished by the Colonial Administration in the early 1930s. However, quite a few *karayuki-san* continued to ply their illicit trade as sly prostitutes or ostensibly as hostesses working for *ryotei* (Japanese-style restaurants). In the pre-war period, there were two *ryotei*,[18] Shin Kiraku in Hylam Street, and Tamagawa in Katong, where there were young *geisha*, some of whom were from Nagasaki prefecture. Many of the *geisha* were detained by the British Army on the outbreak of the Pacific War in December 1941, and were subsequently transported to India (Shinozaki 1978a: 53–4).

When Singapore came under the control of the Japanese Army, the Japanese military authorities revived the sex industry. Many comfort stations and *ryotei* were set up to meet the sexual demand of troops and other Japanese, especially since large numbers of Japanese soldiers and officers, conscripted in Japan and China, were first brought to Syonan, and were then sent to various parts of Southeast Asia. Moreover, there were many employees of Japanese companies in the island, creating a further demand for sexual services.

Comfort stations

In Syonan, comfort stations were located at different places, including Pulau Bukum for the Japanese Navy (with comfort women being Indonesians). Pulau Blakang Mati (present-day Sentosa Island), Bukit Pasoh, Tanjong

Katong Road and Cairnhill Road (where there were Korean and Malay comfort women, as well as Japanese women who were reserved for high-ranking officers) (Hayashi Hirofumi 1994: 36–7).

According to Nagase Takashi, more than ten Korean women were brought to Pulau Blakang Mati in either September or October 1942, and were forced to become comfort women (OHI Nagase). One of these women seems to have been Kim Yun Shimu, who had been taken away with her friend by the Japanese Army on the way home from a photo shop in Korea. Although she attempted suicide, she failed and was made a comfort woman in Syonan (Yoon 1997: 196). Most of the other Koreans seem to have been forcibly recruited by the Japanese.

In the Katong area there were many local and Japanese brothels which were visited by Japanese military men and civilians alike (OHI Gay). In the Seletar naval station, almost all the comfort women were Chinese or Koreans (Hayashi Hirofumi 1994: 35, 38–9). The commissariat also sequestered a section of Cairnhill Road, and set up a comfort station there for the army. A 'boss' (probably a Japanese brothel-keeper) was brought from Korea to run it with a Taiwanese woman (Shinozaki 1976: 83). Hashimoto Tokuju, the ship-building manager of Eifuku Sangyo wrote in his diary on 1 November 1942 that he witnessed Japanese soldiers streaming into a comfort station, called Sakura Club, in Emerald Hill Road (Hashimoto 1964: 93).[19]

In China the large majority of Japanese comfort women were aged between 25 and 30, and were prostitutes, former prostitutes, waitresses or low-grade *geisha*. They were called *yamato nadeshiko* (women of Japan), and served mainly high-ranking Japanese officers charging much higher fees than those charged by Korean and other non-Japanese comfort women (Kim 1976: 95). In Syonan there were also Japanese comfort women serving high-ranking officers in Cairnhill Road (Hayashi Hirofumi 1994: 36–7). Besides them, there were many Japanese women in *ryotei*, filling the sexual needs of Japanese officers.

A certain Japanese who was a sergeant during the occupation period has testified that around October 1943 there were six comfort stations in Syonan, each of which kept 20 to 30 comfort women (Hayashi Hirofumi 1994: 39). This means that there were between 120 and 180 comfort women. But he evidently understated their numbers. Indeed, at the end of the war, there were some 600 Korean women alone in Syonan, the large majority of whom were comfort women. Since there were many comfort women of other nationalities, the total number would have been much larger than what the ex-sergeant claims. As a matter of fact, there were over 300 women who were attached to the comfort stations in the Cairnhill area alone (Shingaporu Nihonjinkai 1978: 85).

How did the Japanese army run comfort stations? Article 7 of the regulations concerning the running of comfort stations and hotels, issued by the Military Administration on 11 November 1943, stipulated that 'whereas the management of comfort stations should in principle be restricted to Japanese nationals, their employees [i.e. comfort women] ought to be locals as far as possible, and the employment of Japanese [women] ought to be kept to a minimum' (Hayashi Hirofumi 1993: 73). This was the main reason why the large majority of comfort women were Koreans, Chinese and local women. However, besides these Asian women there were also some Caucasian prisoners of war, who were forced to work at comfort stations (*Asahi Shimbun*, 22 July 1992).

On 5 March 1942, i.e. 20 days after the Japanese Army occupied Singapore, an advertisement for the recruitment of 'hostesses' appeared in the Chinese-language newspaper, *Syonan Jit Poh*, which was published by the propaganda corps of the Japanese Military Administration. The advertisement said that 'one hundred "hostesses" of any race aged between 17 and 28 were required, and those employed will be paid at least $150 per month'. The same advertisement appeared in the 7 and 8 March issues of the newspaper (*Syonan Jit Poh*, 5, 7 and 8 March 1942). However, as there were no applicants, Japanese soldiers under orders of the military authorities rounded up several hundred local women here and there, and allocated them to each military unit. Among the women were daughters of respectable families (Hung 1986: 149). The overseas Chinese women were in particular targeted for this purpose, partly because the Japanese Army wanted to punish the overseas Chinese in retaliation for their anti-Japanese activities. However, although the imposition of the 'gift money' of $50 million upon the overseas Chinese has been much discussed, the fate of the local women has been virtually forgotten in the history of Singapore (Hicks 1995: 92).

In Southeast Asia there were cases in which former *karayuki-san* were employed to run comfort stations. In the Malay Peninsula, the commissariat of the Twenty-Fifth Army was mainly concerned with the task of rear support, including the provision of necessary materials, but they also undertook the setting-up and running of comfort stations as well as the recruitment of women. According to an ex-soldier who belonged to the commissariat, he entered Kuala Lumpur on 23 May 1942, and was engaged in preparations for the opening of a comfort station there. He recruited 14 Japanese women in the city, of whom 12 were former *karayuki-san*. These women were all put in charge of gathering comfort women, and of running the comfort station. The remaining two were ordered to undertake the running of a military canteen (Hayashi Hirofumi 1993: 77–8). In fact, this is more or less confirmed by George Hicks, who writes that 'a special feature in Malaya was that about fourteen of the earlier generation of expatriate Japanese prostitutes who had settled in the country were employed managing comfort stations' (Hicks 1995: 93).

It should be noted that some Japanese companies benefited from the prosperity of comfort stations. In 1942, 6,450,000 condoms were sent to the military headquarters in Syonan by the Imperial Army Headquarters in

Tokyo. Moreover, the field workshop of the Twenty-Fifth Army ordered the Yokohama Gomu Manufacturing Company to produce condoms as well as rubber gloves for medical operations (Hayashi Hirofumi 1994: 40). According to a survey conducted by the research office of the general affairs department at the Military Administration on 8 February 1942, the company's first factory in Pasir Panjang Road mainly produced rubber hoses, belts, rubber shoes, pneumatic tyres, Bakelite products, and condoms (NIDS, no. 29, March 1943).

Ryotei

Besides the comfort stations, large numbers of *ryotei* were set up in Syonan under the auspices of the navy or the army. Sukemura Iwao, who was the chief of the engineering works section at the Syonan Special Municipality recalls that:

> From the early period of the occupation, there was a wide variety of Japanese *ryotei* and the like, ranging from high-class *ryotei* to cafés, and their owners and employees came from Japan, Manchuria, Taiwan, and Korea. There was no shortage of these places.
>
> (Shingaporu Shiseikai 1986: 292)

In fact, many of the women who worked at *ryotei* acted not only as hostesses but also as prostitutes (Hayashi Hirofumi 1994: 40).[20]

On 2 October 1942 Hashimoto Tokuju of Eifuku Sangyo went out to have lunch with Eifuku Akio, Eifuku Tora's younger bother, to a place called Asahi Kaikan, near their office. As Asahi Kaikan was designated by the Japanese Navy, only navy men could drink beer during the day-time, whereas ordinary customers were allowed to drink only after 6 p.m. There were many *kimono*-clad Japanese women there, brought from Canton, who were mainly natives of Amakusa in Kumamoto prefecture, Japan (Hashimoto 1964: 73).

It should be noted that there was military support behind the establishment of *ryotei* and other such places in the services industry in Syonan. Kim Il Myun argues:

> All the *ryotei* without exception were backed up by either the Army or the Navy. Indeed, it was on the recommendation of the military authorities that several luxurious houses in the city were converted into *ryotei* where geisha's gay voices and shamisen resounded.
>
> (Kim 1976: 191)

The owner of Yamatoya Ryokan (Yamatoya Hotel) in Izu Nagaoka Onsen in Japan, for example, recuited many women, and took them to Syonan where he opened *ryotei* for military officers at the hotels and restaurants which the

Military Administration had requisitioned (*ibid*.; Yamada Meiko 1992: 74–5).

Imai Koshizu managed a *ryotei* called Chikamatsu in Harbin in Manchuria before the outbreak of the Pacific War, and moved to Syonan in 1942 at the instance of a military man, who had formerly been a chief engineer (Shingaporu Shiseikai 1986: 297–8). With the financial support of Komatsu, a well-known *ryotei* in Shinbashi, Tokyo, she landed in Syonan in August 1942 with her executive staff. She was backed up by the army to open a high-class *ryotei*, also called Chikamatsu, on the shore in the Katong area. At first she targeted Japanese civilians as clients, expecting that the military personnel would account for some 30 per cent of her customers. But since the banquet charge was fixed at ¥50 for military personnel, and at ¥75 for civilians, the majority of customers turned out to be high-ranking officers. At the *ryotei*, according to Kamata Hisako who was a typist at the General Affairs Department of the Syonan Special Municipality, there were a total of 90 *geisha*, of whom 50 were from Tokyo, 30 from Osaka, and ten from Nagoya (Kamata 1978: 552). However, Hashimoto Tokuju who went there for pastime in mid-April 1943, claims that, as the *ryotei* originated in Nagoya, more than 50 per cent of the *geisha* (or more than 70 *geisha*) were Nagoya women (Hashimoto 1964: 144). At present, it is not possible to find out the Japanese hometowns of the *geisha*.

Moreover, the Nan-Hua Girls' School was closed after the fall of Singapore, and was sequestered by the Military Administration. It was then converted into a *ryotei* called Tsuruya, which had originally been a crab-dish restaurant in Omori, Tokyo (Shingaporu Shiseikai 1986: 202–4). Tsuruya occupied all the three storeys of the school, and had *tatami* mats on the floors. It employed some 80 Japanese women who were clad in *kimono* of different colours, and took only military personnel as customers. Indeed, one could not imagine that the war was going on at the time, for Tsuruya was doing a flourishing business (Hashimoto 1964: 138). However, as military personnel visited the *ryotei* every night, making great uproar, local residents in the neighbourhood made complaints to the owner of the *ryotei*. Subsequently, several houses around the *ryotei* were sequestered by the military authorities, and officers were frequently seen with Japanese women leaving the *ryotei* for these houses. Odate Shigeo, the Mayor of the Special Municipality, tried to sort it out with the owner of Tsuruya several times but was unsuccessful. He therefore had no choice but to make representations to Field Marshall Terauchi Hisaichi, with the result that the *ryotei* was finally closed down. However, it took six months before the closure (Shingaporu Shiseikai 1986: 202–4).

Military officers were not the only Japanese who frequented *ryotei*. Miyamoto Tatsuichi of the Mitsubishi Kobe Shipyard worked as the chief of the general affairs section of the Syonan Shipyard from May 1944 until the end of the war. He recalls:

> I was fairly busy to entertain our clients, including staffs of general trading companies, at Ryotei Minami, Tsukushi, and Taiga-So (Villa Tiger), the last of which was located in Pasir Panjang and managed by Mr Kadowaki, a former manager of the OSK.[21]
>
> (Minamikai 1968: 79)

Some Japanese company employees also visited local brothels (OHI Chong; OHI Nagase). Although brothels charged as much as $10 for one sexual encounter (OHI Nagase), such an amount may have been a pittance for Japanese customers.

At the end of June 1945 local people were suffering from both hyper-inflation and food shortage. However, Japanese *ryotei* were doing a brisk business thanks to their Japanese customers. Indeed, there was a privileged class in Syonan, comprising high-ranking military personnel, paramilitary personnel, staffs of trading and manufacturing firms, and some other Japanese (Hayashi Hirofumi 1994: 41).

The services industry, including comfort stations, brothels and *ryotei* prospered thanks to their close connections with the army and the navy, but it quickly disappeared from Singapore when Japan was defeated in the Pacific War. It seems obvious that, since the large majority of the comfort women were Taiwanese, Koreans and local women, the Japanese military authorities' declared objective of 'the liberation of Asians' in the Great East Asian War was nothing more than the Japanese rule over other Asians by racial discrimination.

CONCLUDING REMARKS

During the occupation period, Japan was engaged in economic activities in Syonan largely for the prosecution of the war. However, she was not able to achieve a great deal, not only because the occupation lasted for only three and half years, but also because the war situation moved against her. Nevertheless, one could point out several characteristics of her economic activities.

First, the structure of her economic activities was very different from that of the pre-war period. In the pre-war period, large Japanese trading companies, including Mitsui & Co. and Mitsubishi Corporation, were engaged in foreign trade, and Japanese banks, shipping companies and warehousing companies were active. But there were no large-scale Japanese firms in the manufacturing sector, with the notable exception of the Eifuku Sangyo Koshi, a locally incorporated fisheries company, which was engaged in ice-making and iron-working, *inter alia*. However, as soon as Singapore was captured by the Japanese Army, large numbers of Japanese manufacturing firms advanced into the island, and began to produce mainly military goods on orders of the Military Administration.

It should also be noted that, prior to the Pacific War, numerous Japanese shop-keepers were in the retail trade, but there were no Japanese department stores. However, in the early period of the occupation, three large department stores, namely Daimaru, Matsuzakaya and Shirakiya moved into Syonan, and were all engaged not only in retail trade but in other economic activities in collaboration with the military authorities. On the other hand, the Military Administration initially placed severe restrictions on the return of former shop-keepers.

Second, the Japanese fishing methods of the pre-war and occupation periods were adopted by local inhabitants in the post-war period. Prior to the Pacific War, the British collected licensing fees for boats and fishing gear from local fishermen, but made little effort to improve their productivity, apart from preserving territorial waters for their use. However, during the Japanese occupation period, the Japanese military authorities set up a Fisheries Training School in Syonan where local students were given training in fishing, fish breeding and other subjects for six months (*The Syonan Shimbun*, 27 March 1944; *idem*, 5 March 1945). In addition, Eifuku Sangyo employed many local fishermen since there was a grave shortage of Japanese fishermen in Singapore. It is likely that the local Chinese and Malays, trained at the school or employed by the company, acquired modern fishing techniques and made use of them in the post-war period.

In the immediate post-war years, there was a dire shortage of fresh fish caused by the absence of Japanese fishermen, and the British colony imported large quantities of fresh fish from Indonesia and the Federation of Malaya. In 1947, imports accounted for some 76.7 per cent of the fresh fish auctioned at the local fish markets (Le Mare 1950: 98). However, Chinese fishermen filled the gap created by the Japanese to a certain extent. They hired Japanese power boats from the Custodian of Property, conducting fishing in the waters of the Netherlands Indies, and purchasing fresh fish from the fishermen at sea to sell in Singapore. Additionally, the Chinese fishermen inherited the *muro ami* system from the Japanese, even though there was a shortage of skilled divers (*Blue Book,* 1949: 435). In 1951 the *muro ami* catch amounted to 332.5 tons (8 per cent of total catches by fishermen in Singapore), 354.7 tons (6.4 per cent) in 1952, and 250.9 tons (4.5 per cent) in 1953 (Tham 1954: 218).

Third, it was ironic that in the economic field the Japanese were most successful in encouraging the development of import-substitution industries. This was the direct result of the shipping shortages which forced local and Japanese firms to make use of locally available materials. Paper was produced with pulp from *lalang* (a kind of reed), bamboo and pineapple leaves, while ropes and twisted thread were made from pineapple fibre. Other substitutes included grease, lubricant, soap, toothbrushes and tooth powder. However, very few of the import-substitution industries survived the war or continued production in the post-war period (Turnbull 1977: 205; Thio 1991: 104).

Lastly, we would need to consider the impact of Japan's economic activities on the return of Japanese companies to Singapore and also on the Singapore government's plan for industrialisation in the post-war period. Although the occupation period lasted only for three and half years, Japan's economic activities were extensive, covering a wide range of economic fields. However, with the deterioration of the war, Japanese companies had great difficulties in obtaining raw materials, parts, and machinery from Japan and other parts of Southeast Asia because of the critical shortage of shipping, with the result that their Syonan factories and workshops were obliged to operate at a level far below their production capacity. Nevertheless, their experiences in economic activities in the Syonan era seem to have facilitated their return to Singapore in the post-war period. It seems certain that quite a few of the Japanese companies benefited, to a certain extent, from their familiarity with the local conditions and their personal relations with certain local people when they planned to return to Singapore and other parts of Southeast Asia in the post-war period. Moreover, as will be studied in the next chapter, the Singapore government, which tried to achieve industrialisation after the mid-1950s, was very anxious to obtain Japanese co-operation from the very beginning. It is probable that the industrial activities of the Japanese companies might have impressed some future Singaporean leaders immensely, even though the cruelty of the Japanese military rule was not forgotten by them.

6

JAPAN'S RETURN TO SINGAPORE
IN THE POST-WAR PERIOD

Japan lost all her overseas assets when she was defeated in the Pacific War, but she nevertheless began to return economically to Southeast Asia in the late 1940s. Her trade relations with the region started again in 1947 when her restricted private foreign trade began, while Japanese companies resumed their economic activities there well before the commencement of the payment of war reparations to Southeast Asian countries in the second half of the 1950s.

However, Japanese scholars have hitherto paid hardly any attention to Japan's economic relations with Singapore during the period from the late 1940s to the late 1950s. The reasons for it are not hard to find. First, Southeast Asian studies have largely focused on Japan's war responsibility and her return to Southeast Asia in relation to the payment of war reparations. The cases of Malaya and Singapore, however, have simply been ignored, mainly because Britain, on their behalf, renounced the right to demand war reparations. It was only in the 1960s, when the blood-debt issue arose, and incidentally to it, that the Japanese government had to negotiate with the two former British colonies about what was called the 'quasi-reparations'. Second, in their Far Eastern strategy, the Americans positioned Southeast Asia as a main source of raw materials and mineral fuels for the reconstruction of post-war Japan, and it happened that their positioning was identical with that of the *nanshin-ron* (Japan's southward advance concept) advocates. As Singapore was poor in natural resources, Japan did not seem to show much interest in the British colony. Lastly, Japan became less interested in Singapore, largely because she assumed that, as a result of its independence and the economic development of Southeast Asian countries, the British colony would play a decreasing role in the transit trade for the region in the future.

It is therefore not surprising that the period from the late 1940s until the mid-1950s is often regarded as a 'void period' of Japan's economic relations with Southeast Asia. For example, Yano Toru and Kobayashi Hideo maintain

147

that Japan's relations with the region in the post-war period began with the reparations payments (Yano 1975: 174–81; Kobayashi 1983: 2–4). Similarly, Igusa Kunio writes that, from the end of the Pacific War to the Korean War (1950–3), Japan did not have any economic policy on Asia, and it was only after a series of negotiations with Southeast Asian countries regarding war reparations that her economic relations with them became the object of public attention again (Igusa 1991: 206–7). Shibata Yoshimasa also argues that the payment of the war reparations to Southeast Asian countries for human and physical damages laid the grounds for Japan's return to the region's economic and political fields (Shibata 1995: 673).

The main object of this chapter is to study the circumstances in which Japan resumed economic relations with Singapore in the late 1940s and the 1950s, and examine how the colonial authorities and the government in Singapore responded to the return of Japanese firms. We attempt to prove that, contrary to the commonly held view, from the early years of the 'void period' Japan regarded Singapore as the base for her economic return to Southeast Asia in connection with the reconstruction of the Japanese economy, while at the same time the Singapore government regarded Japan as an indispensable partner for the country's industrialisation.

INTERNATIONAL FACTORS IN THE RETURN OF JAPAN TO SOUTHEAST ASIA

The Cold War and the American policy towards Japan

Immediately after Japan's defeat in the Pacific War in August 1945, occupation authorities were created under General Douglas MacArthur, the Supreme Commander of the Allied Powers (SCAP). At that time, there were two main objectives in the US policy on Japan, namely democratisation and demilitarisation. The Allies claimed that they had no responsibility for the reconstruction of the Japanese economy, for that task should be left to the Japanese people's own devices. To make the matters worse for Japan, a reparations survey mission headed by Edwin W. Pauley came to Tokyo in the autumn of 1945. In his final report of November 1946, Pauley recommended that military and industrial facilities totalling ¥2,466 million (at the 1939 prices) should be removed out of Japan, and used for the reconstruction of the Asian countries which had been under Japanese rule during the Pacific War (Nakamura 1981: 31). The Far Eastern Commission then attempted to implement the recommendation.[1] However, as its members could not agree on the allocation of reparations, in April 1947 the US government ordered the SCAP to go ahead with removing the facilities and machinery, and distributing them to China, the Philippines, Indonesia, Burma and the former British Malaya (Malaya and Singapore) (Hara 1994: 156; Kratoska 1998: 334–5).

However, there were growing communist influences throughout the world. The whole of Eastern Europe had come under the effective control of the Soviet Union by the time Germany surrendered in May 1945. In China civil war broke out in June 1946 when talks between the Communists and Nationalists broke down, while the North and South Korean regimes both began to claim control over the entire peninsula after the north Korean Workers' Party was formed in Pyongyang in August. Moreover, in Indo-China the war broke out between France and Vietnam in December when the French army attacked Vietnamese forces.

It was against this background that in March 1947 President Harry S. Truman announced the Truman Doctrine of providing military aid to Greece and Turkey with a view to financially assisting these East Mediterranean states in checking the threat of totalitarianism. In May, the under-secretary of the State Department, Dean Acheson, made a speech saying that the US intended to make Japan the workshop of Asia, for the Korean Peninsula was split into two, while China was politically unstable with the civil war going on (Igarashi 1995: 172). Moreover, George F. Kennan, head of the Policy Planning Staff of the State Department, who returned to Washington from Moscow in August 1947 where he had been an American diplomat for many years, argued that, as there was a danger of Japan becoming a Communist state, the US should give priority to the reconstruction of the Japanese economy by means of offering financial aid and removing obstacles such as reparations. Similarly, William Draper, the under-secretary of the Army, maintained that it would be necessary for the Americans to reconstruct and revive Japan for the sake of preserving political stability in Asia (Nakamura 1998: 289–90; Hagiwara 1978: 115). In early 1948, Kenneth C. Royall, secretary of the Army, stated that Japan should be turned into a bulwark against Communist threats in the region, while Draper announced in March that the reparations would be cut to ¥662 million (Nakamura 1981: 35). Finally, in May of the following year, the American representative of the Far Eastern Commission, McCoy, announced an end to the removal of war facilities and industrial plant out of Japan.

In Japan, the SCAP removed trade restrictions step by step, in accordance with the new American policy for Japan. Since its establishment in December 1945, the Board of Trade was the only organisation authorised to conduct foreign trade through the SCAP. However, in August 1947, it permitted foreign merchants to enter Japan and resume restricted private trading, thereby opening the way for Japanese trading companies and foreign merchants to negotiate directly, even though they could not as yet negotiate for prices. In October 1949, the SCAP issued 'a memorandum concerning export without permission', with a view to facilitating Japanese exports, and, at the same time, it backed up the economic activities by trading companies in foreign countries as it suggested that Japan ought to retaliate to 'those countries which refuse the entry of employees of Japanese trading companies' (Tsusho Sangyo Seisaku-shi 1990a: 208). Moreover, in January 1950, the SCAP allowed Japan to restore the pre-war private trading system, including negotiations for prices between Japanese trading companies and foreign merchants, and began to assist the country in exporting goods to Southeast Asia.

When restricted private foreign trade was resumed in 1947, the Japanese government sent a trade mission to India with the purpose of securing a source of raw materials and an export market for Japanese manufactures. Moreover, in July 1951 a joint SCAP–Japan investigation mission led by K.D. Morrow was sent to Bangkok, where it was split into sub-groups to visit Ceylon, Singapore, Indonesia, Borneo, Philippines, Taiwan, Burma, India and Pakistan. They visited these countries to explore the possibilities of expanding Japan's import and export trades with them, and of effectively tying in these trades with the Colombo Plan and the United Nations' Economic Commission for Asia and the Far East (ECAFE) (PRO, British Embassy in Tokyo to Foreign Office, 6 July 1951, FO731/92642).

By the mid-1950s, Japan had more or less re-established her export-promotion system. In 1947, the Bank of Tokyo was set up as a commercial bank, taking over the assets and employees of the Yokohama Specie Bank, and by a law of 1954 it became a specialised foreign exchange bank. In 1950, the Japan Export Bank (renamed the Japan Export-Import Bank in 1952), fully financed by the government, was established to grant loans to Japanese firms in connection with exports. Moreover, in 1954 the Kaigai Shijo Chosakai (Research Organisation of Overseas Markets),[2] the Kokusai Mihonichi Kyogikai (the International Trade Fair Council) and the Nihon Boeki Assenjo (Japan Trade Centre) were put together to form the Kaigai Boeki Shinkokai (the Overseas Trade Organization) which was renamed the Japan External Trade Organization (JETRO for short) in 1958, while the Saiko Yushutsu Kaigi (the Supreme Export Council) was created in the Cabinet (Nihon Boeki Shinkokai 1988: 5–7).

In 1953 an Export Transaction Law enacted in the previous year was revised, and was renamed the Export and Import Transaction Law. Under the revised law, various export associations were formed in respect to specific export items. As of March 1954, such associations numbered 34. Besides, as from 1953, the Japanese government began to assist trading companies financially by export-promotion measures, including tax deduction on profits arising from exports, and subsidies for setting up branches overseas (Tomen 1991: 122).

In the meantime, in September 1949, Secretary of State Dean Acheson decided once again to step up the conclusion of a peace treaty with Japan, which had been much delayed. In April 1950, John F. Dulles was appointed as special envoy, and sent to Japan in June to study possibilities of securing a peace treaty. Although the Korean War broke out in June, Dulles endeavoured to achieve a peace settlement, simply because he wanted to secure

Japan as a long-term ally in the Cold War (Igarashi 1995: 174). Naturally, there were some countries, notably the Philippines, Australia and New Zealand, which were vehemently opposed to any peace settlement with Japan, out of fear that Japan might re-emerge as a major military power (Kibata 1996: 46–50, 59). Therefore, Dulles made an arrangement for the ANZUS Securities Treaty, and the US–Philippines Mutual Defence Treaty, while at the same time drafting the Japan–US Security Pact.

Eventually, in September 1951 the peace conference was convened in San Francisco, and the Treaty of Peace with Japan was signed by 48 countries including the US and the UK. On 29 May 1952 Japan was able to join the International Monetary Fund and the International Bank for Reconstruction and Development (the World Bank), thanks to the American sponsorship, thereby paving the way for Japan's return to the international economic community (Hagiwara 1978: 142–3). However, Article 14 of the peace treaty stipulated that Japan had an obligation, in principle, to pay reparations; but in consideration of her inability to pay in cash, she could pay them in goods and services, including the raising of sunken ships, after negotiations with the countries concerned (Tsusho Sangyo Seisaku-shi 1990b: 40). Consequently, Japan conducted negotiations on reparations with various Southeast Asian countries, and managed to conclude reparations treaties with Burma in 1954, the Philippines in 1956, Indonesia in 1958 and South Vietnam in 1959, while she signed economic co-operation agreements with Cambodia in 1957 and Laos in 1958.[3]

In the meantime, in 1949 the Communists defeated the Nationalists in China, and the People's Republic of China was born. Although Britain recognised the new state, the US refused to do so, and wanted Japan to take the same position. In December 1951, Dulles was sent to Japan to make sure that the Japanese government would recognise Taiwan instead of China. However, since Prime Minister Yoshida attached great importance to his country's economic relations with the latter, he was reluctant to accept the US special envoy's proposal right away. On 24 December 1951 Yoshida informed Dulles in an official letter that Japan would not recognise China, for he wanted to have the peace treaty ratified by the US (Igarashi 1995: 176). Consequently, the US Senate ratified the peace treaty with Japan on 30 March 1952, while the Japanese government recognised Taiwan on 28 April.

As Japan had thus lost a huge Chinese market, she needed to step up her economic advance into Southeast Asia. Moreover, she needed large outlets for her goods, particularly since she was suffering from the economic recession after the end of the Korean war-boom.[4] Moreover, it was costly for her to import raw materials from the US (*Sekai*, December 1951: 56–69). Transport costs by American ships were particularly high. Since Japan needed to import cheap raw materials for the rehabilitation of domestic industries, Japanese shipping companies would need not only to rejoin international shipping routes which were then dominated by American shipping companies, but also to import raw materials from Southeast Asia instead of the US (*ibid.*: 66–7). Besides, Japan could count on Southeast Asia which would provide markets for her industrial goods thanks to the reparations payment in goods and services (Sudo 1992: 30, 34).

The return of Britain and Western firms to Singapore

In September 1945 the British returned to Singapore and Malaya, and the British Military Administration ran these territories until April 1946. However, at that time, there was a rising tide of independence movements in various parts of Southeast Asia. The Western colonial powers therefore had great difficulties in exercising direct control over their colonies as they had done in the pre-war period, for the image of Western prestige and invincibility had been much tarnished, largely because of the Japanese occupation of the region for three and a half years. Indeed, Sukarno and Mohammad Hatta declared the independence of Indonesia from the Netherlands on 17 August 1945, and Ho Chi Ming the independence of Vietnam from France on 2 September of the same year. The British were obviously anxious to keep their strong political and military position in the former British Malaya, but were also aware that they would not be able to hold it for many years against the wishes of the local inhabitants. They were also concerned with the possibility that the US and China might demand that they abandon the British territories in Southeast Asia (Takeshita 1995: 24–5).

Despite these changing political circumstances, in April 1946 the British separated Singapore from Malaya to create a crown colony, and appointed Sir Franklin Gimson to the governorship. They also made another crown colony, the Malayan Union, consisting of Malacca, Penang and the nine Malay states, but met with strong opposition from Malays, partly because the proposed citizenship laws offered an equal political status to all the citizens irrespective of races, while sultans had to relinquish their rights. Therefore, in 1948 the Malayan Union was replaced by the Federation of Malaya, with special political rights reserved for the Malays and the recognition of sultans as sovereigns with all the power and prestige they had formerly enjoyed. In 1957 the federation achieved complete independence from Britain.

In the economic field, the British Military Administration had to revive the war-damaged economy. By the end of the occupation period, essential services such as water, gas and electricity supplies had run down, while the docks, roads, railways and factories had also been severely damaged by Allied bombing. Seven firms were selected by the military authorities to provide essential services to the local community as soon as possible, and were given military support for securing employees and importing necessary materials. These firms were Singapore Cold Storage, Wearne/Borneo Motors, United Engineers, Singapore Traction Company, Hume Pipe Company, Fraser & Neave Breweries and Malayan Colliery (Turnbull 1977: 226, 255).

In the immediate post-war years, many other Western firms also resumed operations in the colony. For example, the Straits Trading Company had been engaged in tin-smelting at Pulau Brani before the Pacific War, but when the Japanese army reached Singapore in February 1942, seven European technicians of the company and the British military attempted to destroy the plant. Moreover, during the occupation, the Japanese abused the ten furnaces, for they attempted to smelt antimony, lead, bismuth, copper and cartridge cases instead of tin, while the Japanese and Allied bombers also destroyed the wharf and other facilities (Tregonning 1962: 56, 59, 61).

Shortly after the war, the Straits Trading Company wanted to rehabilitate Pulau Brani, and asked the British government for financial assistance. However, as it could not get any official support, the rehabilitation was left to their own devices. Fortunately, as the company had a 75-year association with the Chartered Bank, it was able to obtain loans from the bank. Also, some of the former European members of staff and many of the former Asian employees came back to Pulau Brani to resume their work (*ibid.*: 59–61).

The car assembly plant of Ford Motor Company at Upper Bukit Timah Road, which had been operated by Nissan Motors Co. Ltd during the occupation period had suffered severe war damage. However, by the end of 1945, the plant had been almost completely rehabilitated, and Ford resumed the assembling of passenger cars in 1946. It was also used by the British Military Administration for the repair of vehicles (*The Straits Times*, 12 February 1996). Completed cars were sold not only in Singapore but also in Malaya, North Borneo, Indonesia, Thailand, India, Burma and other parts of South and Southeast Asia (McKerron 1947: 61; SICC 1979: 134).

In the commerce sector, Cold Storage, Robinson & Co., John Little Ltd and other retail stores re-opened. Robinson's building at Raffles Place had been used by the Matsuzakaya Department Store during the occupation period, but as soon as the British returned to Singapore, it was requisitioned by the Military Administration, and was used as the headquarters by the Services' canteens and entertainment organisations, NAAFI and ENSA. Robinson & Co. resumed its retailing trade in the middle of 1946, when its premises was de-requisitioned, and it managed to make a profit of $1 million for the first year. It then continued to expand its business, dealing in high-quality goods, and attracting large numbers of customers. In 1955 it took over John Little Ltd (Robinson & Co. Ltd 1958: 16).

The Return of Japan to Southeast Asia and the British Response

The post-war world economy was dominated by the US, thanks to the Bretton Woods Agreement of 1944 which established two new institutions, namely the International Monetary Fund (IMF) and the International Bank for Reconstruction and Development. The two objectives of the IMF were to maintain exchange stability and to deal with problems of balance of payments. The US dollar became a key currency that was convertible with gold, while par value for the currencies of member countries was established in terms of gold or the US dollar. However, apart from the US, most other countries suffered a grave shortage of gold and had great difficulties in conducting foreign trade. They therefore needed to cut down payments in gold or US dollars as much as possible, by balancing their trade.

Japan's trade relations with other countries had been cut off in the immediate post-war years, but when the country's restricted private trade was permitted by the SCAP in 1947, she needed trade and payment agreements with other countries. However, since Japan was under occupation, it was not the Japanese government but the SCAP which negotiated on her behalf. As the sterling area had been very important as a source of raw materials and markets for her industrial goods, the SCAP and the British representative in Tokyo concluded various agreements concerning Japan's trade with the area. For example, in November, the SCAP on behalf of the Japanese government concluded with Britain an Interim Agreement for Financing Private Trade with Japan, which was the first post-war trade agreement between Japan and the sterling area. In May of the following year this agreement was replaced with an Overall Payment Agreement concerning the trade between Japan on the one hand and Britain, its colonies (excluding Hong Kong) and certain countries in the sterling area on the other. Subsequently, a 'Trade Agreement between Certain Countries in the Sterling Area and Occupied Japan' was concluded in November 1948 on the basis of an Overall Payment Agreement. All these agreements contained a clause that trade accounts were to be settled in US dollars every six months (Gaimusho and Tsusansho 1949: 2–8; Tsusho Sangyo Seisaku-shi 1990a: 168).

However, Britain had accumulated huge trade deficits with the US during World War II, and this led to a pound crisis in July 1946. The crisis continued to deteriorate until September 1949 when the pound sterling was devalued from US$4.03 to US$2.80. In August 1949 Britain began to negotiate for a new trade agreement with the SCAP on behalf of Japan, but the major issue was whether the currency of settlement should be changed from the US dollar to the pound sterling. This agreement was signed in November, and under its terms the value of the trade between Japan and the sterling area was fixed at a total of £143 million (some US$400 million), and the pound sterling became the currency of settlement. Moreover, as Japan continued to have a large surplus in trade with the sterling area, she was asked to increase imports of raw materials from it (*Asahi Shimbun*, 23 November 1949).

After private foreign trade became completely free in Japan in January 1950, the British could foresee the expansion of Japanese trade into Southeast Asia. While the British were engaged in negotiations for a peace settlement with Japan, they did not wish to see the re-emergence of the country as an economic power, or to compete with her especially in the markets of their colonies and dependencies (Kibata 1996: 33–5). For example, since the beginning of 1948 the ECAFE endeavoured to develop the Southeast Asian economies through the expansion of Asian trade, notably the trade with Japan, but Britain, together with the Philippines, continued to strongly oppose Japan's return to Southeast Asia (Sudo 1992: 32). This was simply because Britain regarded the Southeast Asian region as its sphere of influence, and feared that Japan's return would infringe on her interests notably in Singapore and Malaya which were 'money-makers' for her (Hagiwara 1991: 200–1). However, under strong American pressure, Britain had no choice but to accept America's Far Eastern strategy, in which Japan would be rehabilitated through the expansion of her trade with Southeast Asia. She renounced her rights to demand reparations for Malaya, Singapore and Hong Kong at the peace conference in San Francisco.

On 28 November 1951 the Commissioner-General for the UK in Southeast Asia reported to the British Foreign Office in a telegram:

> The early viability of Japan is a cardinal point in United States policy and although no official declaration has been made it seems fairly clear that it is the intention of the United States government that Japan shall achieve this viability by economic expansion in South East Asia. Japanese efforts to expand into South East Asia will therefore almost certainly receive United States backing. . . . It must be recognised, however, that Japanese expansion in South East Asia will affect important British interest in that area.
>
> (PRO, Commissioner General for the United Kingdom in Southeast Asia to Foreign Office, Telegram, 28 November 1951, FO371/99439)

He then suggested two things to London in the same telegram; first, Britain had to have talks with the US government concerning the Japanese problem at an early date, and second, she had to take 'advantage of the friendly and co-operative attitude of the Japanese government towards the United Kingdom to secure their collaboration in an orderly expansion of trade. . . . Their return to South East Asia should be viewed with friendly understanding' (*ibid.*).

In Britain, however, Japan was understandably not popular. On 27 November 1951, Asami Koichiro, the director of the London office of the Japanese Foreign Ministry, reported in a telegram to Tokyo:

> The peace treaty with Japan did not seem to be enthusiastically welcomed by the British. . . . It should be understood that at the House of Commons a bill for the ratification of the Treaty of Peace in San Francisco was passed only because of necessity.

He also reported that the following points were made by some MPs: (a) under the reparations system, raw materials are sent to Japan, and goods made thereof may lead to the Japanese monopoly of markets; (b) as the Japanese ceramics manufacturers have copied the patterns developed by Britain at a high cost, they are in a position to produce ceramics at one-third of the British cost; (c) quotas should be introduced for Japanese goods in British colonies; (d) since the US does not permit Japan to trade with China, there will be intensified Japanese competition in the British colonial markets (DRO, B' 4.1.1.2, 27 November 1951).

However, the editorial of the *Manchester Guardian* of 26 February 1952 elucidated the following points: as far as Britain was concerned, Japan was as important as China; since Asian countries still had high regard for Japan, there would be a great impact upon them if Japan took a neutral political stand; although the British Parliament made a fuss about cheap Japanese goods, if the British firms could produce cheap and high quality goods, local people in the territories under British control would naturally buy them; the main issue was how the British could have a politically friendly relationship with Japan despite the fact that they were in conflict with each other economically.

Actually, the British later changed their view on Japan, as they wanted to maintain their own prestige in Southeast Asia by allowing Japan to resume her trade relations with the region. As noted in Chapter 3, in the 1930s they had dealt with severe Japanese competition in the markets of their colonies and dependencies by erecting tariffs and non-tariff barriers against foreign imports. However, in the post-war years, when there was a rising tide of nationalism and independence movements in the developing world, it was very difficult for the British to deprive local inhabitants of a cheap source of necessities (notably Japanese imports) simply to protect their own interests even in the territories under their control.

THE RESUMPTION OF JAPANESE ECONOMIC ACTIVITIES IN SINGAPORE

Japan's trade with Singapore

As noted earlier, in August 1947 the SCAP revised the state-controlled foreign trade system by allowing the resumption of Japan's private foreign trade with some restrictions. Private Japanese exporters could now negotiate with foreign merchants directly, and the Japanese trade with Singapore began from that time onwards (Tsusho Sangyo Seisakus-hi 1990a: 141–3; Nishikawa 1995: 241–5). According to *Nihon Boeki Seiran (The Detailed Survey of Japan's Foreign Trade)*, in 1947 Japan exported to Singapore ¥156,661,000 worth of goods, and imported from it ¥4,380,000 worth of goods. The exports and imports in 1949 were ¥3,658,140,000 and ¥44,330,000 respectively (Toyo Keizai Shimposha 1975b). These figures reveal that Japan had large trade surpluses with Singapore in these years, though no information is given as to the commodity composition of the trade.

However, we have more detailed information on the trade from 1949 to 1955. As Table 6.1 shows, in the early 1950s there was a huge expansion of the trade between the two countries, which was probably due to the international trade boom triggered by the Korean War.[5] Singapore continued to have a deficit in trade with Japan every year, with the notable exception of 1955 when she had a surplus of $4.4 million. In 1955, Japan was responsible for 6 to 7 per cent of Singapore's foreign trade. As Table 6.2 reveals, rubber accounted for over 80 per cent of Singapore's total exports to Japan up till 1951, and even after that year it remained by far the largest export item. Other important items of exports were tin, scrap iron, liquid fuel and motor spirit. In 1955, Japan was the fourth largest importer of rubber, coming after Britain, the US and West Germany, while she ranked third as a tin importer after the US and France (COS 1958: 85–6).

As for the composition of imports from Japan, in 1949 cotton piece goods accounted for over 60 per cent of the total, and other imports included cement, vegetables and salted and dry fish. However, in the 1950s cotton textiles gave way to rayon goods in importance, and the decline in salted/dry fish and dried/preserved vegetables was coupled with a rise in cement and steel. The Singapore government abolished an import restriction on Japanese cotton and rayon piece goods in March 1955 and on Japanese cement and sundry in the following month, and this helped Japan to increase her exports to the British colony (Shingaporu Nihonjinkai 1978: 86; Singapore Chamber of Commerce 1955: 9). At any rate, there was a steady progress in the economic rehabilitation of Japan, which was now in a position to manufacture varied and more sophisticated industrial goods for export.

Table 6.1 Singapore's trade with Japan, 1949–55 (in $1,000)

	Import		Export	
	Value	*%*[a]	*Value*	*%*[a]
1949	39,139	3.0	10,252	1.0
1950	80,621	3.8	72,324	2.9
1951	207,920	5.8	108,742	2.7
1952	207,330	7.3	102,550	4.0
1953	105,113	4.5	96,192	4.9
1954	120,050	5.2	100,370	4.9
1955	194,182	6.8	198,621	7.1

Source: Constructed from COS Commerce and Industry Department, 1954 and 1955.
Note
[a] Japan's shares in Singapore's imports and exports.

Table 6.2 The structure of Singapore's trade with Japan, 1949–55

	1949	1950	1951	1952	1953	1954	1955
Exports (in $1000)	10,252	72,324	108,742	102,550	96,192	100,370	198,621
Percentages							
Rubber	83.97	89.08	84.08	71.11	59.72	72.22	70.10
Tin	0.00	0.07	5.22	3.75	11.80	7.17	6.85
Motor spirit	0.96	0.00	1.10	5.48	7.03	8.88	5.32
Steel ingot	0.00	0.03	2.60	6.49	4.01	2.69	1.50
Liquid fuel	0.00	2.37	1.66	5.86	4.42	0.10	1.14
Imports (in $1000)	39,139	80,621	207,920	207,330	105,113	12,050	194,182
Percentages							
Cotton piece goods	64.82	28.35	26.29	18.21	19.74	24.89	23.57
Rayon piece goods	4.16	29.62	33.18	32.28	12.6	20.39	26.97
Cement	2.05	2.34	4.32	4.30	4.71	4.66	3.58
Steel bars & ingots	0.04	0.00	0.59	1.52	2.03	0.61	3.14
Crockery	0.00	2.94	1.78	1.41	2.48	1.79	1.43
Sewing machines	0.03	1.35	1.84	1.81	2.05	2.42	1.27
Aluminium sheets	0.00	0.73	1.47	1.99	0.52	0.62	0.54
Steel sheets	0.00	0.00	1.59	2.39	0.06	0.13	0.41
Salted & dried fish	3.45	6.17	3.57	3.58	0.36	0.10	0.16
Dried & preserved vegetables	1.41	3.39	1.40	1.35	0.01	1.42	0.06

Source: COS Commerce and Industry Department,1954 and 1955.

Return of Japanese nationals and resumption of Japanese economic activities

In April 1950 the SCAP lifted a ban on the overseas activities of private Japanese shipping, and it permitted Japanese ships to obtain fuels, water and tinned foods at Singapore in June, when the Korean War broke out (Yoneda 1978: 397–8). Foreign travel by Japanese nationals then became possible in principle, thanks to the conclusion of the San Francisco Peace Treaty in September 1951. When the treaty and the US–Japan Security Pact came into effect on 28 April 1952, the Japanese government officially announced the appointment of diplomats in various countries.

Japan's diplomatic relations with Singapore began in October 1952 when Ninomiya Ken was appointed as Consul-General. The number of Japanese entering the country began to rise considerably thereafter (Shingaporu Nihonjinkai 1978: 89). It should be noted that the colonial authorities issued entry visas only to those Japanese who were diplomats, businessmen and such professionals as doctors and lawyers, but not to Japanese manual workers or shop proprietors (PRO, Commissioner General for the UK in South-east Asia to Clutton, Confidential Despatch, 4 March 1952, CO1022/218). Also, none of the Japanese who had resided in Singapore and/or Malaya during the occupation period was allowed to return there in the post-war period (PRO, High-Commissioner to the Colonial Secretary, Confidential Despatch, 16 September 1952, CO1022/218). Apparently, these restrictions on Japanese immigration were kept intact at least until October 1955.

The 1953 annual report of the Immigration Department shows that a total of 222 Japanese (198 males and 24 females) went through the Singapore Customs Office, but unfortunately it gives no information about the period of their stay or the type of passes (i.e. visas) granted to them. However, the annual reports for the years 1957 and 1959 do provide information on the type of passes. In 1957, there were 127 Japanese, of whom 87 obtained business visit passes, 21 social visit passes which were granted to professionals and researchers, and 19 transit passes. In 1959 there were a total of 162 Japanese, of whom the respective numbers were 54, 92 and five. In addition, eleven student passes were obtained by Japanese in the same year (COS Immigration Department 1953, 1957, 1959). Although the purposes of their visits became varied in the second half of the 1950, most of the Japanese visitors were nevertheless employees of Japanese firms, through whom Japan's economic relations with the British colony continued to develop.

In January 1951 the *Shinyo Maru*, a Japanese ship which was chartered by the Toyo Kisen Kaisha, was at anchor off Singapore on the way to Batu Pahat to load bauxite ores. It was Shinozaki Mamoru, the ex-head of the Education and also Health Departments of the war-time Syonan Special Municipality, who made the allocation of the ship for this purpose. Although he was not permitted to land in Singapore, he met with visitors from the British colony on board, and after he negotiated with them for several days, he succeeded in unloading 8,500 metric tons of the Onoda Cement Company's cement (Shingaporu Nihonjinkai 1978: 86). Thereafter, the *Kansai Maru*, owned by the Kansai Kisen Kaisha (Kansai Steamship Company), and other Japanese ships began to carry cement, sundry goods and other Japanese goods to Singapore.

According to the *Minami Jujisei,* Shinozaki was the first Japanese to visit Singapore in the post-war period to initiate Japan's trade with Singapore (Shingaporu Nihonjinkai 1978: 86). However, he was obviously not the first to land there, for five Japanese (two men, one woman and two girls) had entered Singapore in May 1949 and four men in June 1950 (*Government Gazette*, various issues). Moreover, it was not the *Shinyo Maru* but a Japanese tanker which was the first Japanese ship to call at Singapore in August 1948. It was one of seven oil tankers which were permitted to sail by the SCAP to load heavy oil at Bahrain. It should be noted that all the imports to Japan at that time had to be carried in American vessels, and until the restriction on private Japanese shipping was completely removed in April 1950, all the Japanese ocean liners had to obtain permission from the SCAP for each of their shipping overseas (Osaka Shosen Mitsui 1969: 66–7).

After the Japanese Consulate-General was set up there in October 1952, some Japanese firms resumed economic activities in Singapore. In March 1953, the Bank of Tokyo obtained permission from the colonial authorities to send a resident representative to Singapore, and in the following year established a representative office there. In December 1953 the Kato Kaiun Kaisha (Kato Shipping Co. Ltd) was granted permission for its workers to reside in Singapore temporarily for dismantling sunken ships, and therefore sent 32 workers to the British colony in January 1954. Curiously, there are no official figures to show that Japanese trading companies sent their employees to Singapore at that time. This was largely because, until the end of 1953, the colonial authorities permitted only Japanese diplomats and their families in the total number of 19 to reside in Singapore, and granted other Japanese a maximum of two-month visas for sight-seeing (*Mainichi Shimbun*, 18 December 1953). It may be reasonable to assume that a certain number of employees of Japanese trading companies entered the British colony for a short stay. Indeed, according to Otaka Zenzaburo and *Niigata Nippo* (*Niigata Daily*), there must have been some Japanese businessmen in Singapore (OHI Otaka; *Niigata Nippo*, 11 August 1955).

SINGAPORE'S EXPECTATIONS FOR JAPANESE CO-OPERATION IN INDUSTRIALISATION

Singapore's new policy towards Japan

In April 1955 David Marshall formed the first internal government in Singapore, and this marked a new phase of the economic relations between Japan and Singapore. In July 1955, the Singapore and the Federation of Malaya governments informally decided to grant permission to Japanese businessmen to engage in economic activities in Singapore and Malaya. Furthermore, in September, Echigoya Gofukuten, a long-standing retail shop in the pre-war period, was permitted to resume retail business, and it was actually the first case in the post-war period where Singapore granted permission for the re-establishment of a Japanese business (OHI Marshall;

160

Plate 2.1 The three-storeyed shophouses in Bugis and Malabar Streets, shortly before demolition for the construction of the Bugis Junction shopping centre (photographed in September 1991). It is likely that they were used as Japanese brothels before licensed Japanese prostitution was abolished in 1920, for the streets constituted part of the major Japanese red-light district in Singapore.

Plate 2.2 The Japanese Cemetery at Chuan Hoe Avenue near Yio Chu Kang Road (photographed in September 1997). It was built in 1891, and is the largest Japanese cemetery in Southeast Asia. Large numbers of *karayuki-san*, merchants, military personnel and other Japanese are buried there.

Plate 2.3 The inside of Echigoya Gofukuten's shop, packed with rolls of textile fabrics. In the centre at the back there is a notice in Japanese, saying 'We do not sell on credit'. The draper's shop was founded by Takahashi Chubei in Middle Road in 1908, and was re-organised as Echigoya & Co. in 1932. The date of this photograph is not known, but it is before 1928. (Courtesy of Mr Takahashi Tadayuki.)

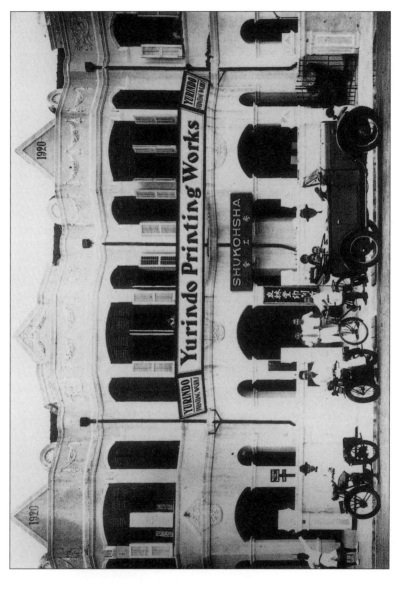

Plate 3.1 Yurindo Printing Works in Waterloo Street, *circa* 1932. It was founded in 1920 by Hayashida Shigeo, a former Sumo wrestler from Nagasaki. (Courtesy of the Japanese Association, Singapore.)

Plate 3.2 Raffles Place in the late 1930s. There were banks, trading companies, shipping firms and other large Japanese firms operating there. (Source: Shingaporu Nihonjin Kurabu 1942.)

Plate 3.3 The Japanese retail shops along Middle Road before World War II. (Courtesy of the Japanese Association, Singapore.)

Plate 5.1 The Syonan Shipyard during the Japanese occupation period. It was run by the Kobe Shipyard of the Mitsubishi Heavy Industries Ltd, and was used mainly for the repair of Japanese warships. (Source: Minamikai 1968.)

Plate 5.2 A military banknote (*gunpyo*). As there was a drawing of bananas on the recto, it was known as a 'banana note'.

Plate 7.1 The Maruzen Toyo Oil Co. Ltd's refinery at Tanjong Berlayer, Pasir Panjang in February 1962 (Source: Maruzen Sekiyu 1987).

Plate 7.2 Jurong Shipyard, *circa* 1968. Jurong Shipyard Ltd was set up as a joint venture between the Singapore government and Ishikawajima-Harima Heavy Industries, Ltd in 1963. (Courtesy of Mr Sakurai Kiyohiko.)

Plate 7.3 The opening ceremony of the Bridgestone Malaysia plant in Singapore on 3 April 1965. The speaker is Ishibashi Shojiro, the chairman of Bridgestone Tire Co. Ltd. Seated in the front row, second and third from the left are, respectively, Tunku Abdul Rahman, the prime minister of Malaysia, and Goh Keng Swee, the finance minister of Singapore. (Courtesy of Bridgestone Tire Co. Ltd.)

Plate 7.4 The inside of the Bridgestone Malaysia plant in April 1965. (Courtesy of Bridgestone Tire Co. Ltd.)

Shingaporu Nihonjinkai 1992: 10). Moreover, in October the Singapore government formally announced that the restriction on the entry of the Japanese was relaxed (Shingaporu Nihonjinkai 1978: 86), and from this time onwards Japanese firms, particularly trading companies, started undertaking economic activities openly.

The reasons behind the change in Singapore's policy towards Japan are not hard to find. In an interview conducted by Sugino Kazuo, the secretary-general of the Japanese Association, on 18 September 1995, David Marshall explained the background to granting permission for the return to Singapore of Japanese companies saying:

> We were scared of the influence of the Chinese Communist Party. We thought that if Japan regained her [economic] strength, she would play a main part against communism. Therefore, we granted permission to the Bank of Tokyo and Mitsubishi Corporation for the establishment of business offices.[6]
>
> (Marshall 1996: 71)

Similarly, the British government and the Colonial Administration also began to entertain the idea that the problems of population increase and unemployment would be solved by industrialisation, which would in turn prevent the spread of Communism in Singapore and Malaya. They came to realise that Japan would be useful in assisting Singapore's industrialisation, for she had reconstructed her war-devastated economy within a fairly short period of time. Thus, in November 1957, in his talks with Prime Minister Kishi, Sir Robert Brown Black, Governor of Singapore, accepted the Singapore government's idea of obtaining Japan's co-operation in Singapore's industrialisation, with the object of countering increasing Communist influence in the region.[7] Lim Yew Hock, who succeeded Marshall as the Chief Minister in June 1956, also expressed his expectations for the return of Japanese firms (DRO, A' 1.5.1.5, 27 November 1957; A' 1.5.1.5–2, undated November 1957).

Both the colonial authorities and the Singapore government wanted to see the development of new manufacturing industries in order to eliminate the source of Communism, i.e. poverty. Indeed, in the middle of the 1950s there was hardly any major manufacturing industry in Singapore apart from rubber footwear production. An Industrial Promotion Board, which had been set up as the government's statutory body in March 1957 with the object of securing the promotion and development of industries, selected five out of the 60 firms which had applied and gave financial assistance to them: these were granite quarrying works; a pencil-manufacturing factory; a printing house for tickets for buses, cinemas and other uses; steel and metal works; and a noodle-making factory. In addition, the Ministry of Commerce and Industry commissioned the board to survey specific industrial and marketing problems, namely (a) Indonesian competition in copra cakes, (b) pelagic fisheries and fish-canning, (c) construction of a sugar refining factory in Singapore, (d) competition in footwear from Japan, (e) production of metal doors and window frames, and (f) production of glue from starch (COS Industrial Promotion Board 1958: 5–15).

It seemed obvious that, as Singapore was not able to achieve industrialisation by itself, it needed to seek co-operation from an industrialised country. The Singaporean leaders therefore looked towards Japan. However, it was just over a decade since the end of World War II, and many Singaporeans had not forgotten Japanese rule. Indeed, during the Japanese occupation period, local inhabitants, notably overseas Chinese, suffered terrible hardships, the hardships which they had never experienced during the British colonial rule, and inevitably came to bear ill feeling against Japan. The memories of the cruelty of Japanese rule probably contributed, to a certain extent, to the causes of the economic friction between Japanese firms and local interests which we shall describe shortly. Nevertheless, on 19 June 1956 the Japanese Consul-General at Singapore, Ninomiya Ken, reported to the Foreign Minister in Tokyo:

> There has been much improvement in the feelings of the local inhabitants towards Japan in the past two or three years. As a matter of fact, the government began to relax step by step the restrictions on the entry of Japanese nationals, though some Singaporeans continued to have animosity against the Japanese.
>
> (DRO, A' 1.3.1.1, 19 June 1951)

It should be borne in mind that the Japanese Army defeated the British military forces, creating entirely new circumstances for the locals, and although British rule was restored in the wake of the defeat of Japan at the end of the Pacific War, as far as the Singaporeans were concerned, Singapore was not the same as it had been in the pre-war period. In other words, the freedom restored after the end of the Japanese occupation was not only political, but economic and social; however it was not simply the restoration of the *status quo ante* (SOS 1959: 31). Now the Singaporeans came to be aware of their status as completely subjugated to the colonial rule, and this gave rise to independent minds among the Singaporeans. It seems that the Japanese occupation produced not only anti-Japanese feelings but also a certain degree of appreciation for Japan at the expense of the diminishing prestige of the colonial power.

Besides, as the industrialisation of Syonan was systematically carried out by the Japanese Military Administration during a short period of three and a half years, it might have given a good impression to those who were to become leaders in post-war Singapore. In other words, Japan's industrial strength and technological level might have been appreciated by them.

Probably this was one of the major reasons for a change in feelings towards Japan among the Singaporeans at an early date, and caused the Singapore government and the colonial authorities to adopt a pragmatic attitude *vis-à-vis* Japan with a view to promoting industrialisation with Japanese help in the face of Communist threats.[8]

Thus, when the Japanese Prime Minister Kishi Nobuskue visited Singapore in November 1957, Chief Minister Lim Yew Hock asked Kishi to make arrangements with Japanese firms for capital investment, as he had a plan for setting up tuna-canning, cement and fertiliser factories. Indeed, he made it clear to the Japanese premier that he had 'no objection to the establishment of these factories with 100 per cent Japanese capital, and profits can be remitted to Japan freely'[9] (DRO, A' 1.5.1.5, 27 November 1957; A' 1.5.1.5–2, undated November 1957).

The tuna-canning factory was planned to undertake the processing, freezing and canning of tuna and other fish caught in the Indian Ocean. It should be noted incidentally that the negotiations for the factory had already begun to take place between the Singapore government and a Japanese pelagic-fishery company in November 1956, i.e. one year before the Japanese premier's visit to Singapore. According to an annual report of the Singapore Industrial Promotion Board, a certain Japanese company sent a technical survey mission to Singapore for this purpose, and continued to negotiate with the government for the adoption of Japanese-style organisation and fish-processing methods (COS Industrial Promotion Board 1958: 10–11).[10] Unfortunately, there is no information as to the name of this fishing company. At that time, Banseimaru Goshi and Taiyo Gyogyo (formerly Hayashikane Shoten and the present Maruha Co. Ltd) had technical links with certain local fishing companies for the supervision of trawlnet fishing, while Okinoshima Suisan and Sacchu Suisan had sent their technical experts and several fishing boats to Singapore (Nihon Keizai Chosa Kyogikai 1967a: 26). One of these fishing firms seem to have negotiated with the Singapore government for the tuna-canning factory project. At any rate, nothing came out of the negotiations in the end.[11] As for the cement-factory plan, the Japanese partners for a joint venture were the Onoda Cement Company and Daiichi Bussan. However, it was not until the early 1960s that a cement factory was finally constructed. There is no available information about the fertiliser factory.

The Japanese side also endeavoured to strengthen Japan's economic relations with the British colony. For example, the Singapore office of the Kaigai Boeki Shinkokai (the Overseas Trade Promotion Organisation), was set up in 1956, and was renamed the Singapore–Japan Trade Centre in 1962. The Kaigai Boeki Shinkokai was engaged in gathering information on overseas markets, introducing overseas trading partners to Japanese merchants, organising trade fairs abroad, and other activities related to the promotion of Japan's trade with foreign countries.

In October 1957, the Japanese Consul-General applied to the Colonial Administration for permission to hold a trade fair in Singapore, and was granted it at the end of the year. From 14 to 28 February 1958, the trade fair was held under the auspices of the Overseas Trade Promotion Organisation in the Happy World Amusement Park (*Tsusho Koho* No. 2,590, 28 March 1958; Nihon Boeki Shinkokai 1973: 47). Tens of thousands of people visited it every day. Japanese cars, textile goods, optical instruments (including cameras), household electrical appliances (including transistor radios) and other industrial goods were particularly popular at the fair. Japan was therefore able to show Singaporeans her industrial strength in general (*Tsusho Koho*, No. 2,590, 28 March 1958). Moreover, 21 members from the Japanese Chamber of Commerce and Industry, and the Southeast Asia Trade and Industrial Technology Co-operation Survey Mission (Tonan Ajia Boeki oyobi Kigyo Gijutsu Kyoryoku Chosadan) visited Singapore in June, while the Yokohama City Southeast Asia Survey Mission paid a visit there in August. Furthermore, in the same year the Singapore government organised three trade fairs, one of which was held at the Happy World Amusement Park in December, mainly exhibiting Japanese goods (COS 1958: 96).

Economic friction between Japanese firms and local interests

The colonial authorities and the Singapore government began to look to Japanese co-operation in the British colony's industrialisation, and they permitted the return of Japanese firms for this reason. However, there was, at that time, one main problem with inviting Japanese firms to make direct investment into Singapore, namely the economic friction between Japanese trading companies and the local interests. As already noted, in the second half of the 1950s the restriction on the entry of Japanese into Singapore was lifted, and various Japanese trading companies started operations in Singapore. But their activities came to clash with the interests of the local merchants. Although similar instances of friction frequently took place in Singapore and other parts of Southeast Asia in the 1960s, what is important here is the fact that in the second half of the 1950s they were already an issue to be discussed between the Japanese and Singapore governments.

When the Japanese premier visited Singapore in November 1957, he discussed with Lim Yew Hock the problem of trade friction between Japanese trading companies and local merchants. Lim told Kishi that he had no intention of restricting the activities of Japanese trading companies in Singapore, but as these firms were infringing on the interests of local merchants, he wanted them to act more cautiously. The Japanese Prime Minister then responded by saying that he wanted the Chief Minister to look at the situation in a good light, for they were bound to exercise self-restraint soon (DRO, A' 1.5.1.5, 5 December 1957). In fact, as from June 1957, the Japanese trading companies voluntarily adopted a quota system of textile exports to Singapore and Indonesia, with the object of avoiding economic friction between themselves and the local importers of Japanese textiles in these markets. They were also considering doing the same soon in other Southeast Asian countries (DRO, A' 1.5.1.5–1, undated, November 1957).

The import of certain Japanese goods also caused friction with local interests. Rubber footwear was a case in point. In the 1950s, it constituted one of Singapore's few items of exportable manufacture, and at its peak in 1956 the industry was turning out four million pairs, the bulk of which were exported to neighbouring countries (Huff 1994: 287). As noted in Chapter 3, Japan had been a major supplier of rubber footwear for the British Malayan market in the pre-war period. In the post-war period, large quantities of low-priced Japanese goods found their way into the Singapore and Malayan markets once again, and local manufacturers faced renewed Japanese competition. For example, the Bata Shoe Company, which had been formed in 1930, was obliged to dismiss 100 out of its 300 workers in September 1958 (*Tsusho Koho,* no. 2,752, 9 October 1958).

The Singapore Rubber Goods Manufacturers and Traders Association accused Japan of dumping rubber footwear on the market, and pressed the government for the imposition of a restriction on Japanese imports. But the Industrial Promotion Board took no measure against Japan. Actually, when it investigated the complaints, it discovered a number of reasons behind the weak position of local manufacturers. Although Japanese workers were low-paid and worked long hours, they were proud of their work, and had a high level of productivity. Also, Japanese product designs were attractive to local consumers. On the other hand, the local manufacturers used outdated machines as well as inefficient production methods. Therefore, the board recommended that the local manufacturers modernise their factories, improve the quality of workmanship and production methods, and cut down costs greatly (COS Industrial Promotion Board 1958: 10–13 *Tsusho Koho,* no. 2,752, 9 October 1958). Consequently, the local rubber industry was left to its own devices to compete with Japanese goods, but it nevertheless seems to have made itself competitive. Indeed, the Bata Shoe Company gradually improved the quality of its products, employing better materials and more skilled workers. In 1963, the company produced 419,000 pairs of shoes, and it set up a new factory in Telok Blangah Road in 1964 (SICC 1979: 114).

Another source of friction was the problem of issuing licences to Japanese fishing firms. In April 1958, the Singapore government issued four licences to Japanese fishing companies. However, at the Legislative Assembly an MP asked whether the government intended to foster Singapore's fishing industry or destroy it by granting fishing licences to the Japanese. He maintained that the Japanese merely wanted to exploit cheap local fishing crew, for they provided them with only rudimentary training, and there was therefore no transfer of fishing technology to Singapore. The government then counter-argued that their pay was not small, and, although 170 men had been recruited by the Japanese firms locally, only six remained working with them after six months, simply because the majority of them did not have strong willpower (SLA 1958: 101–2, 140–1, 197–8).

Obviously, the activities of the Japanese trading companies and the import of Japanese footwear were very different in nature from the granting of fishing licences to Japanese fishing companies, for they directly affected the local interests, whereas the fishing companies were apparently not in direct competition with the local fishermen who mainly operated in the territorial waters, not in the open sea.

JAPANESE FIRMS IN SINGAPORE IN THE SECOND HALF OF THE 1950s

Main features of Japanese firms

As the restrictions on the entry of Japanese nationals were gradually removed, Japanese companies became increasingly active in Singapore from the mid-1950s onwards. According to a Singapore Legislative Assembly document, there was only one Japanese capital investment during the period from January 1956 to May 1959. It amounted to $1.2 million and was made in the Singapore Cement Industrial Co. Ltd by Japanese companies (SLA 1963a). This obviously does not mean that there were no other Japanese companies operating in the British colony. At that time, banking and insurance companies, trading companies, shipping firms and other Japanese companies set up representative offices or branches, though their capital investments were not recorded in Singapore's official statistics.

As Table 6.3 shows, in the 1950s there were 18 Japanese companies in the British colony, of which ten were trading companies. As the entry requirements for Japanese nationals were relaxed in October 1955, Daiichi Bussan (the present Mitsui & Co.) and Mitsubishi Corporation set up branches.[12] In the next two years, other trading companies including Nichimen Jitsugyo (the present Nichimen), Marubeni-Iida (the present Marubeni), Toyo Menka (the present Tomen), Sumitomo Corporation and Nissho established offices or branches. In the field of banking and insurance, the Bank of Tokyo (the present Tokyo Mitsubishi Bank) was registered in September 1956 (the representative office was opened in September 1954, and was promoted to a branch in January 1957), while the Tokio Marine & Fire Insurance Co. Ltd began business in August 1957, and the Taisho Marine & Fire Insurance Co. Ltd (the present Mitsui Marine & Fire Insurance Co. Ltd) in February 1958. As for the manufacturing sector, the Bridgestone Tire Company began operations in October 1956, while the Onoda Cement Company (the present Chichibu-Onoda) was registered in June 1958. It should be noted that, as Table 6.3 shows, the return of Japan to Singapore in the post-war period

166

Table 6.3 Japanese companies in Singapore in the 1950s

Firm names	Type of work	Start of work	Type of Investment[a]
Echigoya & Co.	Draper's trade	Nov. 1955	Joint venture
Mitsubishi Corporation	Foreign and domestic trade	Nov. 1955	Branch
Daiichi Bussan	Foreign and domestic trade	July 1955	Branch
Nichimen Jitsugyo	Foreign and domestic trade	Aug. 1955	Branch
Bank of Tokyo	Banking	Sept. 1954	Branch
Bridgestone Tire Co. Ltd	Rubber trade	Oct, 1956	Branch
Marubeni-Iida	Foreign and domestic trade	Nov. 1956	Branch
Toyo Menka	Foreign and domestic trade	Jan. 1957	Branch
Sumitomo Corporation	Foreign and domestic trade	Aug. 1955	Branch
Nissho	Foreign and domestic trade	Mar. 1957	Branch
Holden Trading Co. (Pte) Ltd	Manufacturing and sales of cosmetics, etc.	May 1957[b]	Joint venture
Iwai Corporation	Foreign and domestic trade	Oct. 1957	Representative office
Tokio Marine & Fire Insurance Co. Ltd	Insurance	Aug. 1957	Sole agency
Taisho Marine & Fire Insurance Co. Ltd	Insurance	Feb. 1958	Sole agency
Japan Airlines Co. Ltd	Air transport	Apr. 1958	Branch
Singapore Cement Industrial Co. (Pte) Ltd	Import and sale of cement	Nov. 1958	Joint venture
Kasho Co. Ltd	Foreign trade	July 1958	Branch
Nomura Trading Co. Ltd	Foreign trade	Feb. 1959	Branch

Source: Constructed from Nihon Shingaporu Kyokai 1976a, b; Nihon Shingaporu Kyokai *et al.* 1990; Nihon Keizai Chosa Kyogikai 1967b, and various company history books.
Notes
[a] Some companies set up representative offices, and then promoted them to branches.
[b] Date of registration or establishment of an office.

began with Echigoya & Co. (the pre-war Echigoya Gofukuten), a draper's shop, and the trading companies. Most of the Japanese companies began their operations before the dates of registration, for they had sent their resident representatives informally to undertake business activities well in advance.

However, according to the Japanese Association (Singapore), as of April 1956 there were a total of 23 founding members of the association. They were the Japan Trade Centre, the Asahi Shimbunsha (Asahi Newspaper Co.), the Mitsui Senpaku Kaisha, the Nippon Yusen Kaisha, the Osaka Shosen Kaisha, the Bank of Tokyo, Asahi Bussan, Ataka Sangyo, Daiichi Bussan, Daido Yoshi Ten, Echigoya, Gosho, Ito Chu, Mitsubishi Corporation, Morioka Kogyo, Marubeni-Iida, Nichimen Jitsugyo, Okaya Koki, Sumitomo Corporation, Takisada, Toyo Menka, Kinoshita Shoten and Matsukura Shoten (Shingaporu Nihonjinkai 1978: 90). It should be noted that, of these firms and organisations, some trading and wholesale companies (including Ataka Sangyo, Daiichi Bussan, Gosho, Morioka Kogyo, Okaya Koki and Kinoshita Shoten), and the three major shipping companies (the Nippon Yusen Kaisha, the Osaka Shosen Kaisha and the Mitsui Senpaku Kaisha) are not shown in Table 6.3. The reason for it is not clear. At any rate, in the second half of the 1950s most of the Japanese firms in Singapore were in the fields of foreign and domestic trade, banking, insurance and shipping. It is true that the Onoda Cement Co. Ltd and the Bridgestone Tire Co. Ltd were in the manufacturing sector, but the former was chiefly engaged in the import and distribution of Japanese cement, and the latter in the purchasing and export to Japan of raw rubber as well as in the sales of tyres and tubes.

Echigoya and Japanese trading companies

Echigoya & Co. was the first Japanese company to return to Singapore in the post-war period. It was closed when Japan was defeated in 1945, and all its assets were sequestered by the British authorities. However, in 1954 Mr Hu, a resident in Singapore, informed Fukuda Kurahachi, the former manager, that he wanted to import silk goods, piece goods, sundry goods and other products from Japan. Taking this as an opportunity, Fukuda returned to Singapore in November 1954. At that time, the Colonial Administration had a policy of not granting an entry visa to any Japanese who had resided in Singapore during the occupation period. Nevertheless, Fukuda managed to return to the British colony, thanks to a special arrangement made by a certain Briton who had been one of his good customers in the pre-war period, and who was then a director of the Immigration Department (Muranushi 1997: 54).

In July 1955 Fukuda managed to obtain a permission from the Singapore government for the re-opening of Echigoya. A retail store was re-established with a capital of $150,000, most of which was subscribed by Lai En Ho, an overseas Chinese who was British by nationality and who was married to a Japanese woman. Lai's capital investment is said to have been arranged by Lim Chong Geok, an executive member of the Badminton Association and an influential person (Nakane 1976: 120). On 9 November Echigoya resumed retail business in Coleman Street with Fukuda as the general manager.

When Fukuda returned to Singapore in late 1954, there were already some Japanese there. In August 1955, he temporarily returned to his hometown in Niigata, and wrote in a local newspaper that there were some 20 Japanese residents in the British colony, who belonged to the Consulate-General or Japanese trading companies (*Niigata Nippo*, 11 August 1955). Daiichi Tsusho set up a representative office in Singapore in 1955, before it was merged with Daiichi Bussan in the same year, and, as of 1 November, there were three Japanese resident representatives, including Otaka Zenzaburo (the head). As far as Otaka remembers, the company had sent to Singapore two members of staff, Ogawa and Nagai, as representatives in 1951, and Otaka himself arrived there in 1953 (OHI Otaka). However, Tan Iwen (Ueda Seiko by Japanese name), Tan Keong Choon's[13] wife, who was the first Japanese to go to Singapore in the post-war period, maintains that the first Japanese she met there in the middle of 1952 was Ishii Yasuo of the Bank of Tokyo, not the two men from the trading company (Tan 1995: 133). If she is right, then Daiichi Tsusho's two staff members could have gone over to Singapore in the second half of 1952, not in 1951 as Otaka claims. Incidentally, in late 1949 the SCAP began to encourage Japanese trading companies to send their employees abroad with a view to expanding Japanese exports, while in 1951 it became possible, in principle, for Japanese nationals to enter Singapore. In these circumstances, it is highly likely that Daiichi Tsusho's employees entered the British colony during the period from 1951 to 1953.

As for Nichimen Jitsugyo, it sent a member of staff to Singapore in March 1955, i.e. about one and half years before its registration and the start-up of its operation, and in September of the following year it established a branch with Oishi Tokuji as the branch manager (Nichimen Jitsugyo 1962: 390). Also, Toyo Menka set up a representative office in January 1955, two years before the establishment of a branch (Tomen 1991: 536). Moreover, Sumitomo Corporation sent its first resident representative to Singapore in August 1955, and established a branch in Robinson Road in October 1957. Singapore was the fifth country in Southeast Asia to which Sumitomo sent its representatives. Prior to that, it had sent representatives to Bangkok and Jakarta in 1953, Manila and Hong Kong in 1954 (Sumitomo Shoji 1972: 737).

What were the activities of the trading companies in Singapore? Daiichi Bussan imported from Japan steel bars, cement, galvanised iron sheets, tyres for motor vehicles, diesel engines, paper, textiles, *shiitake* and other Japanese goods, and sold these imports through overseas Chinese agencies not only in Singapore but in Malaya and Indonesia (OHI Otaka). According to Otaka Zenzaburo, consumer goods such as textiles were handled by Teochiu merchants, while building materials such as steel bars and cement were dealt in by Hokkien merchants. As for exports to Japan, rubber was by far the most important item for Daiichi Bussan. The company bought natural rubber locally and sent it to the Bridgestone Tire Co. Ltd in Japan. At that time, there was a strict foreign exchange control in Japan, and manufacturers were required to export industrial goods in order to import raw materials. Partly because they were allocated with foreign exchange for import, they commissioned Daiichi Bussan and other trading companies to import raw materials and export finished goods (OHI Otaka).

The Singapore branch of Sumitomo Corporation imported fishing nets and ropes from Japan, and sold them in Malaya in the second half of the 1950s. At that time, the material for this fishing gear was in the process of changing from cotton to synthetic fibre, and after an inquiry from Ts'ai Co. Ltd in Malaya, the company contracted Morishita Seimo (Morishita Fishing Net Manufacturing Co. Ltd) in Okayama prefecture to manufacture fishing nets with the synthetic fibre threads produced by Toyo Rayon, Teijin, Asahi Kasei and other Japanese textile companies. Sumitomo continued to export them to Malaya until the late 1960s (Sumitomo Shoji 1972: 591).

Although the Japanese trading companies were initially concerned largely with the sales of Japanese goods in Singapore and the Federation of Malaya, and the export of primary commodities to Japan, they gradually began to diversify their activities into mining in Malaya, and developing the tripartite trade linking Southeast Asia with South Asia. The Singapore branch of Nichimen Jitsugyo, for example, imported cotton piece goods, synthetic textiles, and woollen and hemp goods from Japan, and was also engaged widely in the export and import of machinery, foodstuffs and other goods. It also went ahead with the tripartite trade with Pakistan, India, Burma and other countries, and had a mine-exploitation project in the Federation of Malaya as an important part of its activities. Starting in 1958, the branch undertook more than one hundred full-scale mining surveys there (Nichimen Jitsugyo 1962: 391).

Nevertheless, it seems clear that the trading companies regarded the tripartite trade with South Asia and mining exploitation as a minor part of their activities, for they set up offices or branches in Singapore, the leading international entrepôt in Southeast Asia, mainly aiming at the Singapore, Malayan and Indonesian markets. However, as their number and activities increased greatly, they began to compete fiercely with local overseas Chinese merchants in both the domestic trade and the re-export trade. As noted earlier, it eventually grew into a critical problem of commercial rivalry between them, which was one of the subjects for discussion between Japanese Prime Minister Kishi Nobusuke and Lim Yew Hock in November 1957.

Japanese banks and insurance companies

The Bank of Tokyo was founded in 1947 to succeed the Yokohama Specie Bank which had been actively engaged in finance and foreign exchange businesses in British Malaya in the inter-war period and during the occupation period, and it was the first Japanese bank to advance into Singapore. According to the bank, it set up a representative office there in September 1954, and then opened a branch in Philips Street in January 1957.[14] However, as noted earlier, Tan Iwen maintains that, as early as 1952, she saw its resident representative, Ishii Yasuo, in the British colony. Moreover, the Japanese Association in Singapore claims that the Bank of Tokyo sent the representative in 1953, not 1952 (Shingaporu Nihonjinkai 1978: 88). There is no firm evidence to ascertain whose information is right.

At any rate, according to Mrs Tan, Ishii was undertaking work in her husband's office on a temporary basis, getting help from him until the Bank of Tokyo obtained the permission from the colonial authorities to conduct financial business in Singapore. This temporary office was located on the second floor of a coffee shop next to the OCBC building (Tan 1995: 133–7). Ishii must have been sent to Singapore as the first resident representative well before the opening of the branch, as Mrs Tan seems to have met Ishii before the re-establishment of the Japanese Consulate-General in October 1952. Ishii was succeeded by Sato Hideo who became the first branch manager in January 1957.[15] Incidentally, Sato was appointed the first president of the Japanese Association, and kept the position until 1959.

Singapore was, along with Hong Kong, one of the two major foreign exchange centres in the sterling area in Asia, and this was the main reason for the opening of the branch by the Bank of Tokyo in Singapore at an early date. The representative office (and later the branch) was mainly concerned with conducting financial business with local merchants, many of whom seemed to be overseas Chinese merchants, and undertaking foreign exchange business for Daiichi Bussan and other Japanese trading companies. It is beyond doubt that, in the second half of the 1950s, almost all the Japanese trading companies in Singapore were its clients. As for the method of raising necessary funds, there is no detailed information, but as was commonly done at that time, the branch seems to have obtained them from the Bank of Tokyo's London branch.

Let us look at Japanese non-life insurance companies in Singapore. The resumption of Japan's insurance business abroad also dates back to August 1947 when restricted private foreign trade began. Since the private foreign traders needed insurance, the Japanese Association of Non-life Insurance Companies asked the SCAP, the Ministry of Finance and the Board of Trade for authorisation to deal in marine insurance in foreign currency, while leading Japanese insurance companies began to build up a network of overseas insurance agencies in anticipation of the authorisation. Besides, 'as there were often inquiries about the possibility of cif export trade by buyers in developing regions of [the world], especially Southeast Asia' (Tokyo Kaijo 1964: 494), the demand for foreign currency insurance increased. As soon as the authorisation was given in April 1950, the leading Japanese insurance companies sent resident representatives to large cities in Asia, Europe and the US in order to build up a world-wide insurance business network through the system of resident representatives together with a network of overseas agencies.

By the end of 1957, the Tokio Marine & Fire Insurance Co. had established a network of overseas agencies for ceding business in the US (the states of New York, Alaska, Washington, Hawaii, Tennessee and California), Canada (the state of Ontario), Britain, Holland, Belgium, Singapore, the Federation of Malaya and Hong Kong. It also began to send resident representatives abroad from 1957 onwards, and established an overseas resident representative system in 1959 (Tokyo Kaijo 1964: 404). Similarly, the Taisho Marine & Fire Insurance Co. commissioned Toyo Menka's Bangkok office to act as its ceding insurance agency in September 1954, and by July 1958 it had signed with nine other companies for similar agency agreements in London, Hong Kong, Singapore, Hamburg and four American states (New York, Washington, Texas and California). Singapore was, along with Hong Kong, the strongpoint for its overseas insurance business in Asia.

It was in August 1957 that Tokio Marine acquired a licence for ceding-company status in Singapore and began insurance business there. Its agency was the Overseas Assurance Co. It was not until 1963, however, that the insurance company sent its first resident representative to Singapore. Tokio Marine started operations in Singapore, primarily because there were many Japanese trading companies there. Its clients for goods insurance reveal that at that time:

> General trading companies have become important customers for goods insurance, constantly occupying 9 to 10 out of the top 15 companies paying insurance premium. They nearly always included Mitsubishi Corporation, Kanematsu, Marubeni-Iida, Toyo Menka, Ito Chu, Ataka Sangyo, Nichimen Jitsugyo, and Iwai Sangyo.
> (Nihon Keieishi Kenkyujo 1982: 446–8)

The largest customer was Mitsubishi Corporation, for the insurance company was also a member of the former Mitsubishi *zaibatsu* (family combine).

As for the Taisho Marine & Fire Insurance Co., it started ceding business in Singapore in February 1958, i.e. six months behind the Tokio Marine & Fire Insurance Co. It was the sixth overseas ceding business, following after Bangkok and London in April 1956, New York in May 1957, Hong Kong in September 1957 and Washington in October 1957, and used the Asia Insurance Co. Ltd as its agency. The company sent its first resident representative to London in May 1953. In Asia outside Japan, Hong Kong was considered to be the most important location, and therefore a resident representative was sent there in 1958. Although Singapore came second in importance in the region, the company kept no representative there (Taisho Kaijo 1961: 276–7).

Taisho Marine undertook ceding business in Singapore for the same reason as that of Tokio Marine. As its company history book says, the overseas activities of Japanese trading companies were a prerequisite for embarking on ceding business abroad (Taisho Kaijo 1961: 276). Indeed, from the start, Singapore was considered as an important strongpoint for overseas insurance business, largely because the Japanese trading companies were engaged mainly in the export of Malayan primary commodities to Japan and the import of Japanese industrial goods.

Incidentally, Tokio Marine and Taisho Marine were Japan's largest and second largest companies for overseas insurance business.[16] However, at that time almost all the premiums (from ceding business) were earned in Europe and America. In 1959, for example, Tokio Marine received over 90 per cent of its premiums from America, 0.9 per cent from Hong Kong, 0.4 per cent from Singapore and the Federation of Malaya (Nihon Keieishi Kenkyujo 1982: 408). One could therefore assume that they set up agencies in Asia probably to prepare for a promising future.

Sales offices of Japanese manufacturing companies

In the 1950s there were some Japanese manufacturing companies operating in Singapore. Here we shall examine the activities of the Bridgestone Tire Co. Ltd, the Onoda Cement Co. Ltd. (the present Chichibu Onoda Co. Ltd),[17] and the Ajinomoto Co. Ltd.

From 1954 to 1960, Bridgestone was actively engaged in the export of its products. The value of its exports rose thrice from ¥1,145 million in 1954 to ¥3,712 million in 1957, while the share of exports in its total proceeds rose from 11.7 per cent to 21.9 per cent in the same years. In 1957, Asia took ¥2,200 million (58 per cent) worth of its exports, the Middle East ¥1,000 million (26 per cent), the American military bases in Japan ¥300 million (9 per cent), and Africa ¥200 million (6 per cent). At that time, the company was operating an active export promotion policy. Since imports of raw materials for tyres, including natural rubber and carbon black, accounted for some 25 per cent of the total costs of tyres, the company endeavoured to export 25 per cent of the total production (Burijisuton 1982: 239).

In October 1956, Bridgestone established its first overseas branch in Singapore with an operating capital of US$30,000. The branch, which was initially staffed with two Japanese and one local employee, was engaged in the export to Japan of rubber and the import from Japan of tyres and related products through Daiichi Bussan (*ibid.*: 241). As for its sales activities in Singapore, Bridgestone sold tyres initially through the Fock Chin Tai, but, as this overseas Chinese company got into financial difficulty, it had an agency agreement with the Hong Leong Co. Ltd in 1960, thereby boosting its sales greatly.[18] It is worth noting that, as we shall see in the next chapter,

Bridgestone set up a tyre factory in Singapore in a joint venture with Hong Leong in 1963 (Burijisuton 1982: 241).

When Japan's private foreign trade was resumed in 1947, the Onoda Cement Co. Ltd began to rapidly increase its export of cement, leaving its Japanese rivals far behind. During the period from October 1947 to June 1948, Japan exported 27,900 metric tons (when a FOB price per ton was US$22), of which Onoda was responsible for 5,100 metric tons (18 per cent of total), and the Osaka Yogyo Cement Company[19] (the present Sumitomo Osaka Cement Co. Ltd) 10,800 metric tons (39 per cent). However, from November 1948 to March 1949, the FOB export price per metric ton fell to US$16 due largely to cut-throat competition among the Japanese cement manufacturers. During the period, Japan's cement exports amounted to 211,265 metric tons, of which Onoda was responsible for 54,796 metric tons (25.9 per cent), emerging as the largest exporter. Onoda's export markets included Hong Kong, India, Korea and Indonesia. In 1949, the FOB export price had fallen to as low as US$12, due to a fall in demand for Japanese cement caused by the devaluation of the pound sterling and the world-wide economic recession. Nevertheless, in that year Onoda exported 127,294 metric tons of cement (28.7 per cent of Japan's total exports), of which 13,620 metric tons found its way to Singapore and the Federation of Malaya. In 1950, its exports amounted to 196,007 metric tons (28.1 per cent of Japan's total exports), of which 67,235 metric tons was exported to the same markets. Onoda's other main export markets were Burma and Indonesia (Onoda Semento 1952: 146–54).

One would naturally wonder why the company was so successful. According to Onoda, it managed to increase its exports greatly, because:

> During the period from 1947 to 1950, it carefully studied the international situation and the demand for cement. As the company was unable to satisfy itself with Hong Kong, Philippines, [the former] British Malaya, and other neighbouring countries to which Japan had previously held the monopoly in the supply of cement, in April 1950 it took the initiative in finding out new markets. Beginning with the export of 4,000 metric tons of cement to Costa Rica in Central America, it exported large quantities of cement to French Tahiti, Jeddah in Arabia, Beira in East Africa (Mozambique), Bushehr in Iran, and others.
>
> (*Ibid*.: 145–54)

Onoda exported cement to the Federation of Malaya through Daiichi Bussan, and used Hong Leong as its agency after 1956 with a view to further increasing the local sales. This was the background to the establishment in November 1958 of a joint-venture company, the Singapore Cement Industrial Co. Ltd which undertook the sales of Onoda cement. Onoda planned to invest in Singapore because of the growing demand for cement caused by the expansion of construction works. It made preliminary surveys on the project through Daiichi Bussan, and on the local partner through the Bank of Tokyo. It chose Hong Leong as the local partner because the latter was not only its sole agency but also had a wide sales network as well as influence over the government. The president of the Singapore Cement Industrial Co. Ltd, was Kwek Hong Png who was then the president of Hong Leong. Onoda Cement, Daiichi Bussan and Hong Leong provided 33.3 per cent each of the capital. But since the two Japanese companies were responsible for two-thirds of the capital, the Japanese side dominated the management of the new company. In 1959 the joint-venture company set up a $2 million cement-packing plant with two large storage tanks. Onoda was thereafter able to increase the share of the market greatly in Singapore (Nihon Keizai Chosa Kyogikai 1967b: 195–7, 203; *Singapore Trade*, March 1964: 15).

In short, in the second half of the 1950s leading Japanese manufacturers of export goods invested in Singapore, basically with the object of increasing the sales of their products or facilitating the purchase of raw materials. Also, Japanese trading companies were often involved in their economic advance into the British colony in some ways. It should also be noted that the rapid growth of a newly emerged local enterprise, Hong Leong, was partly thanks to its close relations with such Japanese firms as Bridgestone and Onoda in Singapore.

Finally, we shall study the Ajinomoto Co. Ltd, a producer of MSG (monosodium glutamate) for cooking. Ajinomoto was one of the large Japanese firms actively engaged in the export of their products in the pre-war period. In 1927 it sent a resident representative to Singapore, and endeavoured to cultivate the British Malayan market through him.[20] In 1947 it resumed exports, and in February 1953 Saeki Takeo, the resident representative in pre-war Singapore and a director of the company, accompanied by Saito Koichi, the chief of the first foreign trade section, visited Singapore. In November 1954, Ajinomoto Co. set up an office in Singapore at the same time as the establishment of offices in São Paulo, Paris, Bangkok and Hong Kong, and appointed Takeda Kiyoshi as its resident representative. As Takeda could not easily get a pass in time, it was not until March 1955 that he managed to enter the British colony.[21]

Shortly after the establishment of the representative office, Ajinomoto sold some 50 metric tons of its products per month in Singapore and Malaya, and by 1956 it had come to hold a predominant position in these markets.[22] In the meantime, in Kuala Lumpur, Ajinomoto established a representative office in 1960, and in the following year the Ajinomoto (Malaya) Co. Ltd, a joint-venture company with local partners (99.6 per cent of the capital provided by Ajinomoto, and 0.4 per cent by the local side).[23] The local partners were T.H. Tan, the Secretary-General of the United Malaya

National Organisation (holding 0.1 per cent of the capital), Y.H. Fok (holding 0.2 per cent of the capital), and others (Malays and other residents) in Malaya (0.1 per cent of the capital). Tan in particular played an important role in establishing a good relationship between the company and the government of Malaya (Ajinomoto 1990: 318–19). As the Ajinomoto (Malaya) Co. Ltd started building a factory in Kuala Lumpur in 1963, there was no need to build another one in Singapore. At any rate, the Federal Chemical Industries Ltd, Ajinomoto's rival, was granted pioneer industries status by the Singapore government in October 1962, and began to construct a factory for the production of MSG in Singapore (*ibid.*: 320, 326).

Japanese shipping companies

In the immediate post-war years the Japanese shipping industry was under the SCAP's strict control, but, as soon as it was privatised in April 1950, Japanese shipping firms applied to the SCAP for permission to re-open overseas shipping routes. When the Korean War broke out in June, the SCAP began to negotiate with other countries for a blanket clearance for Japanese ships. Consequently, on 4 August Japanese shipping companies were given permission to pass through the Panama Canal, while on 15 August Japanese tramp ships were permitted to call at American ports. Moreover, on 31 August the SCAP announced that a blanket clearance was granted to Japanese shipping companies by the US, Argentine, Burma, Egypt, India, Pakistan and certain other countries. At the same time, Japanese ships were permitted to enter the ports of Singapore, Hong Kong, Cape Town and Durban for fuel, water, tinned foods and other supplies. However, Britain, Australia and New Zealand refused to grant the Japanese the blanket clearance, simply because they were concerned at the revival of Japanese shipping, which could lead to the re-emergence of Japan as a major naval power. It was only after the San Francisco Peace Treaty came into effect in April 1952 that they finally approved it. Although the Japanese shipping companies faced various problems, they managed to re-establish many overseas shipping routes,[24] and virtually regained their pre-war tonnage by the end of the 1950s when the total shipping tonnage amounted to 6 million gross tons, of which those ships on overseas routes were responsible for 5.02 million gross tons (Osaka Shosen Mitsui 1969: 314).

The Nippon Yusen Kaisha began the allocation of ships for overseas routes again in 1951. It began to provide regular services for the India/Pakistan route in May, the New York route in July, and the Calcutta and the Seattle routes in October. In the following year, it resumed the Europe route via the Suez Canal in June, and the Australia route in August. In April 1953 it launched the South and Central America/Gulf route, and in February 1954 the Europe route via the Panama Canal. By 1955, the company's pre-war shipping routes had been almost all re-established (Kizu

1984: 329). As for the Osaka Shosen Kaisha, it started providing a regular service to Bombay and Karachi in June 1951, after obtaining approval from the SCAP in April, and also opened the Rangoon/Calcutta route in September. In November 1958, it newly instituted the Bangkok/Colombo route (Osaka Shosen 1966: 301–7).

It became possible for Japanese ships to call at Singapore and other territories under British control in 1950. Largely because of its strategic position, Japanese shipping companies chose Singapore as a transit port in Southeast Asia for its main routes including the Bombay/Karachi route, Rangoon/Calcutta route, Bangkok/Colombo route, India/Pakistan route, and a round-the-world route.

From 1952 onwards, the Mitsui Senpaku Kaisha began to set up representative offices at its main ports of call in the world. In January 1954 Singapore became the ninth place where the company had a resident representative in the post-war period, coming after New York and Bangkok in March 1952, London and Calcutta in April, San Francisco in May, and some others thereafter. As for the Osaka Shosen Kaisha, it opened representative offices first in Bangkok, Calcutta and New York in November 1950, and then various places in Europe, America and Asia. It was in October 1953 that the firm established a representative office in Singapore where it had a branch in the pre-war period. The representative office was in charge of Singapore, Malaya, Indonesia and British Borneo, and had a lot of work to do because:

> Various regular ships on the Europe, the South America, the Southeast Africa, the West Africa, the Bombay/Karachi, and the Rangoon/Calcutta routes call at the Straits area for the loading of cargoes and the filling up of oil and water, and there were also many tramp ships calling there to load iron ore and bauxite.
>
> (Osaka Shosen 1966: 623)

Similarly, the Nippon Yusen Kaisha, which also had a branch in pre-war Singapore, opened a resident representative office around October 1955 in the Borneo Company which acted as an agency for the shipping firm.

CONCLUDING REMARKS

Those scholars who work on Japan's return to Southeast Asia in the post-war period pay much attention to Japan's war responsibility and war reparation negotiations, and often refer to the period from the end of World War II until the mid-1950s as a 'void period' of Japan's economic relations with the region. However, during this 'void period', Japan resumed her trade with Singapore, while Japanese trading and shipping companies had already

7

THE BLOOD-DEBT ISSUE AND JAPAN'S ECONOMIC ADVANCE

The People's Action Party (PAP), formed with Lee Kuan Yew as Secretary-General in 1954, won 43 seats out of 51 to the Legislative Assembly in May 1959, and formed a new government. In June of that year Singapore achieved internal self-government, and subsequently became a member of the British Commonwealth. In the first half of the 1960s, however, the country was politically unstable at home, and had difficult relations with the neighbouring countries. Prime Minister Lee Kuan Yew had to struggle with the left wing inside his party for the next few years. In 1961 the dissident faction formed a new political party, the Barisan Sosialis (Socialist Front), and continued to challenge the PAP's supremacy until 1963 when the new party collapsed.[1]

In the meantime, in May 1961 Tunku Abdul Rahman, the prime minister of the Federation of Malaya, put forward a proposal to Lee Kuan Yew for a larger Malaya comprising the Federation of Malaya, Singapore, North Borneo (Sabah), Brunei and Sarawak. As far as the PAP was concerned, it seemed worth while for Singapore to join the scheme, for the British colony was geographically part of the Malay Peninsula and could act as a base for industrialisation and check the influence of the Communist forces (Rodan 1989: 50). However, Singapore's plan to join the Federation of Malaysia met with a strong protest from Indonesia and the Philippines. President Sukarno of Indonesia, who saw the merger of the former British territories as a threat to the region, and an obstacle in the way of his pan-Indonesian concept, i.e. to unite the Malay world, accused Britain of neo-colonialism, while the Philippines claimed dominion over North Borneo (Turnbull 1977: 281–2). On 16 September 1963, when Malaysia came into existence, Indonesia adopted a confrontation policy against the new state, while, in protest, the Philippines announced that its embassy at Kuala Lumpur would be demoted to a consulate. In response, the Malaysian central government under Prime Minister Rahman broke diplomatic relations with these countries (Takeshita 1995: 185–9).

However, Singapore was part of Malaysia for only 23 months. In the Malay Peninsula, the United Malays National Organisation (UMNO), led by Rahman, was the dominant political party, and it was in alliance with the Malaysian Chinese Association (MCA) and the Malaysian Indian Congress. However, the PAP attempted to replace the MCA in the alliance, in order to have a greater influence over the central government, posing a major threat to the MCA and the UMNO. Moreover, the PAP was in favour of multiracialism, whereas the UMNO wanted to defend Malay privilege. Furthermore, the former was eager to make Singapore the financial and commercial centre as well as the major industrial base in Malaysia, an idea which was rejected by Rahman who wanted to have a balanced economic development in the new country. There were also a number of other differences between them (Josey 1980: 166–300; Rodan 1989: 78–84; Iwasaki 1996: 66–74).

Following Singapore's independence in August 1965, in June 1966 the Philippines recognised Singapore, and established relations with it. Indonesia also recognised the new nation in June 1966, agreed to resume foreign trade with it in August 1966, and finally established diplomatic relations with it in September 1967. As Singapore had suffered a sharp decline in the volume of entrepôt trade in primary commodities during the confrontation period, the resumption of trade particularly with Indonesia was a great relief to the country (Takeshita 1995: 299–301). However, at that time, hardly anyone was optimistic about the future existence of the small 'Chinese' city state surrounded by Indonesia and Malaysia, the two large Malay states.

In the midst of these problems, there was the 'blood-debt issue', which turned out to be the most critical problem in Japan–Singapore relations since World War II. Although it was finally settled by 'quasi-reparations' in 1967, the issue caused a rapid deterioration in the feelings of the Chinese towards the Japanese.[2] In spite of this, at that time large numbers of Japanese companies, particularly those in the manufacturing sector, advanced into Singapore. It is true to a certain extent that these Japanese firms had a great interest in a large common market to be created as a result of the formation of Malaysia, and therefore advanced into Singapore to take advantage of it. However, the prospect for the large common market alone does not account for the Japanese investment boom during the period of political instability and heightened anti-Japanese feelings among the Chinese.

Behind the investment boom lay the Singapore government's active policy of attracting Japanese manufacturing investments. The main purpose of this chapter is to explore the background to this policy, and to shed light on the activities of Japanese companies in Singapore in the first half of the 1960s.

POLICY FOR IMPORT-SUBSTITUTION INDUSTRIALISATION

Singapore's development plan

In the first half of the 1960s Singapore experienced its lowest economic growth during the period from the early 1960s until 1997. It is true that there was a minus growth rate in 1985, but, taking the average growth rate of a five-year period, the first half of the 1960s experienced the lowest since independence. The average yearly GNP growth rate was 6.9 per cent for 1961–5, 13.9 per cent for 1966–70, 18.3 per cent for 1971–5, 12.3 per cent for 1976–80 and 10.8 per cent even for 1981–5 (DSS 1983 and 1996). According to official statistics, the value of foreign trade declined by 14 per cent from $7.3 million in 1959 to $6.3 million in 1964. As those figures do not take into account Indonesian trade figures, not included in Singapore's official statistics since the year of the confrontation, the actual value would not have fallen as much as the above. Nevertheless, one cannot deny that Singapore's foreign trade was in recession (Buchanan 1972: 66–7).

However, in the second half of the 1950s Singapore started to prepare for industrial development, and in the first half of the 1960s it completed the groundwork for launching into industrialisation. During the period from 1955 to 1961, three reports were made on Singapore's economic development. The first was the 1955 report which was made by a mission organised by the International Bank for Reconstruction and Development (IBRD) at the instance of the Singapore government along with the governments of Britain and the Federation of Malaya. The second was the 1959 report made by F.J. Lyle, a Canadian industrial development specialist, under the Colombo Plan, and came to be known as the Lyle Report. The third and most important was the Winsemius Report of 1961. As soon as the PAP came to power in 1959, it asked the IBRD for advice, and consequently a United Nations Industrial Survey Mission headed by Albert Winsemius visited Singapore from October to December 1960 to study, *inter alia*, possibilities of industrialisation (Cheng 1991: 188–9; Rodan 1989: 64).

The Lyle Report, like the IBRD (1955) report, emphasised the need for industrialisation as a solution to the unemployment problem, and advised the government to establish an efficient organisation for industrial development. The Pioneer Industries Ordinance of 1959 was based on this report, and under this new law those firms which were granted pioneer-industries status were to be exempted from paying the prevailing 40 per cent corporate tax for five years.

However, it was the Winsemius Report which had the strongest impact on the government, for the State Development Plan (1961–4) was based on it. The report pointed out that, since Singapore could not rely on foreign trade alone to cope with the annual average population growth rate of 4 per cent in spite of its position as the world's leading trade centre, it was necessary for the Singapore government to make an industrial development plan. Moreover, it contained not only the measures to solve the immediate problem of unemployment but also a ten-year industrialisation programme. The Winsemius Report advised that success in industrial development would lead to the enlargement of the domestic market, and would require the country to make an export drive for overseas markets. Winsemius advised the Singapore government to look towards far-distant foreign markets rather than the markets of the neighbouring countries which would be limited in size, while recommending the establishment of an Economic Development Board as a special organisation (United Nations 1961: i–ii, 46).

The report also made recommendations to the government that promising industries should be those which could utilise the ability and skill of the local workforce to produce quality goods for overseas markets and which would be able to contribute to the immediate expansion of the domestic market. Those industries included ship-building, steel-rolling, electrical appliances and parts, and chemicals. For example, ship-breaking and ship-building could create employment within a short period of time, while metal products, upholstery and electrical switch gears would be required for Singapore's building and construction plan (*ibid.*: 128–9).

The role of state in economic development

According to the Winsemius Report, the intervention of the state should be restricted to only certain selected industries, and the initiative for the industrialisation programme should be taken primarily by the private sector in the light of comparative advantages. The Singapore government ought to make the utmost efforts to attract well-known foreign companies to make direct investment into Singapore, and to promote joint ventures between local manufacturers and these foreign companies (United Nations 1961: 129–30).

However, contrary to the recommendations made in the report, the government began to play an immensely large role in industrialisation. In August 1961 the Economic Development Board (EDB) was set up to replace the Industrial Promotion Board in accordance with the State Development Plan which later became a Five-Year Development Plan. It was provided with a budget totaling $100 million for the 1961–4 period (or $25 million per year on average), a huge jump from an annual budget of $1 million which had previously been allocated to the Industrial Promotion Board (Cheng 1991: 190). It had the objective of developing new industries and accelerating the growth of existing ones, and provided loans and technical support to local industrialists to set up and run factories.

In December 1960 the Singapore government invited a team of six Japanese technical experts headed by Yanagisawa, Y., the president of the International Construction Engineers' Association of Japan, to prepare a detailed plan for an industrial estate at Jurong. For two months the Japanese team conducted a survey in the country in close consultation with the UN Industrial Survey Mission (Tonan Ajia Chosakai 1961: 178; Matsuo 1962: 151–2). Based on the plan, the newly created EDB set out to build the industrial estate (the Jurong Industrial Estate) in 1961, with the object of attracting foreign firms to set up subsidiaries as pioneer industries in such areas as steel-rolling, ship-building and ship-repairing, plywood and paper (SOS 1961: 101).

As the government came to realise the need for the protection of local industries by tariffs against unfair foreign competition, in July 1962 it passed a Tariff Advisory Commission Ordinance No. 23 in the Legislative Assembly, and set up a Tariff Advisory Commission in November. The commission then advised the government to impose tariffs on certain imported goods for the purpose of protecting local industries which were already in existence or were about to be set up (SOS 1962: 127). When a common market was launched as a result of the formation of Malaysia in 1963, the Singapore government adopted a development policy promoting further the growth of import-substitution industries. In 1963 import quotas were instituted, and by May 1965 as many as 230 imported items became subject to quantitative restrictions and import licensing (Lim and Associates 1988: 284; Tan & Ow 1982: 282).

In the field of public housing the government also played an important role. In the early 1960s, as the population of Singapore had risen steeply from 978,000 in 1947 to 1.5 million in 1959, there was a serious housing problem. Therefore in 1961 a Housing and Development Board (HDB) was set up with the object of dealing with this problem. The HDB completed over 50,000 low-cost housing units during 1961–5, and over 60,000 in the next five years (DSS 1983: 100).

As seen above, in the first half of the 1960s the Singapore government under the leadership of Lee Kuan Yew came to play the leading role in implementing an import-substitution industrialisation policy, and set a basic pattern of state-led development, a pattern which was to be employed in the post-independence period; and it was Japan which was most sought after by the government for this purpose.

THE REPARATIONS ISSUE AND THE LEE REGIME'S POLICY TOWARDS JAPANESE FIRMS

The blood-debt question

As seen in the previous chapter, the colonial power on behalf of Singapore and Malaya renounced the right to claim war reparations from Japan. Consequently, although the Singapore Joint Appeal Committee of Japanese-

Massacred Chinese wanted to demand compensation from Japan in 1946, the issue was not taken up by the British government (Kratoska 1998: 336). However, in early 1962 large quantities of human remains were unearthed at a housing construction site on the east coast of the country. With this discovery, Chinese began to denounce the massacre of Chinese committed by the Japanese Army shortly after the start of the occupation in 1942. Then the blood-debt movement, led by the Chinese Chamber of Commerce, began to take shape, with demands for compensation for the massacre. Although the issue was not settled until September 1967,[3] it did not seem to stand in the way of Japanese capital investment in Singapore. On the contrary, in our view it was definitely a factor facilitating the advance of Japanese firms into Singapore. In what follows, we shall examine the background to the blood-debt issue, and then attempt to show the basis for our argument.

In May and June 1962 there were heated discussions on the blood-debt issue at the Singapore Legislative Assembly. As Lee Kuan Yew had visited Japanese Prime Minister Ikeda Hayato on 25 May, Tee Kim Leng, a Chinese MP for Pasir Panjang, questioned him as to whether or not he had discussed with Ikeda the question of compensation for the incident. Lee then replied that he had told the Japanese Prime Minister that Japan would have to make atonement to Singapore for the massacre of the overseas Chinese. However, he emphasised that although Japan ought to give compensation for the massacre on moral grounds, since Britain had renounced the right to claim for war reparations and signed a peace treaty with Japan at San Francisco in 1951, Singapore was not in a position to claim for it now (SLA 1962: 285–8).

In this matter, Japan for her part maintained her firm position that the reparations issue no longer existed. Indeed, Maeda Kensaku, the Japanese Consul-General at Singapore told the colonial authorities in December 1962 that, as far as the Japanese government was concerned, the question of Japan's war reparations payment was over, for the San Francisco Peace Treaty stipulated that Japan agreed to pay war reparations once for all, including the forfeiture of billions of dollars' worth of Japanese assets left in Singapore and Malaya. Nevertheless, he told them that Japan would be prepared to finance the building of a park or monument, not as compensation, but as a gesture of friendship from one country to another (PRO, British Embassy, Tokyo to FO, Enclosure, 28 December 1962, FO 371/170788).

In the meantime, as the Chinese in Singapore were not happy with the Japanese government's position, on 25 August 1963 they held a mass rally to demand compensation from Japan. It was mainly organised by the Chinese Chamber of Commerce and attended by some 120,000 people. The Chinese decided to organise a boycott of Japanese goods, and made the following resolutions: (a) the peoples of Singapore, Malaya, North Borneo and Sarawak will co-operate in demanding compensation from Japan; (b) unless the blood-debt is compensated, people will start a non-cooperation movement against Japan; (c) unless compensation is paid, the people will exert pressure on the Singapore government to refuse the entry of Japanese nationals (*Asahi Shimbun*, 26 August 1963; Shingaporu Nihonjinkai 1978: 103).[4] Prime Minister Lee stated in a public speech at the mass rally that in order to speed up industrialisation it was the government's policy to introduce industrial technology from all over the world, and Japan could provide it at the lowest costs. He also said that no visit passes should be issued to Japanese for new commercial and industrial activities after the rally of that night (Takeshita 1995: 521–2). However, Lee's real intention was that Singapore ought to make use of Japan for its economic development, and treat the incident as something in the past (*ibid.*: 521).

It should be noted that the Chinese Chamber of Commerce planned to organise the boycott of Japanese goods from 16 September onwards, unless the Japanese government agreed to pay compensation for the blood-debt issue. But this happened to coincide with the date of the formation of Malaysia, in which Singapore was to join. As noted earlier, the merger led Indonesia to adopt a confrontation policy, while the Philippines made a vigorous protest. Consequently, there was hardly any time left for the Chinese to talk about the demand for the blood-debt compensation. To make matters worse for them, Tunku Abdul Rahman, the Prime Minister of newly-formed Malaysia, was placed in charge of the negotiations with Japan. It is therefore not surprising that the Chinese boycott of Japanese goods had to be postponed indefinitely.

As regards Lee Kuan Yew's statement, there is no evidence to suggest that the Singapore government curtailed Japanese capital investment and the entry of Japanese nationals in relation to the blood-debt issue. Although we have not been able to obtain any information about the number of passes issued to Japanese in 1964 and 1965, it is highly unlikely that the government stood in the way of the entry of Japanese nationals into Singapore. In fact, many Japanese firms made direct investments in the country at that time, and the number of Japanese company employees sent there must have increased greatly.

Incidentally, there is an interesting fact concerning the issuance of passes to Japanese. In the 1950s the Japanese were issued mainly with business visit passes, but in the first half of the 1960s most of the passes issued to them were professional visit passes. According to the Immigration Department, the number of professional visit passes rose from 29 in 1960 to 122 in 1961, and then declined to 115 in 1962, and 86 in 1963. As for the number of business visit passes, it declined sharply from 45 in 1960 to 16 in 1961 and 11 in 1962, but then recovered somewhat to 28 in 1963, while the numbers of social visit passes were 50, 64, 13 and 77 respectively (SOS Immigration Department, 1960–3).

Today, professional visit passes are normally issued to short-term foreign visitors such as journalists, entertainers and participants at conferences, but not to company employees. However, on 24 July 1963 the Singapore government released information on professional visit passes in the Legislative Assembly with the purpose of shedding light on the activities of the Japanese companies and the number of Japanese staff working for these companies: the number of professional visit passes issued to Japanese was 129 in 1961, 88 in 1962, 32 in the first six months of 1963, and as of July 1963 there were 164 Japanese working in Singapore (SLA 1963a: 98–100). It should be noted that these figures were different from those of the Immigration Department. The reason for the discrepancy is not very clear.

It is evident from the above that professional visit passes, rather than business visit passes, were issued to Japanese company employees. As the Lee regime was in high expectation of Japanese co-operation for Singapore's industrialisation, it tried to attract those Japanese firms which were indispensable for that purpose, by issuing professional visit passes to their Japanese employees who had technical knowledge and other expertise.

The Singapore government's attitude towards Japan

One would nonetheless wonder why it was that Japanese nationals and companies were not whole-heartedly boycotted by the Chinese who were demanding compensation from Japan for the blood-debt issue. According to Sakurai Kiyohiko, the ex-managing director of Jurong Shipyard Ltd, the blood-debt issue did not stand in the way of Japanese investment at all. Indeed, the Singapore government made it abundantly clear that the issue would not make any negative impact on the advance into the country of Japanese companies, and it kept its firm position in this respect (OHI Sakurai).

In fact, ever since the PAP won a land-slide victory in the general election of May 1959, Lee Kuan Yew continued to have high expectations of Japanese co-operation in implementing Singapore's industrialisation plan.[5] In October of that year, Finance Minister Goh Keng Swee requested the Japanese Foreign Ministry and the Japan External Trade Organisation (Nihon Boeki Shinkokai) to arrange for capital investment by Japanese firms in such areas as iron, ship-building, electrical machinery and textile industries. The form of investment could be either joint ventures or 100 per cent Japanese ownership, and Singapore would be ready to grant various benefits to Japanese companies (*Asahi Shimbun*, 29 October 1959). According to *Asahi Shimbun* (a leading Japanese newspaper), at that time the Japanese Ministry of Trade and Industry was aware of certain merits of capital investment into Singapore, but was concerned with the following problems: (a) The Lee Kuan Yew government was a Socialist government formed only a few months before, and the internal political situation was unstable; (b) Singapore was at variance with Malaya; (c) as the government strongly rejected capital investment from Britain, there was a possibility of British interference in Japanese investment; (d) in addition to a lack of supporting industries, Singapore was not really in a position to start trade with neighbouring countries right away (*ibid.*, 29 October 1959).

As noted earlier, Lee Kuan Yew asked Japan for co-operation in making a plan for construction of the Jurong Industrial Estate, and in response, the Japanese government sent a survey team of six experts to Singapore in late 1960. In March 1962, the EDB established an office in Tokyo with the main purpose of inviting Japanese companies to set up plants in Singapore (*ibid.*, 31 March 1962). Singapore came to have a high opinion of Japan, because, as noted in the preceding two chapters, the Singaporeans were awakened to self-reliance thanks to the fact that Japan had easily defeated the Western military forces in Southeast Asia at the beginning of the Pacific War and exercised military control over the region for three and a half years. Moreover, as suggested in Chapters 5 and 6, the industrialisation policy of the Japanese military authorities during the occupation period might have given Singaporean leaders a strong impression of the country. One cannot entirely dismiss, for example, the possibility that the government decided to invite the Ishikawajima-Harima Heavy Industries (IHI), a Japanese ship-building firm, to set up a joint-venture company, Jurong Shipyard Ltd in 1963, partly because some of the PAP leaders had been impressed by the management of the Syonan Shipyard.

Unlike the IHI, the Bank of Tokyo and Japanese trading companies reacted sensitively to the blood-debt rally. A group of six Singapore branch managers of the bank and the five leading trading companies (Mitsui & Co., Mitsubishi Corporation, Marubeni-Iida, Ito Chu and Nissho[6]) returned temporarily to Japan in September 1963, i.e. one month after the anti-Japanese mass rally, and made a petition to the government and the business circles for the early settlement of the blood-debt issue (Takeshita 1995: 523). It was Nakayama Kazumi, the Singapore branch manager of Nissho, who worked particularly hard for this.[7]

Nakayama Kazumi and Sakurai Kiyohiko reacted differently to the blood-debt issue on several grounds. Nakayama was fluent in Chinese, establishing close relations with the Chinese Chamber of Commerce, which exerted strong pressure on the government to demand compensation from Japan.[8] He became aware of the Chinese people's anti-Japanese feelings through the Chinese language, and was compelled by moral obligations to endeavour to solve the blood-debt issue. In sharp contrast, Sakurai was working for Jurong Shipyard Ltd, a joint-venture enterprise with the Singapore government, and kept close contacts with Singapore's English-educated political leaders, partly thanks to his good command of English. He felt the enthusiasm of the Lee government for achieving industrialisation with Japanese support, and in fact co-operated with the government actively. Indeed, he did not seem to feel any uneasiness about the anti-Japanese movement.

It should be borne in mind that at that time there existed a hostile relationship between Lee Kuan Yew's PAP regime on the one hand and the Chinese Chamber of Commerce and the Chinese public on the other. It was a political factor which played a part in influencing the government to choose foreign enterprises instead of local Chinese enterprises in order to promote industrialisation later on (Iwasaki 1990: 160). The PAP government was dominated by people who had been educated in Britain and mainly used English,[9] whereas members of the Chinese Chamber of Commerce were predominantly Chinese speakers and were strongly opposed to the government. The conservative group of Chinese entrepreneurs who were attached to the Chinese Chamber of Commerce had formed the Democratic Party in February 1955.

The strife between the two groups mentioned above had a deep impact on major political decisions and behaviours. For instance, on 25 August 1963 Lee Kuan Yew attended the mass rally for the blood-debt organised by the Chinese Chamber of Commerce, because, 'seeing the heightening blood-debt movement incited by the Malayan Communist Party, he was determined to bring it under control so as not to lose Japanese co-operation which was indispensable for the industrialisation of his country' (Takeshita 1995: 521–2). Moreover, at the blood-debt negotiations with Japan after the 1965 independence, the government made it clear that 'it did not have good relations with the Chinese Chamber of Commerce, and intended to conduct the negotiation at its own pace without any pressure from the chamber' (*ibid.*).

There was also, more specifically, at the same time a power struggle between the Lee regime and those Chinese, notably Communists, who were in favour of the demand for blood-debt compensation. A well-known figure in this conflict was Tan Lark Sye, a director of the Oversea-Chinese Banking Corporation (OCBC), and also the chairman of the Chinese Chamber of Commerce in the early 1950s. Tan was a staunch supporter of the Barisan Socialis, and was critical of the PAP government for not attaching importance to Chinese education and culture (Turnbull 1977: 284–5).[10] According to Iwasaki Ikuo, he was, 'deprived temporarily of Singapore citizenship because of his financial support to a communist candidate in the 1963 election' (Iwasaki 1990: 160–1). However, the large majority of those who demanded compensation for the blood-debt were not prominent persons like Tan, as they were largely students, workers and other ordinary Chinese who were in support of Communism, and were opposed to the Lee Kuan Yew regime.

Although Lee put emphasis on Japan's moral responsibility, added to the fact that the UK had renounced the right to demand war reparations from Japan, he had to consider, first of all, how to bring his political opponents under control. Similarly, since those who led the blood-debt campaign were engaged in a power struggle with the Lee government, they could not afford simply to concentrate on the anti-Japanese movement. In fact, according to Hara Fujio, although the blood-debt demand movement began after the discovery of skeletal remains in 1962, similar remains had been found in Singapore and Malaya before that, and monuments for the victims had been built in many cities and towns (Hara 1994:173). The discovery of the remains in 1962 does not therefore seem to have been the only reason or even a decisive one for the beginning of the blood-debt movement.

The Lee government employed an effective way to simultaneously get rid of the root cause of the problems between the Chinese on the one hand and the Japanese nationals and companies on the other. It seems that while stressing Japan's moral obligations, the government made skilful use of those obligations to invite Japanese firms to make capital investment into Singapore. As we shall study in detail shortly, it was done in the form of control over the activities of influential Japanese trading companies in the country. However, one cannot be sure whether or not this control was exercised as part and parcel of the policy regarding the blood-debt issue alone. It must be said nevertheless that control was imposed on Japanese trading companies in 1963 when the movement for the blood-debt demand was at its height, and it did have the effect of diminishing the anti-Japanese feelings among the Chinese.

The blood-debt issue heightened the anti-Japanese feelings among local Chinese, but, since the Singapore government was in the process of making preparations for real industrialisation along the line of the UN reports, notably the Winsemius Report, it kept itself away from the blood-debt related anti-Japanese movement, and compelled Japanese trading companies to make contributions to the country's industrialisation.

Controls over the activities of Japanese trading companies

In 1963 the PAP government informed the Japanese trading companies in writing of seven clauses concerning restrictions on their activities in Singapore. Although we have been unable to obtain detailed information about the contents of all the conditions, one of them was a ban on tripartite trade and domestic commerce including retailing and wholesaling, and another concerned the contributions by the Japanese firms towards Singapore's industrialisation. There is little doubt that the ban on tripartite trade dealt the greatest blow to the trading companies. They had already begun to undertake this kind of trade in the 1950s, and it had become the mainstay of their economic activities by the early 1960s.[11] They were obviously very anxious to have the ban removed as soon as possible, but it was not until the end of the 1960s that it was finally lifted.[12] However, the condition concerning Japanese contributions to industrialisation was stressed particularly heavily by the government. In other words, its inclusion shows clearly the government's enterprising spirit for industrialisation and its high expectations for the role of the Japanese trading companies as project organisers.[13] Indeed, Nakayama Kazumi had a high opinion of the Singaporean leaders saying that 'since the government could foresee the leading role of the trading companies in the country's industrial promotion as early as 1963, it had indeed a sharp eye for the future' (Nakayama 1976: 8–9).

Japanese trading companies were obliged to induce Japanese manufacturing companies to make capital investment in Singapore if they wanted to establish branches there and obtain and/or renew passes for their resident representatives. They therefore made active use of this stipulation in order to advance into the country, get passes for their staffs, and expand their economic activities. As a matter of fact, it was said that, at times, they high-handedly induced Japanese manufacturing companies to invest in Singapore, especially when they were involved in setting up joint-venture enterprises with them (OHI Satta).

It seems that the ban on Japanese involvement in domestic trade helped subdue, to a certain extent, the anti-Japanese feelings among the Chinese merchants and the general public, for Japanese competition in this field could be easily seen. On the other hand, the pragmatic attitude of the Lee regime towards Japanese capital investment seemingly meant that, as the Japanese companies were trusted by the government, they and the Japanese community in general came to feel a sense of security in the country. In short, the Singapore government exercised strict control over the activities of the Japanese trading companies which were encroaching on the interests of local Chinese merchants, while, at the same time, making active use of them to attract Japanese manufacturing investment for the sake of the country's industrialisation.

Interestingly, today, control over the activities of Japanese trading companies is hardly known among those Japanese who are concerned with Singapore, including the present members of the Japanese Chamber of Commerce and Industry in Singapore and the Japan Singapore Association in Tokyo. Similarly, although the blood-debt issue remains an unforgettable incident in the history of Japan–Singapore relations, there is no evidence to suggest that Japanese companies in Singapore were much troubled by it. Indeed, as we have noted above, Japanese companies could undertake economic activities with some restrictions even during the height of the blood-debt movement, and did not therefore need to pay special attention to the issue.

JAPANESE CAPITAL INVESTMENT IN SINGAPORE IN THE FIRST HALF OF THE 1960s

Main features of Japanese companies in Singapore

According to Nakayama Kazumi, in 1962 there were over 300 Japanese including dependants present in Singapore (Nakayama 1979: 30–1). As of

July 1963, there were 53 Japanese companies operating in Singapore, and 157 Japanese nationals holding professional visit passes. Among these companies, Maruzen Sekiyu kept the largest number of Japanese staff at its Singapore subsidiary, the Maruzen Toyo Oil Co. Ltd (44 persons), followed by Japan Air Lines (twelve persons), and the Bank of Tokyo (ten persons). Large trading companies, namely Mitsubishi Corporation, Mitsui & Co., Toyo Menka, Marubeni-Iida, Nichimen Jitsugyo and Nomura Boeki each employed several Japanese. Most of the other firms employed one or at most a few Japanese each (SLA, 1963a: 98–100).

It should be noted that, according to Yoshihara Kunio, the first Japanese manufacturing investments in post-war Singapore were made in the early 1960s in response to the Singapore government's industrialisation policy and also to a high expectation in the common market that would result from Singapore's participation in Malaysia (Yoshihara 1976: 50; *idem* 1978: 20). It is true that there was a Japanese investment boom at that time, but as already pointed out, they were obviously not the first Japanese investments, for some Japanese firms had made capital investment in the1950s.[14]

What, then, were the main characteristics of the Japanese companies in Singapore in the first half of the 1960s? During the period from January 1960 to August 1965, 34 Japanese companies were registered in Singapore. Of these,17 were registered in 1963, and their registration was done mainly in July and August of that year just before the formation of Malaysia, revealing their expectations of the advantages to be gained from a common market. Of the remaining 17 companies, four each were registered in 1962, 1964 and 1965, and three in 1961. As for the start-up period of operations, of those companies whose information is available, three began in 1963, seven in 1964, and eight in 1965. Indeed, it is highly unlikely that the blood-debt issue had a negative effect on Japanese investments in Singapore.

As in the 1950s, some companies were involved in foreign trade and/or related activities, including the Nippon Fire & Marine Insurance Co. Ltd, Ito Chu, the Mitsui Bank (the present Sakura Bank) and Akatsuki Kaiun (Akatsuki Shipping), while there were also manufacturers, including Sanyo Denki (Sanyo Electric) and Piasu Keshohin (Piasu Cosmetics), which hoped to promote the sales of their products by setting up subsidiaries.

In sharp contrast to these two types of company, however, in the 1960s manufacturing companies made large investments for the purpose of production in Singapore. They can be classified into four main categories. First, companies which were initially based on the traditional entrepôt trade and then expanded into other parts of Southeast Asia include Maruzen Sekiyu (oil-refining) and the Ishikawajima-Harima Heavy Industries Ltd (ship-building and ship-repairing). Second, companies which were concerned with infrastructural and related works in the Malaysian common market (including Singapore), or which supplied mechanical equipment, machine parts and materials there, include Onoda Cement (cement-production), Nippon Paint and Kansai Paint (paint-manufacturing), Yuasa Denchi and Airo Boeki (electrical parts), Eidai Sangyo (plywood and veneer), Kawasaki Seitetsu (zinc sheets), Sekisui Kagaku, Maruichi Kokan and Nippon Kokan (vinyl and steel pipes), Furukawa Denko (electric wire), Shin Nihon Seitetsu (iron wire) and Momoi Seimo (fishing-net weaving). Third, companies which aimed at the Singapore and Malaysian markets for consumer goods include Yuasa Denchi (batteries for motor bikes), Bridgestone Tire (tyres and tubes), Mitsui Seito (sugar-refining), Toyo Rayon and Teijin (textiles), and Kao Sekken – the present Kao (shampoo and washing powder). Finally, there were construction companies such as Daiwa Hausu, Kajima Kensetsu (the present Kajima), Toa Kensetsu and Mizuno Gumi (the present Goyo Kensetsu).

Although the first half of the 1960s witnessed slow economic growth in Singapore, it was nevertheless a brisk period for the construction industry thanks to a sharp increase in public investment. Indeed, from 1961 onwards the government directed public investment largely into the fields of housing and education, and to a lesser extent into the construction of industrial infrastructure, in particular in the development of the Jurong Industrial Estate. Housing investment accounted for 22 per cent of Singapore's fixed capital formation in the decade from 1955 to 1965, and helped to lay the grounds for future economic growth in the post-independence period (Buchanan 1972: 68). Indeed, Japanese manufacturing firms advanced into Singapore, aiming at the rapidly growing demand for building materials in connection with public housing and other construction works, and also at providing the Malaysian market with consumer goods. Many of these manufacturing investments were directed into those industries which were listed in the Winsemius Report.

Another feature of Japanese companies in Singapore was an increase in the size of each investment. The investment made by Onoda Cement amounted to $6 million, while the IHI and Teijin made $50 million investment each. Other large capital investments included $65 million by Maruzen Sekiyu and Toyo Menka in the Maruzen Toyo Oil Co. Ltd, $5 million by Eidai Sangyo and Iwai Sangyo in the Pan Malaysia Industries Ltd, and $5 million by Kawasaki Seitetsu in the Singapore Galvanizing Industries Ltd.

It was the trading companies which played a major role in these investments. There was a total of 34 investments, of which 20 (or 59 per cent of the total) involved the trading companies. Moreover, if one refers only to the manufacturing sector, then 17 out of 22 investments (or 77 per cent of the total) were in a joint venture with the trading companies which often acted as the largest or equal investors. It may be interesting to compare these percentages with those of the trading companies' involvement in joint ventures in a later period. Tran Van Tho has analysed Japanese investments in five ASEAN countries, using the data contained in the 1981 issue of the *Kaigai Kigyo Shinshutsu Kigyo Soran* (General Survey of Japanese Firms

Abroad) (Toyo Keizai Shimposha 1981), and has concluded that, of the 195 cases of Japanese investment in Singapore, there were 39 (or 20 per cent of the total) involving Japanese trading companies: four cases involved trading companies alone, and 35 cases were joint ventures between them and manufacturing companies. As for the five ASEAN states as a whole, there were 248 cases of Japanese investment (or 34 per cent of the total) either by trading companies alone or jointly by trading companies and manufacturing companies (Tran 1982: 23–5). These percentages were much smaller than those of the pre-independence period. It is true that he has taken into consideration only nine large general trading companies, omitting small and medium-sized trading companies as well as specialised trading companies. Had he also studied all kinds of trading companies, the percentage of the investments involving them would have been somewhat larger.

In the first half of the 1960s, the trading companies launched a series of joint ventures, mainly because they came to play the role of project organisers. It is true, however, that their joint-venture partners were not confined to Japanese firms. Mitsui & Co., for example, chose the Hong Leong Group as a joint-venture partner to set up the United Industrial Paper Products Manufacturing Co. Ltd in July 1963.

The trading companies played a crucial role in attracting Japanese manufacturing investments into Singapore. At that time, manufacturing companies were not well acquainted with overseas market conditions, and did not have a sufficient number of staff who had good command of foreign languages and who had working experiences abroad. They therefore needed to rely on trading companies for these. The Singapore government obliged the Japanese trading companies to make contributions towards industrialis-ation as one of the conditions for their activities, and considered their organising role extremely important. Indeed, it must be said that the govern-ment succeeded in so doing, as demonstrated by many Japanese investments involving trading companies.

Japanese manufacturing companies

As noted above, large numbers of Japanese manufacturing firms advanced into Singapore in the first half of the 1960s, but information on most of them is very limited.

In the early 1960s, manufacturers of textiles and plywood made capital investments. For example, in March 1963 Pan-Malaysia Industries Ltd was set up with an authorised capital of $5 million, and was granted pioneer-industries status by the Singapore government. It was a Japan–Singapore joint venture with a paid-up capital of $2,247,000, of which 29 per cent was subscribed by two Japanese firms, Eidai Sangyo and Nissho. It built a modern 30,000 sq ft factory in the Jurong Industrial Estate to produce some 20 million sq ft of wood veneer and plywood annually, using timber from the Malayan and Bornean forests (Harada 1969: 89–90; *Malayan Trade Digest*, 1 December 1963).

In 1963, several joint-venture companies were also formed in the textile industry in Singapore. Swan Socks Manufacturing Co. (Malaysia) Ltd was, for example, set up as a joint venture with an authorised capital of $5 million, of which $1 million was paid up by three Japanese firms (Ataka Sangyo, Toyo Rayon and Ikeo Socks) and Siakson Trading Co. Ltd, and was granted pioneer-industries status. It was engaged in the production of nylon socks and nylon threads (Harada 1969: 78–9; *Malayan Trade Digest*, 1 June 1964).

We shall now examine in some detail Maruzen Sekiyu, Ishikawajima-Harima Heavy Industries (IHI), Bridgestone Tire and Kawasaki Seitetsu, for their investments are considered fairly important and there is also some useful information about them.

Maruzen Sekiyu (Maruzen Oil Co. Ltd)

Maruzen Sekiyu (the present Cosmo Sekiyu) set out to diversify its activities in 1952 when Wada Kanji was appointed to the post of president. In Japan, the company set up Maruzen Tochi in 1957 to embark on the ownership and management of real estates, and to develop housing sites. In the following year, it established Maruzen Hodo with a view to increasing sales outlets for asphalt, and Maruzen Gasu Kaihatsu for supplying gas in small cities, making use of propane and butane gases which were produced through oil-refining processes. In foreign countries, Maruzen Sekiyu set up the Maruzen Oil Company of the US in 1956 to provide bunker fuel to Japanese ships calling at American ports, and also established the Unimar Co. Ltd (Hong Kong) as a joint venture with the Union Oil Co. Ltd of the US in 1959.[15]

It was during this period of Maruzen Sekiyu's rapid expansion both at home and abroad that the company established the Maruzen Toyo Oil Co. Ltd with a capital of $65 million in Singapore in September 1960 (*Singapore Trade*, May 1963: 13). It was a fifty–fifty joint venture with Toyo Menka, a Japanese trading company, aimed at oil-refining and sales of its petroleum products in the Southeast Asian region. As it was a full-scale Japanese investment, it did not fail to draw public attention in Japan (*Asahi Shimbun*, 30 March 1960). In February 1962, its oil-refinery was completed at Tanjong Berlayer, Pasir Panjang (Maruzen Sekiyu 1987: 20–1).

In the late 1950s petroleum products were Singapore's second most important export item coming only after rubber. Of Singapore's total exports, rubber accounted for 42.5 per cent ($1,029.1 million), and petroleum products 12.1 per cent ($299.3 million) (COS 1959:105, 109). Singapore had excellent oil-storage facilities, and became the major petroleum distribution centre in Southeast Asia. Indeed, it was on the threshold of emerging as the leading oil-refining base for Southeast Asia in 1961 when the Royal Dutch Shell Group built the first oil-refinery which was given the first pioneer-industries status by the Singapore government. Maruzen Sekiyu was the second foreign oil company to advance into Singapore, and Esso, Mobil, British Petroleum and the Singapore Refining Company joined the oil-refining industry later on (Sharma 1989: 5).

Undoubtedly, Maruzen Sekiyu took part in the investment boom in the oil industry. Apparently, the Singapore government had a high expectation of its investment, simply because, as noted earlier, it had issued as many as 44 professional visit passes to the company's employees by July 1963. However, the oil-refining operations of the Maruzen Toyo Oil Co. Ltd did not last long, mainly because the parent company had financial difficulties.

From the 1956 Suez crisis until 1959, oil companies in Japan were busily engaged in the expansion of their refining facilities in response to a growing demand for refined oil. Then in January 1960 the Japanese government announced that crude oil imports should be liberalised in the near future, and relaxed the import restriction. In June of the same year, it abolished the system of foreign currency allocations. Consequently, in the early 1960s the oil companies competed with one another in increasing oil imports and expanding further their refining capacity. They soon began to engage in cut-throat competition among themselves with the result that the wholesale price of petrol per kilo litre (kl) fell from ¥14,942 in 1960 to ¥11,695 in 1961, ¥10,680 in 1962, and ¥11,165 in 1963, while that of fuel oil also declined from ¥8,850 to ¥8,020, ¥6,917 and ¥7,042 in the same years (Sekiyu Renmei 1981: 190). In order to put an end to this cut-throat competition, the government enacted an oil industry law in May 1962 to exercise control over the volume of crude oil imports, *inter alia*. By this time, all the oil companies in Japan sustained heavy losses, but it was Maruzen Sekiyu which suffered most severely from low oil prices. In February 1960, Maruzen Seikyu had increased its capital to ¥11,025 million to emerge as the largest oil company in Japan, but it had serious financial difficulties by October 1962. In the early 1960s the oil company had made long-term charter contracts with three shipping firms, namely, the Mitsui Senpaku Kaisha, Japan Line and Yamashita Shin Nihon Kisen. However, the market rate for charters subsequently declined steeply, but, because of the contracts, Maruzen Sekiyu had no choice but to continue to pay high charter rates to the shipping firms (Maruzen Sekiyu 1987: 26, 28 and 150).

In October 1962 Maruzen Sekiyu planned to dispose of its tankers and the Maruzen Toyo Oil Co. Ltd (*Asahi Shimbun*, 2 October 1962). Moreover, in November 1962, Vice-President Sugimoto Shigeru and four executive directors resigned from the company, while in February 1963 President Wada Kanji also resigned on the ground of mismanagement. In May 1963, Maruzen Sekiyu was able to increase its capital to ¥16,425 million, thanks to Union Oil's equity participation in a total amount of US$15 million (¥5,400 million), but it nevertheless continued to have difficulties. In June 1963, it decided to reconstruct its Singapore subsidiary by asking British Petroleum and Shell Oil through Union Oil for co-operation. By this time, the Maruzen Toyo Oil Co. Ltd had accumulated a deficit of ¥300 million, and was still making a financial loss of ¥10 million a month due to its low-level operations and limited sales of petroleum products. Maruzen Sekiyu therefore asked the two European firms to subcontract its oil-refinery subsidiary with a view to raising the level of its operations greatly (*Asahi Shimbun*, 2 June 1963). However, this plan did not work, and all the facilities of the Maruzen Toyo Oil Co. Ltd had to be sold to British Petroleum in June 1964 for the sake of the reconstruction of its parent company in Japan (Maruzen Sekiyu 1987: 29).

Ishikawajima-Harima Heavy Industries Ltd

Jurong Shipyard Ltd was set up by the Ishikawajima-Harima Heavy Industries Ltd (IHI) in joint venture with the Singapore government in 1963. The ship-building industry had hitherto developed in association with the growth of the free port, both in building new ships and repairing those ships calling there. Indeed, Jurong Shipyard Ltd became also largely concerned with ship-repairing, for as late as 1970 some 80 per cent of its work was undertaken by its ship-repairing section (Higaki 1970: 35).

As already noted, the 1961 UN report (Winsemius Report) saw much prospect in the ship-building and ship-repairing industry, for it was an industry which was expected to create much employment. As soon as the recommendation was made in the report, the government thought that it would become a strategic industry for the country's industrialisation, and determined to look for a foreign ship-building company willing to make direct investment into Singapore.

When Lien Ying Chow, the founder of the Overseas Union Bank Ltd, and a political supporter of the PAP, was in Hong Kong in 1961, he asked the IHI management through Mr Tsumura of the Hong Kong branch for the possibility of making investment into Singapore, and this was the first time that Singapore approached the Japanese company (OHI Sakurai).[16] Prime Minister Lee Kuan Yew, Finance Minister Goh Keng Swee and some other political leaders then worked hard to attract the ship-building company to make direct investment into their country. For example, Goh Keng Swee visited Japan three times for this purpose in the two years before the IHI decided to send a survey mission to Singapore in 1962, and endeavoured to press for the realisation of the joint venture between the IHI and the Singapore government (Loh and Tey 1995: 14).

However, the IHI was of the view that the time was not yet ripe for investment in the country. As the Singapore government asked it again at the ECAFE's Tokyo Conference in March 1962, the company decided to send a survey mission to Singapore. The mission was headed by Sakurai Kiyohiko and included six specialists who had been involved in investment in Brazil, and it undertook feasibility studies (Sakurai 1982: 6; Higaki 1970: 38–9). In January 1963 the IHI eventually signed an agreement with the Economic Development Board (EDB) for the establishment and operation of a shipyard at Pulau Samulun in Jurong. The shipyard was a joint-venture enterprise with an authorised capital of $30 million (a paid-up capital of $9.5 million). The EDB and IHI held 49 per cent and 51 per cent of the shares respectively (Loh and Tey 1995: 1). In April 1963 the shipyard was incorporated.

The PAP leaders showed much interest in the IHI, but not in any other Japanese ship-building company, apparently because they highly valued the company which had made direct investment in Brazil in 1959. We may also assume that the PAP government wanted to invite a Japanese ship-building firm to set up a ship-building company in Singapore, for some of the leaders had seen the activities of the Syonan Shipyard during the occupation period, but on political grounds, they could not have asked the Mitsubishi Heavy Industries Ltd, which had been involved in the running of the shipyard.

Moreover, unlike other Japanese ship-building companies, the IHI was very eager to make direct investment abroad. The IHI had been created as a result of the merger of two comparatively small companies, Ishikawajima and Harima in December 1960. According to Tanaka Takao, the company did not have a huge shipping firm within its financial group, whereas the Mitsubishi Heavy Industries Ltd had the Nippon Yusen Kaisha, the Mitsui Zosen the Mitsui Senpaku Kaisha, and the Kawasaki Heavy Industries Ltd had the Kawasaki Kisen. As a result, it did not have a solid base in the domestic market, and did not have much prospect for further expansion within Japan, a handicap which forced the IHI to make direct investment abroad (Tanaka 1979: 147).

Grace Loh and Tey Sau Hing stress the importance of the positive policy adopted by the management concerning the company's overseas activities. Doko Toshio, the president and Shinto Hisashi, the managing director were both eager to venture abroad (Loh and Tey 1995: 19–21). In fact, as early as 1959 the IHI had set up a shipyard in Brazil. It was then considering the possibility of investing into other countries including Singapore, Taiwan, India, Pakistan, Greece and Bangladesh, and regarded Singapore as the best country for its next investment (Loh and Tey, 1995: 25). Therefore, when Doko was asked by Goh Keng Swee for investment, he responded positively and sent Shinto to Singapore. Shinto had talks with the political leaders including Lee Kuan Yew, Goh Keng Swee and Hon Sui Sen, and sympathised with Prime Minister Lee's policy of creating 'a Singapore for Singaporeans' by putting an end to Singapore's traditional relations with Britain (ibid.: 21, 24). Moreover, according to Sakurai, Goh Keng Swee and the bureaucrats who were involved in attracting IHI investment, as well as other Singaporeans whom he met while undertaking a survey in Singapore, had a strong desire for the country's economic development (OHI Sakurai).

Initially, the IHI planned to build many small vessels (with a carrying capacity of less than 1,000 gross tons each) to be anchored at Singapore for coastal trade in Southeast Asia (*Malayan Trade Digest*, October 1, 1962). At that time, its survey mission was of the opinion that if it built quality boats it could penetrate the market for boats and make large profits. However, when Jurong Shipyard began to build such boats, it ended in failure. This was largely because Chinese boat owners bought up far more boats in speculation than the survey mission had expected, and did not think of making efficient use of them for trading purposes. Therefore, the management of Jurong Shipyard was groping for what kind of work they should mainly undertake at the beginning of its operations. At that time, there were some British and Swedish ship-building companies in Singapore. But they were small in size of operations, and were mostly engaged in building ships for speculative purposes. The fact was that the main Western ship-building firms built ships in their own countries, and did not bother investing in Singapore (OHI Sakurai).

In 1965 Sakurai embarked on repair work for tankers at the shipyard, and opened the way for it to become an independent industry, making full use of Singapore's strategic location in the face of changing international shipping conditions (Sakurai 1975: 3).[17] Formerly, huge oil-tankers had just passed through the Straits of Malacca *en route* to Japan, and ship-repairing had been merely auxiliary to the port. However, shortly after Jurong Shipyard began to repair ships, Norwegian ship-owners became its best customers, for they were engaged at that time in transporting crude oil to Japan, and found it convenient to have their ships repaired at Singapore. Then Greek ships also made use of Jurong Shipyard for the same reason (OHI Sakurai). Although the repairing charges were higher in Singapore than those in Japan, many foreign tankers preferred to undergo repair work at Jurong Shipyard because Singapore had locational advantages over Japan. Ozawa Ushio explains:

> It is necessary to have a repair dock on a shipping route. As ships cost a lot to sail a day, they need to take the shortest possible route. For this reason, most of ships, which ply between Europe/the Middle East and the Far East, pass through the Straits of Malacca/Singapore. Normally, they enter the most-conveniently-located docks after unloading cargoes, and in the case of Far Eastern routes they mainly go to docks in Japan or Singapore. In the case of tankers carrying crude oil, all the gas trapped inside tankers has to be completely removed, because if any gas remains inside, it is very dangerous at the time of repair work. It takes about one week to do so. It [also] takes about one week to sail from Japan to Singapore. It is uneconomical to keep costly ships idle even for a single day. If ships head for Singapore as soon as they have unloaded crude oil, they can

have their gas removed on the way, and go straight to docks in Singapore. . . . This is the greatest advantage for repairing tankers at Singapore.

(Ozawa 1976: 32–3)

It should be borne in mind that in the first half of the 1960s Japan was experiencing high-speed economic growth, and her import of crude oil from the Middle East was rising sharply, for there was an expansion of oil consumption in the country. The volume of her crude-oil imports rose sharply from 8,553,000 kl in 1955 to 31,183,000 kl in 1960, 59,246,000 kl in 1963, 83,601,000 kl in 1965 and 140,534,000 kl in 1968. The bulk of these imports came from the Middle East (Sekiyu Renmei 1981). By trial and error Jurong Shipyard therefore realised what its locational advantages were at an early date, and managed to establish a footing for its development by changing its major work from ship-building to ship-repairing (Shingaporu Nihonjinkai 1987: 109).[18]

It is worth noting, incidentally, that the establishment of Jurong Shipyard helped facilitate the rationalisation and productivity improvement of the Singapore Port Authority's existing shipyard, which had hitherto continued to monopolise repair work for large ships. In 1966 the shipyard asked Britain's Swan Hunter Group to join the management, and it was re-established as Keppel Shipyard (with its shares wholly owned by the government) after becoming independent from the Port Authority in 1968. Also, the IHI set up Jurong Shipbuilders Ltd with the object of building large ships in 1969. By the late 1960s, ship-building and ship-repairing had emerged as one of the major industries in Singapore (Isobe 1990: 248–50).

Bridgestone Tire Co. Ltd

The Bridgestone Tire Co. Ltd set up a branch in Singapore in 1956 , primarily for the purpose of promoting the sales of its products in Southeast Asia. Malaya and Singapore were regarded by Bridgestone as an important base for the Southeast Asian markets.

At that time, rickshaws were still in wide use in the region, and bicycle tyres used by them accounted for a considerable part of its products. But these soon lost importance, and were replaced by tyres for motor bikes and vehicles. The number of cars registered in Singapore was 85,668 at the end of 1963 and 95,349 at the end of 1964 (*Singapore Trade*, March 1965: 25).

The company began to consider the manufacturing of tyres in the Federation of Malaya in expectation of a common market in 1961 when Singapore's merger with the Federation of Malaya was planned. In fact, the Malayan government had just given pioneer industries status to Dunlop Co. Ltd, and it did not intend to grant the same status to another tyre manufacturer. In view of this, Bridgestone had no choice but to abandon its initial plan to build a factory in Singapore (Burijisuton 1982: 243). However, in April 1963, Marubeni-Iida (the present Marubeni) made a proposal to Bridgestone Tire for setting up a joint-venture company in Singapore with Dato Low Yat of the Pan-Malaya Rubber Industries Ltd, which was then actively engaged in diverse activities in the Federation of Malaya, including cement production. The idea behind was to get pioneer status from the Singapore government instead of a preferential treatment from the Malayan government. Dato Low Yat was very anxious to set up a joint venture company with Bridgestone as soon as possible, for he was convinced that unless they obtained pioneer status from the Singapore government before the planned formation of Malaysia in August 1963, they would never get it from a new Malaysian government, especially in view of the fact that Dunlop had already been granted it by the Malayan government (Burijisuton 1982: 244–5).

In June 1963, Bridgestone sent to Singapore a survey mission headed by the vice-president Matsudaira, and it concluded a joint-venture agreement with the Pan-Malaya Rubber Industries Ltd in the following month. In August, a new company, Bridgestone Malaysian Co. Ltd was established with an authorised capital of $20 million ($10 million paid-up capital) (*The Straits Times*, 3 April 1975). The capital investment ratio was on an equal basis, i.e. 50 per cent subscribed by each side. Bridgestone rented from the Singapore government an area of 146,000 sq m for its factory site in the Jurong Industrial Estate, and then sent 31 Japanese engineers and supervisors to Singapore, including Fukuyama Hisashi who became the managing director of the new company, and others who were involved in factory construction. On 28 August, the Bridgestone Malaysia Co. Ltd was granted a five-year pioneer industries status by the Singapore government (Burijisuton 1982: 244–5). In April 1965 its factory began operations with a production capacity of 126,000 tyres and 126,000 tubes a year, and initially employed some 400 workers who worked in two shifts (*The Straits Times*, 3 April 1975; *Singapore Trade*, March 1965: 35). Its products were sold in Singapore as well as in the neighbouring countries.

However, the Bridgestone Malaysia Co. Ltd (renamed the Bridgestone Singapore Ltd in 1968) was plagued by regional politics. A few months after the company began production in April 1965, Singapore left Malaysia to become independent. Bridgestone's anniversary book describes that Singapore's separation from Malaysia was a great blow to the company, for its Singapore factory was set up to take advantage of the Malaysian common market (Burijiston 1982: 246). The Bridgestone Tire Co. Ltd made every effort to assist Bridgestone Malaysia by allocating to it on a priority basis some of the production orders which it secured. Partly because of such efforts, the subsidiary managed to take the business out of the red in the middle of 1967. Moreover, in 1969 the parent company invested an additional $5.5 million for the modernisation of the plant in Jurong (*The Straits*

Times, 3 April 1975). However, in 1970 the period of pioneer status expired. Besides, in 1980 the Singapore government removed a 40 per cent customs duty on imported tyres with the result that Bridgestone Singapore rapidly lost its competitive edge, and was obliged to cease its operations in the year (Burijiston 1982: 246).

Kawasaki Seitetsu (Kawasaki Steel Corporation)

Like ship-building and ship-repairing, the iron and steel manufacturing industry was one of the main industries recommended to Singapore in the Winsemius Report. In the first half of the 1960s, five iron and steel firms were set up in the Jurong Industrial Estate for the production of iron and steel goods including bar steel, electrolytic welded tubes and galvanised sheet iron. These were the National Iron Steel Mills Ltd (NISM; capital of $16 million) which was established by the EDB in 1961, the Simalpan Steel Industries Ltd (capital of $4,575,000; 14.64 per cent each subscribed by Nippon Kokan and Marubeni-Iida) which began operations in 1964, the Malaysia Steel Pipe Manufacturing Co. (capital of $15 million; 30 per cent each subscribed by Nissho and Maruichi Kokan), the Eastern Wire Manufacturing Co. Ltd (capital of $2,280,000; 16 per cent subscribed by Mitsui & Co. and 11 per cent by Fuji Seitetsu) and the Singapore Galvanising Industries Ltd (capital of $5 million: 20 per cent each subscribed by Kawasaki Steel, Marubeni-Iida, and two other Japanese companies) (Awayama 1971: 8–9).

The government-owned NISM was by far the largest. The other four were joint-venture enterprises involving not only Japanese trading companies and Japanese steel companies but also local financial groups, even though we have only shown in brackets the percentage shares of the capital subscribed by the Japanese firms. For example, the Simalpan Steel Industries had the Tan Eng Hong Group as the local partner, while the Singapore Galvanising Industries' local partner was the Hong Leong Group. As for the Eastern Wire Manufacturing, the local partners were the NISM and the Hong Leong Group.

In July 1963, Kawasaki Seitetsu set up the Singapore Galvanising Industries Ltd for the production and sale of galvanised sheet iron in a joint venture with Marubeni-Iida, Yodogawa Seiko, Ito Chu and the Hong Leong Group contributing 20 per cent of the capital each, and it began production in June 1965. At that time, Malaysia imposed an import duty on galvanised sheet iron for the protection of the local iron and steel industry. As Singapore was expelled from Malaysia in August 1965, the products manufactured by the Singapore Galvanising Industries Ltd became subject to an import tariff in Malaysia, and the company was virtually obliged to cease its sales in Ipoh and Malacca, which constituted large markets for its products. However, from 1967 to 1969 the company exported its products to Ceylon and

Indonesia, and managed to make profits, eliminating its cumulative deficits, although when galvanised factories were set up in these countries, it could no longer export large quantities of goods to them.

In Singapore itself, there was a gradual decline in demand for galvanised iron sheets due to the construction in large numbers of high-rise flats. Moreover, in January 1972 the government abolished an import duty on coated steel goods for ducts and roofs to meet an increasing demand for these products. As a result, the joint-venture company faced direct competition from imports, and incurred huge losses. The five share-holding companies discussed its increasing problems and decided to liquidate it. They agreed that all the shares held by the Japanese companies were to be sold to the Hong Leong Group at a liquidation cost (Kawasaki Seitetsu 1976: 725–7). Consequently, Kawasaki Steel withdrew from Singapore completely.

Construction companies

Kajima Kensetsu (the present Kajima) was the first Japanese construction company to advance into Singapore when it won a contract in 1960 for foundation work for the oil-refinery facilities of the Maruzen Toyo Oil Co. Ltd at a cost of ¥66 million. In 1964 it was contracted to construct the first dock and a quay for Jurong Shipyard Ltd at a cost of ¥494 million (Yuya 1988: 23).

Another Japanese construction company which advanced into Singapore was Mizuno Gumi (the present Goyo Kensetsu). As early as 1957, Mizuno Gumi had sent technical experts to Indian Goa, then under the control of Portugal, to undertake construction work for an iron ore-loading harbour, and in 1961 it won a contract for repair work at the Suez Canal by international tender (Goyo Kensetsu 1971: 66). Indeed the company had experience in construction activities abroad when it was contracted to build the wharf base of a repairing dock for Jurong Shipyard Ltd at ¥504 million, and also for a soil survey at a housing development site in Bedok district at ¥20 million in 1964. Moreover, in 1965 it managed to win a contract for the first phase of the coastal reclamation work at Tanjong Rhu in Bedok district at ¥5,278 million (Yuya 1988: 23).

It is often argued that in the post-war period Japanese construction companies advanced into Southeast Asia in order to undertake works in relation to the war-reparations payment. However, since Britain had renounced the right to demand reparations from Japan for Singapore, this popular view cannot explain their advance into the country. In fact, Japanese construction companies advanced there on a commercial basis from the very beginning. In most cases they first won contracts for construction works in Singapore from other Japanese companies, and then extended their activities into the preparation of housing sites, coastal reclamation and other construction works.

CONCLUDING REMARKS

During the period of import-substitution industrialisation in the first half of the 1960s, Singapore was politically unstable, while there were anti-Japanese feelings among the Chinese caused by the blood-debt issue. Nevertheless, large numbers of Japanese firms, notably those in the manufacturing sector, made direct investment into the country, for they were indispensable in the implementation of the Singapore government's industrialisation programme along the lines of the Winsemius Report. Indeed, the Lee regime did not exclude Japanese companies even during the height of the blood-debt movement, but it imposed, instead, various restrictions on Japanese trading companies, including contributions to industrialisation. The result was that many Japanese manufacturing companies were encouraged by the trading companies to make direct investment in the country.

The Japanese manufacturing companies on their part began to regard an enlarged Malaysia as an attractive market for their products. However, since many of them had hardly any experience in overseas operations, they preferred to rely on the trading companies for setting up factories in Singapore. Therefore it can be argued that the condition concerning the contributions to industrialisation imposed on the trading companies worked to the advantage of the manufacturing firms.

However, the expectations of the Japanese companies with regard to the Malaysian common market were dashed when Singapore was separated from Malaysia to become an independent state. The Singapore government had no choice but to change its industrial strategy from import-substitution to export-oriented industrialisation, and accordingly the country's economic relations with Japan had to take a new form in the post-independence period. Consequently, many of the Japanese manufacturing firms which had advanced into Singapore to take advantage of the common market had to withdraw from the country even before they set their business on a path. However, the case of Maruzen Sekiyu was very different from all the others. It suffered from financial difficulties in Japan so that its Singapore subsidiary, the Maruzen Toyo Oil Co. Ltd had to be sold off and was not even given sufficient time to show its operational performance.

Obviously, there were many companies which managed to survive Singapore's separation for a variety of reasons. Jurong Shipyard Ltd, for example, was able to find a new market, largely thanks to the growth of the Japanese economy in the 1960s. Paint and cement manufacturers as well as construction companies were able to continue to operate in the country, for they found ready markets at home thanks to the development of the port and/or a sharp increase in construction works, and to the expansion of domestic consumption. Moreover, trading companies and those engaged in financial business also continued to thrive by adapting themselves to new conditions.

It is worth noting, incidentally, that in the first half of the 1960s the advance of Japanese manufacturing companies into Singapore was largely realised in line with Singapore's import-substitution industrialisation policy. However, one also needs to view it in the light of Japan's overseas economic expansion strategy. At that time, the Japanese government adopted an economic policy with a view to developing the manufacturing sector in Japan, and therefore encouraged manufacturing firms to invest abroad, provided that they intended to find or expand local markets for their goods. Indeed, Japanese companies often advanced into Southeast Asian countries when an import-substitution industrial policy was adopted by some of them, and they manufactured goods locally, using raw materials and semi-finished goods imported from Japan into the region. But when locally manufactured goods were exported to Japan, and were about to compete with domestically manufactured goods, then the Japanese government took tough measures to exclude them from the Japanese market. Obviously, such cases were still limited in number at that time, but, recalling the activities of the trading companies in Singapore, Nakayama Kazumi points out that the export to Japan and the US of plywood, manufactured by a certain Japanese-controlled company in Singapore, was banned by the Japanese government (Nakayama 1976: 7).[19]

Finally, we would like to put forward two topics for further discussion. First, large numbers of Japanese manufacturing companies (particularly in the electrical and electronics industry) advanced into Singapore in the 1970s, giving rise to a second Japanese investment boom there. However, most of these firms chose the country as a production base for export to the European and American markets, and they, together with American and European MNCs, came to play an important role in transforming Singapore into one of the NIEs. Nevertheless, they seem to owe much to their predecessors, i.e. the Japanese companies which had advanced into Singapore in the first half of the 1960s. For example, the period of import-substitution industrialisation provided the Lee regime with ample opportunities to gain experience not only in state-led industrialisation but also in inviting Japanese firms to set up factories particularly in the Jurong Industrial Estate. These experiences must have helped the government to pursue export-oriented industrialisation later on. Moreover, in the 1960s Japanese trading companies acted as joint-venture partners to invite Japanese firms to set up factories in Singapore, and this type of joint venture remained an effective means of attracting Japanese manufacturing companies in the post-independence period, even though there were other Japanese firms which made direct investment without the co-operation of trading companies. These points would need to be taken into account when one makes an analysis of Japanese direct investment into Singapore after 1965.

Second, although we have referred only briefly to the Chinese financial groups which acted as joint-venture partners for Japanese firms in the previous chapter and this chapter, their role in attracting Japanese capital investment needs to be further examined. In the post-independence period, the role of Japanese and Western firms in the development of the Singapore economy has increased greatly, but it is worth noting that such newly emerged Chinese financial groups as Hong Leong seem to have grown rapidly by means of setting up joint-venture companies with Japanese firms.[20] One would need to study what kind of relationships they have had with Japanese and Western firms after independence.

CONCLUSION

The main object of this study has been to trace Japan's economic activities in Singapore in the context of the world economy from the last quarter of the nineteenth century until 1965, focusing on such areas as fisheries, the sex industry, foreign and domestic trade, financial business, and manufacturing industries, and, in the light of these, to re-evaluate the popular views on the subject. In this conclusion, we shall first summarise our findings and elaborate on them wherever necessary. We shall then attempt to give a bird's-eye view of how Japan has advanced into Singapore since 1965 to provide readers with some understanding of their economic relations since independence.

JAPAN'S ECONOMIC ADVANCE BEFORE 1965

In Chapters 2 and 3 we showed that, contrary to the *nanshin-ron* (the southward advance concept), Japan's economic advance into Singapore and other parts of Southeast Asia is not to be credited solely to 'Japan proper', that is, *karayuki-san*, other early Japanese immigrants, Japanese firms and the Japanese government. At the time when *karayuki-san* emerged in Southeast Asia, in the last few decades of the nineteenth century, overseas Chinese merchants in Japan began to export Japanese goods to Southeast Asia, making use of intra-Asian Chinese commercial networks. However, this fact has been brushed aside and has been largely ignored in the modern history of Japan–Southeast Asian relations.

Prior to World War I, the bulk of Japan's trade with foreign countries was conducted mainly by the overseas Chinese and Western merchants in Japan. Apart from Mitsui & Co. and a few others, Japanese merchants were not as yet engaged in international trade in a true sense, and acted mainly as intermediaries between Japanese manufacturers on the one hand and foreign merchants in Japan on the other hand. It was not the Japanese exporters but the overseas Chinese merchants in Japan (particularly those of Kobe) who began to cultivate the Southeast Asian markets for marine products, lacquer ware, rickshaws, textile goods and other Japanese goods in the last quarter of

207

the nineteenth century and the early twentieth century. It was only during World War I that the domination by the overseas Chinese of Japan's trade with British Malaya and other parts of Southeast Asia began to be increasingly challenged by Japanese merchants.

It is obviously wrong to deny entirely that the *karayuki-san* played a certain role in laying the foundations of Japan's later economic advance into the British colony and other parts of Southeast Asia. Drapers, hairdressers, dentists, doctors, sundry-goods store-keepers and other early Japanese immigrants were attracted to Singapore largely by the custom of the *karayuki-san*. However, apart from Echigoya Gofukuten and such professionals as doctors and dentists, only a few of them could successfully expand their businesses. Moreover, although part of the *karayuki-san*'s earnings was invested in rubber plantations and other Japanese ventures in British Malay, many such investments ended in failure: most of the small rubber estates owned by individual Japanese went bankrupt in the post-World War I recession and were sold off. Indeed, during World War I, merchants, banks, shipping companies and some other Japanese were able to expand their economic activities in the British colony, not thanks to the *karayuki-san*, but largely because of the wartime boom. Most of the Japanese trading companies and individual merchants simply followed in the footsteps of the overseas Chinese merchants in Japan who were largely responsible for the cultivation of the British Malayan and other Southeast Asian markets for Japanese goods.

In Chapter 4 we traced the development of the Japanese fisheries based in Singapore, and analysed the effects of Japanese fishing activities on the local economy and the fisheries policy of the colonial administration. In the mid-1920s large numbers of Japanese fishermen began to migrate into Singapore, and in the 1930s there were around 1,000 Japanese fishermen who were mainly Okinawans. There is little doubt that the position of the British colony as an international transit port with a highly developed distribution system was crucial for the development of the Japanese fisheries, for Japanese-caught fresh fish needed to be quickly distributed not only in the domestic market but also in the Malay Peninsula. For instance, the existence of the port facilities and an excellent distribution system also led the Kyodo Gyogyo Co. Ltd (the present Nihon Suisan Co. Ltd) to set up its operating base in the British colony for trawling in the Southeast Asian region.

The Japanese fisheries were manned only by Japanese fishermen who remitted the bulk of their earnings to their families in Japan. Nevertheless, one cannot say that they formed an economic enclave in Singapore, since almost all the catches were marketed in Singapore and the Malay Peninsula. The Japanese fishermen were highly productive as compared to local Chinese and Malay fishermen, and were responsible for 40 to 50 per cent of the fresh fish traded in the local fish markets. Indeed they helped to change the local food culture and lower the prices of fresh fish which constituted the main source of protein for local Chinese, Malays and Indians. Moreover, there was a close relationship between the Japanese fishermen and overseas Chinese traders, for the latter controlled the internal distribution system in British Malaya, and the bulk of Japanese-caught fish was sold through them. Nevertheless, overseas Chinese traders in general were often portrayed by the contemporary Japanese as 'evils of some kind', for they were said to deliberately place obstacles in the way of Japan's trade expansion. At any rate, this relationship came to an end in the late 1930s, when the overseas Chinese in British Malaya boycotted Japanese goods in protest against the Japanese invasion of China.

Chapter 5 considered Japanese economic activities in Syonan. There is a substantial literature on Syonan and other parts of Southeast Asia under Japanese rule, but their main focus is on the military, political and cultural aspects. Besides, those works written by the British and Singaporeans often emphasise the cruelty of Japanese rule. Obviously, the massacre of overseas Chinese, the harsh treatment of POWs and other misdeeds by the Japanese Army are very important topics, and need to be further studied. But, along with these, Japanese economic policy and the activities of Japanese firms should also be critically examined in order to get a more accurate picture of Japanese rule.

Prior to World War II there were large Japanese companies in Singapore, including two large trading companies (Mitsui & Co. and Mitsubishi Corporation), banks, shipping companies and warehousing companies. But apart from the Eifuku Sangyo Koshi (formerly known as the Taichong Kongsi), a leading Japanese fisheries company in the British colony which diversified its activities into commerce and manufacturing industry (ice-making and iron-working), there were no major Japanese manufacturing companies there. During the occupation period Japan needed Southeast Asia's mineral fuels and raw materials for the prosecution of the war, and placed Singapore at the centre of her economic activities in Southeast Asia. However, during the occupation period, as in other parts of Southeast Asia, a wide variety of large Japanese companies moved into Singapore, and were engaged in economic activities largely for the Japanese Army.

The occupation period also saw the revival of prostitution. The Acting Japanese Consul-General banned Japanese prostitution in 1920, while the colonial authorities finally abolished licensed prostitution in the early 1930s. However, considerable numbers of *karayuki-san* remained in Singapore and the Malay Peninsula, and after the commencement of the Japanese occupation some of them co-operated with the Japanese army, either willingly or involuntarily, in recruiting local women and running comfort stations in various parts of the former British Malaya. It is worth noting that the large majority of the comfort women were non-Japanese Asians with some Caucasian POWs, serving mainly the sexual needs of low-ranking Japanese soldiers, while Japanese comfort women, whose number was fairly limited, were largely reserved for high-ranking Japanese officers, and were probably better treated than their Asian counterparts. Indeed, under the lofty slogan of 'the Greater East Asia Co-prosperity Sphere', large numbers of Korean, Chinese and other Asian women were condemned to become comfort women simply to satisfy the Japanese men. Besides, high-ranking officers and company employees were 'entertained' at *ryotei* by Japanese women, who were brought in from Japan, China, the Korean Peninsula and other part of Asia under Japanese control. The issue of comfort women clearly reveals Japanese colonialism, racism and sex discrimination against women.

The Japanese rule lasted only for three and a half years, and the Japanese companies which undertook economic activities under the orders of the Japanese Military Administration were far from producing sufficient quant-ities of goods, owing to the grave shortages of skilled workers, raw materials, machinery and spare parts. Nevertheless, there is a possibility that the experiences gained by the Singaporeans through the large-scale industrial activities of Japanese firms during the period may have been useful in some way to the country's industrialisation in the post-war period. Moreover, one could suggest that some of the post-war Singaporean leaders had been impressed by Japan's economic activities in the Syonan era, and were there-fore anxious to obtain Japanese co-operation in the country's industrialis-ation. This might partly explain why, as shown in Chapter 7, the Lee Kuan Yew government was very eager to encourage Japanese manufacturing firms to advance into Singapore in the first half of the 1960s, in spite of the strong anti-Japanese feelings among local Chinese.

Chapters 6 and 7 illustrated how Japan resumed her economic activities in Singapore in the post-war period. The period from the end of the Pacific War to the mid-1950s is often regarded as a 'void period' in the economic relations between Japan and Southeast Asia, for it is commonly argued that Japan's return to the region began only after the commencement of the payment of war reparations in the mid-1950s. However, since Britain renounced the right to demand Japan war reparations for Singapore and Malaya in the post-war period, as far as the former British Malaya is concerned this argument cannot be supported. In fact, in the post-war period Japan's economic relations with Singapore began again as early as 1947 when Japanese trading companies were permitted by the SCAP to resume restricted private trade with foreign countries, and the volume of trade between them started increasing rapidly in 1950 when restrictions on private foreign trade were entirely removed. Besides, in the first half of the 1950s some Japanese shipping companies sent their staff to Singapore, while the Bank of Tokyo and several Japanese trading companies also made preparations for the resumption of their operations there. In the second half of the decade the restrictions on the entry into Singapore of Japanese nationals were relaxed, and a number of Japanese companies set up branches/representative offices in the British colony.

Japan's return to Singapore and other parts of Southeast Asia must be studied in the context of America's Far Eastern strategy, in which Japan was expected to act as the major industrial nation in Asia, importing raw materials and mineral fuels from Southeast Asia and exporting industrial goods to the region. Consequently, Singapore became the principal base for the activities of Japanese firms. In the meantime, in Singapore unemployment rose sharply with a rapidly expanding population, while there were signs of growing Communist influences. With a view to dealing effectively with these problems, the British colony showed increasing interest in promoting its own industrialisation, and came to expect Japanese co-operation in achieving its object. Indeed, it is significant that Lim Yew Fock, the Chief Minister of the internal government, asked Prime Minister Kishi Nobusuke for Japanese investments in tuna-canning, cement and fertiliser plants as early as 1957 when Kishi was on a visit to Southeast Asia. This expectation of Japan continued after the PAP under Lee Kuan Yew came to power in 1959, and in fact there was a Japanese investment boom in the first half of the 1960s. A popular view claims that many Japanese firms made direct investment into the country simply in order to reap the benefit of a common market which was planned to be formed in 1963 by the merger of the Federation of Malaya with Singapore, Sabah and Sarawak. Indeed, Japanese manufacturing companies had high expectations for the merger, for they foresaw the difficulties in exporting Japanese goods direct to Singapore and the Malay Peninsula once the Malaysian common market was formed. However, this explanation is not very convincing, for, as well as a desire to take advantage of the merger, there were, behind the Japanese investment boom, effective measures taken by the Lee Kuan Yew regime to attract Japanese manufacturing companies to Singapore.

The anti-Japanese movement began to grow in 1962 in relation to the massacre of overseas Chinese committed by the Japanese Army shortly after the occupation of Singapore in 1942, but it did not affect the PAP government's expectation of Japan. At the height of the anti-Japanese feelings among local Chinese, the Singapore government, while imposing a ban on Japanese trading companies engaging in domestic and tripartite trade, obliged them, at the same time, to encourage Japanese manufacturing companies to invest in Singapore if they wanted to obtain permission to set up branches, and to apply for visas or renewal of visas for their Japanese employees in the country.

However, unexpectedly from the Japanese firms' point of view, in September 1965 Singapore was separated from Malaysia to become an independent state, and many Japanese firms which had made investments aiming at the common market were subsequently obliged to withdraw from Singapore. Those which continued to operate there were in financial business, foreign trade and the ship-building and repairing industry, which all benefited from the expansion of the world economy (especially the

Japanese economy), and in construction and certain manufacturing industries (including cement and paints), which profited particularly from the expansion of the domestic market. In short, those Japanese firms which survived the separation of Singapore from Malaysia in Singapore were able to continue their economic activities, largely because they were in a position to respond to changes in internal and international economic circumstances.

Finally, we shall now outline the structure of the Japanese community in Singapore. In the pre-war period, broadly speaking, the Japanese community consisted of two distinct groups of Japanese residents, namely the *gudang zoku* (the '*élite*' class) and the *shitamachi-zoku* (the downtown people). Most of the *gudang zoku* resided in the colony for two or three years, and comprised employees of trading companies, banks, shipping firms and other large Japanese companies located in the commercial centre around Raffles Place and Battery Road (Yano 1975: 124–9; Shimizu Hajime 1982: 204–6). As for the *shitamachi-zoku*, they lived mainly in the Japanese town around High Street and Middle Road, and comprised largely the long-term settlers, such as shop-keepers and *karayuki-san*, even though they were later joined by short-term immigrants such as fishermen. After the abolition of licensed Japanese prostitution in British Malaya in 1920, the number of Japanese prostitutes declined sharply, even though some of them continued to ply the trade clandestinely. There were also those who were married to Japanese or other Asians, or became their concubines, and settled down in Southeast Asia. Some fishermen also became long-term settlers in Singapore opening retail shops there.

There existed social barriers between the two groups, and they normally kept distance from each other. However, Eifuku Tora, the successful owner of the Eifuku Sangyo Koshi, often mixed with the *gudang zoku* (Kataoka 1991: 82–8). Moreover, although dentists and doctors belonged to the élite class, they were long-term settlers, residing mainly in the Japanese town. They treated all classes of Japanese patients, while some of them were actively engaged in looking after non-Japanese patients as well.

During the occupation period not many of the former *shitamachi-zoku* remained, not only because, as soon as the Pacific War broke out in December 1941, large numbers of Japanese shop-owners, fishermen and other Japanese in Singapore were taken by the British to India as internees, but also because the Japanese Military Administration restricted the return of the former shop-keepers who had taken refuge in Japan. However, comfort stations were set up by the military authorities, while *ryotei* began business often under the auspices of either the army or the navy. In consequence, the Japanese community largely comprised military men, paramilitary personnel, company employees, officials of the Syonan Special Municipality, *geisha*/prostitutes and other civilian Japanese.

In the post-war period, as the colonial authorities in Singapore permitted economic activities only by Japanese company employees, while the Japanese government strictly controlled foreign exchange outflows, shop-keepers and other individual Japanese could not enter the British colony. Consequently, the Japanese community comprised predominantly the *gudang-zoku*, not the *shitamachi-zoku* of the pre-war type. Even today, the large majority of Japanese residents are Japanese company employees and their dependants.

SINGAPORE AND JAPAN'S ECONOMIC ADVANCE SINCE 1965

Today, Singapore is one of the four Asian NIEs, boasting GDP per capita of US$30,942 in 1996, which was much larger than that of US$19,723 enjoyed by Britain, the former colonial power (Somucho Tokeikyoku 1998: 79–80). It is now one of the MNCs' major production bases for the world market, and continues to strengthen its economic position as a major regional centre for Southeast Asia. The turning point for Singapore's economic development dates back to its separation from Malaysia in 1965. Although Singapore became an independent nation, it had a small domestic market and could no longer pursue its import-substitution industrialisation policy designed for the Malaysian common market. In the second half of the 1960s it therefore had to change its development strategy to an export-oriented industrialisation policy. At that time, MNCs had great difficulties in carrying on manufacturing in their home countries due to high wages and frequent strikes, and were in the process of relocating the labour-intensive part of their production to selected developing countries where they could make use of low-cost labour (Fröbel *et al.* 1980: 33–6). Singapore was one of the countries in which MNCs decided to undertake offshore production.

The Singapore government adopted various measures with a view to attracting MNCs to set up factories in the country. In 1967 it enacted an Economic Expansion Incentives Act, which incorporated the Pioneer Industries Ordinance of 1959 and introduced export-promotion measures. Foreign firms were now allowed to repatriate capital and remit earnings abroad freely. In 1968 the Jurong Town Corporation was set up to take over from the EDB the responsibility for managing not only the Jurong Industrial Estate but also other industrial estates. Moreover, in November 1969 the government began to set up Singapore Investment Centres in various countries including the US, Japan, Germany and Britain with the object of encouraging MNCs to make direct investment in Singapore (Matsuo 1973: 56; Deyo 1981: 56).

The banking systems were also consolidated to provide facilities to foreign and local firms. When the Asian Dollar Market was created in Singapore in 1968, the offshore banking system began to develop.[1] Commercial banks (and merchant banks after 1970) were permitted to set up Asian Currency Units (ACU) for the purpose of accepting foreign currency deposits and making loans in foreign currencies. No tax was imposed on interest on deposits in foreign currencies kept by non-residents. The Bank of America was anxious to collect deposits particularly from Chinese in Southeast Asia, and became the first bank to establish an ACU in 1968. In the same year, the Development Bank of Singapore was established by the government to relieve the EDB of the financial functions of providing manufacturers with long-term loans at a low interest rate and making capital investment in industry. Moreover, in 1971 the Monetary Authority of Singapore was created with all the functions of a central bank except the issue of currency, for which the Singapore Currency Board has been responsible since 1967.

However, one should not assume that Singapore was unique in offering various incentives to MNCs, for other Asian countries were also doing more or less the same at that time. In fact, Singapore's average wages were higher than those in Taiwan, South Korea and Hong Kong, which were to emerge as Asian NIEs in later years. In 1972, the average monthly wage of a semi-skilled worker was US$66 in South Korea, US$73 in Taiwan, US$84 in Hong Kong and US$87 in Singapore (Yoshihara 1976: 192). Nevertheless, Singapore was able successfully to attract foreign direct investments thanks to its strategic location and excellent infrastructure, enabling MNCs to import raw materials and export finished goods at low costs (Ho 1995: 115).

Japan was one of the advanced countries from which the PAP government was anxious to obtain co-operation in achieving export-oriented industrialisation. The blood-debt issue was eventually settled on 21 September 1967 when Japan signed with Singapore an agreement on 'quasi-reparations', consisting of grants of $25 million (¥2,940 million) and an equal amount of loans in yen on liberal terms. According to the Japanese Ministry of Trade and Industry, during the period from 7 May 1968 to 31 March 1972 the Singapore government spent the grants on the ground communication base for an earth satellite (¥456 million), cranes for the Jurong Harbour (¥396 million), machinery for the Public Works Department (¥419 million), and the construction of a shipyard (¥1,669 million), which seems to have been Jurong Shipbuilders Ltd (Tsusansho 1995: 264–5). As for the yen loans, the Japanese and Singapore governments concluded a separate agreement on 28 January 1971, under which ¥2,548 million was to be spent on new ocean-going ships (an interest rate of 5.5 per cent with a repayment period of 18 years, and a deferment period of five years), and ¥392 million on the construction of a station for the ground communication base of an earth satellite (an interest rate of 4.5 per cent with a repayment period of 20 years, and a deferment period of five years) (ibid.). As new ships would have been built at Jurong Shipbuilders Ltd, a substantial part of the quasi-reparations could have been spent on the new ship-building company which was set up in 1969.[2]

Japanese firms themselves began to make export-oriented investment abroad in the late 1960s and early 1970s, and regarded Singapore as one of their low-cost production bases in Asia for exports to the European and American markets. This was not only because they began to suffer from a grave shortage of unskilled and semi-skilled labour, with a resultant rise in wages, but also because high land prices made it very difficult for them to increase their production capacity in their country. Moreover, the Japanese government relaxed its currency restriction in October 1969 and abolished it altogether in July 1971. Besides, in 1971 the fixed exchange rate of ¥360 per US$1 was finally abandoned, and subsequently the yen appreciated to reach ¥280–¥300 per US$1 by 1973. Finally, because of Japan's increasing trade friction with the US and Europe, it became increasingly difficult for Japanese firms to export large quantities of industrial goods direct to these markets. The subsidiaries set up in Asian countries were largely engaged in labour-intensive assembly operations using the components mainly imported from their parent companies in Japan, and the bulk of finished products found their way into the European and American markets (Allen 1981: 172–7). According to the Japanese Ministry of International Trade and Industry, in March 1974 the Japanese manufacturing firms in Singapore obtained locally 21.9 per cent of the stock goods (including raw materials and semi-finished products) used in their factories, 60.2 per cent from Japan (of which 49.1 per cent from their parent companies), and 17.9 per cent from other countries. As for the electrical and electronics manufacturers, they imported 76.1 per cent of those stock goods from Japan alone (of which 72.2 per cent from their parent companies) (Tsusansho Tsusho Sangyo 1975: 174).

In the early 1970s Japanese direct investments in Singapore in terms of numbers were mostly found in consumer electronics (including electrical goods) and textiles. As of 31 March 1974 there were 13 Japanese firms in the electronics industry, of which five were 100 per cent Japanese-owned, and six were with 50 to 99 per cent Japanese equity ownership (Yoshihara 1978: 166). Until about the mid-1970s the large Japanese electronics manufacturers, including Hitachi and Sanyo, were primarily engaged in the assembly of consumer electronics products, including radios, TVs and cassette tape recorders, mainly for export to the US, Europe and other foreign countries (Chusho Kigyo 1989: 36–43). As for Japanese textile firms, there were 14 which were all in joint ventures with local capital and Japanese trading companies (Yoshihara 1978: 115, 120–1). Trading companies performed many essential functions, including the search for local partners, the import of textile materials, and the export of finished goods.

In the late 1960s and early 1970s several ship-building and repairing companies were set up in a joint venture between Japanese ship-building firms and the Singapore government/local capital. As noted in Chapter 7, the Ishikawajima-Harima Heavy Industries Ltd and the Singapore government set up a joint-venture company, Jurong Shipyard Ltd in 1963. In 1968, the Mitsubishi Heavy Industries Ltd established the Mitsubishi Singapore Heavy Industries Ltd also as a joint venture with the Singapore government, while in 1970 the Hitachi Zosen Ltd and the Robin Group jointly set up the Hitachi Zosen Robin Dockyard Ltd. Moreover, in 1969 Jurong Shipbuilders Ltd was established with a total capital of $15 million in the form of a joint venture between the Ishikawajima-Harima Heavy Industries (33 per cent), the Singapore government and Jurong Shipyard Ltd, and started operations in December 1971. At the end of 1972 there were 340 workers (of whom 36 were from the IHI) working for the firm (Toyo Keizai Shimposha 1973: 124 and 261). But the new company suffered from the world-wide recession caused by the first oil crisis of 1973, and was absorbed by Jurong Shipyard Ltd in 1976 (Isobe 1990: 252).

In the early 1970s the Singapore government asked Japan to undertake two major projects in Singapore. The first was the construction of an integrated steel-manufacturing plant at Pulau Tekong to produce 5 million tons of steel per year. In the Jurong Industrial Estate there existed at that time a number of iron and steel-manufacturing firms, which had been set up as joint ventures between Japanese firms and local financial groups in the 1960s to produce wire, pipes, galvanised iron sheets and other steel products, but there was no integrated iron and steel mill in the country. The EDB made this plan in 1970, and asked the steel-manufacturing interests in Japan for co-operation. It could be either a 100 per cent Japanese ownership, or a joint venture with the Singapore government. However, the Japanese steel-manufacturing interests rejected the proposal on the ground that the plan was too difficult to carry out (Awayama 1971: 10). Eventually the Singapore government abandoned the plan, largely because the disadvantaged position of the steel industry, which consumed a lot of energy, became evident in the wake of the first oil crisis of 1973.

The second project was the establishment of the Petrochemical Corporation of Singapore (PCS) at Pulau Merbau, which was the first genuine petrochemical industry in Southeast Asia. In 1971, Lee Kuan Yew asked President Hasegawa Shigenori of the Sumitomo Chemicals Co. Ltd, who was then visiting Singapore, if his company could undertake a PCS project. In 1973 Sumitomo Chemicals carried out a feasibility study, and found favourable factors such as the strategic location at the mid-point between the Middle East and Japan, political stability under the PAP leadership, the availability of highly educated workers, and the existence of the third largest oil-refining base in the world (*Kokusai Keizai*, vol. 24, no. 2, 1987: 187–9). In 1974, it was agreed to set up a joint-venture company between the EDB and Sumitomo on an equal basis, but in the following year the project was suspended owing to the prolonged recession in the wake of the first oil crisis. However, in 1977 Singapore made it a national project, and Prime Minister Lee Kuan Yew visited Japan to ask the Japanese government for its co-operation. The PCS was eventually established in 1977 with 50 per cent of the capital subscribed by the Japanese side (consisting of the Japanese government, Sumitomo Chemicals and ten other petrochemical companies, and eleven banks and trading companies). Unfortunately, the second oil crisis occurred in 1979, causing a sharp rise in oil prices and a steep decline in demand for petrochemical products in the world market. Consequently, although the construction works had been virtually completed by the end of 1982, it was not until February 1984 that the operations at the petrochemical complex centred around the PCS commenced. In the meantime, in the early 1980s the Polyolefin Company (Singapore) Pte Ltd, the Phillips Petroleum Singapore Chemicals Pte Ltd, and the Denka Singapore Pte Ltd were set up as joint ventures involving Japanese and other petrochemical firms for the production of refined oil products such as ethylene and acetylene; these companies were all related to the Petrochemical Corporation of Singapore (Iwaki 1990: 240). The total amount of capital invested in the petrochemical complex was as much as ¥220 billion (*Kokusai Keizai*, vol. 24, no. 2, 1987: 187–9; Shimizu Hiroshi 1993b: 59–60). In 1987 the Singapore government privatised the PCS so that Shell Oil acquired 30 per cent of the shares. By December 1992 Shell and the Japanese side had come to hold 50 per cent each of the total (*Nihon Keizai Shimbun,* 9 December 1992).

Obviously, Japanese firms did not restrict their capital investment to the manufacturing sector alone, for there were those which invested in banking, finance and retailing. In Singapore, Japanese banks and other financial institutions played a large role in the development of the international financial centre. As noted in Chapter 6, the Bank of Tokyo was the first Japanese bank to advance into the country in the post-war period, to be followed by the Mitsui Bank, and after 1971, the Sanwa Bank, the Daiichi Kangyo Bank, the Daiwa Bank and some other banks followed suit (Hashimoto Akira 1974: 24). Also, in 1972, the Daiwa Securities Co. Ltd and the Nomura Securities Co. Ltd began operations there. Clearly, the Japanese banks advanced into the city state not only to provide banking services to the growing number of Japanese firms in Singapore, but also to take advantage of the country as an international financial centre.

The first half of the1970s also witnessed the advance into Singapore of two Japanese retail companies. The first was Isetan Co. Ltd, which set up the Isetan Emporium (S) Pte Ltd (renamed Isetan Singapore Ltd in 1981) in a joint venture with Apollo Enterprises Pte Ltd in 1970 to manage a department store at Apollo Hotel in Havelock Road, primarily with the object of selling goods to Japanese residents and tourists.[3] The second was the Yaohan Group, a medium-sized supermarket in Shizuoka prefecture, Japan, which established a joint-venture company, Yaohan International, in 1974 to run a department store at Plaza Singapura in Orchard Road.[4] Unlike Isetan, it targeted largely at the local consumers, whose purchasing power had continued to rise since the independence of 1965 thanks to Singapore's steady economic growth.[5] As they continued to conduct their retail business successfully, increasing the number of their stores, they were joined by several other large Japanese department stores including Daimaru and Takashimaya in the following two decades. Indeed, along with their local rivals such as C.K. Tang and Metro, the Japanese department stores dominate the large-scale retail trade in Singapore today.

In the second half of the 1970s the number of Japanese electrical and electronics firms operating in the city state increased greatly, while by this time the Japanese companies in general had come to undertake the assembly operations of more sophisticated products, including video tape-recorders and audio equipment, or to manufacture electronic components, including IC and silicon transistors as well as brown tubes for colour TVs (Nakamura and Koike 1986: 253). In 1978 the Singapore government revised the Economic Expansion Incentives Act with the result that those foreign companies with less than $1 million of fixed capital expenditure could invest in Singapore (Nihon Noritsu Kyokai 1987: 209). This revised law helped to encourage small and medium-sized but high-technology Japanese firms to set up subsidiaries to act as subcontractors and component producers to Japanese MNCs in the country.

In 1979 Singapore adopted a high-wage policy with a view to replacing labour-intensive and low value-added industries with high-technology and capital-intensive industries (Hirakawa 1987: 205). The government raised the rate of the CPF (Central Provident Fund) from 37 per cent of workers' monthly earnings in 1979 to 38.5 per cent in 1980, 42.5 per cent in 1981, and 45 per cent in 1982. Taking 1979 as 100, the wage index rose to 144.3 in 1981, and continued to increase in the next few years (Shimizu Hiroshi 1993b: 54). The government gave tax incentives and financial assistance to those industries with a promising future, whereas it ruthlessly abandoned labour-intensive and low value-added industries. For example, the preferential treatment for car-assembly and tyre-manufacturing industries was scrapped on 1 August 1980, when a 45 per cent customs duty was imposed on locally assembled cars, while a 40 per cent duty on imported tyres was removed. As a consequence, both Ford and Bridgestone had to close down their factories in that year. Also, other manufacturing industries were affected by the government's policy. Actually, Minebea and other Japanese firms relocated their bases of production to neighbouring countries because of a loss of comparative advantages in Singapore.

Indeed, in the first half of the 1980s, the level of Japanese direct investment in Singapore's manufacturing sector was fairly low. Its value amounted to $135.3 million in 1980, $73.3 million in 1982 and $166.6 million in 1984, although it was $319.4 million in 1979 (Nihon Noritsu Kyokai 1987: 208; DSS 1990). However, these figures do not include huge Japanese investment in the petrochemical complex at Merbau. Moreover, it should be noted that in 1984 the Singapore International Monetary Exchange started operations, and it began to have US$/¥ futures trading in September 1984, while introducing the Nikkei Average (the Japanese stock index futures contract) two years later. At this time, besides Japanese banks, Japanese manufacturing companies, which had stepped up direct investments in Asia for the purposes of sales and production, set up group-finance subsidiaries in Singapore with the object of group-financing and offshore investment. According to the Nomura Research Institute, Mitsubishi Denki set up the Mitsubishi Electric (Singapore) Pte Ltd in May 1979, Ajinomoto the AIF Investment in May 1984, Minebea the Minebea Investment Pte Ltd in June 1985, and Asahi Glass the AG Investment (Singapore) Pte Ltd in December 1985 to embark on financial business (*Nomura Ajia Joho*, March 1987: 13).

In the middle of 1984 Singapore began to suffer a serious recession, and experienced an economic growth rate of −1.6 per cent in 1985, the worst economic performance since independence in 1965. The oil-refining industry suffered from world-wide over-production, as the demand for Singapore's oil products (mainly refined oil) was low in the world market. The ship-building and ship-repairing industry had continued to have excess capacity since the first oil crisis of 1973. The Mitsubishi Heavy Industries Ltd withdrew *in toto* from Singapore in 1984, while the other ship-building companies diversified their activities into the production of oil-rigs and marine engines in order to weather the recession. The electrical and electronics industry also suffered a major setback due to a sharp fall in demand for its products. To make the matters worse for the Singapore economy, there was a recession in the construction industry.

In April 1985 an Economic Committee was set up to study the internal causes of the economic downturn, and it was headed by Lee Kuan Yew's elder son, the Junior Minister for Defence, Lee Hsien Loong. The committee then released a report, *The Singapore Economy: New Directions* in February 1986, recommending that Singapore should be made a 'total business centre' with manufacturing and services (international services, transport and communications, finance and banking) sectors as the backbones of the economy, in view of the limitation of Singapore's human and natural resources (Economic Committee 1986: 4–20; Nihon Boeki Shinkokai 1989: 130).[6] As it was found that Singapore lost competitiveness because of the fact that wages rose faster than productivity, the government froze wages for two years and lowered the rate of corporate taxes from 40 per cent to 33 per cent. The employers' CPF contribution was brought down from 25 to 10 per cent, while keeping the workers' contribution intact at 25 per cent. The services industry became eligible for pioneer status which had hitherto been granted only to manufacturing firms. Moreover, those companies which set up OHQ (operational headquarters) and IPO (international procurement offices) in Singapore could enjoy various tax reductions.

The Singapore economy subsequently recovered, as the economic growth rates were 9.4 per cent in 1987, 9.2 per cent in 1989, and 9.3 per cent in 1990. One of the main reasons for the recovery was a sharp increase in Japanese direct investment. In the wake of the Plaza Agreement in September 1985, the exchange value of the yen continued to rise sharply against other currencies. The result was that Japanese firms were anxious to relocate production to Asia including Singapore. The yen rose from 89.9 cents per ¥100 in 1984 to $1.30 in 1986, and $1.57 in 1988 (Economic Intelligence Unit 1989: 8). Besides the rise in the yen, Singapore was attractive to Japanese firms on account of its high-level education, political stability, highly developed infrastructure, the availability of various incentives and the importance of the city state as the major supplying base for the other ASEAN countries (Shimizu Hiroshi 1993b: 67). The value of Japanese direct investment in Singapore rose from $244.1 million in 1985 to $601.1 million in 1987 and $708.2 million in 1990 (DSS 1991: 124).

Since the recession of 1985, Japanese firms have tended to make capital investment into the non-manufacturing sectors of the economy. In 1981, manufacturing firms accounted for 64 per cent of total Japanese investments, but their share then continued to decline to 32 per cent in 1990 and 30 per cent in 1996 (Kawada 1997: 115). As of the end of 1996 there were 3,018 Japanese firms registered with the Registry of Companies and Businesses, and of these, 701 were in the manufacturing sector (including 245 in electronics and electrical machinery, 108 in machinery and 84 in petrochemical), and 2,317 in other industries (including 1,066 in domestic and foreign trades, 459 in services, 222 in finance and insurance and 161 in construction) (Kawada 1997: 115).[7] Since 1990 the number of new Japanese firms, notably manufacturing companies, which are registered with the registry has continued to decline, largely because of high wages and the shortages of both labour and industrial estates. In fact, subsidiaries of many Japanese manufacturing firms have maintained high technology operations in Singapore, while shifting labour-intensive operations to neighbouring countries and China where they enjoy lower costs of production.

This tendency may further accelerate in future, since the Singapore government has in recent years been eager not only to make the city state an international business hub by encouraging MNCs to set up operational and business headquarters, but also to encourage foreign firms to establish more R & D (research and development) and design centres. Indeed, Hitachi, Sony International Singapore Pte Ltd, Yokogawa Electric and Aiwa have begun to conduct R & D in the country. Sony International Singapore Pte Ltd was the first Japanese company to get OHQ status in 1987, and was followed by Fujikura International Management Pte Ltd in 1988, Omron Management Centre of Asia Pacific Pte Ltd and Matsushita Asia in 1989, Hitachi Asia in 1990, Toshiba Electronics Asia and NEC Electronics in 1991, and Fuji Xerox in 1992 (Kawada 1997: 21–3). These cases confirm that Japanese firms maintain manufacturing operations in China and Southeast Asia, and position Singapore as a centre for exercising general control over international intra-firm division of work. Indeed, it shows the locus of development of Singapore in line with the globalisation of world economies .

Finally, we shall briefly examine the role of tourism in Japan's economic relations with Singapore, for the tourist industry occupies an important position in the Singapore economy today. A Singapore Tourist Promotion Board (renamed the Singapore Tourist Board in 1997) was created in 1964, and an office was set up in Tokyo as early as 1970 to attract Japanese tourists. Moreover, in 1974, a Singapore Convention Bureau was created by the STPB with the object of attracting international conventions, exhibitions and incentive tours. In fact, among the international convention cities recognised by the Union of International Associations in Brussels, Singapore has continued to host the largest number of international conventions in Asia every year since 1983, and has ranked in the top ten in the world since 1983. Today, those who participate in international conventions, trade fairs and incentive tours account for a considerable proportion of foreign visitors to Singapore, including Japanese (OHI Kikuchi). Indeed, the number of foreign visitors rose steeply from 98,500 in 1965 to 1,169,300 in 1975, 3,191,100 in 1986 and 7,197,963 in 1997, and during the period the average annual growth rate was 14.9 per cent (DSS 1983: 154; STB 1998a).

The number of Japanese visitors to Singapore rose sharply from a mere 25,546 in 1965 to 113,400 in 1973, 209,300 in 1978, 404,300 in 1986 and 1,094,047 in 1997 (STPB 1969, 1975, 1994; STB, 1998a). It is true, however, that, largely because of the deteriorating economic situation in Japan, the number declined by nearly 30 per cent in the first six months of 1998 as compared with the same period in 1997 (STB 1998b: 4). As for the purposes of visits, those for 'business' and 'business and pleasure' accounted for 42.5 per cent in 1969, but their combined share continued to decline to 20.9 per cent in 1975, and 14.9 per cent in 1997. This means that those with other purposes (mainly 'holidays') continued to increase over the same period (STPB 1969, 1975, 1994; STB 1998a).

The popularity of Singapore among Japanese has grown enormously in recent years. In 1985 the number of Japanese visitors to Singapore was 377,700, as compared to 1,496,200 to the US, 638,900 to South Korea, 635,800 to Hong Kong, 488,600 to West Germany (as it was then), and 470,300 to France. However, in 1993, Singapore ranked fourth (1,001,000), coming after the US (3,542,500), South Korea (1,492,100) and Hong Kong (1,280,900) (Sorifu 1968: 50; idem 1994: 110). Since Hong Kong was returned to China in July 1997, the number of Japanese to visit the former British colony have declined, and this might help strengthen further Singapore's position as a tourist spot. As for the sex ratio, in 1969 males accounted for 88.3 per cent of total Japanese visitors to Singapore, but their share declined to 57.4 per cent in 1997 (STPB 1969; STB 1998a).

To conclude, in the late nineteenth and early twentieth centuries large numbers of *karayuki-san* with those related to them were attracted to Singapore, a prosperous international entrepôt, and they accounted for a high proportion of the Japanese population there. However, within a century or so, the composition of this population has changed completely, for company employees and their dependants constitute the large majority of the Japanese residents in the city state today. Indeed, large numbers of Japanese firms in the manufacturing and services sectors position Singapore as an important base for their international economic activities, while numerous Japanese tourists, participants in international conventions and others visit the country.

NOTES

INTRODUCTION

1 These figures represent the Japanese companies which were registered with the Registry of Companies and Businesses in Singapore as of the end of 1996, but they include those which had already withdrawn from the country but were still on record.

2 As of May 1998, there were 1,968 pupils at the Japanese Primary School in Singapore.

3 For example, Chris Dixon (1991), WG Huff (1994), and Ian Brown (1997) omit the Japanese occupation of Singapore or Southeast Asia from their works.

4 *Ryotei* were Japanese restaurants where guest were entertained by *geisha* and other females.

5 Detailed information about the *nanshin-ron* can be found in Shimizu Hajime's English-language article (1987: 386–402).

6 Yano Toru's methodology has been severely criticised by Mori Hisao in his review of Yano's other book, *Nihon no Nanyo Shikan* (Japan's Historical Views on the South Seas). See Mori (1979).

1 EMERGENCE OF SINGAPORE AND JAPAN IN THE WORLD ECONOMY

1 The Straits Settlements was initially under the control of the East India Company, but was transferred to the control of the India Office in London when the company was dissolved in 1858. In 1867, it became a Crown Colony under the Colonial Office in London.

2 Raffles was an employee of the East India Company, and was the founder of Singapore. For information about him, see Alatas (1971) and Raffles (1991).

3 The P & O received 450,000 a year for its weekly service to Bombay and a fortnightly one to China and Japan. These subsidies, which accounted for nearly half of all British mail subsidies, enabled the firm to purchase the most modern steamers (Headrick 1988: 39).

4 In the pre-war period, Singapore had neither an important agricultural sector, nor major export goods, apart from polished rice, smelted tin, sago products, and tinned pineapples. In fact, the Straits Trading Company's tin-smelting at Pulau Brani was the only major export-oriented industrial undertaking in the colony. Other manufacturing industries were concerned largely with the production of daily necessities including shoes, soap, beverages and food, and building materials (Wong 1991: 42).

5 It was rare for the Singapore branches of the Western banks to give loans to rubber plantations, tin-mining, copra-producing and other industries in the

Malay Peninsula (Huff 1994: 87–8; Naito 1942: 319). They normally provided funds to European merchant houses which had high credit standing, but were not very willing to make loans to overseas Chinese merchants. In fact, as of 1896 there were not more than 50 overseas Chinese merchants who kept accounts with the European banks, and these banks did not really encourage small and medium-sized overseas Chinese merchants to open an account with them even in the inter-war period (Huff 1994: 230–1).

6 For further information about Chinese banks based in Singapore before World War II, see Huff (1994: 230–5) and Lee Sheng-Yi (1990: 37–42).

7 The remittance shops numbered 70 in Singapore alone in the middle of the 1930s of which 36 were Hokkien, 17 were Cantonese, 15 were Teochiu, and two were other dialect-groups (Fukuda 1939: 150).

8 Large numbers of Chinese left China for Singapore through the ports of Hong Kong, Amoy, Swatow and others, but it was Hong Kong which was by far the most important port for this purpose.

9 In 1911, the total population of Singapore was 303,321, of whom 5,711 were Westerners (4,539 Britons), 219,577 overseas Chinese, 41,932 Malays, 27,770 Indians, 4,671 Eurasians, 1,409 Japanese, and 2,251 were others (Makepeace et al. 1991a: 360–1).

10 However, there were some Chinese merchants in Southeast Asia, who imported industrial goods direct from Europe. According to Allen and Donnithorne, at the beginning of the twentieth century a number of Chinese merchants in the Straits Settlements and on the east coast of Sumatra were engaged in the import of manufactured goods from Europe, while Kian Gwan, a major Chinese firm which was based in the Netherlands Indies with a branch in Singapore, was actively importing a wide range of goods from the West in the 1930s (Allen and Donnithorne 1957: 236–7).

11 Mitsui & Co. had been formed as a result of the amalgamation between the Senshu Kaisha and Mitsui's Kokusan Kata (The National Products Company) in 1876.

12 The share of agriculture in total labour force was a mere 19 per cent in Britain in 1871, 43 per cent in France in 1866, 36 per cent in Germany in 1882, 51 per cent in the US in 1870, and 72 per cent in Japan in 1872 (Minami 1986: 33).

13 These figures represent the Japanese nationals who migrated to Southeast Asia with valid passports, and, in addition, there must have been large numbers of stowaways, especially before World War I.

2 *KARAYUKI-SAN* AND JAPAN'S ECONOMIC ADVANCE INTO SINGAPORE

1 The term *karayuki* is sufficient to describe Japanese prostitutes abroad, but *karayuki-san* is commonly used by attaching an honorific term, *san*.

2 For information about the economic activities of the *karayuki-san* in the Netherlands Indies, see Shimizu Hiroshi (1992: 17–43).

3 One *shaku* is 0.994 ft.

4 S.H. Alatas argues that the myth of 'the lazy natives' was created by colonial capitalists (Alatas 1977: *passim*).

5 Although Shimizu Hajime says that *karayuki-san*'s customers were mainly Chinese coolies, they also included many soldiers in the British forces in Singapore, sailors, and others (Shimizu Hajime 1992: 143–4).

6 According to Mak Lau Fong, most of the Chinese prostitutes in Singapore were Cantonese (1995: 66–7). J.F. Warren has made a detailed study of Chinese prostitutes in pre-war Singapore from a social historian's point of view (Warren 1993).

7 According to Kani Hiroaki, Chinese prostitutes in Victoria Street, Rochor Road, North Canal Road and Chin Chew Street took Caucasian men as customers (Kani 1979: 125).

8 It is estimated that, in addition, there were some 60 prostitutes and 200 concubines in British Malaya in 1919 who were not registered with the Japanese Consulate in Singapore (DRO, 4.2.2.27, undated).

9 Mori Katsumi has undertaken research on the Amakusa region in relation with *karayuki-san* (Mori 1959:14–100).

10 It is worth noting that in 1960 *Muraoka Iheiji Jiden* (The Autobiography of Muraoka Iheiji) was published by a Japanese publishing company, Nanposha. Muraoka Iheiji wrote about his experiences in pre-war Southeast Asia in the book, claiming that he had been one of the kingpins controlling the supplies of Japanese women to Southeast Asia during the period from the early 1890s to the 1930s. This work constituted a standard reference book on *karayuki-san*, and was widely quoted in many books on them. Mori Katsumi, for example, published a scholarly book in 1959, *Jinshin Baibai* (The Flesh Trade), drawing heavily on the manuscript of Muraoka's autobiography, even though it is also based partly on his personal interviews with the former *karayuki-san* and those who had lived in Southeast Asia before World War II.

However, in 1972 Yamazaki Tomoko published a non-fiction story on *karayuki-san*, entitled *Sandakan Hachiban Shokan* (Sandakan No. 8 Brothel), casting doubt on the authenticity of Muraoka's work. (An English summary of Yamazaki's non-fiction work has appeared under the title, 'Sandakan No. 8 Brothel' in *Bulletin of Concerned Asian Scholars*, vol. 7, no. 4, 1975). According to Yamazaki, there are many inaccuracies in historical facts in Muraoka's autobiography, while there is nobody who could recognise him and there are no works published before World War II referring to him. Her arguments have been further strengthened by Yano Toru and Hara Fujio in their works (Yano 1975: 36–40; Hara 1987, 94–101). In Australia, David C.S. Sissons published '*Karayuki-san*: Japanese Prostitutes in Australia,1887–1916 (Part I)' in 1976, in which he discusses the question of authenticity of Muraoka's autobiography (Sissons 1976: 330–6).

In spite of the controversy, authors are still making use of Muraoka's autobiography as a source material. For example, both *Tonan Ajia wo shiru Jiten* (*Encyclopedia of Southeast Asia*) (Ishii *et al*. 1986: 61–2), and Jim Warren's *Ah Ku and Karayuki-san* (Warren 1993: 198–9, 213–14, and *passim*) draw on it. To our surprise, Yamazaki Tomoko herself, who was the first person to point out the inaccuracies of Muraoka's autobiography, in actual fact makes use of the autobiography in her recent book, *Ajia Josei Koryu-shi* (A History of Asian Women's Intercourse), arguing:

> Although there is doubt about the authenticity [of Muraoka's autobiography], we can barely get to know, by putting together this record with other fragmentary source materials, a picture of flesh traffickers and *karayuki-san*, who tend to be buried in the shadow of history.

> (Yamazaki 1995: 23)

Moreover, Terami (-Wada) Motoe has maintained in her two articles that with reference to the Philippines, the information given by Muraoka is fairly accurate (Terami-Wada 1986, 291–6; Terami 1989, 39–42). If Terami were correct, then one would naturally wonder why it is that Muraoka could write accurately about his activities in the Philippines but not about those in other Southeast Asian countries.

We have not come across Muraoka Iheiji's name in any of the documents and secondary works on British Malaya and the Dutch East Indies which we have so far read, and feel that he was no more than a petty pimp in Southeast Asia. Since the autobiography contains a lot of information, anyone working on *karayuki-san* would be tempted to make use of it. But when there are so many inaccuracies and exaggerations in any work, one would naturally wonder which parts of it are reliable, and should therefore avoid using it as research material.

11 The Japanese red-light district of the pre-war period, comprising Malay Street, Hylam Street, Malabar Street and Bugis Street, was redeveloped in the first half of the 1990s, and is now called 'Bugis Junction', a huge shopping centre, where the Seiyu Department Store, Parco, Inter-Continental Hotel and other Japanese-controlled companies are located.

12 It is worth noting that Muraoka Iheiji claims in his autobiography that he was responsible for the creation of the Japanese Cemetery in Singapore (Muraoka 1960:75–9).

13 In 1912 the Singapore branch of the Bank of Taiwan was opened, and was concerned with foreign exchange transactions and loans to local Japanese business and rubber planters (Robertson 1986: 16). It is highly unlikely, however, that the branch made loans to the Japanese brothels in Singapore.

14 Unlike the colonial authorities in British Malaya, the Dutch authorities in the Netherlands Indies did not recognise Japanese medical qualifications (Kobayashi and Nonaka 1985: 285).

15 As for large-scale rubber estates owned by Japanese companies, the first Japanese firm to own a rubber estate was Sango Koshi with its head office in Taiwan and its president Akuzawa Naoya. It owned an estate of 8,300 acres in 1906 in Pengerang, Johore (Nanyo oyobi Nihonjinsha 1938: 178 and 180).

16 According to Naito Hideo, prior to the abolition of licensed Japanese prostitution in 1920, some $600 million, which the pimps had squeezed out of the *karayuki-san*, was invested in rubber estates in Malaya (Naito 1941: 142).

17 According to Nanyo oyobi Nihonjinsha, Shibuya Ginji returned to Yokohama, but the period of his return is not known (Nanyo oyobi Nihonjinsha 1938: 510–11).

18 Kobayashi Chiyomatsu, who was one of the most influential bosses in the Japanese community at that time, escaped arrest, for he had left Singapore a few months before the 'hunting out' (DRO, 4.2.2.27, 30 May 1914).

19 The Japanese Consulate at Singapore was promoted to the status of Consulate-General in 1919.

20 Takemura Tamio is wrong to argue that in 1920 the colonial authorities abolished all the brothels in British Malaya, for it was in 1930 that licensed prostitution was finally abolished (Takemura 1982: 91).

21 At that time, pearl-oyster fishing was very profitable around the Aru Islands. In 1910, for example, the total catches amounted to 63,770 kg by weight, and 1,276,655 guilders by value (about ¥1,021,300) (Okayagura 1911: 76).

22 According to the Japanese Consulate at Batavia, the number of such prostitutes was between 60 and 70 (DRO, 4.2.2.27, 19 March 1913).

3 JAPAN'S TRADE EXPANSION INTO BRITISH MALAYA: WITH SPECIAL REFERENCE TO SINGAPORE

1 The Suez Canal drastically cut down distances from Europe to the East. The distance from London to Singapore was, for example, 15,486 km via the canal, as compared to 21,742 km via the Cape. Further information about the technological change in ship-building after 1869 can be found in Headrick (1988: 26–31).

2 However, Peter Post and the present writer (Shimizu) have written about the role of Japan's overseas Chinese merchants in the development of Japan's trade with pre-war Southeast Asia. See Post (1995: 154–76) and Shimizu Hiroshi (1995: 85–96; 1997b: 1–18).

3 Prior to World War II, British Malaya was heavily dependent upon the US, which took the bulk of its two main exports, rubber and tin. For example, in 1935 the US imported 40,408 tons of tin (64.9 per cent of total tin exports), and 308,383 tons of rubber (52.2 per cent of total rubber exports) (Mills 1942: 554, 556).

4 Before World War II, the area around Raffles Place was known among Japanese residents as *gudang* (warehouses in Malay) where trading companies, banks, shipping companies and some other large Japanese companies set up branches and/or representative offices.

5 The overseas Chinese merchants at Kobe were mostly engaged in both the import and export trade, but since their main interests lay in the export trade, this chapter concerns that rather than the import trade. Their imports included rice from Thailand, rubber and tin from British Malaya, hemp from the Philippines, and soybeans and cotton from China (Kyo 1983: 131–2).

6 Some of the influential overseas Chinese merchants at Kobe invested in industrial concerns which turned out matches and other export goods. For further information about this, see Shiba (1995: 192–5) and Koyama (1979: 32–4).

7 See, for example, Kobe Boeki Kyokai (1968).

8 It is possible that the figure included those overseas Chinese who moved from Yokohama to Kobe (Shokosho Boekikyoku 1938: 132).

9 Some of Kobe's Chinese merchant houses, including Yue Ching Cheong and Seng Kee & Co., were branches of the Nam bak hang commercial houses (Kobe Shoko Kaigisho 1929: 29–30). Nam bak hang literally means 'the South and North trade', and originates in those Hong Kong merchants who traded with both the North (China) and the South (Southeast Asia).

10 Some scholars argue that overseas Chinese stood in the way of Japan's trade expansion into Southeast Asia before World War II, for they boycotted Japanese goods from time to time (Horimoto 1997239–40; Takei 1932). It is obviously wrong, on two main grounds, to think only of the antagonistic relationship between the Japanese and the overseas Chinese. First, the overseas Chinese merchants in Japan and intra-Asian Chinese commercial networks were instrumental in the development of Japan's export trade with Southeast Asia, particularly in the last quarter of the nineteenth century and the early twentieth century, and most of the Japanese merchants simply followed their footsteps.

Second, the Japanese merchants had to rely heavily on overseas Chinese wholesalers and retailers for the distribution of Japanese goods in Southeast Asian markets. There was indeed co-existence of the symbiotic and antagonistic relationships between the two races, and one cannot take into account only the antagonistic one.

11 By the early twentieth century Mitsui & Co. had come to export the bulk of Japanese coal to the Straits Settlements. For example, in 1917 Japan exported to Singapore and Penang 421,400 metric tons of coal, of which the firm handled 358,000 metric tons (Mitsui Bunko, Bussan 338/11, June 1918: 11–12).

12 James F. Warren has written a major book on the social history of rickshaw coolies in pre-war Singapore (Warren 1986).

13 The representative office of Mitsubishi Goshi (which was later promoted to a branch) acquired a rubber dealer's licence in 1917, paying an annual fee of $150 and a deposit of $1000 (Mitsubishi Shashi Kankokai 1981b: 4311).

14 Choya Gomei in Tokyo was reorganised as the Choya Shokai Co. Ltd with a capital of ¥500,000 on 25 April 1917. However, as it expanded too rapidly, the company was in financial difficulty in May 1918, and was restructured with Nomura Shoten's capital participation in October of that year. In this book, we employ only the new company name, Choya Shokai, for the sake of simplicity (Choya Hyakunen-shi 1986: 42–4).

15 The South Seas Association was formed in Tokyo in January 1915, with the main purpose of facilitating Japan's economic expansion into Southeast Asia, and it subsequently established branches in Singapore and other parts of the region. It published a monthly journal, *Nanyo Kyokai Zasshi* (*Journal of the South Seas Association*) (later renamed *Nanyo* or *The South Seas*).

16 The Bank of Taiwan was set up with a capital of ¥5 million in September 1899, and acted as the central bank for the Taiwan government. It also undertook foreign exchange business, while financing a large part of Japan's trade with Taiwan and Southeast Asia before World War II. It was liquidated in September 1945 under the order of the Supreme Commander of the Allied Powers.

17 In the 1920s, the Bank of Taiwan continued to give large loans to Suzuki Shoten, a major Japanese trading company, which had financial difficulties in the immediate post-World War I years. Its loans amounted to ¥80 million at the end of 1920, and reached ¥380 million in March 1927, when the bank finally suspended transactions with the company (Yoshihara 1982: 66). As the bulk of its loans was directed to Suzuki Shoten, it was in great straits, and was barely saved by the Japanese government's financial assistance.

18 For example, in the inter-war period the Singapore branch of the Yokohama Specie Bank made a loan of $150,000 to the Ishizu Gyogyo Koshi (Robertson 1986: 16).

19 Many Japanese trading companies in the Netherlands Indies also went bankrupt for similar reasons, shortly after World War I (Shimizu Hiroshi 1991: 44).

20 In the late 1920s, the Singapore Chamber of Commerce expressed serious concern about the adverse effects of growing Japanese competition on the import of British goods (Singapore Chamber of Commerce 1929: 31, and 1930: 19–21).

21 The combined share of cotton and rayon piece goods in total imports from Japan rose from 16.1 per cent in 1920 to 35.8 per cent in 1929 and 41.2 per cent in 1933 (Shokosho Boekikyoku 1931: Foldout Table 3; Mantetsu 1941: 379).

22 Cheapness of Japanese goods in British Malaya is confirmed by Singaporeans. For example, Lakshmi Naidu, a Singaporean woman of Indian origin, recalls that in

the 1930s Japanese goods were extremely cheap, mainly costing 20 cents and 30 cents each. At that time, she could buy 3 dresses for children at $1 (OHI Naidu). Similarly, Ismail bin Zain, a Malay, says that, as Japanese goods were cheap and of high quality, they were bought not only by the poor but by the middle-class people (OHI Ismail).

23 Information about the Ottawa Conference and the ensuing British foreign trade policy can be found in I.M. Drummond (1972: Chapter III) and Shimizu Hiroshi (1986: 34–55).

24 Japan rapidly increased her share in the world market for cotton piece goods particularly after the Great Depression, and eventually overtook Britain as the largest exporter of cotton piece goods in 1933 (Shimizu Hiroshi 1986: 30–3). At the Anglo-Japanese commercial talks between the representatives of British and Japanese cotton interests, which began in September 1933, Britain and Japan clashed against each other over export markets. In the end, the talks broke down in March 1934 (Sugiyama 1994: 52–60).

25 In the 1930s, besides the UK, other Western powers imposed various import restrictions mainly to deal with severe Japanese competition in their Southeast Asian colonies, while overseas Chinese boycotted Japanese goods. In order to deal with these problems, various Japanese economic organisations were established in various parts of Southeast Asia (Horimoto 1997: 237–55; Hashiya 1997: 224–34).

26 Further information about the quota system in British Malaya can be found in Nomura (1941: 243–52) and Mills (1942: 150–61).

27 As of 1929, there were four Indian commercial houses in Kobe, which were engaged in the export of silk and other goods to Singapore and other parts of Asia (Kobe Shoko Kaigisho 1929: 39–50).

28 The Overseas Chinese Exporters' Association of Kobe was founded in November 1933, and, as of 1938, it consisted of 32 members (24 Cantonese and eight Hokkiens) (Kikakuin 1939: 354–5).

29 For information about the development of nascent industries in Singapore before World War II, see Huff (1994: 218–30); Ward *et al.* (1994: 289–337); Chan and Chiang (1994).

4 THE RISE AND FALL OF THE JAPANESE FISHERIES BASED IN SINGAPORE

1 Fish were marketed in three forms, namely, boiled, salted and dried, and fresh. This chapter concerns only the last as almost all Japanese-caught fish were sold fresh.

2 According to the information given by the colonial authorities, the number of Japanese fishermen was 1,050, not 971, in 1934. See Table 4.1.

3 A *koleh* is a canoe-like boat which is sailed or paddled, and is used by local Malay fishermen.

4 *Muro ami* fishing is also known in Japanese as *oikomi ami* (drive-in net) fishing.

5 Eric Robertson is wrong to argue that the drift netting was the most important Japanese fishing method, followed by the *muro ami* fishing before World War II. See Robertson (1986: 53).

6 For further information about the *muro ami* method, see German (1930: 199), Kee (1966: 57) and Hiroyoshi (1987: Chapter 6).

7 Masukado Kon'ei, an Okinawan fisherman aged 20, committed suicide on a

fishing boat in January 1933. Just before he died, he uttered some words in a dialect which was not understood by any of the other crew who were also Okinawans (Singapore Subordinate Courts, AD-019, S/no. 20, 5 January 1933).

8 Although Robertson says that the Kyodo Gyogyo Co. Ltd was a subsidiary of the Oriental Development Company (Robertson 1986: 57), the fishery company was independent until 1934 when it came under the control of the Nippon Sangyo Co. Ltd (Nissan).

9 The Kyodo Gyogyo Co. Ltd was not the first company to engage in trawling in the waters of Southeast Asia. In 1912, a certain Chinese conducted trawling, employing the *Golden Crown*, a 100-ton trawler, with a crew consisting of a captain and a mate, both British, as well as ten Chinese and Malays, in the waters of the Straits Settlements. However, he incurred huge losses due to the crew's inexperience in trawling and bad choice of fishing grounds, and was obliged to cease the operations after three months (Takayama 1914: 324).

5 JAPAN'S ECONOMIC ACTIVITIES IN SYONAN

1 Syonan can also be spelt Shonan in Japanese.

2 A list of the Japanese companies in Syonan can be found in Boei Kenkyujo Senshibu (The War History Department of the National Institute of Defence Studies) (1985: 202–5). Also, the Japanese companies in Southeast Asia under Japanese control are classified by company and the type of undertakings in 'Nanpo rikugun chiku shinshutsu kigyo kaisha ichiran' (A List of the Japanese Firms in the Southern Regions under the Jurisdiction of the Japanese Army) (DRO, E2.2.1/3–40). Although the list includes large numbers of the Japanese companies in Syonan, it omits some important companies such as department stores. Moreover, these two lists show neither the number of workers nor the production capacity of Japanese firms.

3 In the Japanese Army, a yellow flag was attached to the front of a general's car, a red flag to that of a field officer's car, and a blue flag to that of a car belonging to an officer below the rank of major.

4 Prior to World War II Malaya was British Malaya except Singapore, but during the Japanese occupation period it included Syonan (Singapore). However, in order not to confuse readers, in this chapter we shall employ the term Malaya in the same way as for the pre-war period.

5 In 1937, for example, ¥100 was equivalent in value to $54.55 and 51.82 guilders (Nanyo Kyokai 1943: 339).

6 The Southern Regions Development Bank's notes were also called banana notes because there were drawings of bananas on them.

7 The Teikoku Suisan Tosei Kaisha (the Imperial Fisheries Control Co. Ltd), founded in 1942 as a national policy company, took over Nihon Suisan's ice-manufacturing and cold-storage facilities in Japan and the Japan-occupied Asian territories including Singapore in 1943.

8 Many Chinese were engaged in illegal importation, carrying rice by junks, while the military authorities did not impose strict control over their activities (Kurasawa 1997: 150–1). As the shortage of rice became increasingly serious, the Japanese set up a Private Rice Importers Association in mid-1944 with a view to encouraging local traders to import rice by junks (Kratoska 1998: 251).

9 Economic activities of Matsuzakaya in Southeast Asia under Japanese rule can be found in Matsuzakaya (1981: 67) and Takenaka (1964: 513–17).

10 In the 1930s, a considerable number of Japanese migrated into the Cameron Highlands under the protection of Nanyo Kyokai (the South Seas Association). At the peak, Japanese households numbered some 20. They were mainly engaged in the cultivation of vegetables, but there were some like Takeuchi Taihei, who owned tea plantations (Hara 1986: 77–115).

11 Satake Toshio was born in 1886, and opened Satake Shokai in 1918. Sugiyama Shozo was born in 1902, and began to run Nanyo Shoko in 1920. As for Uchida Takeo, he was born in 1904, and opened Baba Shoten in 1924 (Nanyo oyobi Nihonjinsha 1938: 689, 690, 694).

12 Fukuda Kurahachi was interned with other Japanese residents by the British Army in Singapore when the Pacific War broke out, and was subsequently sent to India. However, like Eifuku Tora, he was one of those Japanese who were exchanged with British prisoners of war at Lourenço Marques, and he was able to return to Singapore in September 1942.

13 Even some Japanese were engaged in purchasing car parts on a black market, and used them for maintenance of their cars (OHI Ang).

14 The Ho Hong Oil Mills constituted part of the Ho Hong Conglomerate. For further information about the conglomerate, see Iwasaki (1990: 106–8) and Huff (1994: 147, 225, 233).

15 For detailed information about Japanese education policy during the Syonan era, see Wilson (1978: 85–113).

16 Dr Edred Corners, who worked for the Syonan Museum during the occupation period, learned from a local mechanic that in April 1942 the former Ford Assembly factory was re-opened by Nissan, and turned out 20 to 30 vehicles a day. He himself saw many completed limousines and military lorries outside the factory (Corners 1981: 55–6). If one assumed that Nissan had started assembling Ford cars using parts in stock well before it began to assemble Japanese cars, then there would be no problem with his description. However, it is highly unlikely that the factory was re-opened by Nissan as early as April 1942.

17 The Japanese Army, in imitation of the pre-war British Army, had extracted Vitamin B from yeast, made it into tablets, and distributed them to Japanese troops (OHI De Souza).

18 *Ryotei* literally meant a place where food and drink were served and *geisha* attended to guests through conversation and entertainment. It could also mean establishments where *geisha* also provided customers with sexual services.

19 Goh Sin Tub, who lived in Emerald Hill Road during the occupation period, wrote a novel entitled *The Nan-Mei-Su of Emerald Hill*, based on a comfort station which existed near his place. In his story, Nan-Mei-Su, a comfort station, was set up by the Japanese Army, and managed by a Japanese woman, keeping young Singaporean girls.

20 Kim Il Miyun relates that *ryotei* in the Japanese-occupied territories were high-class comfort stations where high-ranking officers were entertained by Japanese women (Kim 1976: 192).

21 The OSK is probably an abbreviation for the Osaka Shochiku (Shojo) Kagekidan (the Osaka Shochiku Girls' Operetta Troupe Company).

6 JAPAN'S RETURN TO SINGAPORE IN THE POST-WAR PERIOD

1 The Far Eastern Commission was set up in Washington by the Allied Powers in December 1945 as a policy-making body with regards to Japan. However, MacArthur, the SCAP, distrusted it and carried out his occupation policies without consulting it.

2 The Kaigai Shijo Chosakai was set up in 1951 in Osaka on the model of Britain's Export Trade and Research Organisation (Nihon Boeki Shinkokai 1973: 1).

3 At the San Francisco Peace Treaty, the British plenipotentiary Kenneth Younger expressed the British government's decision to renounce the right to demand war compensation for Malaya, Singapore and Hong Kong (Nishimura Kumao 1971: 221; Kobayashi 1993: 192–3). This was largely because Britain was obliged to agree on the American Far East policy. In fact, colonial Singapore was not in a position to negotiate with Japan for war reparations under an international law (SLA 1962: 285).

4 The American relief aid to Japan amounted to approximately US$3 billion as of June 1951 when it was suspended, while Japan was able to derive the special procurements income of approximately US$1 billion from the American military expenditures during the Korean War from 1950 to 1953.

5 The Korean War initially increased Singapore's foreign trade enormously, thanks to a sharp rise in the prices of primary commodities on the world market. The value of the colony's total foreign trade rose from $2,358 million in 1949 to $4,605 million in 1950, and $7,610 million in 1951, but it declined suddenly to $5,393 million in 1952 and $4,305 million in 1953 (COS Commerce and Industry Department, 1954: 3).

6 It is worth noting that in 1938 Marshall joined the Singapore Volunteers Corps which constituted part of the Straits Settlements Voluntary Force, and became a prisoner of war in February 1942 when Singapore was occupied by the Japanese Army. In May 1943, he and other prisoners were sent to Hokkaido in Japan, where they worked in the coal mines until the end of the Pacific War. When he learned that Japan had surrendered, Marshall 'felt he did not want to meet another Japanese for the rest of his life' (Chan 1984: 38, 44–50).

7 Japanese Consul-General Hinata Seizo at Singapore reported to Tokyo that in their talks R.B. Black told Prime Minister Kishi:

> It is a great concern for Britain to prevent the spread of Communist influence in Asia, as Communist forces were gradually growing in strength . . . I have recently advocated for developing local industry in order to deal with the twin problems of the population increase and unemployment, and to dispel economic uncertainty.
>
> (DRO, A' 1.5.1.5, 5 December 1957)

8 As for Singapore's response to the return of Japanese companies, Iwasaki Ikuo, for example, writes in his recent work:

> Singapore, which had gone through harsh Japanese military rule during the Second World War, showed rejection symptoms of Japan. But as it began industrialisation in the 1960s, it took the policy of opening doors to foreign capital. It treated the Japanese rule as a past problem, and opened the doors to Japan for the sake of industrialisation. Thereafter, beginning with the

ship-building investment as a joint venture with the Singapore government in the 1960s, [Japan's economic activities] expanded into electrical industry and foreign trade in the 1970s.

(Iwasaki 1996: 91–2)

However, what Iwasaki has overlooked is the fact that the Singapore government was very anxious to attract Japanese companies to invest in the colony in the 1950s.

9 In November 1957, Prime Minister Rahman of the Federation of Malaya visited Japan and asked Prime Minister Kishi for Japan's co-operation in setting up a tuna-fishing company as a joint venture and in constructing a fish-canning factory. There was, therefore, competition between Singapore and the Federation of Malaya in winning Japanese investment at that time (DRO, A' 1.5.1.5–3, 24 November 1957).

10 The SCAP placed a ban on fishing by all Japanese fishing ships in August 1945, but, because of the grave shortage of foodstuffs, in September it permitted fishing by Japanese within the limited sea area of some 630,000 square nautical miles around Japan. The line delineating this area was known as the MacArthur Line. Although the fishing area was extended several times thereafter, it was too limited to catch fish. As a result, the quantities of catches declined from 4,330,000 metric tons in 1936 to 1,820,000 metric tons in 1945, and remained at about 2 million metric tons in the next few years. In April 1952 fishing operations by the Japanese fishing companies in Southeast Asia and the Indian Ocean became possible thanks to the abolition of the MacArthur Line just before the San Francisco Peace Treaty came into effect. Japanese fishing companies were then able to resume offshore fishing. They were particularly interested in the Indian Ocean and Southeast Asian seas because of the existence of tuna-fishing grounds (Kawai 1994: 53–5).

11 Taiyo Gyogyo had technical links in fisheries with Singapore at that time, but it had never managed any fish-processing and tinning factory in Singapore in the past, even though it showed some interest in the Singapore region at one time. This information was given to Hirakawa Hitoshi by the Maruha Co. Ltd on 10 March 1995.

12 Both Mitsui & Co. and Mitsubishi Corporation were dissolved by the SCAP in 1947, and a large number of small and medium-sized companies were created by the former employees out of them thereafter. However, they were reborn in the 1950s through mergers. For further information about the dissolution and re-emergence of these trading companies, see Yoshihara (1982: 95–113).

13 Tan Keong Choon is a nephew of Tan Kah Kee, a well-known overseas Chinese entrepreneur.

14 This information was given to Hirakawa Hitoshi in written form by the Singapore branch of the Bank of Tokyo through its head office in Tokyo on 16 March 1993, in reply to his enquiry.

15 *Ibid.*

16 In 1957, the Japanese insurance companies paid foreign countries a total of ¥9.6 billion as reinsurance fees, of which the Tokio Marine Insurance Co. Ltd was responsible for 30 per cent, and the Taisho Marine Insurance Co. Ltd 14 per cent, while they received ¥4.4 billion as reinsurance fees from foreign countries, of which the Tokio Marine Insurance Co. Ltd and the Taisho Marine Insurance

Co. Ltd were responsible for 34 per cent and 14 per cent respectively (Nihon Keieishi Kenkyujo 1982: 210–11).

17 In 1994, the Onoda Cement Co. Ltd was amalgamated with the Chichibu Cement Co. Ltd to form a new company, the Chichibu Onoda Co. Ltd.

18 The Hong Leong Co. Ltd was set up with a capital of $7,000 in 1941 by Kwek Hong Png, who had migrated to Singapore from Hokkien Province in China in 1929. During the occupation period, the company made large profits by handling in ironware and by running a paint factory thanks to the grave shortage of various goods in Syonan. In 1946, he set up a joint-venture company in Penang to trade in ironware, and invested in rubber estates in the Malay Peninsula, making a fortune thanks to a sharp rise in demand for rubber during the Korean War. From the second half of the 1950s, Hong Leong started growing rapidly largely because of its various undertakings with Japanese companies (Iwasaki 1990: 49–52).

19 In 1926 the Osaka Yogyo Cement Co. Ltd was founded, and was renamed the Osaka Cement Co. Ltd in 1963. In 1994 the company was absorbed by the Sumitomo Cement Co. Ltd to form the Sumitomo Osaka Cement Co. Ltd.

20 This information was provided to Hirakawa Hitoshi in written form by the Company-History Editorial Group of the General Affairs Section of Ajinomoto Co. Ltd on 13 February 1997, in reply to his enquiries about the actual conditions of resident representatives at the Singapore office.

21 *Ibid.*

22 *Ibid.*

23 The Ajinomoto (Malaya) Co. Ltd was renamed the Ajinomoto (Malaysia) Sdn Berhad when Malaysia was formed in 1963.

24 A typical trouble occurred when Japanese shipping firms were refused leave to join an ocean-shipping route by Western shipping conference members which feared severe Japanese competition. They therefore had no choice but to allocate ships outside the conference unilaterally. The worst trouble occurred in November 1951 when the Mitsui Senpaku Kaisha, a newcomer, was refused membership of the European Freight Conference, which was a closed conference controlled largely by the influential British and European shipping firms. Since the Nippon Yusen Kaisha and the Osaka Shosen Kaisha had been its members before World War II, they were granted membership in the early 1950s. Mitsui Senpaku therefore began to allocate ships outside the conference. In January 1956 the three Japanese shipping firms had talks under the mediation of Yoneda Fujio, the director of the Shipping Association of Japan (Nippon Senpaku Kyokai). Moreover, in May of that year, the representatives of P & O, the Blue Funnel Line and the East Asiatic were invited to Japan to have talks with the representatives of the Japanese firms. Eventually, in June 1957 Mitsui Senpaku was permitted to operate its ships on the Asia–Europe route under the wing of the Nippon Yusen Kaisha (Osaka Shosen Mitsui 1969: 107–9; Yoneda 1978: 399–418; Ariyoshi 1981: 267–9). This meant that Mitsui Senpaku's ships were operated under the name of the Nippon Yusen Kaisha which was in charge of collecting cargoes, issued its own bills of lading and used its own agencies.

7 THE BLOOD-DEBT ISSUE AND JAPAN'S ECONOMIC ADVANCE

1 Further information about the political struggle between the PAP and the Barisan Sosialis can be found in Lee Kuan Yew (1998: 385–524), Rodan (1989: 66–84) and Takeshita (1995: 149–73).

2 In the previous chapters we have mainly employed the term 'overseas Chinese' to denote Chinese residents in Singapore and Malaya, but in this chapter we use the term 'Chinese', for in the 1950s and the 1960s, the 'overseas Chinese' came to have a special meaning in Southeast Asia including Singapore and Malaya.

As it is well known, the term, 'overseas Chinese' means 'Chinese residing abroad temporarily'. However, Singapore gained complete autonomy in 1959, while the Federation of Malaya achieved independence from Britain in 1957. On the other hand, China adopted in the middle of the 1950s a policy that overseas Chinese in Southeast Asia should be encouraged to acquire the nationalities of the countries where they lived, and to participate actively in the nation-building of these countries. Moreover, there was a growing Communist threat in Singapore and Malaya under the influence of the Chinese Communist Party, and since Communist activities were undertaken largely by overseas Chinese, the term, 'overseas Chinese', came to mean those who had close relations with the Chinese Communist Party. This led the Chinese people in the region to call themselves 'Chinese' instead of 'overseas Chinese', in order to show their loyalty to the local community, while they themselves chose to use it because they felt that they were self-reliant, being independent from Communist China (Okabe 1968: 18).

In the 1960s, the people in Singapore were fully committed to the nation-building of their country, and the local Chinese called themselves 'Chinese', to be independent from China. At any rate, by this time, the first-generation overseas Chinese (i.e. those born in China) constituted a minority in Singapore (43.1 per cent of total Chinese in 1947, and 35.7 per cent in 1957), and this must have caused the overseas Chinese to accept the concept of Singaporean nationality (Kani 1994: 84).

3 In September 1967, the Japanese government signed an agreement with the Singapore government, under which Japan was to pay the country a $25 million grant and an equal amount of loans in yen on liberal terms (Shingaporu Nihonjinkai 1978: 102–6; Shingaporu Nihon Shoko Kaigisho 1990: 184).

4 With regards to the blood-debt issue, Shimizu Hajime seems to overstate the severity of Chinese hostilities towards Japanese in Singapore, as he argues that:

> The anti-Japanese movement for the blood-debt issue mainly took the form of anti-Japanese meetings, attacks by rioters, refusal for loading and unloading of Japanese goods at the port, and others, affecting the Japanese community directly in Singapore. The Japanese community was in a state of panic for a while, but the movement in effect came to an end thanks to the tough negotiations by the Japanese government and the change of negotiator for the blood-debt issue to Prime Minister Rahman as a result of the formation of Malaysia in September 1963.
>
> (Shimizu Hajime 1994a: 274)

Contrary to Shimizu Hajime's argument, there is apparently a general agreement among the Japanese concerned that many Japanese at that time were comparatively well composed, coping with the 'crisis', even though there was a situation where the Japanese became tense for a time in Singapore. At any rate, the PAP government dealt with the incident calmly.

5 However, such a stance taken by the Lee Kuan Yew government has been completely ignored by scholars. Iwasaki Ikuo writes:

> While struggling politically against the communist group, the People's Action Party government began to implement the industrialisation and social development policies. In 1961, it made several development plans including the 'Four-Year Development Plan' (which later became the Five-Year Development Plan), the only one ever made in Singapore, and the 'Five-Year Housing Programme'. However, as the People's Action Party had to spend all its energy on its desperate struggle against its political enemy, the Barisan Sosialis, it could hardly afford the economic development.
>
> (Iwasaki 1996: 62)

Moreover, Iwasaki maintains that the Singapore government opened its doors to Japanese companies in the 1960s. This is the view which has hitherto been commonly held by almost all the scholars who have worked on the advance of Japanese firms into post-war Singapore.

6 In 1968 Nissho Co. Ltd amalgamated with Iwai Sangyo to form a new company, Nissho-Iwai Co. Ltd.

7 When the group of Japanese petitioners returned to Japan, they energetically worked for an early settlement of the blood-debt issue, explaining the actual situation of the anti-Japanese movement in Singapore, meeting cabinet ministers, such as Foreign Minister Ohira Masayoshi and Finance Minister Tanaka Kakuei, and the representatives of various economic associations, and appearing on TV and radio. The Japanese Association of Singapore's *Minami Jujisei* describes that 'at the time of the petition, Nakayama Kazumi, who based his power of persuasion on his constant study of Southeast Asia and overseas Chinese, did not fail to draw the attention of his audience' (Shingaporu Nihonjinkai 1978: 106). Nakayama became both the Singapore branch manager and the Malaysian area manager in 1968 when Nissho amalgamated with Iwai Sangyo.

8 Nezu Kiyoshi befriended Nakayama Kazumi in Singapore when he was a news reporter in charge of Asia for Yomiuri Shimbunsha (Yomiuri Newspaper Co. Ltd). He recalls now that Nakayama was fluent in Mandarin and Hokkien as well as in Cantonese (OHI Nezu).

9 For example, Lee Kuan Yew was educated at Cambridge University, while Goh Keng Swee, Toh Chin Chye and S. Rajaratnam studied at London University.

10 In 1953, Tan Lark Sye made a proposal for the establishment of a Chinese-medium university, the Nanyang University, and became the chairman of the council in 1956 when the university was eventually opened.

11 For example, the Singapore branch of Nichimen Jitsugyo began to engage in tripartite trade with Pakistan, India, Burma and others in the 1950s (Nichimen Jitsugyo 1962: 391).

12 At the round-table talk on the tenth anniversary of the Japanese Chamber of Commerce and Industry in 1979, Sakurai Kiyohiko of Jurong Shipyard Ltd said that the first fruit of the establishment of the chamber in August 1969 was the removal of the ban on tripartite trade (excluding traditional goods). When Sakurai

had a talk with Finance Minister Goh Keng Swee shortly after the establishment of the chamber, he was told verbally about it by Goh (Sakurai 1979: 36).

Also, Sato Shusaku of Mitsui & Co. attended the Southeast Asian Regional Trade Joint Conference organised by the Japanese government in Taipei in April 1970 and said at the conference that in November 1969 the Singapore government had removed a ban on Japanese trading companies engaging in tripartite trade (excluding 12 items of traditional goods as well as Indonesian goods), thanks to the efforts made by the Japanese embassy (Sato 1970: 19).

13 According to Yoshihara Kunio, when a Japanese trading company applied to set up a branch in the early 1960s, the Singapore government stated that the application would be considered if a main object of the branch was to promote the establishment of joint industrial ventures. Apparently, Yoshihara does not think that it was a unique case (Yoshihara 1976: 59). It is highly likely that the sentences quoted by Yoshihara constituted part of the document on the seven conditions restricting the activities of Japanese trading companies to which Nakayama referred. At any rate, as Yoshihara assumes, these conditions seem to have been applied to all the Japanese trading companies in Singapore.

14 Yoshihara Kunio says that the number of Japanese-controlled manufacturing firms by the year of establishment was one in 1961, two in 1962, and eight in 1963 (Yoshihara 1976: 183, Table 4.1). His figures are based on the EDB's 1972 list for pioneer industries, and the 1972/73 membership list of the Singapore Manufacturers' Association. However, as noted in the previous chapter, in the non-manufacturing sector there were already Japanese investments in the 1950s, and as shown in this chapter, even in the manufacturing sector there were several times more Japanese companies which invested in Singapore in the first half of the 1960s. Yoshihara has taken no account of capital investments by non-manufacturing companies, and seems to have overlooked those companies which had withdrawn from the country.

15 The Unimar Co. Ltd (Hong Kong) was named by combining 'Uni' of Union with 'mar' of Maruzen.

16 Although most members of the Chinese Chamber of Commerce took an anti-Lee Kuan Yew stance at that time, Lien Ying Chow was close to the prime minister politically (Iwasaki 1990: 48–9).

17 According to Sakurai Kiyohiko, in 1964 the repairing facilities for Jurong Shipyard Ltd were transported from Japan, and repair work for small ships of a 3,000 gross ton class began, in preparation for the repair of large ships. However, the commencement of the repairing work was not officially announced until 1965 when the 9-ton dry dock was completed (OHI Sakurai).

18 At the round-table talks arranged by the Japanese Association, Singapore, in March 1984, Sakurai Kiyohiko agreed with Hashimoto Kenjiro that Singapore's development was related greatly to the growth of the Japanese economy, and then said:

> The development of Jurong Shipyard Ltd was, in a way, also thanks to it. In other words, Japan's high-speed economic growth with the rise in industrial productivity led to the huge expansion in oil consumption in the country. Oil tankers plying between Japan and the Middle East's oil-producing countries entered Singapore's port, while passing through the Straits of Malacca. 'Jurong' could make money by undertaking repairing and maintenance works for them.
>
> (Shingaporu Nihonjinkai 1987: 109)

19 This Japanese-controlled company, which seems to have been the Pan-Malaysia Industries Ltd, was banned by the Japanese government from exporting plywood to the US as well as to Japan, because it was feared that the company would compete with Japanese manufacturers of similar products on the American market.

20 It is said that today the Hong Leong Group is powerful enough even to overtake the traditional family combines of three largest banking/industrial groups, namely the OCBC (Oversea-Chinese Banking Corporation Ltd) Group, the UOB (United Overseas Bank Ltd) Group, and the OUB (Overseas Union Bank Ltd) Group (Iwasaki 1990: 49).

CONCLUSION

1 For further information about the Asian Dollar Market, see Lee Sheng-Yi (1990: 97–103).

2 We have not been able to find any Singapore source materials concerning the relationship between the 'quasi-reparations' and Jurong Shipbuilders Ltd. Incidentally, it is interesting to note that, according to the Ministry of Culture, Singapore, 'The memorial [the Cenotaph] was partly financed with money paid by the Japanese Government to the Singapore Government as atonement for the atrocities committed during Japan's occupation of Singapore' (Ministry of Culture 1984: 85). However, the Japanese government has never stated publicly that it made financial contributions to the Singapore government for this purpose.

3 Isetan was not one of the three Japanese department stores (Daimaru, Matsuzakaya and Shirakiya) which were actively engaged in retailing and other activities in Syonan during the Japanese occupation period. However, Kato Fukuhei, the first managing director of the Isetan Emporium (S) Pte Ltd, had been in Padang, Sumatra during the Pacific War where he and Kosuge Shozo managed a department store under orders from the Japanese Army, and was responsible for negotiating with the president of Apollo Enterprises Pte Ltd for the joint venture in Singapore (Isetan Koho, 1990: 85 and 282).

4 Yaohan's joint-venture partners were the Development Bank of Singapore, Tiger Pte Ltd, Temasek Holdings and Singapore Nomura Merchant Banking.

5 In 1990, the Yaohan Group moved its headquarters from Japan to Hong Kong, but was eventually liquidated owing to financial difficulties in 1997.

6 Shortly after the release of the report, Lee Hsien Loong was promoted to Acting Minister of Trade and Industry.

7 As of the end of 1996, there were 3,018 Japanese firms which were registered with the Registry Office of Companies and Businesses in Singapore, but it is assumed that some 30 per cent of these firms had already withdrawn from the country (Kawada 1997: 115).

BIBLIOGRAPHY

I   UNPUBLISHED SOURCES

1   PRO (Public Record Office), Kew, Richmond, England

CO 273 Series: Correspondence Relating to the Straits Settlements, 1838–1946.
CO 852 Series: Original Correspondence, General Economic, 1935–55.
CO 1022 Series: Original Correspondence, South East Asia Department, 1951–3.
FO 371 Series: Original Correspondence, Political (and Economic), 1906–54.

2   Singapore Subordinate Courts, Singapore

Coroners' Inquests and Enquiries, 1882–1939.

3   DRO (Diplomatic Record Office), Tokyo: Diplomatic Documents

Pre-War and War Period

4. 2. 2. 27: *Honpojin fuseigyo torisimari kankei zakken* [Miscellaneous Matters concerning Controls over Japanese Flesh Traffickers] (7 vols).

4. 2. 2. 34: *Honpojin fuseigyo torisimari kankei hoki zassan* [Miscellaneous Matters concerning the Regulations for Controls over Japanese Flesh Traffickers] (2 vols).

4. 2. 2. 99: *Kaigai ni okeru honpo shugyofu no insu oyobi sono jokyo to nen nikai hokokugata kuntatsu ikken* [Notification for making a bi-annual Report on the Number and Activities of Japanese Prostitutes overseas] (11 vols).

7. 1. 5. 4: *Kaigai zairyu hojin shokugyo-betsu jinko chosa ikken* [Survey on Overseas Japanese Residents by Occupation] (32 vols).

B. 9. 10. 0/1-1-1: *Kokusai renmei fujin jido mondai ikken: Toyo ni okeru fujo baibai jittai chosa no ken junbi chosa (baishofu no jitsujo torishirabe no ken)* [League of Nations' Issue of Women and Children: A Preliminary Enquiry into Traffic in Women and Children in the East (An Enquiry into the Actual Conditions of Prostitutes)] (1 vol.).

E. 0. 0. 0/8: *Dai toa senso-chu no teikoku no tai nanpo keizai seisaku kankei zakken: Shinajihen oyobi dai niji oshu senso wo fukumu* [Miscellaneous Matters concerning

Imperial Economic Policy for Southeast Asia during the Greater East Asia War (including the Sino-Japanese War and World War II)] (3 vols).

E. 0. 0. 0/8–1: *Nanpo ni okeru shigen kaihatsu jigyo shinchoku jokyo shirabe* [An Enquiry into the Level of Progress in the Exploitation of Natural Resources in the Southern Regions] (1 vol.).

E. 1. 1. 0/8: *Teikoku no taigai keizai hattensaku kankei zakken* [Miscellaneous Matters concerning the Imperial Policy for Overseas Economic Expansion] (2 vols).

E. 2. 2. 1/3-37: *Nanpo kaihatsu kinko chosaka hen, Nanpo kankei kaisha yoran* [Research Section of the Southern Regions Development Bank, ed., The Survey of the Japanese Firms which had relations with the Southern Regions] (11 vols).

E. 2. 2. 1/3-40: *Nanpo rikugun chiku shinshutsu kigyo kaisha ichiran (jigyo-betsu)* [A List of Japanese Firms in the Southern Regions under the Jurisdiction of the Japanese Army (classified by type of undertakings] (1 vol).

E. 2. 7. 0/1-1: *Honpo shohin chinretsujo kankei zakken: zaigai no bu* [Miscellaneous Matters concerning Japanese Commercial Museums: in Foreign Countries] (8 vols).

E. 3. 1. 1/4: *Teikoku boeki seisaku kankei zakken* [Miscellaneous Matters concerning Imperial Trade Policy] (24 vols).

E. 3. 1. 1/4-10: *Teikoku boeki seisaku kankei zakken: Yushutsunyu kumiai kankei* [Miscellaneous Matters concerning Imperial Trade Policy: Import and Export Guilds] (8 vols).

E. 3. 1. 2/X1-B9: *Kakkoku kanzei narabi hoki kankei zakken: Marai no bu (Kita Boruneo oyobi Sarawakku wo fukumu)* [Miscellaneous Matters concerning Custom Duties and Regulations in various Countries: British Malaya including North Borneo and Sarawak] (11 vols).

E. 3. 2. 0/J3: *Shogaikoku shijo ni okeru honpo yushutsu-hin shinshutsu oyobi kyoso kankei zakken* [Miscellaneous Matters concerning the Inroads of Japanese Goods and Japanese Competition in various Overseas Markets] (4 vols).

E. 4. 8. 0/X4-B1: *Gaikoku kozan oyobi kogyo kankei zakken: Eikoku no bu (Zokuryo chi wo fukumu)* [Miscellaneous Matters concerning Foreign Mines and Mining Industry: Britain and the territories under British Control] (1 vol.) .

E. 4. 9. 0/7-7: *Honpo gyogyo kankei zakken: Nanyo gyogyo kankei* [Miscellaneous Matters concerning Japanese Fisheries: Fisheries in Southeast Asia] (6 vols).

E. 4. 9. 0/7-8: *Honpo gyogyo kankei zakken: Kaigai ni okeru honpojin gyogyo jokyo chosa* [Miscellaneous Matters concerning Japanese Fisheries: A Survey on the State of Overseas Japanese Fisheries] (1 vol.).

F. 1. 6. 0/7: *Honpo kisen kaisha gaikoku koro kankei zakken* [Miscellaneous Matters concerning the Overseas Shipping Routes of Japanese Shipping Firms] (7 vols).

I. 1. 10. 0/2-4: *Honpo ni okeru kyokai oyobi bunka dantai kankei zakken: Nanyo kyokai kankei* [Miscellaneous Matters concerning Associations and Cultural Organizations: The South Seas Association] (1 vol.).

J. 1. 2. 0/J8-2: *Imin ni kansuru tokei oyobi chosa kankei zakken – Zaigai honpojin jin'in narabi sokingaku chosa* [Miscellaneous Matters concerning the Statistics and Surveys on Emigrants: A Survey on the Number of Japanese overseas and the Amount of Remittances] (7 vols).

K. 3. 7. 0/5: *Zaigai honpo ni kansuru torishirabe zassan* [Miscellaneous Matters concerning An Enquiry into Japanese overseas] (3 vols).

Post-war Period

A' 1. 3. 1. 1: *Nihon-eikoku kankei gaiko* [Anglo-Japanese Diplomacy].

A' 1. 5. 0. 3: *Yoshida sori obei homon kankei ikken* [Prime Minister Yoshida's visit to the US and Europe] (5 vols).

A' 1. 5. 1. 5: *Kishi sori tonan ajia shokoku, osutoraria, nyujirando homon kankei ikken* [Prime Minister Kishi's visit to Southeast Asian Countries, Australia, and New Zealand] (5 vols).

A' 1. 5. 1. 5-1: *Kishi sori tonan ajia shokoku, osutoraria, nyujirando homon kankei ikken: Junbi shiryo* [Prime Minister Kishi's visit to Southeast Asian Countries, Australia, and New Zealand: Prepared Materials].

A' 1. 5. 1. 5-2: *Kishi sori tonan ajia shokoku, osutoraria, nyujirando homon kankei ikken: Homon ni kansuru hokoku* [Prime Minister Kishi's visit to Southeast Asian Countries, Australia, and New Zealand: Report on his Visit].

A' 1. 5. 1. 5-3: *Kishi sori tonan ajia shokoku, osutoraria, nyujirando homon kankei ikken: homon koku shuno tono kaidan kiroku* [Prime Minister Kishi's visit to Southeast Asian Countries, Australia, and New Zealand: Records on his talks with the leaders in these countries].

B' 4. 1. 1. 2: *Nihon koku tono heiwa joyaku kankei ikken: Shogaikoku hijun kankei* [The Peace Treaty with Japan: Ratification by Various Foreign Countries].

4 NIDS (National Institute of Defence Studies), Tokyo: Military Administration Documents

No. 17: Nanpo gunsei sokanbu chosabu [Research Department of the Southern Regions Military Administration Headquarters], 'Marai no jidosha no tenbo' [Prospect for Automobiles in Malaya], *Nanpo gunsei sokanbu chosa shiryo* [Survey materials of the Southern Regions Military Administration Headquarters], October 1943.

No. 18a: Nanpo gunsei sokanbu chosabu [Research Department of the Southern Regions Military Administration Headquarters], 'Syonan tokubetsushi wo chushin to suru bukka taisaku' [A Measure to counter Inflation mainly in the Syonan Special Municipality], *Nanpo gunsei sokanbu chosa shiryo* [Survey materials of the Southern Regions Military Administration Headquarters], March 1944.

No. 18b: Marai gunseikanbu chosa shiryo [Research Department of the Southern Regions Military Administration Headquarters], 'Marai ni okeru jidosha yusoryoku zokyo wo chushin to suru shomondai' [Various Matters concerning the Increase in the Capacity of transportation by motor vehicles in Malaya], *Nanpo gunsei sokanbu chosa shiryo* [Survey materials of the Southern Regions Military Administration Headquarters], May 1944.

No. 29: Gunseikanbu somubu chosashitsu [Research Office of the General Affairs Department at the Military Administration Headquarters], 'Syonan tokubetsushi juyo kojo genkyo gaikyo' [A General Survey of the Present Conditions of Main Factories in the Syonan Special Municipality], *Nanpo jijo chosa hokoku kankei tsuzuri* [A File of Survey Reports on the Conditions of Southern Regions], March 1943.

No. 97: Fukuinsho shizaika [Materials Section of the Ministry of Demobilisation], 'Shusen-ji ni okeru nanpo rikugun gunsei chiiki no jigyo kiroku-hyo' [A Document concerning the undertakings in the region under the Southern Regions Military Administration at the time of Japan's Defeat], *Dai toa senshi gunsei sangyo no bu bessatsu* [A Supplementary to the Military Administration's Industries in the Greater East Asian War History], June 1946.

5   Mitsui Bunko [Mitsui Archives], Tokyo: Historical Documents

Bussan 338/11: Moji Sekitan Shibu[Moji Coal Branch], '*Shitencho kaigi shiryo*' [Source Materials for the Meeting of Branch Managers], *Dai rokkai shitencho kaigi shiryo* (12), [Materials for the Sixth Meeting of Branch Managers (12)], June 1918.

Bussan 348/8: Sekitan Bucho [Coal Manager], '*Shitencho kaigi sekitanbu hokoku*' [Report by the Coal Section at the Meeting of Branch Managers], *Dai hachikai shitencho kaigi shiryo* (11), [Source Materials for the Eighth Meeting of Branch Managers (11)], June 1921.

Bussan 357/1: Tokyo Honten Sanji Joho Kakari [Tokyo Head Office's Secretary in Charge of Information], '*Hantaisho shirabe*' [An Enquiry into Rival Merchants), *Dai hachikai shitencho kaigi shiryo* (10), [Source Materials for the Eighth Meeting of Branch Managers (10)], April 1921.

Bussan 394/1-7: Honten Gyomuka [Head Office's Business Section], '*Zappin toriatsukai hikaku-hyo*' [A Comparative Table for Handling of Sundry Goods], July 1931.

Bussan 51/38: '*Mitsui bussan kabushiki kaisha shokuinroku*' [Mitsui & Co. Personnel Directory], 42nd edition, 30 September 1941.

Bussan 51/39: '*Mitsui bussan kabushiki kaisha shokuinroku*' [Mitsui & Co. Personnel Directory], 43rd edition, 30 April 1942.

Bussan 51/40: '*Mitsui bussan kabushiki kaisha shokuinroku*' [Mitsui & Co. Personnel Directory], 44th edition, 31 October 1942.

Bussan 51/44: '*Mitsui bussan kabushiki kaisha shokuinroku*' [Mitsui & Co. Personnel Directory], 45th edition, 1 April 1943.

6   OHI (Oral History Interviews)

Singapore National Archives, Singapore

Ang Seah San: Interview conducted by Low Lay Leng, 25 June 1983, A000419/07.

Aziz bin Rahim Khan Surattee: Interview conducted by Low Lay Leng, 28 March 1984, A000284/06.

Barth, R.H.: Interview conducted by Pitt Kuan Wah, 10 February 1984, A000394/26.

Cheah, Charlie Fook Ying: Interview conducted by Low Lay Leng, 30 December 1983, A000385/14.

Chong, Robert: Interview conducted by Tan Beng Luan, 4 June 1983, A000273/16.

De Souza, Jocelyn Simon: Interview conducted by Yagarajeh Yogiui, 11 November 1981, A000126/04.

Gay Wang Leong: Interview conducted by Tan Beng Luan, 16 March 1985, A000535/07.

Heng Chang Ki: Interview conducted by Chua Ser Koon, 2 February 1982, A000152/08.

Ismail bin Zain: Interview conducted by Tan Beng Luan, 5 September 1985, A000601/05.

Lee Tian Soo: Interview conducted by Low Lay Leng, 21 May 1983, A000265/07.

Marcus, Philip Carlyle: Interview conducted by Chua Ser Koon, 4 August 1982, A000183/09.

Nagase Takashi: Interview conducted by Daniel Chew, 8 June 1987, A000789/004.

Naidu, Lakshmi: Interview conducted by Tan Beng Luan, 24 February 1982, A000110/11.

Oehlers, F.A.C.: Interview conducted by Low Lay Leng, 13 April 1984, A000421/20.

Sachdev, Durgadass: Interview conducted by Lim How Seng, 9 September 1982, A000153/07.

Soo Kim Seng: Interview conducted by Tan Beng Luan, 3 April 1985, A000543/11.

Tan Cheng Hwee: Interview conducted by Low Lay Leng, 22 March 1984, A000416/14.

Yamashiro Masamichi, *et al.*: Interview conducted by Henry Frei, 19 June 1994, A001701/06-07.

Others

Choo Yam Wai (ex-Librarian at the National University of Singapore): Interview conducted by Shimizu Hiroshi, 7 September 1996, Singapore.

Kikuchi Shigeru (Deputy Regional Director in Japan of the Singapore Tourist Board): Interview conducted by Hirakawa Hitoshi, 28 July 1998, Tokyo.

Marshall, David: Interview conducted by Sugino Kazuo, 18 September 1995, Singapore.

Negishi Masao, Yamashiro Masamichi, Kozai Rikuo and Ishikawa Ken (ex-Shonan Special Municipality Officials): Interview conducted by Hirakawa Hitoshi, 5 and 26 April 1996, Tokyo.

Nezu Kiyoshi (ex-reporter at *The Yomiuri Shimbun* Singapore Office): Interview conducted by Hirakawa Hitoshi, 12 July 1997, Tokyo.

Nukata Hiromitsu (ex-Shonan Special Municipality Official): Interview conducted by Hirakawa Hitoshi, 26 April 1996, Tokyo.

Otaka Zenzaburo (The First Head of Daiichi Bussan's Singapore Branch): Interview conducted by Hirakawa Hitoshi, 13 December 1995, Tokyo.

Sakurai Kiyohiko (ex-Managing Director of Jurong Shipyard Ltd): Interview conducted by Hirakawa Hitoshi, 17 August 1995, Tokyo.

Satta Kazutoshi (ex-Resident Representative of the Singapore Office of Mitsui & Co.): Interview conducted by Hirakawa Hitoshi, 13 February 1996, Tokyo.

Sugino Kazuo (Secretary General of the Japanese Association, Singapore): Interview conducted by Hirakawa Hitoshi and Shimizu Hiroshi, 10 September 1997, Singapore.

II NEWSPAPERS AND PERIODICALS

Asahi Shimbun [Asahi Newspaper], Tokyo.

Bataviasch Nieuwsblad, Batavia.

Boeki Jiho [The Trade Journal], Commercial Museum, the Ministry of Agriculture and Commerce, Japan, Tokyo.

Dai-Nippon Suisan Kaiho [Journal of the Great Japan Fisheries Association], Dai-Nippon Suisankai, Tokyo.

Government Gazette, the Straits Settlements (pre-war period), the Colony of Singapore (1946–59), and the State of Singapore (1959–65).

Java Gazette, Batavia.

Jitsugyo no Nihon [The World of Japanese Business], Jitsugyo no Nihonsha, Tokyo.

Kakushin [The Purity], Kakusinkai, Tokyo.

Kokusai Keizai [The International Economy], Kokusai Hyoronsha, Tokyo.

Mainichi Shimbun [Mainichi Newspaper], Tokyo.

Malaya, The British Association of Malaya, London.

Malayan Trade Digest, The Straits Times, Singapore.

Nagoya Shoko Kaigisho Geppo [Monthly Report of the Nagoya Chamber of Commerce and Industry], Nagoya.

Naigai Shoko Jiho [Journal of Domestic and Foreign Commerce and Industry], (before 1925) Commercial Museum, the Ministry of Agriculture and Commerce, Tokyo, and (after 1925) the Ministry of Commerce, Tokyo.

Nanyo [The South Seas], Nanyo Kyokai [South Seas Association], Tokyo.

Nanyo Keizai Jiho [Review of the South Seas Economies], Singapore Commercial Museum, Singapore.

Nanyo Kyokai Zasshi [Journal of the South Seas Association], Nanyo Kyokai, Tokyo.

Nanyo Suisan [South Seas Fisheries], Association for South Seas Fisheries, Tokyo.

Nihon Keizai Shimbun [Japan Economic Newspaper], Tokyo.

Niigata Nippo [Niigata Daily], Niigata.

Nomura Ajia Joho [Nomura Journal of Asian Information], Nomura Sogo Kenkyujo, Tokyo.

Osaka Asahi Shimbun [Osaka Asahi Newspaper], (Okinawa edition), Osaka.

Sekai [The World], Iwanami Shoten, Tokyo.

Shingaporu [Singapore], Nihon Shingaporu Kyokai [The Japan Singapore Association], Tokyo.

Singapore Trade, The Straits Times, Singapore.

(The) Straits Times, Singapore.

Suisan Iho [Fisheries Information], Bureau of Fisheries, Ministry of Agriculture and Forestry, Tokyo.

Suisankai [The World of Fisheries], Dai-Nippon Suisankai [Great Japan Fisheries Association], Tokyo.

Syonan Jit Poh [Syonan Daily], Singapore.

Syonan Shimbun [Syonan Newspaper], Singapore.

(The) Syonan Times, Singapore.

Tsusho Isan [Trade Compilation], Trade Bureau of the Foreign Ministry, Tokyo.

Tsusho Koho [Trade Information], (before July 1958) Kaigai Boeki Shinkokai [the Foreign Trade Promotion Organization], and (after July 1958) Nihon Bokei Shinkokai [Japan External Trade Organisation], Tokyo.

III BOOKS, ARTICLES, YEARBOOKS AND OTHERS

Aichiken Suisan Shikenjo (ed.) (1932) *Nanyo Gyogyo Chosa Hokoku* [A Survey Report on Fisheries in the South Seas], Miya: Aichiken Suisan Shikenjo.

Ajinomoto (1972) *Ajinomoto Kabusiki Kaisha Shashi* [The Company History of Ajinomoto Co. Ltd], Part II, Tokyo: Ajinomoto Kabushiki Kaisha.

—— (1990) *Aji wo tagayasu: Ajinomoto Hachijunen-shi* [Cultivation of the Taste: The Eighty-Year History of Ajinomoto Co. Ltd], Tokyo: Ajinomoto Kabushiki Kaisha.

Akashi Yoji (1968) 'Nanyang Chinese anti-Japanese boycott movement, 1908–1928: A study of Nanyang Chinese nationalism', *Journal of the South Seas Society*, vol. 23, Singapore.

Alatas, Hussein Syed (1971) *Thomas Stamford Raffles, 1781–1826: Schemer or Reformer?*, Singapore: Angus and Robertson.

—— (1977) *The Myth of the Lazy Natives*, London: Frank Cass.

Allen, G.C. (1981) *The Japanese Economy*, London: Weidenfeld and Nicolson.

Allen, G.C. and Donnithorne, A.G. (1957) *Western Enterprise in Indonesia and Malaya: A Study in Economic Development*, London: George Allen & Unwin.

Ando Yoshio (1975) *Kindai Nihon Keizaishi Yoran* [A Handbook of Modern Japanese Economic History], Tokyo: University of Tokyo Press.

Arisawa, Hiromi (general editor) and Nakamura Takafusa (ed.) (1990) *Nihon Keizai Saiken no Kihon Mondai* [The Basic Problem of the Japanese Economic Reconstruction], Tokyo: University of Tokyo Press.

Ariyoshi Yoshiya (1975) *Kaiun Gojunen* [The Fifty Years of Shipping], Tokyo: Nihon Kaiji Shimbunsha.

—— (1981) *Kaiso-roku: Nihon Kaiun to tomoni* [Memoirs: With Japanese Shipping], Tokyo: Nihon Kaiji Koho Kyokai.

Asano Isao (1968) 'Syonan Zosenjo Shimatsu-ki' [A Story of the Circumstances about the Syonan Shipyard], Minamikai, *Syonan Zosenjo no Omoide* [Recollection of the Shonan Zosenjo], Kobe: Minamikai.

Ashworth, W. (1975) *A Short Economic History of the International Economy since 1850*, London: Longman.

Awayama Akira (1971) 'Shingaporu no Tekko Jijo oyobi Tonan Ajia Tekko Kyokai ni tsuite' [The conditions of steel industry in Singapore and the steel associations in Southeast Asia], *Geppo* [Monthly Report], November, Japanese Chamber of Commerce and Industry, Singapore.

Ayabe Tsuneo and Nagazumi Akira (eds) (1982) *Motto Shiritai Shingaporu* [Singapore about which we want to gain Wider Understanding], Tokyo: Kobundo.

Ayabe Tsuneo and Ishii Yoneo (eds) (1994) *Motto Shiritai Shingaporu* [Singapore about which we want to gain Wider Understanding] (second edition), Tokyo: Kobundo.

Azato Minobu (1941) *Okinawa Kaiyo Hatten-shi: Nihon Nanpo Hatten-shi Josetsu* [A History of the Oceanic Development in Okinawa: An Introduction to Japan's Advance into the Southern Regions], Naha: Okinawaken Kaigai Kyokai.

Beasley, W.G. (1987) *Japanese Imperialism, 1894–1945*, Oxford: Clarendon Press.

Birtwistle, W. (1933–9) *Annual Report of the Fisheries Department, Straits Settlements and Federated Malay States*, Singapore.

Blue Book (1870–1939, 1946 and 1949) Singapore: Straits Settlements Government.

Boei Kenkyujo Senshibu (1985) *Shiryoshu: Nanpo no Gunsei* [A Collection of Source Materials: Military Administration in the Southern Regions], Tokyo: Asagumo Shimbunsha.

Brown, Ian (1994) 'The British merchant community in Singapore and Japanese commercial expansion in the 1930s', in Sugiyama Shinya and Milagros C. Guerrero (eds) (1994), *International Commercial Rivalry in Southeast Asia in the Interwar Period*, New Haven: Yale Southeast Asian Studies.

—— (1997) *Economic Change in South-east Asia, 1830–1980*, Kuala Lumpur: Oxford University Press.

Buchanan, I. (1972) *Singapore in Southeast Asia*, London: G. Bell and Sons Ltd.

Burdon, T.W. (1955) *The Fishing Industry of Singapore*, Singapore: Donald Moore.

Burijisuton Taiya Soritsu Gojushunen Shashi Hensan Iinkai (1982) *Burijisuton Gojushunen-shi* [The Fiftieth Anniversary of the Bridgestone Tire Co. Ltd], Tokyo: Burijisuton Taiya Kabushiki Kaisha.

Butcher, John G. (1979) *The British in Malaya*, Kuala Lumpur: Oxford University Press.

Census of Returns (1881, 1901, 1911), Singapore.

Chan Heng Chee (1984) *A Sensation of Independence: A Political Biography of David Marshall*, Singapore: Oxford University Press.

Chan Kwok Bun and Chiang, Claire (1994) *Stepping Out: The Making of Chinese Entrepreneurs*, Singapore: Prentice Hall.

Cheng Siok Hwa (1991) 'Economic change and industrialization', in Ernest C.T. Chew and Edwin Lee (eds) (1991).

Chew, Ernest C.T. and Lee, Edwin (eds) (1991) *A History of Singapore*, Singapore: Oxford University Press.

Chou Chu Chi (1986) 'Shingaporu Gunko Rodosha no Jigoku Seikatsu Kaisoroku' [Reminiscences on hellish life of workers at the naval port in Singapore], in Shü Yun Ts'iao and Chua Ser Koon (eds) (1986).

Choya Hyakunen-shi Henshu Iinkai (1986) *Choya: Isseiki no Ayumi* [Choya: A Hundred-year History], Tokyo: Choya Kabushiki Kaisha.

Choya Shatsu Hachijunen-shi Kanko Iinkai (1974) *Choya Shatsu Hachijunen-shi* [The Eighty-Year History of the Choya Shirts Co. Ltd], Tokyo: Kabushiki Kaisha Choya Shatsu.

Choya Shokai (1918–20) 'Dai 12 Kai–15 Kai Kessan Hokokusho' [The twelfth to fifteenth financial statements], Tokyo: Choya Shokai.

Chua Ser Koon (1986) 'Nihongun ni yoru Kensho Daigyakusatsu no Giseisha-su wo Kento suru' [Reviewing the inspected number of the victims at the hand of the Japanese Army], in Shü Yun Ts'iao and Chua Ser Koon (eds) (1986).

Chusho Kigyo Kin'yu Koko Chosabu (1989) *Yakushin suru ASEAN no Sangyo to Kin'yu* [Rapidly Growing Industry and Financial Business in the ASEAN], Tokyo: Toyo Keizai Shimposha.

Corbin, Alain (1978) *Les filles de noce: Misère sexuelle et prostitution (19e et 20e Siècles)*, Paris: Aubier-Montaigne.

Corners, Edred J.H. (1981) *The Marquis: A Tale of Syonan-To*, Singapore: Heinemann Asia.

COS (Colony of Singapore) (1958) *Colony of Singapore Annual Report 1956*, Singapore.

—— (1959) *Colony of Singapore Annual Report 1958*, Singapore.

——, Commerce and Industry Department (1954, 1955) *Report of the Department of Commerce and Industry*, Singapore.

——, Immigration Department (1953, 1957, 1959) *Annual Report of the Immigration Department*, Singapore.

——, Industrial Promotion Board (1958) *The Singapore Industrial Promotion Board First Year Report* (March 1957 to April 1958), Singapore.

Daimaru Nihyakugojunen-shi Henshu Iinkai (1967) *Daimaru Nihyakugojunen-shi* [Two Hundred-Fifty-Years History of Daimaru], Osaka: Kabushiki Kaisha Daimaru.

Dai-Toa-Sho Renraku Iinkai Daiichi Bukai (1943) *Nanpo Keizai Taisaku* [Economic Policy for the Southern Regions] (Revised Edition), Tokyo: Dai-Toa Renraku Iinkai.

Deyo, F.C. (1981) *Dependent Development and Industrial Order: An Asian Case Study*, New York: Praeger.

Dixon, Chris (1991) *South East Asia in the World-Economy*, Cambridge: Cambridge University Press.

Drabble, J.H. (1991) *Malayan Rubber: The Inter-war Years*, Basingstoke and London: Macmillan.

Drabble, J.H. and Drake, P.J. (1981) 'The British agency houses in Malaysia: Survival in a changing world', *Journal of Southeast Asian Studies*, vol. 12, no. 2, September, Singapore.

Drummond, I.M. (1972) *British Economic Policy and the Empire 1919–1939*, London: Allen & Unwin.

DSS (Department of Statistics Singapore) (1983) *Economic and Social Statistics Singapore 1960–1982*, Singapore.

—— (1990, 1991, 1996, 1997) *Yearbook of Statistics Singapore*, Singapore.

Duus, P., Myers, R.H. and Peattie, M.R. (eds) (1996) *The Japanese Wartime Empire, 1931–1954*, Princeton: Princeton University Press.

Economic Committee (1986) *The Singapore Economy: New Directions* (Report of the Economic Committee), Singapore: Singapore National Printers Ltd.

Economic Intelligence Unit (1989) *Country Report: Singapore*, no. 4, London.

Endo Masako (1996) *Shingaporu no Yunion Jakku* [The Union Jack of Singapore], Tokyo: Shueisha.

Firth, Raymond (1966) *Malay Fishermen*, London: Trench, Trubner & Co. Ltd.

Foreign Imports and Exports, Malaya (1930–9), Singapore: Government Printing Office.

Frank, Andre G. (1969) *Capitalism and Underdevelopment in Latin America: Historical Studies of Chile and Brazil*, London and New York: Monthly Review Press.

Fraser and Neave Ltd (1927) *The Singapore and Malayan Directory 1927*, Singapore: Fraser and Neave Ltd.

Fröbel, F. *et al.* (1980), *The New International Division of Labour*, London: Cambridge University Press.

Fukuda Shozo (1939) *Kakyo Keizai-ron* [On the Overseas Chinese Economics], Tokyo: Ganshodo Shoten.

Gaimusho (1928) 'Nanyo no Gyogyo oyobi Yosangyo' [Fisheries and silk-worm raising in the South Seas], Nanyo Shigen Chosa Hokokusho (mimeographed).

Gaimusho and Tsusansho (Kanri Boeki Kenkyukai) (eds) (1949) *Sengo Nihon no Boeki*

Kin'yu Kyotei [Financial and Trade Agreements between Occupied Japan and other Countries], Tokyo: Jitsugyo no Nihonsha.

Gaimusho Tsushokyoku (1918) *Kaikyo Shokuminchi Gairan* [An Overview of the Straits Settlements], Tokyo: Keiseisha.

German, R.L. (1930) *Handbook of British Malaya, 1930*, London: Waterlow & Sons Ltd.

Goh Sin Tub (1989) *The Nan Mei Su Girls of Emerald Hill*, Singapore: Heinemann Asia.

Goto Ken'ichi (1993) 'Gyogyo, Nanshin, Okinawa' [The fisheries, the Southward Advance, and Okinawa], in Oe Shinobu *et al.* (eds) (1993).

—— (1995) *Kindai Nihon to Tonan Ajia: Nanshin no 'Shogeki' to 'Isan'* [Modern Japan and Southeast Asia: The Impact and Legacy of the Southward Advance], Tokyo: Iwanami Shoten.

Goyo Kensetsu (1971) *Goyo Kensetsu Nanajugonen no Ayumi* [The Seventy-Five Years of the Goyo Construction Company's History], Tokyo: Goyo Kensetsu Kabushiki Kaisha.

Green, C.F. (1927) *Annual Report on the Fisheries Department, 1926*, Singapore.

Hagiwara Yoshiyuki (1978) 'Sengo Nihon to Tonan Ajia no Ichizuke: Haisen kara Junen no Kiseki' [Positioning of Japan and Southeast Asia in the post-war period: The ten-year locus since the end of World War II], in Shoda Ken'ichiro (ed.), *Kindai Nihon no Tonan Ajia Kan* [The Outlook of Modern Japan on Southeast Asia], Tokyo: Institute of Developing Economies.

—— (1991) 'Sengo Nihon no Nanpo Kaiki' [Japan's return to Southeast Asia in the post-war period], in Yano Toru (ed.) (1991).

Hamashita Takeshi and Kawakatsu Heita (eds) (1991) *Ajia Koeki-ken to Nihon Kogyoka 1500–1900* [The Asian Trade Sphere and Japanese Industrialisation 1500–1900], Tokyo: Libro Porto.

Hara Fujio (1978) 'Taiheiyo Senso mae ni okeru Maraya e no Shihon Shinshutsu' [Capital investment in Malaya before the Pacific War] in *Ouchi Tsutomu Kyoju Kanreki Kinen Ronbunshu* [Essays for the Sixtieth Anniversary of Professor Ouchi Tsutomu], Tokyo: University of Tokyo Press.

—— (1986) *Eiryo Maraya no Nihonjin* [The Japanese in British Malaya], Tokyo: Institute of Developing Economies.

—— (1987) *Wasurerareta Nanyo Imin* [Forgotten Japanese Immigrants in the South Seas], Tokyo: Institute of Developing Economies.

—— (1994) 'Nihon to Mareishia Keizai: Dai-Niji Taisen Chokugo no Baisho Mondai Ketchaku no Keii to sono Keizaiteki Igi' [Japan and the Malaysian economy: The background to and the significance of the settlement of the war reparations issue shortly after War War II], in Hara, Fujio (ed.), (1994) *Mareishia ni okeru Kigyo Gurupu no Keisei to Saihen* [The Formation and Re-organization of Industrial Groups in Malaysia], Tokyo: Institute of Developing Economies.

Harada Tadao (1969) *Shingaporu no Soshi Sangyo* [Pioneer Industries in Singapore], Tokyo: Institute of Developing Economies.

Hashimoto Akira (1974) 'Shingaporu ni okeru Hogin Jimusho no Katsudo ni tsuite' [On the business activities of Japanese banks' offices in Singapore], *Geppo*, November, Japanese Chamber of Commerce and Industry, Singapore.

Hashimoto Tokuju (1952) *Nihon Mokuzosen Shiwa* [A Historical Story of Japanese Wooden Ship-building], Tokyo: Hasegawa Shobo.

—— (1964) *Sokei no Hana* [Jasmine Flowers], Tokyo: Seien Hakkojo.

Hashiya Hiroshi (1985) 'Senzen-ki Firipin ni okeru Hojin Keizai Shinshutsu no Keitai' [A type of Japanese economic advance into the Philippines in the pre-war period], in Shimizu Hajime (ed.) (1985).

—— (1993) 'Nihon-Tonan Ajia Kankei-shi Kenkyu no Seika to Gendaiteki Igi' [The result and the significance for the contemporary period of studies in the history of Japan–Southeast Asian relations], *Ajia Keizai*, vol. 34, no. 9, September, Tokyo.

—— (1997) 'Tonan Ajia ni okeru Nihonjinkai to Nihonjin Shogyo Kaigisho' [Japanese Associations and Japanese Chamber of Commerce in Southeast Asia], in Namikata Shoichi (ed.) (1997).

Hayashi Hirofumi (1993) 'Marei Hanto ni okeru Nihon Gun Ianjo ni tsuite' [Comfort stations of the Japanese Army in the Malay Peninsula], *Kanto Gakuin Daigaku Keizai Gakubu Ippan Kyoiku Ronshu*, vol. 15, July, Yokohama.

—— (1994) 'Shingaporu no Nihongun Ianjo' [Comfort stations of the Japanese Army in Singapore], *Senso Sekinin Kenkyu* [Studies in War Responsibility], vol. 4, Summer, Tokyo.

Hayashi Kingoro (ed.) (1917) *Nanyo* [The South Seas], Tokyo: Kiryuya Shuppanbu.

Hayashi Toshiaki (ed.) (1990) *Shingaporu no Kogyoka: Ajia no Bijinesu Senta* [The Industrialisation of Singapore: Asia's Business Centre], Tokyo: Institute of Developing Economies.

Headrick, Daniel R. (1981) *The Tools of Empire: Technology and European Imperialism in the Nineteeth Century*, New York and Oxford: Oxford University Press.

—— (1988) *The Tentacles of Progress: Technology Transfer in the Age of Imperialism, 1850–1940*, New York and Oxford: Oxford University Press.

Heussler, Robert (1982) *British Rule in Malaya*, Westport (Connecticut): Greenwood Press.

Hicks, George L. (1995) *The Comfort Women*, Singapore: Heinemann Asia.

—— (ed.) (1993) *Overseas Chinese Remittances from Southeast Asia 1910– 1940*, Singapore: Select Books.

Higaki Shigeru (1970) 'Singaporu ni okeru Zosengyo' [The shipbuilding industry in Singapore], *Geppo* (Monthly Report), August, Japanese Chamber of Commerce and Industry, Singapore.

Hikida Yasuyuki (ed.) (1995) *Nanpo Kyoeiken: Senji Nihon no Tonan Ajia Keizai Shihai* [The Southern Regions Co-prosperity Sphere: Japan's Economic Control over Southeast Asia during the War], Tokyo: Taga Shuppan.

Hirakawa Hitoshi (1987) 'Ajia Shin Kogyoka to Shingaporu' [Asia's new industrial-ization and Singapore], in Okumura Shigetsugu (ed.), *Ajia Shin Kogyoka no Tenbo* [A Survey of Asia's New Industrialization], Tokyo: University of Tokyo Press.

—— (1996a) 'Sengo Nihon no Shingaporu e no Keizaiteki Kaiki' [Japan's economic return to Singapore in the post-war period], *Ajia Keizai*, vol. 37, no. 9, September, Tokyo.

—— (1996b) 'Yunyu Daitai Kogyoka-ki no Shingaporu to Nihon Kigyo' [Singapore and Japanese firms during the period of import-substitution industrialisation], *Ajia Keizai*, vol. 37, no. 10, October, Tokyo.

Hiroyoshi Katsuji (1987) 'Oikomiami Gyogyo no Seisei to Hatten' [The formation and growth of drive-in net fishing], in Nakadate Ko (ed.) (1987).

Ho, K.C. (1995) 'Singapore: Maneuvering in the middle league', in Gordon L. Clark and Kim Won Bae (eds), *Asian NIEs and the Global Economy*, Baltimore and London: Johns Hopkins University Press.

Horimoto Naohiko (1997) 'Shingaporu no Kajin Konichi Undo to Nihon-gawa Keizai Dantai' [Anti-Japanese Movement by Chinese and Japanese Economic Organisations in Singapore], in Namikata Shoichi (ed.) (1997).

Hosaka Hikotaro (1916) *Nanyo Tsuran* [A Survey of the South Seas], Tokyo: Keiseisha Shoten.

Howe, Christopher (1996) *The Origins of Japanese Trade Supremacy*, London: Hurst & Company.

Huff, W.G. (1994) *The Economic Growth of Singapore: Trade and Development in the Twentieth Century*, Cambridge: Cambridge University Press.

Hung Chin T'ang (1986) 'Kiki Kaikai na sono Seiji' [The outrageous politics], in Shü Yun Ts'iao and Chua Ser Koon (eds) (1986).

Hyam, Ronald (1986) 'Empire and sexual opportunity', *Journal of Imperial and Commonwealth History*, vol. XIV, no. 2, January, London.

—— (1990) *Empire and Sexuality: The British Experience*, Manchester: Manchester University Press.

Ide Yoshinori (1987) 'Okinawa Sangyo no Hensen to Suisangyo no Ichi' [A change in industrial structure, and the position of the fisheries in Okinawa], in Nakadate Ko (ed.) (1987).

Igarashi Takeshi (1995) 'Senso to Senryo 1941–1951' [The war and the occupation], in Hosoya Chihiro (ed.), *Nichibei Kankei Tsushi* [A General History of the US–Japan Relations], Tokyo: University of Tokyo Press.

Igusa Kunio (1991) 'Nihon no Tai Tonan Ajia Keizai Shinshutsu no Kozu' [The structure of Japan's economic advance into Southeast Asia], in Yano Toru (ed.) (1991).

Inoue Masaji (1915) *Nanyo* [The South Seas], Tokyo: Fuzanbo.

Irie Toraji (1942a, b) *Hojin Kaigai Hatten-shi* [A History of Japanese Overseas Expansion] Parts I and II, Tokyo: Ida Shoten.

—— (1943) *Meiji Nanshin Shiko* [A Historical Writing on the Southward Advance in the Meiji Period], Tokyo: Ida Shoten.

Isetan Koho Tanto Shashi Hensan Jimukyoku (ed.) (1990) *Isetan Hyakunen-shi* [One Hundred Years of Isetan], Tokyo: Kabushiki Kaisha Isetan.

Ishii Taro (1978) 'Jawa Hojin Kusawake Monogatari' [A story of the earliest Japanese in Java], in Jagartara Tomo no Kai (ed.) (1978).

Ishii Yoneo *et al.* (general eds) (1986) *Tonan Ajia wo Shiru Jiten* [Encyclopedia of Southeast Asia], Tokyo: Heibonsha.

Ishikawajima-Harima Jukogyo Somu Sokatsubu Shashi Hensan Tanto (ed.) (1992a) *Ishikawajima-Harima Jukogyo Shashi* [The Company History of Ishikawajima-Harima Heavy Industries] (*Gijutsu/ Seihin Hen*) [Volume on Technology and Products], Tokyo: Ishikawajima-Harima Jukogyo Kabushiki Kaisha.

—— (1992b) *Ishikawajima-Harima Jukogyo Shashi* [The Company History of Ishikawajima-Harima Heavy Industries] (*Enkaku/ Shiryou Hen*) [Volume on History and Source Materials], Tokyo: Ishikawajima-Harima Jukogyo Kabushiki Kaisha.

Isobe Keishi (1990) 'Zosen Shurigyo' [Ship-building and ship-repairing industry], in Hayashi Toshiaki (ed.) (1990).

Iwaki Akio (1990) *Sekiyu Seisei, Sekiyu Kagaku* [Oil-Refining and Petro-chemicals] in Hayashi Toshiaki (ed.) (1990).

Iwasaki Ikuo (1990) *Shingaporu no Kajin-kei Kigyo Shudan* [The Chinese Enterprise Groups in Singapore] Tokyo: Institute of Developing Economies.

—— (1996) *Ri Kuanyu: Seiyo to Ajia no Hazama de* [Lee Kuan Yew: An Interstice between the West and Asia], Tokyo: Iwanami Shoten.

Iwatake Teruhiko (1981a, b) *Nanpo Gunsei-ka no Keizai Shisetsu: Marai, Sumatora, Jawa no Kiroku* [The Economic Facilities under the Military Administration in the Southern Regions: Records of Malaya, Sumatra and Java], Parts I and II, Tokyo: Kyuko Shoin.

—— (1989) *Nanpo Gunsei Ronshu* [Collected Papers on the Military Administration in the Southern Regions], Tokyo: Gannando Shoten.

Iwatsuki Yasuo (1978) *Hatten Tojokoku e no Iju no Kenkyu* [A Study of Emigration into Developing Countries], Tokyo: Tamagawa Daigaku Shuppanbu.

Iwauchi Ishimi (1978) 'Batabia Hojin no Omoide' [Recollections on the Japanese in Batavia], in Jagatara Tomo no Kai (ed.) (1978).

Jagartara Tomo no Kai (ed.) (1978) *Jagatara Kanwa: Ran'in Jidai Hojin no Kiroku* [Jagatara Idle Talks: A Chronicle of Japanese during the Netherlands Indies Period], Tokyo: Jagatara Tomo no Kai.

Jamann, Wolfgang (1994) *Chinese Traders in Singapore: Business Practices and Organizational Dynamics*, Saarbrucken: Bielefeld University.

Jinsen Nanajugonen-shi Henshu Iinkai (1981) *Mitsubishi Kobe Zosenjo Nanajugonen-shi* [The Seventy-Year History of the Mitsubishi Kobe Shipyard Ltd], Kobe: Mitsubishi Jukogyo Kabushiki Kaisha Kobe Zosensho.

Josey, Alex (1980) *Lee Kuan Yew: The Crucial Years*, Singapore: Times Book International.

Kagotani Naoto (1989) 'Senhappyaku-hachijunen-dai no Nihon wo torimaku Kokusai Kankyo no Henka: Chugokujin Boekisho no Ugoki ni Chumoku shite' [A change in the international situation surrounding Japan in the 1880s: With special reference to the activities of Chinese merchants], *Keiei Kenkyu* [Studies in Management], vol. 2, no. 2, Aichi Gakusen Daigaku Keiei Kenkyujo, Toyota (Japan).

Kajima Shuppankai Henshukyoku (1974) *Kajima Kensetsu: Hyakusanjugonen no Ayumi* [Kajima Corporation: One Hundred and Thirty Five Years of History], Tokyo: Kajima Kenkyusho Shuppankai.

Kamata Hisako (1978) 'Chikamatsu no Okami "Imai Koshizu"' [Imai Koshizu, the Chikamatsu's proprietress], in Shingaporu Nihonjinkai (1978).

Kanan Ginko (1931) *Singaporu ni okeru Hojin Suisangyo* [Japanese Fisheries in Singapore], Taipei: Kabushiki Kaisha Kanan Ginko.

Kaneko Fumio (1993) 'Sengo Nihon Shokuminchi Kenkyushi' [A history of post-war colonial studies], in Oe Shinobu *et al.* (eds), *Iwanami Koza Kindai Nihon to Shokuminchi: Togo to Shihai no Ronri* [Iwanami Lecture on Modern Japan and Colonies: Logic of Unification and Rule], vol. 4, Tokyo: Iwanami Shoten.

Kani Hiroaki (1979) *Kindai Chugoku no Kuri to Choka* [Coolies and Prostitutes in Modern China], Tokyo: Iwanami Shoten.

—— (1994) 'Minzoku to Gengo' [The races and the languages], in Ayabe Tsuneo and Ishii Yoneo (eds) (1994).

Kataoka Chikashi (1991) *Senzenki Nanyo no Nihonjin Gyogyo* [Japanese Fisheries in the Pre-War South Seas], Tokyo: Dobunkan Shuppan.

Katayama Kunio (1996) *Kindai Nihon Kaiun to Ajia* [Asia and Modern Japanese Shipping], Tokyo: Ochanomizu Shobo.

Kawada Atsusuke (1997) *Shingaporu no Chosen* [The Challenge of Singapore], Tokyo: Nihon Boeki Shinkokai.

Kawai Tomoyasu (1994) *Nihon no Gyogyo* [Japanese Fisheries], Tokyo: Iwanami Shoten.

Kawasaki Seitetsu (1976) *Kawasaki Seitetsu Nijugonen-shi* [The Twenty-five-year History of the Kawasaki Steel Co. Ltd], Tokyo: Daiyamondo-sha.

Kee Yeh Siew (1966) 'The Japanese in Malaya before 1942', *Journal of the South Seas Society*, vol. 20, Singapore.

Kibata Yoichi (1996) *Teikoku no Tasogare: Reisen-ka no Igirisu to Ajia* [The Empire at Dusk: Britain and Asia in the Cold War Period], Tokyo: University of Tokyo Press.

Kikakuin (1939) *Kakyo no Kenkyu* [A Study of Overseas Chinese], Tokyo: Shozanbo.

Kikakuin Dairoku Iinkai (1942) *Nanpo Keizai Taisaku* [Economic Policy for the Southern Regions], Part I, Tokyo: Kikakuin Dairoku Iinkai.

Kim Il Myun (1976) *Tenno no Guntai to Chosenjin Ianfu* [The Emperor's Army and Korean Comfort Women], Tokyo: San'ichi Shobo.

Kirin Biru (ed.) (1957) *Kirin Biru Kabushiki Kaisha Gojunen-shi* [The Fifty-Year History of Kirin Breweries Co. Ltd.], Tokyo: Kirin Biru Kabushiki Kaisha.

Kizu Shigetoshi (ed.) (1984) *Nippon Yusen Senpaku Hyakunen-shi* [The Hundred-Year History of Nippon Yusen's Shipping], Sekai no Kansen Bessatsu [Supplementary Issue on Warships of the World], Tokyo: Kaijinsha.

Kobayashi Hideo (1975) *Dai-Toa Kyoeiken no Keisei to Hokai* [The Rise and Fall of the Greater East Asia Co-Prosperity Sphere], Tokyo: Ochanomizu Shobo.

—— (1983) *Sengo Nihon Shihon Shugi to 'Higashi Ajia Keizai-ken'* [Japanese Capitalism and 'the East Asian Economic Sphere' in the Post-War Period], Tokyo: Ochanomizu Shobo.

—— (1993) *Nihon Gunsei-ka no Ajia: 'Dai-Toa Kyoeiken' to Gunpyo* [Asia under Japanese Military Administration: The Greater East Asia Co-prosperity Sphere and Military Bank Notes], Tokyo: Iwanami Shinsho.

Kobayashi Kazuhiko and Nonaka Masataka (1985) *Johoru Kahan: Iwata Yoshio Nanpo-roku* [Johore by the Riverside: the Record of Iwata Yoshio in Southeast Asia], Tokyo: Ajia Shuppan.

Kobe Boeki Kyokai (1968) *Kobe Boeki Kyokai-shi: Kobe Boeki Hyakunen no Ayumi* [A History of the Kobe Foreign Trade Association: The Hundred-Year History of Kobe's Foreign Trade], Kobe: Kobe Boeki Kyokai.

Kobe Shoko Kaigisho (1929) *Kobe Boeki Gyosha Meikan* [A Directory of Trading Firms at Kobe], Kobe: Kobe Shoko Kaigisho.

—— (1936) *Kakyo no Gensei to Kobe ni okeru Kakyo* [The Present Conditions of Overseas Chinese and the Overseas Chinese at Kobe] Source Materials no. 54, Kobe: Kobe Shoko Kaigisho.

Kobe Zosenjo Gojunen-shi Hensan Iinkai (1957) *Shin Mitsubishi Kobe Zosenjo Gojunen-shi* [The Fifty-Year History of the New Mitsubishi Kobe Shipyard], Kobe: Shin Mitsubishi Jukogyo Kabushiki Kaisha Kobe Zosenjo.

Koh, Denis Soo Jin and Tanaka Kyoko (1984) 'Japanese competition in the trade of Malaya in the 1930s', *Southeast Asian Studies*, vol. 21, no. 4, The Centre for Southeast Asian Studies, Kyoto University, Kyoto.

Kojima Masaru (1991) '"Nanshin" no Keifu Igo' [Since the publication of *The Genealogy of the Southward Advance*], in Yano Toru (ed.) (1991).

Kokusai Kyoryoku Jigyodan (1979) *Kaigai Iju no Igi wo motomete* [In Search of the Meaning of Overseas Emigration], Tokyo: Kokusai Kyoryoku Jigyodan.

Konno Toshiro (1978) 'Nanyo Kyokai to Jisshusei' [The South Seas Association and its trainees], in Jagatara Tomonokai (ed.) (1978).

Kono Kohei (ed.) (1920) *Nanyo Soran* [A General Survey of the South Seas], Singapore: Kobunkan Shuppanbu.

Koyama Toshio (1979) *Kobe Osaka no Kakyo: Zainichi Kakyo Hyakunen-shi* [Overseas Chinese at Kobe and Osaka: A Hundred-Year History of Overseas Chinese in Japan], Kobe: Kakyo Mondai Kenkyujo.

Kratoska, Paul H. (ed.) (1995) *Malaya and Singapore during the Japanese Occupation*, Singapore: Journal of Southeast Asian Studies.

—— (ed.) (1996) 'Special Issue: The Japanese occupation in Southeast Asia', *Journal of Southeast Asian Studies*, vol. 27, no. 1, March, Singapore.

—— (1998) *The Japanese Occupation of Malaya 1941–1945: A Social and Economic History*, London: C. Hurst & Co.

Kunigami Mura Kaigai Imin-shi Hensan Iinkai (1992a) *Kunigami Mura Kaigai Imin-shi* (A History of Emigration from Kunigami Village] (the main volume), Kunigami, Okinawa: Kunigami Mura Yakuba.

—— (1992b) *Kunigami Mura Kaigai Imin-shi* [A History of Emigration from Kunigami Village] (Source Materials), Kunigami, Okinawa: Kunigami Mura Yakuba.

Kurahashi Masanao (1989) *Kitano Karayuki-san* [Karayuki-san of the North], Tokyo: Kyoei Shobo.

Kurasawa Aiko (1997) 'Beikoku Mondai ni miru Senryo-ki no Tonan Ajia: Biruma, Maraya no Jijo wo Chushin ni' [The rice issue in Southeast Asia under the Japanese occupation: With special reference to the cases of Burma and Malaya], in Kurasawa Aiko (ed.) *Tonan Ajia-shi no naka no Nihon Senryo* [The Japanese Occupation in the Southeast Asian History], Tokyo: Waseda University Press.

Kyo Shukushin (1983) 'Ryunichi Kakyo Sokai no Seiritsu ni tsuite, 1945–1952: Hanshin Kakyo wo Chushin to Shite [The formation of overseas Chinese Associations in Japan, 1945–1952: With special reference to the overseas Chinese in Kobe and Osaka], in Yamada Nobuo (ed.) (1983).

Lai Ah Eng (1986) *Peasants, Proletarians, and Prostitutes: A Preliminary Investigation into the Work of Chinese Women in Colonial Malaya*, Singapore: Institute of Southeast Asian Studies.

Le Mare, D.W. (1950) *Report of the Fisheries Department, Malaya, 1949*, Singapore.

League of Nations (1932) *Commission of Enquiry into Traffic in Women and Children in the East*, Geneva: League of Nations.

Lee Chung Yuan (1996) *Higashi Ajia Reisen to Kan-Bei-Nichi Kankei* [The Cold War in East Asia and the Relations among Korea, the US and Japan], Tokyo: University of Tokyo Press.

Lee, Edwin (1991) *The British as Rulers: Governing Multiracial Singapore 1867–1914*, Singapore: Singapore University Press.

Lee Kuan Yew (1998) *The Singapore Story: Memoirs of Lee Kuan Yew*, Singapore: Times Editions.

Lee Sheng-Yi (1990) *The Monetary and Banking Development of Singapore and Malaysia*, Singapore: Singapore University Press (Third edition).

Li Dun Jen (1982) *British Malaya: An Economic Analysis*, Kuala Lumpur: Institut Analisa Sosial.

Lim Chong Ya and Associates (1988), *Policy Options for the Singapore Economy*, Singapore: McGraw-Hill Book Company.

Lindblad, J.T. (1998) *Foreign Investment in Southeast Asia in the Twentieth Century*, Basingstoke: Macmillan; New York: St Martin's Press.

Liu, Gretchen (1987) *One Hundred Years of the National Museum Singapore, 1887–1987*, Singapore: The National Museum.

Lockhart, R.H. (1932) *Memoirs of A British Agent*, London: Putnam.

—— (1936) *Return to Malaya*, London: Putnam.

Loh, Grace and Tey Sau Hing (1995) *Jurong Shipyard Limited: What's behind the Name?*, Singapore: Times Academic Press.

McKerron, P.A.B. (1947) *Report on Singapore for the Year 1947*, Singapore: Government Printing Office.

Mak Lau Fong (1995) *The Dynamics of Chinese Dialect Group in Early Malaya*, Singapore: Singapore Society of Asian Studies.

Makepeace, Walter *et al.* (eds) (1991a, b) *One Hundred Years of Singapore*, vols I and II, Singapore: Oxford University Press.

Malayan Year Book (1935–9), Singapore: Straits Settlements and Federated Malay States (Statistics Department).

Mantetsu Toa Keizai Chosakyoku (1941) *Nanyo Kakyo Sosho: Eiryo Marai, Biruma, oyobi Goshu ni okeru Kakyo* [A Series of Studies in Overseas Chinese in the South Seas: British Malaya, Burma, and Australia], Tokyo: Mantetsu Toa Keizai Chosakyoku.

Marshall, David (1996) 'Debbiddo Masharu Hakase Kaikenki' [An interview with Dr David Marshall] (Interviewer: Sugino Kazuo), *Minami Jujisei*, no.1, Japanese Association, Singapore.

Maruzen Sekiyu Shashi Henshu Iinkai (1969) *Sanjugonen no Ayumi* [The Thirty-Five Years of the History], Osaka: Maruzen Sekiyu Kabushiki Kaisha.

—— (1987) *Maruzen Sekiyu no Hanseiki* [A Half Century of the Maruzen Oil Co. Ltd], Tokyo: Cosumo Ado.

Masuda Shozo (1987) 'Itomanshi Itomancho no Chiiki Tokusei' [Regional characteristics of Itoman Town in Itoman City], in Nakatate Ko (ed.) (1987).

Matsuo Hiroshi (1962) 'Keizai Kaihatsu no Tokucho' [Main features of economic development], in Matsuo Hiroshi (ed.), *Maraya Shingaporu no Keizai Kaihatsu* [The Economic Development of Malaya and Singapore],Tokyo: Institute of Developing Economies.

—— (1973) *Shingaporu no Keizai Kaihatsu* [The Economic Development of Singapore], Tokyo: Hyoronsha.

Matsuzakaya Nanajusshunen-shi Henshu Iinkai (1981) *Matsuzakaya Nanajusshunen-shi* [Seventy-Year History of Matsuzakaya], Nagoya: Kabushiki Kaisha Matsuzakaya.

Maugham, W. Somerset (1985) *The Casuarina Tree*, Singapore and Oxford: Oxford University Press.

Midgley, C. (ed.) (1998) *Gender and Imperialism*, Manchester and New York: Manchester University Press.

Mills, L.A. (1942) *British Rule in Eastern Asia*, London: Oxford University Press.

Minami Ryoshin (1986) *The Economic Development of Japan: A Quantitative Study*, Basingstoke and London: Macmillan Press.

Minamikai (1968) *Syonan Zosenjo no Omoide* [Recollections of the Syonan Shipyard], Kobe: Minamikai.

Ministry of Culture (1984), *Singapore: An Illustrated History, 1941–1984*, Singapore: Information Division of the Ministry of Culture.

Mitsubishi Jukogyo Shashi Hensan Shitsu (1956) *Mitsubishi Jukogyo Kabushiki Kaisha Shashi* [A History of the Mitsubishi Heavy Industries Ltd], Tokyo: Mitsubishi Jukogyo Kabushiki Kaisha Shashi Hensan Shitsu.

Mitsubishi Shashi Kankokai (ed.) (1980, 1981a, 1981b) *Mitsubishi Shashi* [Mitsubishi Company Journal] (reprint), Part I of vol. 27, Part II of vol. 28, and vol. 29, Tokyo: University of Tokyo Press.

Mitsubishi Shoji (1986) *Mitsubishi Shoji Shashi* [A History of Mitsubishi Corporation] (Part 1), Tokyo: Mitsubishi Shoji Kabushiki Kaisha.

Miyashita Takuma (1929) *Hojin Katsuyaku no Nanyo* [The South Seas where the Japanese are Active], Tokyo: Kaigaisha.

Mori Hisao (1979) 'Shohyo: Yano Toru Cho, *Nihon no Nanyo Shikan*' [A review of Yano Toru's *Japan's Historical Views on the South Seas*], *Ajia Keizai*, vol. 20, no. 11, November, Tokyo.

Mori Katsumi (1959) *Jinshin Baibai: Kaigai Dekasegi Onna* [Flesh Traffic: The Women Working Abroad], Tokyo: Shibundo.

Morisaki Kazue (1976) *Karayuki-san* [Karayuki-san], Tokyo: Asahi Shimbunsha.

Murakami Shoichi (1916) *Nanyo Zakkai* [The World of the South Seas], Tokyo.

Murakawa Ichiro (ed.) (1991) *Daresu to Yoshida Shigeru: Purinsuton Daigaku Shozo Daresu Bunsho wo Chushin to shite* [Dulles and Yoshida: With Special Reference to Dulles Documents kept at Princeton University], Tokyo: Kokusho Kankokai.

Muranushi Jiro (1997) 'Shingaporu Konjaku' [Singapore, Past and Present], *Minami Jujisei*, no. 2, Japanese Association, Singapore.

Muraoka Iheiji (1960) *Muraoka Iheiji Jiden* [The Autobiography of Muraoka Iheiji], Tokyo: Nanposha.

Murayama Yoshitada (1985) 'Senzenki Orandaryo Higashi Indo ni okeru Hojin Keizai Shinshutsu no Keitai' [A type of Japanese economic advance into the Netherlands East Indies in the pre-war period', in Shimizu Hajime (ed.) (1985).

Nagaoka Shinkichi and Nishikawa Hiroshi (eds) (1995) *Nihon Keizai to Higashi Ajia: Senji to Sengo no Keizaishi* [The Japanese Economy and East Asia: The War-time and Post-War Economic History], Kyoto: Minerva Shobo.

Naikaku Tokei Kyoku (ed.) (various issues) *Nihon Teikoku Tokei Nenkan* [Statistical Yearbook of the Japanese Empire], Tokyo.

Naito Hideo (1941) *Shingaporu* [Singapore], Tokyo: Aikoku Shimbunsha Shuppanbu.

—— (1942) *Marei no Kenkyu* [A Study of Malaya], Tokyo: Aikoku Shimbunsha Shuppanbu.

Nakadate Ko (ed.) (1987) *Nihon ni okeru Kaiyomin no Sogo Kenkyu: Itoman-kei Gyomin wo Chushin to shite* [General Studies on Fishermen: With Special Reference to Itoman Fishermen], Part I, Fukuoka: Universities of Kyushu Press.

Nakamura Shuichiro and Koike Yoichi (1986) *Chusho Kigyo no Ajia muke Toshi* [Asia-oriented Investment by Small and Medium-sized Enterprise], Tokyo:Institute of Developing Economies.

Nakamura Takafusa (1981) *The Postwar Japanese Economy: Its Development and Structure*, Tokyo: University of Tokyo Press.

—— (1983) *Economic Growth in Pre-war Japan*, New Haven and London: Yale University Press.

—— (1998) *A History of Showa Japan, 1926–1989*, Tokyo: University of Tokyo Press.

Nakane Kazuo (1976) 'Sekai ni nobiru Nihon no Ryutsugyo, Doryoku Hitosuji de ganbatta Hanseiki: Shingaporu Echigoya' [Expansion of Japanese distribution trade into the world: A half century of strenuous efforts by the Echigoya of Singapore], *Shogyokai* [The World of Commerce], December, Tokyo.

Nakayama Kazumi (1976) 'Shingaporu Keizai Jugonen no Kaiko to Tembo' [Recollections and review of the fifteen years of the Singapore economy], *Geppo*, April, Japanese Chamber of Commerce and Industry, Singapore.

—— (1979) 'Zadankai: Honsho Sosetsu to sono Yakuwari' [A round-table talk: The establishment and function of the Japanese Chamber of Commerce and Industry], *Geppo*, November, Japanese Chamber of Commerce and Industry, Singapore.

Namikata Shoichi (ed.) (1997), *Kindai Ajia no Nihonjin Keizai Dantai* [Japanese Economic Organisations in Modern Asia], Tokyo: Dobunkan Shuppan.

Nanyo Dantai Rengokai (ed.) (1942) *Dai-Nanyo Nenkan* [The Yearbook of the Great South Seas] , Tokyo: Nanyo Dantai Rengokai.

Nanyo Kyokai (ed.) (1943) *Nanpo-ken Boeki Tokei-hyo* [Statistical Tables for Foreign Trade in the Southern Regions Sphere], Tokyo: Nihon Hyoronsha.

Nanyo Kyokai Taiwan Shibu (1929, 1932) *Nanyo Nenkan* [The Yearbook of the South Seas], Taipei: Nanyo Kyokai Taiwan Shibu.

Nanyo oyobi Nihonjinsha (1938) *Nanyo no Gojunen: Shingaporu wo Chusin ni Doho Katsuyaku* [The Fifty Years of the South Seas: the Activities of Our Compatriots with Special Reference to Singapore], Tokyo: Shokasha.

Nanyo Suisan Kyokai *et al.* (1937) *Kaigai Gyogyo Jijo* [The Conditions of Overseas Fisheries] , Tokyo: Toa Suisan Kyokai.

Nathan, J.E. (1921) *The Census of British Malaya*, Singapore.

Nichimen Jitsugyo Shashi Hensan Iinkai (ed.) (1962) *Nichimen Nanajunen-shi* [The Seventy-Year History of Nichimen Co. Ltd], Osaka: Nichimen Jitsugyo Kabushiki Kaisha.

Nihon Boeki Shinkokai (1972) *Kaigai Shijo Hakusho: Wagakuni Kaigai Toshi no Genjo* [White Paper on Overseas Markets: the Present Situation of our Country's Foreign Investment], Tokyo: Nihon Boeki Shinkokai [Japan External Trade Organization].

—— (1973) *JETRO: Nijunen no Ayumi* [The Twenty Years of JETRO's History], Tokyo: Nihon Boeki Shinkokai.

—— (1988) *Yushutsu Shinko kara Kokusai Kyocho e: JETRO no Sanjunen* [From Export Promotion to International Co-operation: Thirty Years of JETRO], Tokyo: Nihon Boeki Shinkokai.

—— (1989), *Jetro Hakusho: Toshi-hen, Sekai to Nihon no Kaigai Chokusetsu Toshi* [JETRO White Paper on Investment: Direct Investments by Japan and the World], Tokyo: Nihon Boeki Shinkokai.

Nihon Keieishi Kenkyujo (ed.) (1976) *Chosen to Sozo: Mitsui Bussan Hyakunen no Ayumi* [The Challenge and Creation: A Hundred-Year History of Mitsui & Co.], Tokyo: Mitsui Bussan Kabushiki Kaisha.

—— (1982), *Tokyo Kaijo Kasai Hoken Kabushiki Kaisha Hyakunen-shi* [The Hundred-Year History of the Tokyo Marine & Fire Indusrance Co. Ltd], Part 2, Tokyo: Tokyo Kaijo Kasai Hoken Kabushiki Kaisha.

Nihon Keizai Chosa Kyogikai (1967a) *Tonan Ajia no Nihon-kei Kigyo* [Japanese Firms in Southeast Asia], Tokyo: Nihon Keizai Chosa Kyogikai.

—— (1967b) *Tonan Ajia no Nihon-kei Kigyo* [Japanese Firms in Southeast Asia], Fuzoku Shiryo: Jittai Chosa [Annexed Source Materials: A Survey on Actual Conditions], Tokyo: Nihon Keizai Chosa Kyogikai.

Nihon Keizai Kenkyukai (ed.) (1941) *Nanshin Nihon Shonin* [Southward Advance of Japanese Merchants], Tokyo: Ito Shoten.

Nihon Noritsu Kyokai (ed.) (1987) *Ajia NICs ni okeru Kigyo Senryaku* (Companies' Strategies in the Asian NICs), Tokyo: Nihon Noritsu Kyokai.

Nihon Semento Shashi Hensan Iinkai (1963) *Hachijunen-shi* [The Eighty-Year History], Tokyo: Nihon Semento Kabushiki Kaisha.

Nihon Shashi Zenshu Kankokai (1977) *Nihon Shashi Zenshu: Nihon Reizo Nijugonen no Ayumi* [A Collection of Japanese Company Histories: The Twenty-Five-Year History of the Japan Cold Storage Co. Ltd], Tokyo: Tokiwa Shoin.

Nihon Shingaporu Kyokai (1974, 1976a, b) *Hojin Shinshutsu Kigyo narabini Gaishi Shuyo Kigyo Gaikyo Ichiran-hyo* [General Situation of Japanese Firms and Main Foreign Firms], Source Materials nos. 21, 37 and 43, Tokyo: Nihon Shingaporu Kyokai.

Nihon Shingaporu Kyokai *et al.* (ed.) (1990, 1994) *Singaporu no Nikkei Kigyo Soran* [A General Survey of Japanese Firms in Singapore] (1990 and1994 editions), Tokyo: Nihon Shingaporu Kyokai.

Nihon Suisan (1981) *Nihon Suisan no Nanajunen* [The Seventy Years of the Nihon Suisan Co. Ltd], Tokyo: Nihon Suisan Kabushiki Kaisha.

Nihon Yusen (1956) *Nanajunen-shi* [The Seventy-Year History], Tokyo: Nihon Yusen Kabushiki Kaisha.

Nishihara Masashi (1976) *The Japanese and Sukarno's Indonesia: Tokyo-Jakarta Relations, 1951–1966*, Honolulu: The University Press of Hawaii.

Nishikawa Hiroshi (1995) 'Higashi Ajia Keizai-ken to Nihon no Boeki' [The East Asian economic sphere and Japan's foreign trade], in Nagaoka Shinkichi and Nishikawa Hiroshi (eds) (1995).

Nishimura Kumao (1971) 'San Furanshisuko Heiwa Joyaku' [The San Francisco Peace Treaty], in Kajima Heiwa Kenkyusho (ed.) *Nihon Gaiko-shi* [A Japanese Diplomatic History], Tokyo: Kajima Heiwa Kenkyusho Shuppankai.

Nishimura Takeshiro (1941) *Shingaporu Sanjugonen* [Thirty Five Years of Singapore], Tokyo: Tosuisha.

Nishioka Kaori (1997) *Shingaporu no Nihonjin Shakai-shi: Nihon Shogakko no Kiseki* [A Social History of the Japanese in Singapore: Locus of the Japanese Primary School], Tokyo: Fuyo Shobo Shuppan.

Nissan Jidosha Chosabu (ed.) (1983) *Nijuisseiki e no Michi: Nissan Jidosha Gojunen-shi* [The Way to the Twenty-First Century: The Fifty-Year History of the Nissan Motor Co. Ltd], Tokyo: Nissan Jidosha Kabushiki Kaisha.

Nomura Sadakichi (1941) *Shingaporu to Marai Hanto* [Singapore and the Malay Peninsula], Tokyo: Hounsha.

Oe Shinobu *et al.* (eds) (1993) *Iwanami Koza, Kindai Nihon to Shokuminchi, Shokuminchi to Sangyoka* [Iwanami Lecture on Modern Japan and the Colonies: Colonies and Industrialisation], vol. 3, Tokyo: Iwanami Shoten.

Ogawa Taira (1976) *Arafura Kai no Shinju: Kinan no Daiba Hyakunen-shi* [Pearls in the Arafura Sea: One-Hundred-Year History of Kinan's Divers], Tokyo: Ayumi Shuppan.

Ohata Atsushiro (1991) 'Nanshin no Keifu' [A genealogy of the southward advance theory], in Yano Toru (ed.) (1991).

Oishi Amane (1994, 1995) 'Sengo Tai- Ajia Baisho Mondai to Beikoku no Tai-Nichi Senryo Seisaku' [The issue of war reparations for Asia and the American policy for the occupation of Japan in the post-war period], *Osaka Shidai Ronshu*, Part 1, vol. 74, February, and Part 2, vol. 79, July, Osaka City University, Osaka.

Okabe Tatsumi (1968) 'Shingaporu Kajin to Chugoku'[The Chinese in Singapore and China], *Ajia Keizai*, vol. 9, no. 4, April, Tokyo.

Okamoto Nobuo (ed.) (1963, 1964, 1966) *Suisan Nenkan* [The Fisheries Yearbook], the 1963, 1964 and 1966 editions, Tokyo: Suisansha.

Okayagura Utako (1911) 'Nanyo no Koto ni nan no Fujiyu mo nai Nihonjin Machi' [The Japanese town in an isolated island where the Japanese live in comfort] , *Kaigai no Nihon* [Japan Overseas], vol. 6, Tokyo.

Okinawaken Kyoiku Iinkai (ed.) (1972) *Okinawaken-shi: Keizai* [A History of Okinawa Prefecture: The Economy], vol. 3, Naha: Okinawaken Kyoiku Iinkai.

—— (1974) *Okinawaken-shi: Imin* [A History of Okinawa Prefecture: Emigration], vol. 7, Naha: Okinawaken Kyoiku Iinkai.

Onoda Semento Soritsu Nanajunen-shi Hensan Iinkai (1952) *Kaiko Nanajunen* [Recollections: The Seventy Years], Tokyo: Onoda Semento Kabushiki Kaisha.

Osaka Shosen (1934) *Gojunen-shi* [The Fifty Years], Osaka: Osaka Shosen Kabushiki Kaisha.

—— (1966) *Osaka Shosen Kabushiki Kaisha Hachijunen-shi* [The Eighty-Year History of the Osaka Shosen Co. Ltd], Osaka: Osaka Shosen Kabushiki Kaisha.

Osaka Shosen Mitsui Senpaku (1969) *Mitsui Senpaku Kabushiki Kaisha Shashi* [A History of the Mitsui Shipping Co. Ltd], Tokyo: Osaka Shosen Mitsui Senpaku Kabushiki Kaisha.

—— (1985) *Sogyo Hyakunen-shi* [The First Hundred-Year History], Tokyo: Osaka Shosen Mitsui Senpaku Kabushiki Kaisha.

Ozawa Ushio (1976) 'Senpaku yo Toryo (Marine Paint) ni tsuite' [On marine paints for ships], *Geppo*, March, Japanese Chamber of Commerce and Industry, Singapore.

Pang Eng Fong (1993) 'Singapore', in Ng Chee Yuen and Pang Eng Fong (eds), *The State and Economic Development in the Asia-Pacific*, Singapore: Institute of Southeast Asian Studies.

Peattie, Mark R. (1988) *Nan'yo: The Rise and Fall of the Japanese in Micronesia, 1885–1945*, Honolulu: University of Hawaii Press.

—— (1996) 'Nanshin: The "Southward Advance", 1931–1941, as a prelude to the Japanese occupation of Southeast Asia', in P. Duus, R. H. Myers and M.R. Peattie (eds), *The Japanese Wartime Empire, 1931–1945*, Princeton: Princeton University Press.

Post, Peter (1993) 'Tai Ran'in Keizai Kakucho to Oranda no Taio' [The economic expansion into the Netherlands East Indies and the Dutch response], in Oe Shinobu *et al.* (eds) (1993).

—— (1995) 'Chinese business networks and Japanese capital in Southeast Asia, 1880–1940: Some preliminary observations', in R.A. Brown (ed.), *Chinese Business Enterprise in Asia*, London and New York: Routledge.

Purcell, Victor (1948) *The Chinese in Malaya*, London: Oxford University Press.

Raffles, Sophia (1991) *Memoir of Life and Public Services of Sir Thomas Stamford Raffles*, Singapore: Oxford University Press.

Reith, G.M. (1985) *1907 Handbook to Singapore*, Singapore: Oxford University Press (first published in 1907).

Return of Imports and Exports (1909, 1914–19), Singapore: Government Printing Office.

Rimmer, Peter J. (1990) 'Hackney carriage syces and rikisha pullers in Singapore: A colonial registrar's perspective on public transport, 1892–1923', in Peter J. Rimmer and Lisa M. Allen (eds), *The Underside of Malaysian History: Pullers, Prostitutes, Plantation Workers . . .*, Singapore: Singapore University Press.

Robertson, Eric (1986) *The Japanese File*, Singapore: Heinemann Asia (first published in 1979).

Robinson & Co. Ltd. (1958), *The Story of Robinson's 1858–1958*, Singapore: Robinson & Co. Ltd.

Rodan, Garry (1989) *The Political Economy of Singapore's Industrialization: National State and International Capital*, London: Macmillan

Sakurai Kiyohiko (1975) 'Shingaporu Zosen Shurigyo no Rekishi' [A History of Ship-building and ship-repairing industry in Singapore], *Geppo*, November, Japanese Chamber of Commerce and Industry, Singapore.

—— (1979) 'Zadankai: Honsho sosetsu to sono yakuwari'[A round-table talk: The foundation and function of the Japanese Chamber of Commerce and Industry] (With reference to Sakurai's speech), *Geppo*, November, Japanese Chamber of Commerce and Industry, Singapore.

—— (1982) 'Developing human resources overseas: IHI in Singapore', *Business Series Bulletin*, no. 84, Institute of Comparative Culture, Sophia University, Tokyo.

Sato Shusuke (1970) 'Showa Yonjugonen Tonan Ajia Chiiki Boeki Godo Kaigi Hokoku' [Report on the Joint Conference on the Southeast Asian Regional Trade for the Year 1970) (with reference to Sato's speech), *Geppo*, April, Japanese Chamber of Commerce and Industry, Singapore.

Seki Keizo (1954) *Nihon Mengyo-ron* [On the Japanese Cotton Industry], Tokyo: University of Tokyo Press.

—— (1956) *The Cotton Industry of Japan*, Tokyo: Japan Society for Promotion of Science.

Sekiyu Renmei (1981) *Sengo Sekiyu Tokei* [Statistics on Petroleum in the Post-war Period], Tokyo: Sekiyu Renmei.

Sharma, Shankar (1989) *Role of the Petroleum Industry in Singapore's Economy*, Singapore: Institute of Southeast Asian Studies.

Shiba Yoshinobu (1995) *Kakyo* [The Overseas Chinese], Tokyo: Iwanami Shoten.

Shibata Yoshimasa (1995) 'Haisen Shori to Sengo Saishinshutsu' [The post-war settlement and the resumption of (Japan's) advance]', in Hikida Yasuyuki (ed.) (1995).

Shibata Yoshimasa and Suzuki, Kunio (1995) 'Kaisenzen no Nihon Kigyo no Nanpo Shinshutsu' [The economic activities of Japanese firms in the Southern Regions before the outbreak of the Pacific War], in Hikida Yasuyuki (ed.) (1995).

Shima Hidenori (1987) 'Oikomiami Gyogyo no Seisei to Hatten' [The formation and growth of drive-in net fishing], in Nakadate Ko (ed.) (1987).

Shimazaki Hisaya (1989) *Yen no Shinryaku-shi: Yen Kawase Hon'i Seido no Keisei Katei* [The History of the Invasion of the Yen: The Formation Process of the Yen Exchange Standard System], Tokyo: Nihon Keizai Hyoronsha.

Shimizu, Béatrix (1996) 'The exoticism of the Malay world: French and British images', *Aichi Shukutoku Daigaku Gendaishakai Gakubu Ronshu* [The Bulletin of the Faculty of Studies on Contemporary Society, Aichi Shukutoku University], vol. 1, February, Nagakute, Aichiken (Japan).

Shimizu Hajime (1982) 'Nihon tono Koryu' [The relations with Japan], in Ayabe Tsuneo and Nagazumi Akira (eds) (1982).

—— (1985) 'Senzen-ki Shingaporu Maraya ni okeru Hojin Keizai Shinshutsu no Keitai: Shokugyo-betsu Jinko wo Chusin to shite' [Types of Japanese economic advances in Singapore and Malaya: With special reference to the occupations of the Japanese population], in Shimizu Hajime (ed.) (1985).

—— (ed.) (1985) 'Senzen-ki Hojin no Tonan Ajia Shinshutsu' [The Japanese advance into Southeast Asia in the pre-war period], *Ajia Keizai*, vol. 26, no. 3, Tokyo.

—— (ed.) (1986) *Ryotaisenkan-ki Nihon Tonan Ajia Kankei no Shoso* [Various Aspects of Japan-Southeast Asian Relations in the Inter-war Period], Tokyo: Institute of Developing Economies.

—— (1987) 'Nanshin-ron: Its turning point in World War I', *The Developing Economies*, vol. 26, no. 4, December, Tokyo.

—— (1991) 'Nihon Shihonshugi to Nanyo' [Japanese capitalism and the South Seas], in Yano Toru (ed.) (1991).

—— (1992) 'Nanpo Kan'yo' [Involvement in the South Seas], in Yano Toru (ed.) *Koza Tonan Ajia Gaku Bekkan: Tonan Ajia Gaku Nyumon* [Supplement to the Lecture on Southeast Asian Studies: Introduction to Southeast Asian Studies], Tokyo: Kobundo.

—— (1994a) 'Nihon tono Koryu' [The relations with Japan], in Ayabe Tsuneo and Ishii Yoneo (eds) (1994).

—— (1994b) 'Japanese economic penetration into Southeast Asia and the south-ward expansion school of thought', in Sugiyama Shinya and Milagros C. Guerrero (eds) (1994).

—— (1997) *Ajia Kaijin no Shiso to Kodo: Matsura-to, Karayuki-san, Nanshin Ronja* [The Thought and Activity of Asian Maritime People: Matsura Clique, Karayuki-san, and Southward Advance Theorists], Tokyo: NTT Shuppan.

Shimizu Hiroshi (1986) *Anglo-Japanese Trade Rivalry in the Middle East in the Inter-war Period*, London: Ithaca Press.

—— (1988) 'Dutch–Japanese competition in the shipping trade on the Java–Japan route in the inter-war period', *Southeast Asian Studies*, vol. 26, no. 1, Kyoto: Centre for Southeast Asian Studies, Kyoto University, Kyoto.

—— (1991) 'Evolution of the Japanese commercial community in the Netherlands Indies in the pre-war period: From Karayuki-san to Sogo Shosha', *Japan Forum*, vol. 3, no. 1, Oxford.

—— (1992) 'Rise and fall of the Karayuki-san in the Netherlands Indies from the late nineteenth century until the 1930s', *Review of Indonesian and Malaysian Affairs*, vol. 26, Summer, Sydney.

—— (1993a) 'The Japanese trade contact with the Middle East: Lessons from the pre-oil period', in Sugihara Kaoru and J.A. Allan (eds), *Japan in the Contemporary Middle East*, London and New York: Routledge.

—— (1993b) 'The People's Action Party and Singapore's dependent development, 1979–1992', Part II, *Nagoya Shoka Daigaku Ronshu* [The Bulletin of Nagoya University of Commerce and Business Administration], vol. 38, no. 1, March, Nisshin, Aichiken (Japan).

—— (1995) 'Senzen-ki Nihon no Tai-Eiryo Maraya Boeki Kakucho: Kobe Kasho no Yakuwari wo Chusin to shite' [Japan's trade expansion into pre-war Southeast Asia: With special reference to the role of overseas Chinese merchants at Kobe], *Aichi Shukutoku Daigaku Ronshu* [The Bulletin of Aichi Shukutoku University], vol. 20, March, Nagakute, Aichiken (Japan).

—— (1997a) 'Karayuki-san and the Japanese economic advance into British Malaya, 1870–1920', *Asian Studies Review*, vol. 20, no. 3, April, Asian Studies Association of Australia, Clayton.

—— (1997b) 'Kobe's overseas Chinese merchants and Japan's trade expansion into pre-war Southeast Asia: A case study of British Malaya', *Asian Culture*, no. 21, Singapore Society of Asian Studies, Singapore.

—— (1997c) 'The Japanese Fisheries based in Singapore, 1892–1945', *Journal of Southeast Asian Studies*, vol. 28, no. 2, Singapore.

Shimizu Hiroshi and Hirakawa Hitoshi (1998), *Karayuki-san to Keizai Shinshutsu: Sekai Keizai no naka no Shingaporu Nihon Kankei-shi* [*Karayuki-san* and the Economic Advance: A History of Japan–Singapore Relations in the World Economy], Tokyo: Commons.

Shingaporu Nihon Shoko Kaigisho (1990) *Shingaporu ni okeru Kigyo Keiei Gaido* [A Guide to Company Management in Singapore], Singapore: Japanese Chamber of Commerce and Industry.

Shingaporu Nihonjin Kurabu (ed.) (1942) *Sekido wo yuku* [Travelling the Equator], Tokyo: Niriki Shoten.

Shingaporu Nihonjinkai (1978) *Minami Jujisei: Singaporu Nihonjin Shakai no Ayumi* [*The Southern Cross*: The History of the Japanese Community in Singapore], (Tenth Anniversary Re-issue), Singapore: Japanese Association.

—— (1983) *Shingaporu Nihonjin Bochi: Shashin to Kiroku* [The Japanese Cemetery in Singapore: Photographs and Record], Singapore: Japanese Association.

—— (1987) *Minami Jujisei: Sokan Nijusshunen Kinen Fukkoku-ban* [*The Southern Cross*: The Twentieth Anniversary Re-issue], Singapore: Japanese Association.

—— (1992) 'Report on events: Sato Shodai Kaicho ga Raiho' [Report on events: Visit of the First President Sato], *Newsletter*, October, Japanese Association, Singapore.

—— (1997) *Minami Jujisei: Sokan Sanjusshunen Kinengo* [*The Southern Cross*: The Thirtieth Anniversary Re-issue], Singapore: Japanese Association.

Shingaporu Nihonjinkai Shiseki Shiryobu (1998) *Sengo Shingaporu no Nihonjin: Shashin to Kiroku* [The Japanese in Post-war Singapore: Photographs and Record], Singapore: Japanese Association.

Shingaporu Shiseikai (ed.) (1986) *Shonan Tokubetsu-shi* [A History of the Syonan Special Municipality], Tokyo: Nihon Shingaporu Kyokai.

Shingaporu Shohin Chinretsukan (1920) *Shingaporu ni okeru Nihon Shohin* [Japanese

Goods in Singapore], Singapore: Shingaporu Shohin Chinretsukan [The Commercial Museum, Singapore].

—— (1927) *Kaikyo Shokuminchi Shijo ni okeru Nihon Shohin no Ichi* [The Position of Japanese Goods in the Straits Settlements Market], Singapore: Shingaporu Shohin Chinretsukan.

Shinozaki Mamoru (1976) *Shingaporu Senryo Hiroku: Senso to sono Ningenzo* [A Secret Memoir: The War and its Image of Human Beings], Tokyo: Hara Shobo.

—— (1978a) '*Nanyo Shinshutsu no Hyakunen: Shingaporu Hojin Ryakushi*' [The hundred years of the advance into Southeast Asia: A short history of Japanese in Singapore], in Shingaporu Nihonjinkai (1978).

—— (1978b) '*Shingaporu Senryo to "Syonan" Jidai: Watashino Senchu-shi*' [The occupation of Singapore and the Syonan era: My war-time history], in Shingaporu Nihonjinkai (1978).

—— (1982) *Syonan: My Story*, Singapore: Times Books International.

Shirakiya (1957) *Shirakiya Sanbyakunen-shi* [The Three Hundred Years of Shirakiya], Tokyo: Kabushiki Kaisha Shirakiya.

Shokosho Boekikyoku (1930a, b) *Naigai Shijo ni Okeru Honpo Yushutsu Suisanbutsu no Torihiki Jokyo* [Conditions of the Trade in Japanese Marine Products for Export in Domestic and Overseas Markets], Parts 1 and 2, Tokyo: Shokosho Boekikyoku.

—— (1931) *Kako Jukkanen-kan ni okeru Eiryo Marai Taigai oyobi Tai-Nichi Boeki* Jijo [Conditions of British Malaya's Trade with Japan and Foreign Countries in the Past Ten Years], Tokyo: Shokosho Boekikyoku.

—— (1932) *Nanyo narabi Eiryo-Indo Shijo ni okeru Kinu oyobi Jinken Orimono Jokyo* [The Situation of Silk and Artificial Silk Goods in the South Seas and British Indian Markets], Tokyo: Shokosho Boekikyoku.

—— (1938) *Hanshin Zairyu no Kasho to sono Jijo* [Overseas Chinese Merchants at Kobe and Osaka, and their Conditions], Tokyo: Shokosho Boekikyoku.

Shokosho Shomukyoku (ed.) (1925) *Kaigai Shijo ni okeru Honpo Menpu* [Japanese Cotton Piece Goods in Overseas Markets], Tokyo: Koseikai Shuppanbu.

Shu Toku Ran (1997) *Nagasaki Kasho Boeki no Shiteki Kenkyu* [A Historical Study of the Trade by Overseas Chinese Merchants at Nagasaki],Tokyo: Fuyo Shobo Shuppan.

Shü Yun Ts'iao and Chua Ser Koon (1986) *Nihon Gunsei-ka no Shingaporu: Kajin Gyakusatsu Jiken no Shomei* [Singapore under the Japanese Military Occupation: Evidence for the Incident of the Massacre of Chinese], Tokyo: Aoki Shoten (Translation from the Chinese).

SICC (Singapore International Chamber of Commerce) (1979) *From Early Days*, Singapore.

Silver, Lynette R. (1992) *Krait: The Fishing Boat that went to War*, Kuala Lumpur: S. Abdul Majeed & Co.

Singapore Chamber of Commerce (1928, 1929, 1930, 1932, 1935) *Report*, Singapore.

—— (1951, 1952, 1955) '*Proceedings of Extra General Meeting*', Singapore.

Singapore Chinese Chamber of Commerce (1908), *Cheng Hsin Lu* [Showing the Statement of Receipts and Expenditure], Singapore: Singapore Chinese Chamber of Commerce.

Singapore Heritage Society (ed.) (1992) *Syonan: Singapore under the Japanese*, Singapore: Singapore Heritage Society.

Sissons, D.C.S., (1976, 1977) 'Karayuki-san: Japanese prostitutes in Australia 1887–1916', *Historical Studies*, vol. 17, no. 68 (Part I), April, no. 69 (Part 2), October, Melbourne.

SLA (Singapore Legislative Assembly) (1956) 'Singapore Legislative Assembly Debates: Official Report', First Series vol. 2, Part One of Session 1956, Singapore.

—— (1958) 'Singapore Legislative Assembly Debates: Official Report', Third Session of the First Legislative Assembly, Part One, 22, 23, 24 April, Singapore.

—— (1962) 'Singapore Legislative Assembly Debates: Official Report', vol. 18, no. 3, 29 June, Singapore.

—— (1963a) 'Singapore Legislative Assembly Debates, Official Report', vol. 21, no. 1, 24 July, Singapore.

—— (1963b) 'Singapore Legislative Assembly Debates, Official Report', vol.21, no. 5, 30 July, Singapore.

Somucho Tokeikyoku (ed.) (1998) *Sekai no Tokei* [The Statistics of the World] Tokyo: Okurasho Insatsukyoku.

Sone Sachiko (1992) 'The Karayuki-san of Asia 1868–1938: The role of prostitutes overseas in Japanese economic and social development', *Review of Indonesian and Malaysian Affairs*, vol. 26, Summer, Sydney.

Song Ong Siang (1967) *One Hundred Years' History of the Chinese in Singapore*, Singapore: University of Malaya Press.

Sorifu (ed.) (1968, 1994, 1998) *Kanko Hakusho* [White Paper on Tourism], Tokyo: Okurasho Insatsukyoku.

SOS (State of Singapore) (1959, 1961, 1962) *Annual Report,* Singapore.

——, Immigration Department (1960–3) *Annual Report of the Immigration Department*, Singapore.

STB (Singapore Tourist Board) (1998a) *Singapore Annual Report on Tourism Statistics 1997*, Singapore.

—— (1998b) *Performance of the Tourism Sector 1998*, Singapore.

Stead, David G. (1923) *General Report upon the Fisheries of British Malaya with Recommendations for Future Development*, Singapore.

STPB (Singapore Tourist Promotion Board) (1969, 1975, 1994), *Annual Statistical Report on Visitor Arrivals Singapore*, Singapore.

Sudo Sueo (1992) *The Fukuda Doctrine and ASEAN*, Singapore: Institute of Southeast Asian Studies.

Sugihara Kaoru (1991) 'Ajia-kan Boeki to Nihon no Kogyoka' [The intra-Asian trade and the industrialisation of Japan], in Hamashita Takeshi and Kawakatsu Heita (eds) (1991).

—— (1996) *Ajia-kan Boeki no Keisei to Kozo* [The Formation and Structure of Intra-Asian Trade], Kyoto: Minerva Shobo.

Sugiyama Shinya (1988) *Japan's Industrialisation in the World Economy 1859–1899: Export Trade and Overseas Competition*, London: Athlone Press.

—— (1994) 'The expansion of Japan's cotton textile exports into Southeast Asia', in Sugiyama Shinya and Milagros C. Guerrero (eds) (1994).

Sugiyama Shinya and Guerrero, Milagros C. (eds.) (1994) *International Commercial Rivalry in Southeast Asia in the Interwar Period*, Monograph 39, Yale Southeast Asia Studies, New Haven: Yale Center for International and Area Studies.

Sumitomo Shoji Shashi Hensanshitsu (1972) *Sumitomo Shoji Kabushiki Kaisha-shi* [A History of Sumitomo Corporation], Osaka: Sumitomo Shoji Kabushiki Kaisha.

Surveyor General (1924) *Singapore* (F.M.S. Surveys no. 7), Singapore: Survey Department, Federated Malay States and Straits Settlements.

Suzuki Joji (1992) *Nihonjin Dekasegi Imin* [Japanese Migrant Workers Abroad], Tokyo: Heibonsha.

Taisho Kaijo Kasai Hoken (1961) *Yonjunen-shi* [Forty Years' History], Tokyo: Taisho Kaijo Kasai Hoken Kabushiki Kaisha.

Taiwan Ginko (1919) *Taiwan Ginko Nijunen-shi* [The Twenty-year History of the Bank of Taiwan], Taipei: Taiwan Ginko.

Taiwan Ginko-shi Hensanshitsu (1964) *Taiwan Ginko-shi* [A History of the Bank of Taiwan], Taipei: Taiwan Ginko-shi Hensan Shitsu.

Taiwan Sotokufu Gaijibu (ed.) (1942) *Nanyo Nenkan* [The Yearbook of the South Seas], Taipei: Nanpo Shiryokan.

Taiwan Sotokufu Kanbo Chosaka (1932) *Shingaporu ni okeru Hojin Suisangyo* [Japanese Fisheries in Singapore], Taipei: Taiwan Sotokufu.

Taiwan Sotokufu Nettai Sangyo Chosakai (1937) *Meiji Shonen ni okeru Honkon Nihonjin* [The Japanese in Hong Kong in the Early Years of the Meiji Period], Taipei: Taiwan Sotokufu.

Takada Fujio (1989) 'Shingaporu no Itomanjin: Tokuei Maru Jiken wo Chusin ni' [Itoman people in Singapore: With special reference to the Tokuei Maru Incident], Okinawa Bunka Henshujo, *Okinawa Bunka: Okinawa Bunka Kyokai Sosetsu Yonjisshunen Kinen-shi* [Publication for the Fortieth Anniversary of the Okinawa Cultural Association], Naha: Okinawa Bunka Henshujo.

Takayama Itaro (1914) *Nanyo no Suisan* [Fisheries in the South Seas], Tokyo:Dai-Nippon Suisankai.

Takei Juro (1932) *Waga Nanyo Boeki wo Sogai suru Kakyo no Shinso* [Truth about the Overseas Chinese who Stand in the Way of Our South Seas Trade], Tokyo: Toa Keizai Chosakyoku.

Takemura Tamio (1982) *Haisho Undo: Kuruwa no Josei wa do Kaiho Saretanoka* [Movements for the Abolition of Licensed Prostitution: How Women in Brothels were liberated], Tokyo: Chuo Koronsha.

Takenaka Jisuke (ed.) (1964) *Ten-shi Gaiyo: Matsuzakaya* [An Outline History of the Stores: Matsuzakaya], Nagoya: Kabushiki Kaisha Matsuzakaya.

Takeshita, Hidekuni (1995) *Shingaporu: Ri Kuwan Yu no Jidai* [Singapore: The Lee Kuan Yew Era], Tokyo: Institute of Developing Economies.

Takumusho Takumukyoku (1931) *Nanyo ni okeru Suisangyo Chosa* [A Survey on Fisheries in the South Seas], Tokyo: Takumusho.

—— (1938) *Kaigai Suisan Chosa* [A Survey on Overseas Fisheries], Tokyo: Takumusho.

Tan, Augustine H.H. and Ow Chin Hock (1982) 'Singapore', in B. Balassa and Associates, *Development Strategies in Semi-Industrial Economies*, A World Bank Research Publication, Baltimore: Johns Hopkins University Press.

Tan Iwen (1995) *Misesu Tan to yobarete: Kakyo ni natta Nihonjin* [To be called Mrs Tan: A Japanese who became an Overseas Chinese], Tokyo: Bungei Shunjusha.

Tanaka Takao (1979) 'Ishikawajima-Harima Juko no Kaigai Shinshutsu to Takokuseki-kigyoka [The overseas advance of the Ishikawajima-Harima Heavy

Industries and its transformation into a multi-national corporation], in Fujii Mitsuo *et al.* (eds), *Nihon Takokuseki Kigyo no Shiteki Tenkai* [Historical Development of Japanese Multi-National Corporations], Part 1, Tokyo: Otsuki Shoten.

Teo Siew-Eng and Victor R. Savage (1991) 'Singapore landscape: A historical overview of housing image', in Ernest C.T. Chew and Edwin Lee (eds) (1991).

Terami Motoe (1989) 'Manira no Shoki Nihonjin Shakai to Karayuki-san' [Karayuki-san and the early Japanese community in Manila], in Ikehata Setsuho *et al*, *Seiki Tenkan-ki ni okeru Nihon Firipin Kankei* [Japan–Philippines Relations at the Turn of the Century], Tokyo: Tokyo Gaikokugo Daigaku Ajia Afurika Gengo Bunka Kenkyujo.

Terami-Wada, Motoe (1986) 'Karayuki-san of Manila: 1890–1920', *Philippines Studies*, vol. 34, Manila.

Tham Ah Kow (1954) *Report of the Fisheries Division, Department of Commerce and Industry Singapore, 1953*, Singapore.

Thio, Eunice (1991) 'The Syonan Years, 1942–1945', in Ernest C.T. Chew and Edwin Lee (eds) (1991).

Toa Keizai Chosakyoku (1938) 'Zairyu Shina Boekisho'[Chinese merchants in Japan], *Keizai Shiryo* [Economic Source Materials], vol. 14, no. 3, Toa Keizai Chosakyoku, Tokyo.

Tokyo Ginko (ed.) (1981, 1983, 1984) *Yokohama Shokin Ginko Zenshi* [The Complete History of the Yokohama Specie Bank], vols. 2, 5 (Part 1) and 6, Tokyo: Tokyo Ginko Kabushiki Kaisha.

Tokyo Kaijo Kasai Hoken (1964) *Tokyo Kaijo Hachijunen-shi* [The Eighty Years of the Tokyo Marine & Fire Insurance Co. Ltd], Tokyo: Tokyo Kaijo Kasai Hoken Kabushiki Kaisha.

Tomen Shashi Sakusei Iinkai (ed.) (1991) *Habatake Sekai ni: Tomen Nanajunen no Ayumi* [Flapping of Wings Towards the World: The Seventy-Year History of Tomen], Tokyo: Kabushiki Kaisha Tomen.

Tonan Ajia Chosakai (1961) *Tonan Ajia Yoran* [A Survey of Southeast Asia], 1961 edition, Tokyo: Tonan Ajia Chosakai.

Toyo Keizai Shimposha (1973, 1975a, 1981, 1992) *Kaigai Shinshutsu Kigyo Soran* [A General Survey of Japanese Firms Abroad], 1973, 1975, 1981 and 1992 editions, Tokyo: Toyo Keizai Shimposha.

—— (1975b) *Nihon Boeki Seiran* [A Detailed Survey of Japanese Foreign Trade], Tokyo: Toyo Keizai Shimposha.

—— (1995a, b) *Nihon Kaisha-shi Soran* [A General Survey of Companies History], Part 1 and 2, Tokyo: Toyo Keizai Shimposha.

Tran Van Tuh (1982) 'Nihon no Asean Shokoku e no Chokusetsu Toshi: Seizogyo Toshi' [Japanese direct investment into the ASEAN: Investment into manufacturing sector], in Sekiguchi Sueo (ed.), *Kan-Taiheiyo-ken to Nihon no Chokusetsu Toshi* [The Circum-pan-Pacific Sphere and Japanese Direct Investment], Tokyo: Nihon Keizai Shimbunsha.

Tregonning, K.G. (1962) *Straits Tin: A Brief Account of the First Seventy-Five Years of the Straits Trading Company, Limited 1887–1962*, Singapore.

—— (1966) *The Singapore Cold Storage, 1903–1966*, Singapore: Cold Storage Holdings Ltd.

Tsujimura Tamizo (1926) *Shingaporu Tebikigusa* [A Guide to Singapore], Singapore: Hanaya Shokai.

Tsukuda Koji and Kato Michinori (1919) *Nanyo no Shin Nihonjin Mura* [New Japanese Villages in the South Seas], Tokyo: Nanbokusha.

Tsurumi Yoshiyuki (1981) *Marakka Monogatari* [A Story of Malacca], Tokyo: Jiji Tsusinsha.

—— (1982) *Ajia wa Naze mazushiinoka* [Why is Asia Poor?], Tokyo: Asahi Shimbunsha.

—— (1990) *Namako no Me* [Eyes of Sea Cucumbers], Tokyo: Chikuma Shobo.

Tsusansho (1995) *Keizai Kyoryoku no Genjo to Mondaiten* [The Present Conditions and Problems of Economic Co-operation], Tokyo: Tsusho Sangyo Chosakai.

Tsusansho Tsusho Sangyo Seisakukyoku (1975) *Showa Gojunen-ban Wagakuni Kigyo no Kaigai Jigyo Katsudo* [The 1975 Edition, the Overseas Industrial Activities of Our Country's Firms], Tokyo: Okurasho Insatsukyoku.

Tsusho Sangyo Seisaku-shi Hensan Iinkai (ed.) (1990a) *Tsusho Sangyo Seisaku-shi: Sengo Fukko-ki* [A History of Trade and Industry Policy: the Post-war Reconstruction Period], vol. 4, Part 1, Tokyo: Tsusho Sangyo Chosakai.

—— (1990b) *Tsusho Sangyo Seisaku-shi: Jiritsu Kiban Kakuritsu-ki* [A History of Trade and Industry Policy: the Establishment Period of the Self-supporting Base], vol. 6, Part 2, Tokyo: Tsusho Sangyo Chosakai.

Turnbull, C.M. (1977) *A History of Singapore 1819–1975*, Singapore: Oxford University Press.

Uchida Naosaku (1949) *Nihon Kakyo Shakai no Kenkyu* [A Study of Overseas Chinese Community in Japan], Tokyo: Dobunkan Shuppan.

Uchida Naosaku and Shiowaki Koshiro (eds) (1950) *Ryunichi Kakyo Keizai Bunseki* [An Economic Analysis of Overseas Chinese in Japan], Tokyo: Kawade Shobo.

Ueda Fujio (1987) 'Itoman Gyomin no Hatten' [The development of Itoman fishermen], in Nakadate Ko (ed.) (1987).

Ueda Kiyoji (1972) *Waga Kokoro no Jijoden* [An Autobiography of My Heart], Kobe.

United Nations (Industrial Survey Mission (1961) *A Proposed Industrialisation Programme for the State of Singapore*, New York: United Nations.

Wallerstein, I. (1979) *The Capitalist World Economy*, Cambridge: Cambridge University Press.

Wang Gung Wu (1991) *China and Chinese Overseas*, Singapore: Times Academic Press.

Ward, A.H.C. *et al.* (editors and translators) (1994) *The Memoirs of Tan Kah Kee*, Singapore: Singapore University Press.

Warren, J.F. (1986) *Rickshaw Coolie: A People's History of Singapore (1880–1940)*, Singapore: Oxford University Press.

—— (1989) 'Karayuki-san of Singapore 1877–1941', *Journal of Malaysian Branch of the Royal Asiatic Society*, vol. 62, Part II, December, Petaling Jaya (Malaysia).

—— (1993) *Ah Ku and Karayuki-san: Prostitution in Singapore 1870–1940*, Singapore: Oxford University Press.

Watanabe Haruo (1942) *Nanpo Suisangyo* [Fisheries in the Southern Regions], Tokyo: Chukokan.

Watanabe Takeshi (1942) *Nanpo Kyoeiken to Kakyo* [The Southern Regions Co-prosperity Sphere and the Overseas Chinese], Tokyo: Shikensha.

Wilson, H.E. (1978) *Social Engineering in Singapore*, Singapore: Singapore University Press.

Wong Lin Ken (1991) 'The strategic significance of Singapore in modern history', in Ernest C.T. Chew and Edwin Lee (eds) (1991).

Yamada Kiichi (1934) *Nanyo Taikan* [A Great View of the South Seas], Tokyo: Heibonsha.

Yamada Meiko (1992) *Ianfutachi no Taiheiyo Senso* [The Pacific War for Comfort Women],Tokyo: Kojinsha.

Yamada Nobuo (ed.) (1983) *Nihon Kakyo to Bunka Masatsu* [Japan's Overseas Chinese and the Cultural Frictions], Tokyo: Gannando Shoten.

Yamamuro Gunpei (1977) *Shakai Kakushin-ron* [On Social Purification], Tokyo: Chuo Koronsha (first published by Keiseisha Shoten in 1914).

Yamashita Kiyomi (1988) *Shingaporu no Kajin Shakai* [The Chinese Community in Singapore], Tokyo: Taimeido.

Yamazaki Tomoko (1975) *Sandakan Hachiban Shokan* [No. 8 Brothel at Sandakan], Tokyo: Bungei Shunjusha (first published by Chikuma Shobo in 1972).

—— (1977) *Sandakan no Haka* [A Graveyard at Sandakan], Tokyo: Bungei Shunjusha (first published in 1974).

—— (1995) *Ajia Josei Koryu-shi* [A History of Asian Women's Intercourse], Tokyo: Chikuma Shobo.

Yano Toru (1975) *'Nanshin' no Keifu* [The Genealogy of the Southward Advance], Tokyo: Chuo Koron.

—— (1979) *Nihon no Nanyo Shikan* [Japan's Historical Views on the South Seas], Tokyo: Chuo Koron.

—— (ed.) (1991), *Koza Tonan Ajia Gaku: Tonan Ajia to Nihon* [Lecture on Southeast Asian Studies: Southeast Asia and Japan], vol. 10, Tokyo: Kobundo.

Yokohama Shokin Ginko Chosaka (1922) *Senji oyobi Sengo ni okeru Nanyo Boeki Jijo* [Trade Conditions of the South Seas in the War-time and Post-war Periods], Yokohama: Yokohama Shokin Ginko.

Yoneda Fujio (1978) *Gendai Nihon Kaiun Shikan* [Historical Views on Contemporary Japanese Shipping], Tokyo: Kaiji Sangyo Kenkyujo.

Yoon Joung Ok (1997) 'Moto Ianfu wo Ryojoku suru Shazai naki Nihon no Taido' [The attitude of Japan which insults ex-comfort women without apologies], *Ronza*, December, Tokyo.

Yoshihara Kunio (1976) *Foreign Investment and Domestic Response: A Study of Singapore's Industrialization*, Singapore: Eastern University Press.

—— (1978) *Japanese Investment in Southeast Asia*, Honolulu: The University Press of Hawaii.

—— (1982) *Sogo Shosha: The Vanguard of the Japanese Economy,* Tokyo: Oxford University Press.

Yoshimi Yoshiaki (ed.) (1992) *Jugun Ianfu Shiryo-shu* [A Collection of Source Materials for Comfort Women], Tokyo: Otsuki Shoten.

Yoshino Masaharu (1957) *Sengo no Nihon Kaiun* [The Japanese Shipping in the Post-war Period], Tokyo: Kaiun Keizai Shimbunsha Shuppanbu.

Yoshioka Toshiki (1942) *Marei no Jisso* [The Real Conditions of Malaya], Tokyo: Asahi Shimbunsha.

Yuya Tsutomu (1988) 'Shingaporu ni okeru Nikkei Kensetsugyo no Katsudo ni tsuite' [On the activities of Japanese construction companies in Singapore], *Geppo*, September, Japanese Chamber of Commerce and Industry, Singapore.

INDEX